Acclaim for GIOCONDA BELLI's

THE COUNTRY UNDER MY SKIN

"A poetic, penetrating and revelatory tale of love and war, literature and politics . . . lyrical, dramatic and incisive, Belli's soulful self-portrait and paean to her beautiful, beleaguered country is at once timely and timeless, tragic and life-affirming."
—*Chicago Tribune*

"Love and revolution have rarely been so splendidly and provocatively intertwined than in this heretic memoir of a woman's sensual and intellectual voyage of self-discovery in Nicaragua."
—Ariel Dorfman

"Gioconda Belli's memoir reads better than a novel. It recounts her larger-than-life experiences as a revolutionary, lover, and mother with honesty, passion, intelligence and, above all, poetry. *The Country Under My Skin* is as much the story of Nicaragua as it is one extraordinary woman's dreams."
—Cristina García

"The poet and novelist Gioconda Belli has written no ordinary memoir. This book is about American history, North and South; about power and the seeds of revolution; about one woman's life and choices entangled among many lives—and deaths—expended in the unkillable hope for human freedom and love. If her life seems romantic, she writes with the strength and clarity of a realist."
Rich

"Unravels [the] contradic   rful
women—with characteri   us,
surprisingly fluid."   lon

"Engaging. . . . When Belli   ... the depths of her woman's insight . . . her prose pierces the heart. . . . A window to one woman's extraordinary journey."   —*San Antonio Express-News*

"A surprisingly frank picture of the movement. . . . Belli presents a complex picture, revealing the ego clashes and massive blunders as well as moments of incredible bravery under fire."

—*Los Angeles Magazine*

"Belli recalls with engaging candor the course of a life lived to the full. In its twist and turns, moments of danger followed by intense romantic encounters, Belli's memoir can resemble exuberant historical fiction. . . . A luminously written, always insightful account of one woman's encounter with personal and political liberation."

—*Kirkus Reviews*

"Gioconda Belli has had a unique place in modern Nicaraguan history. . . . [Her] progress through her various love affairs mirrors Nicaragua's history during the same period. . . . Introduces us to an astute veteran of two eternal wars, one between the sexes and one that pits the world's poor against its rich."

—*The New York Review of Books*

"A lush memoir . . . both intensely personal and informatively political. . . . An honest, insider's account of the very real debates surrounding this major revolution would be valuable in itself, but Belli offers more: a frank examination of her struggle for love."

—*Publishers Weekly*

"A tribute to beauty, valor, and justice. Belli's giving and clarion book is also an antidote to fear and apathy, and a reminder that freedom is always a work in progress."   —*Booklist*

"Romantic and engaging."   —*Philadelphia City Paper*

GIOCONDA BELLI

THE COUNTRY
UNDER MY SKIN

Gioconda Belli's poetry and fiction have been published in many languages. Her first novel, *The Inhabited Woman*, was an international bestseller; her collection of poems, *Linea de fuego*, won the prestigious Casa de las Americas Prize in 1978. *The Country Under My Skin* was chosen as one of the best books of 2002 by the *Los Angeles Times* and was nominated for a *Los Angeles Times* Book Award in 2003. She lives in Santa Monica and Managua.

THE COUNTRY UNDER MY SKIN

A Memoir of Love and War

GIOCONDA BELLI

Translated by Kristina Cordero with the author

ANCHOR BOOKS
A Division of Random House, Inc. • New York

FIRST ANCHOR BOOKS EDITION, OCTOBER 2003

Translation copyright © 2002 by Gioconda Belli

Grateful acknowledgment is made to Ibidem Consulting for permission to reprint two poems from *Vientos del Pueblo* by Miguel Hernández. Copyright © Vientos del Pueblo S.L. Reprinted by permission of Ibidem Consulting.

The Library of Congress has cataloged the Knopf edition as follows:
Belli, Gioconda.
The country under my skin: a memoir of love and war / Gioconda Belli.—1st ed.
p.   cm.
ISBN 0-375-40370-1
1. Belli, Gioconda, 1948–.   2. Authors, Nicaraguan—20th century—Biography.   3. Revolutionaries—Nicaragua—Biography.   4. Nicaragua—History—Revolution, 1979—Personal Narratives.
I. Title.
PQ7519.2.B44 Z47413   2002
868'.6409—dc22   2002109565

Anchor ISBN: 1-4000-3216-4

Book design by Robert C. Olsson

www.anchorbooks.com

Printed in the United States of America
10   9   8   7   6   5   4   3   2

This book is dedicated to Chepita, Alicia, Eda, Anita, Cristina, María Elsa, Nidia, Petrona; and most especially for Socorro Ruiz, Beatriz Mancilla, Dolores Ortega, and all the women who helped me on the home front, and without whom neither this book nor the life I have led would have been possible.

For my children, Maryam, Melissa, Camilo, and Adriana.
For Charlie

We fill the craters left by the bombs
And once again we sing
And once again we sow
Because life never surrenders.

—anonymous Vietnamese poem

Introduction

Two things decided my life: my country and my sex. Perhaps because my mother went into labor when she was at a baseball game in Managua's stadium, it was my destiny to be drawn to the warmth of crowds. My response to the multitude was an early indication I would fear solitude and be attracted to the world of men, biological functions and domestic life notwithstanding. Outside the stadium from which my mother rushed to the hospital, there stood in those days an equestrian statue of Anastasio Somoza García, the dictator who installed a family dynasty in Nicaragua in 1937. Who knows what signals got mixed up in the amniotic fluid in my mother's womb because although I love crowds and baseball, I didn't choose to become a bat-wielding athlete. Instead I ended up taking up arms against the descendants of that horse-riding despot, drawing on every resource I had, to join in my country's struggle to free itself from one of the most enduring tyrannies in Latin America.

As a child I was no rebel. My parents would never have guessed that their demure, sweet, proper little girl would turn into the defiant woman who caused them so many sleepless nights. I was an adolescent devoted to reading. Jules Verne and my grandfather Francisco—my purveyor of books—were responsible for encouraging me to give free rein to my imagination and to believe my fantasies could come true. Revolutionary dreams found fertile ground in my young mind, as did other, more conventional kinds of dreams, although my knights in shining armor were guerrillas and my heroic exploits would be performed between changing diapers and boiling baby bottles.

I have been two women and I have lived two lives. One of these women wanted to do everything according to the classic feminine code: get married, have children, be supportive, docile, and nurturing. The other woman yearned for the privileges men enjoyed: independence, self-reliance, a public life, mobility, lovers. I have spent the greater part of my life trying to balance and blend these two identities, to avoid being torn apart by their opposing forces. In the end I believe I have found a way that allows both women to live together beneath the same skin. Without renouncing my femininity, I think I have also managed to live like a man.

Reconciling my two lives has been infinitely more complex. It has been geographically wrenching. I have flung my past and my country upon my shoulders and carried them with me not to any place, but to the north, to the country whose carefully laid net captured and conquered so many of my high-flying fantasies. One year after my compatriots and I exultantly celebrated victory, our country reverted back to war and bloodshed. Bullets, not manna, rained down from the heavens. Instead of singing together as one, Nicaraguans were sorely divided; instead of abundance there was want. While my compatriots scrawled "Yankee go home" on the city walls, I fell in love with a Yankee journalist. When all that remained of my revolution were echoes and shadows, love—the one thing I could never resist—led me to seal a pact which sentenced me to live in the country of the man I loved. Having succumbed to the magic spell like a fairy-tale princess, I now live part of my life like a bird in a golden cage singing wistfully for its tropical homeland. And from my cage, surrounded by palm trees warmed by the California sun, I try to come to terms with the country that, like a schoolyard bully, stole the kite I set out to fly. I try to see it through the eyes of the man I love. Lost in the anonymity of a giant American city, I am one among many: a mother who takes her daughter to kindergarten and organizes play dates. To look at me, nobody would ever guess that at one time a military tribunal tried, convicted, and sentenced me to prison for being a revolutionary.

But I did live that life. I witnessed and was involved in the realization of great deeds. I lived through the gestation and birth of a revolution brought forth by the flesh, blood, and will of a nation. I watched masses of people celebrate the end of a forty-five-year dictatorship. I felt the thrilling release of energy that comes from daring to defy fear and the survival instinct, in the name of a goal that transcends self-interest. I cried a lot, but I laughed a lot too. I discovered the joy that comes from surrendering the "I" and embracing the "we." These days when cynicism abounds, when we easily become dismayed, lose faith, and renounce dreams, I write down these memories in defense of the kind of happiness that makes life—and even death—worthwhile.

CITIZEN OF A SMALL COUNTRY

No me conformo, no: me desespero
Como si fuera un huracán de lava.

—Miguel Hernández

I will not resign, no: I despair/As though I were a hurricane of lava.

CHAPTER ONE

Where these memories, dusted with gunpowder, begin

CUBA, 1979

WITH EACH SHOT I fired my body shuddered, the impact reverberating through every last joint, leaving an unbearable ringing in my head, sharp and disturbing. Shame kept me from admitting how much I hated firing a gun. I would squeeze my eyes shut as I pulled the trigger, praying that my arm wouldn't tremble during that brief, blinding moment. After every shot I would feel a sudden, overwhelming urge to throw down the weapon as if it were on fire, as if my body could only be whole again once I let go of that lethal appendage gripped in my hand and pressed against my shoulder.

January 1979. Morning. A brisk northerly wind blew through a clear, cloudless sky. It would have been a perfect day for going to the beach, for lounging on the grass beneath a tree, gazing out at the Caribbean. Instead, I found myself at a shooting range with a group of Latin American guerrillas. In my arms, an AK-47. Behind me, observing us as he spoke with a group of people, was Fidel Castro.

Barely half an hour earlier, in an atmosphere reminiscent of a pleasant elementary school field trip, we had arrived at the modern and well-appointed shooting range of the FAR—the Fuerzas Armadas Revolucionarias, the Cuban armed forces. Inside the munitions warehouse, where we were to select our weapons of choice, we were like children in a toy store, touching and studying the astonishing array of automatics, semiautomatics, machine guns, and pistols laid out before us. I had only shot with pistols before, and I wanted to know what it felt like to fire a rifle. After choosing our weapons, we went out to the field, and lined up to aim and fire at our targets, which were located directly across a ravine. For the first time in my life I felt the pounding in my shoulders, the power of the machine gun blasts, and the way the body loses balance if the feet are not planted firmly in the ground for support. The others began firing away enthusiastically, but I felt dazed and bewildered, floundering through a world of muffled sounds, as if underwater. These weapons gave me no thrill at all. In fact, they had precisely the opposite effect, for I emerged from the experience with a feeling of profound, visceral revulsion. Was I the only one who felt absolutely no fascination for these instruments of war? What would I do when it was my turn to enter combat? I continued firing, furious with myself. By the time I was finished, I was face down on a mound of earth clutching a .50 caliber machine gun, its long barrel rotating on its axis. I remained there, using my thumbs to pull the lever that activated the trigger. It was the most lethal weapon there. As I fired, I heard a dry, sharp boom and this time it didn't pound through me and I was undeterred.

"I see you liked the .50, didn't you?" Fidel mused with a malicious grin when I saw him a few days later. He had come to the hotel to visit the Sandinista delegation and we had been summoned to the presidential suite. I said nothing. I smiled at him. He turned back and continued talking to Tito and the other *compañeros* who had been invited to Havana for the Cuban Revolution's twentieth-anniversary celebration.

I sat back and watched him. It was inevitable that the sight of Fidel would stir a collage of memories in my mind. Fidel was the first revolutionary I had ever heard of. When I was a child I had followed his rebellious feats as if they were episodes in an adventure novel. Sprawled out on our parents' bed, my elder brother, Humberto, and I devoured the *Life* magazine issue with the story on Fidel in the Sierra Maestra. In our house, among the adults, passions always ran high when it came to Fidel.

Around this time, Humberto had perfected his a cappella imitation of Al Hirt's trumpet. His greatest pride, however, was his masterful rendering of Daniel Santos's singing. Santos, a Puerto Rican, had been catapulted into fame thanks to his nasal rendition of the anthem of the Cuban rebel movement. Humberto's voice boomed through the house as he broke into song either in the shower or during other moments of sudden inspiration: "Adelante cubanos, que Cuba premiará vuestro heroismo, pues somos soldados que vamos a la Patria liberar" ("Onward, Cubans; Cuba will reward your heroism, for we are the soldiers who will free the Motherland"). It was listening to that song that I first experienced the call of patriotism. I would repeat it to myself, secretly thinking of Nicaragua's tyrant, Somoza. To me, Fidel was a romantic hero. In Cuba, he and his bearded, fearless, daring young men were accomplishing things that nobody had been able to achieve in Nicaragua—neither my cousins, who were involved in the struggle, nor Pedro Joaquín Chamorro (the opposition leader), nor the Conservative Party. I was only ten years old when Fidel achieved his victory, but I remember how thrilled I felt. I applauded the Cuban Revolution as if it had been a victory for us as well.

Soon after, of course, all that enthusiasm vanished, as if spirited away by a magic spell. I don't know exactly what happened, but between the nuns at school, my parents' friends, the newspaper reports, and the conversations in my house, it began to appear that Fidel and his cronies had fooled the entire world, making themselves out to be good Christians when they were actually dangerous communists.

"Can you believe it?" my mother said. "Fidel appeared in *Life* with an enormous crucifix hanging from his neck, and now he calls himself an atheist. It's an outrage!" The nuns told us horror stories about Cuba: about young children torn from their parents' arms and sent to institutions where the state would reeducate them as communists who would know nothing of God. To be a communist was a terrible stigma—it was a capital sin, the surest path to hell. I remember feeling awful for all those poor Cuban children—that is, until I overheard something my maternal grandfather, Francisco Pereira, said to a Chinese friend of his who came to visit every day. Together they would sit back and enjoy afternoon drinks in their rocking chairs in front of my grandfather's house in León. "It's all lies. They're inventing it all to sabotage Fidel," my grandfather said. He would draw upon his encyclopedic memory and recite, word for word, excerpts of Castro's speeches broadcast on Radio Havana that to me sounded like the homilies I'd heard in church offering solace to the poor. But with so many different perspectives before me, I didn't know quite what to make of him. I was further confused when President Kennedy— my mother's idol—turned to Luis Somoza Debayle, who ruled the country after his father's death, to launch the Bay of Pigs invasion from Nicaragua. I couldn't fathom how or why a president like Kennedy could maintain friendly relations with a government like ours.

Who would have ever guessed, then, that one day I would find myself seated on a fluffy sofa in Havana, talking to Fidel? But we come into the world with a ball of yarn to weave the fabric of our lives. One cannot know exactly what the tapestry will look like, but at a certain moment one can look back and say: Of course! It couldn't have been any other way! That shiny thread, that stitching couldn't have led anywhere else!

CHAPTER TWO

Where I tell of certain bizarre connections between California,
interoceanic canals, and my life

SANTA MONICA, 1998

FROM THE TOP of my house in Santa Monica I can see the ocean. When I feel nostalgic, I get into my car, drive down to the beach, and cross the wide expanse of sand until I reach the edge of the water. The sight of whitecaps unfurling at my feet instantly transports me back home, to Nicaragua. This is the ocean of my childhood memories. I recognize the curl of the waves, the drone of the sea crashing against the sand as it comes and goes tirelessly. The beach here dissolves farther ahead into the silhouette of the pier and its amusement park, but if I close my eyes and see just with my memory, I can glimpse far down the coast to the cabin where I used to spend summer vacations with my family. I can see myself when I was a teenager, watching the sunset from the highest point of Tiger Rock. I would sit quietly there, feeling quite adult in my melancholy, imagining I was a heroine on an intrepid quest.

Now I imagine other things. I imagine the ocean, with its swirling, watery fingers knitting together the two lives I have lived.

That I should see a link between California and Nicaragua through the Pacific Ocean comes as no surprise to me. My country's history was forever altered when gold was discovered by James Marshall in the American River on the West Coast of the United States in 1848. After the Gold Rush began, thousands of people made their way to California. In those days, it was a perilous journey from the East to the West Coast. Travelers had to choose between crossing by land in slow caravans—under the threat of Indian attacks—or a long steamboat trip from the Atlantic to the Pacific Ocean, which meant going down the coast of South America around Cape Horn and back up to San Francisco. Short routes across the continent were in great demand when, in 1849, Commodore Cornelius Vanderbilt, an audacious and powerful New York entrepreneur who owned a steamship company, devised a transit route through Nicaragua which could shorten the trip substantially. The Accessory Transit Route was opened in 1851. Travelers arrived from New York by steamboat to the mouth of Nicaragua's San Juan River. The river connected with Lake Nicaragua. After the trek upriver and through the lake, the "forty-niners" only had to travel less than ten miles on horse-drawn carriages to arrive at a port on the Pacific Ocean and board another steamship to San Francisco. The Nicaraguan route was safer, prettier, and cleaner than the Panama route, which was so unsanitary that insurance companies with-held coverage to any traveler who spent more than twenty-four hours in the Panamanian town of Colón. Unfortunately, such geographic advan-tage soon became a curse for my country. With the help of an enterprising rogue named William Walker, two wealthy businessmen, Charles Morgan and Cornelius Garrison, took over the Transit Route from Vanderbilt while he was vacationing in Europe. Walker's dream to make Nicaragua another star on the United States flag led him to use his cunning and mili-tary expertise to eventually declare himself president of the country. But the Central American populace joined forces to combat him, and in 1860 he was executed by a firing squad in Honduras.

Even though the Transit Route never became an interoceanic canal, the William Walker episode was a precursor to what would become a long history of U.S. involvement in Nicaragua to insure, among other things, that no other world power would dare build a rival canal through it. The United States became both referee and player in this tiny rebel nation, which seemed to be constantly embroiled in some war or another. Over and over again the United States intervened, first defending the Liberals and then the Conservatives, until they encountered a short, scrawny general named Augusto César Sandino, who, from 1927 to 1933, opposed American intervention and whose ragtag army of peasant soldiers fast became a nightmare for the United States, as a good number of Marines fell victim to the shrewd military tactics of that little man in his trade-mark cowboy boots and Stetson hat. The American government pulled out its troops in 1933, and decided it would be best if Nicaragua created its own army, and they helped search for an appropriate leader. They came up with none other than Anastasio Somoza García, a minor bureaucrat from the water company whose merits included his fluent English, his marriage to a niece of President Juan B. Sacasa, and the fact that the U.S. ambassador's wife found him "pleasant." Somoza would soon reveal his cunning and ruthless determination by orchestrating, on February 21, 1934, the murder of Sandino and his generals as they left the presidential building after a banquet offered by President Sacasa in celebration of the recent peace accords. Three years later, Somoza García staged a coup d'etat against his uncle-in-law and declared himself president. "Somoza is a son of a bitch," said President Franklin Roosevelt, "but he's our son of a bitch." When a poet killed Somoza García in 1956, first his elder son, Luis, and then his youngest, Anastasio, succeeded him. Anastasio's English was actually better than his Spanish. He was a graduate of West Point—the perfect *criollo* Marine. Backed by the United States, the Somoza dynasty remained in power until 1979. Almost half a century.

The quest for an interoceanic passageway left its mark on my family as well. My ancestors were northern Italians from the Piedmont, Biella to be exact. Two Belli brothers made it to the Americas: Próspero was an archaeologist, Antonio, a civil engineer. Próspero traveled all the way to Peru, where he eventually founded a museum in the Ica desert. Antonio worked on the Panama Canal. That is, until a certain weekend in which he visited the town of Granada, Nicaragua. Spellbound by the colonial mansions and the breeze that floated off a lake so enormous that the Spanish conquistadors christened it a freshwater sea—"la Mar Dulce"—he fell in love with my great-grandmother. Carlota was a strong, beautiful woman, and she also came from a very prominent family. Her brother was Emiliano Chamorro, a Conservative general who became president of the country twice and who earned the respect and support of the United States for conceding, in perpetuity, the exclusive rights for the construction of the interoceanic canal. In an effort to show how much he admired that great nation to the north, Chamorro also signed an agreement with Somoza imposing a two-party system in Nicaragua. I never knew my Italian great-grandfather Antonio, who they say had one blue eye and one brown eye, but I did know General Chamorro. By the time I met him, he was a wizened, wrinkled old man with a mat of white hair on his head and the face of a sad old bloodhound.

CHAPTER THREE

---

*On how a coin led to my first trip to the United States,
and on my first experience of witnessing bloodshed*

Managua, 1952–1959

Antonio Belli died young, of cirrhosis. Once his children grew up and got married, his widow, Abuelita Carlota, as we called my great-grandmother, had a wall built right down the middle of the interior courtyard of her spacious and stately colonial house—all clay tiles and thick adobe masonry—and divided it in two. She lived with Elena, her daughter (who had married a lawyer), in one half of the house. The other half went to my father, who was more like a son than grandson to her, and that is where we lived. The two houses remained connected by an archway in the wall between them. My aunt Elena's half was full of cheer and activity. Her daughters, María Elena, Eugenia, and Carlota, my cousins, were all older than me. The youngest, whom we called Toti to distinguish her from Abuelita, was only five or six years older than me, and she was my idol. She was mischievous, funny, and charmingly flirtatious, and she would recruit me as unconditional accomplice to her schemes, which mainly consisted of incessant spying on her older sisters, who had begun to date and have boyfriends.

When I was three or four years old, I took to mimicking the women who passed by our street balancing baskets on their heads and announcing their merchandise with a town-crier singsong. I would use the lid from a can of crackers as a tray to support a few rocks on my head. Then I would parade through my house chanting, "Bread for sale! Breads, muffins, cookies!" The grown-ups would pretend to buy my merchandise and I would continue gleefully, searching out the next client. So it was until the afternoon my great-grandmother Carlota gave me a one-peso coin. By then she was quite ancient, always dressed in gray, her white hair pulled back into a bun, and she spent long hours rocking back and forth absently. I looked at her, stupefied by the emotion of my first "real" sale, but her gaze was already far away, lost in contemplating the sunlight that fell on the courtyard. Incredulous, I closed my hand tightly around the coin, only to open it again later, with an air of superiority, to show it off to my brother Humberto, who slept in the bunk above mine. Instead of applauding my sale, Humberto turned me in to our nanny.

"Give it to me," she said sternly, thinking, I imagine, that I had taken the coin without permission. But there was no earthly power that could pry that treasure from me. During the struggle that ensued, in a fit of desperation, I put it in my mouth and swallowed. In those days, one-peso coins were large. My parents thought that the problem would resolve itself, expecting the coin to come out on its own, but it didn't. Instead, it blocked the passage to my stomach. The doctors in Nicaragua wanted to operate, but my father insisted there had to be a way to remove it without leaving a huge scar. I was his little girl, after all, and he did not rest until he found a doctor who specialized in such cases, in Philadelphia, and so he sent me there with my mother.

My mother had been educated at Ravenhill Academy, an exclusive Catholic school in Philadelphia run by nuns. She said she owed Ravenhill her knowledge of the English language and her love for the arts. She called the nuns before we left Nicaragua, and they invited us to stay with them. Even though I still have memories of that trip to the United States— scattered images of enormous buildings, a flurry of crowds and lights that terrified me—I can't recall anything about being on the plane or in the hospital where they finally extracted the coin. I do remember the garden and apple orchard at Ravenhill. My mother took pictures of me there. Many years later, when I found the photographs, I was surprised at the uncanny accuracy of my childhood recollections. I am standing among the trees, a chubby little girl with a round, sweet face, my abundant, golden chestnut hair gathered to the side and fastened with a big satin bow. My mother spoke often, and rather wistfully, about how happy she had been during her Ravenhill years. I think she was always a bit sad that she hadn't grown up in a big city, that she hadn't lived in a more worldly, refined social universe where she might have put her good graces and modern ways to greater advantage. I think she longed for a world like that of Grace Kelly, her classmate in Philadelphia, who my mother claimed had invited her to her wedding with Prince Rainier of Monaco, although I never knew whether to take her seriously or not.

My family's house was on Calle del Triunfo—Triumph Street—one of Managua's main avenues. My aunt Elena's side was next door to Somoza's Liberal Party headquarters. Whenever rallies were held there, we would cover our ears to block out the "Viva Somoza" cheers, which reverberated through the walls like insults hurled directly at us—in our very own home! My cousin Toti would yell "Die!" when on the other side of the wall they shouted "Viva"—that is to say, "Long live Somoza." Occasionally I would echo her sentiments, but never in a very loud voice. Other times, I would beg her to keep quiet as I envisioned the soldiers who would come pounding on our door to take us away to who knew where. I had heard that people were thrown in jail for lesser offenses than the things Toti said.

My parents didn't support our government, but my aunt Elena's family was actively against it. They fervently opposed the dictatorship and would spend long hours plotting hypothetical schemes to overthrow Somoza. Of Aunt Elena's two sons, Mauricio was the most politically involved. One day he simply disappeared. Soon after, we learned that he had participated in the invasion of Olama and Mollejones, a coup attempt organized by a group of conservatives which included Pedro Joaquín Chamorro, the editor in chief of *La Prensa*, the most important newspaper in the country. The invasion was nothing more than a foolish, sloppy military maneuver. Several rebels were imprisoned as a result, while others were executed during so-called escape attempts. The more fortunate ones—my cousin Mauricio was among them—were granted political asylum. Mauricio sought and obtained asylum at the Salvadoran embassy.

One Saturday afternoon, I went with my aunt Elena and my cousins to visit him. The embassy had a large garden filled with mango trees and cement benches, where we sat down and chatted with Mauricio and five or six other young men, acquaintances of my cousins who had also sought refuge there. At the time, they looked to me like students at a boarding school. They all looked healthy, and my aunt brought them things like clothes and candy. Disillusioned, the boys sat around discussing their failed coup attempt, the government's repression, and our country's bleak future. Pedro Joaquín Chamorro had managed to escape to Costa Rica, and the other rebels were in hiding. At six years old, I was too young to understand much, but I do remember the atmosphere of fear that hung over everything during that time. I remember the serious, sad faces of the grown-ups and their disappointment as they bemoaned yet another failed attempt to overthrow the government.

I think it was around this time that we moved to the neighborhood of San Sebastián. My brother Eduardo and my sister Lucía had been born, and my mother had wanted a larger house. The Parodi family, with their gang of jovial, good-looking sons who often buzzed around my cousins, lived nearby. One afternoon, there was a great commotion in the neighborhood; I remember my mother and father wouldn't allow us to play in the street that day. In reaction to the harsh political climate in Nicaragua, the university students had staged massive protests calling for an end to the repression. On that day the National Guard had apparently opened fire on the students. Shots rang out in our neighborhood that afternoon. My parents and the other adults were visibly shaken, and I vaguely heard something about one of the Parodi brothers being shot on the doorstep of his family's home.

Two or three days later, when things had more or less returned to normal, my nanny and I went out to buy some candy. She held my hand as we walked past the Parodi house, which was set back from the street a bit. On the side of the house that faced the front yard, with its little path leading to the front door, I spied a huge, coffee-colored stain. By then I knew the National Guard had killed Silvio Parodi. My cousins were inconsolable, sobbing and seething with rage. I remember I stopped right in front of the stain, my heart pounding. It was there, wasn't it? I asked my nanny, That's where they killed Silvio, right? But the blood is brown. I thought blood was red, I said to her. My nanny yanked me by the arm, trying to get me to cross to the other side of the street. But I resisted. I kept asking her about the blood. Why was the blood brown? "Because it got old," she finally answered me, yanking me again, practically dragging me away. "Come on, if your mother finds out you saw that, she'll be furious with me."

Silvio's parents left that bloodstain on the side of the house, as a testament to the cold-blooded murder of their son. I saw it many more times, over and over again until months later when they finally repainted the house. I can still see it today. It's one of those indelible memories from childhood. I even remember the smell of that day, the whistle of the wind, the sunlight falling on the bouquet of red flowers placed by the front door, alongside that giant brown stain.

I will always associate the end of my childhood with the memory of one specific day. It was like any other day, really. I was sitting in the back seat of my father's car, on my way home from school. All of a sudden, as if a thunderbolt had struck me, I realized that I would be alone in my body forever. I can still feel that surge of adrenaline, the sudden awareness that accompanied this irrefutable fact. In a single, terrifying instant I became acutely aware that nobody could share my inner space, feel what I felt, listen to my innermost thoughts. I could never experience what it would be like to be someone other than the little girl I was, in my uniform of pleated skirt and white blouse. It dawned on me that I could never look at myself directly in the face—I could only do it through a mirror. For a few days I was quite disconcerted by the enormity of my realization. I was baffled by the random design that had made me be born where I was born, arbitrarily deciding I would come into the world with a silver spoon in my mouth, instead of as one of those broken, scraggly little waifs who ran after our car, banging on the windows, begging for change, and in whose eyes I saw, with painful clarity, the very same bewilderment I felt.

CHAPTER FOUR

Of how it was that I had an early introduction to marriage,
maternity, and disenchantment

MANAGUA, 1966–1969

I FINISHED HIGH SCHOOL in Spain and then traveled to the United States to study a one-year course of advertising and journalism in Philadelphia. I had wanted to go to medical school but my father discouraged me. Medicine was not a career for a woman, he said. I would be so old by the time I was done studying that I'd never marry. I was too young to contradict him, so I agreed to learn something "useful" and went off to advertising school. I was sixteen and, as a special concession to my mother, the Asunción nuns allowed me to board at Ravenhill Academy, her alma mater. After the course ended, I left Philadelphia and returned to Nicaragua. One week after my return—I was seventeen—I got my first job as an account executive at an advertising agency in Managua. The agency was located in a rambling, ramshackle old house, and I shared an office with a talkative, friendly man who had been assigned to train me in the rudiments of my job. About a month later, I was invited to a friend's country home for a daytime outing, and during a bucolic walk along the green, shady banks of the Tipitapa River, I met the man who would become my husband. He was a tall, slender, slightly shy man, with little eyes that peeked out from his glasses. I liked him because he shared my interest in books. Sitting on the grass, looking out at the river, we talked about literature. One of the first things I thought of was how much my parents would like him, because he was related to families that moved in the same social circle as ours, and my mother was always saying that

similar educational and cultural backgrounds were the essential ingredi-
ents for a good marriage.

I wanted to get married as quickly as possible. I was in a hurry to live
my life, to get away from the commotion of my parents' house, and my
four brothers and sisters. I wanted my independence. Our courtship
began soon after that June day. My future husband quickly joined the
whirlwind of parties and social activities that filled the summer months
of all the young, high-society Nicaraguans back from a year of studying
abroad. He was my date at the Debutantes Ball, at which I flouted the
unwritten dress code of pastels, designing my own gown which included a
bold swath of red. The ball was in my honor, because that year I had been
designated the belle of the Nejapa Country Club—kind of a homecoming
queen—and it was my duty to open the event by dancing a waltz with
the president of the club. Among my various childhood friends, who were
jovial and glib, my fiancé's lethargy was overshadowed. It wasn't until we
were married that I realized that fun made him uncomfortable. I saw how
his melancholy often drove him to lock himself away in a room in his
aunt's house where he would mournfully play the harmonica for hours at
a time. It was too late when I realized that this was not the behavior of a
man suffering from temporary bouts of sadness, but rather the manifesta-
tion of a frightened, lonely, misanthropic soul.

The wedding was held in February of 1967. I had turned eighteen
scarcely two months earlier. I was still a virgin. My satin silk bridal gown
was simple, with a tulle overskirt and Venetian lace detailing. I was quite
pleased with the way I looked—that is, until my mother arranged the cap
and veil upon my head, and guided each of my hands inside a long, kidskin glove. At that moment, all of a sudden, a sense of ridicule came over
me, I felt I was being packaged up like a gift. There was something humili-
ating about the entire ceremony—my parents symbolically handing me
over to a man. The white clothes made me feel like the sacrificial lamb
from the Bible whose blood was to be offered as a sign of chastity. And as
I walked toward the altar on my father's arm, following the trail of my
two little sisters, Lucía and Lavinia, who were all dressed up in salmon-
colored dresses, carrying tiny bouquets of flowers, I was possessed by the
unsettling thought that as they watched me, all the guests were privately
imagining my wedding night.

The Iglesia del Carmen was one of the most beautiful churches in
Managua, sober and modern. You could hear its bells ringing all the way
to my house in Bolonia, the fashionable neighborhood in those days, with

modern, angular, 1960s-style houses. Many of Managua's wealthy families lived in Bolonia—it was a place for people who didn't want to live in the middle of the city but who didn't want the suburbs, either. Only a few blocks from my house, which had been designed by a prominent Panamanian architect, a more humble level of buildings came into view. Grocery stores, tire repair shops, drugstores, and small-town, colonial-style houses lined up one after the other, painted all sorts of brilliant colors: aquamarine, lemon yellow, pink. We coexisted but never mixed with that world. We knew of their existence simply because they were there. They were everywhere. We read about them constantly in the newspapers, which were always filled with stories about the poor and the hardships they suffered. Or we would learn about their lives firsthand through the maids and drivers that worked for us. Inside the church, however, that world seemed nonexistent. The guests were resplendent. Men in suits, women in hats and gloves, their hands soft and well cared for. Dressed in his tuxedo, with a ceremonious, nervous look on his face, my fiancé waited for me at the altar. I'll make him happy, I thought. I'll make him laugh. I'll be his protector, his fairy. I was the one who convinced him that our combined salaries would be enough for us to live on. With my job at the advertising agency, I was earning as much as he was in the government's Highway Department. Yet, when we announced our intention to get married, both his parents and mine did everything they could to dissuade us. We were so young. And so obstinate. And in the end, they gave in to us.

My wedding reception, held at noon in the banquet halls of the Nejapa Country Club, was quite the social event. My mother, who enjoyed being known for her flair and her social graces, was determined to show her elegance and exquisite taste. She planned the celebration in strict accordance to the rules of her social bible: Emily Post's book of etiquette. Yet, while she was strict about rules regarding decorum and manners, in other areas she was surprisingly liberal. As my wedding reception came to a close, just before I was to leave for my honeymoon, she pulled me aside.

"In her home, a woman should always behave like a lady," she advised. "But not in bed. When you're in bed with your husband, you can do whatever you want. Nothing is forbidden. Nothing."

From the time I was a little girl, my mother always spoke of the human body with the utmost reverence. She even said the words "human body" in the same tone that other women—her own friends—used to invoke the name of Jesus Christ. To her, the human form was divine, and prudishness was provincial and backward. On the trip we made through Europe when I was fourteen, on my way to the boarding school I would attend in Spain, my mother took me to the Folies Bergère in Paris. Officially, it was off-limits to anyone under the age of sixteen, and so my mother deftly made up my face to sneak me in. It took my breath away— the sumptuous decor, the feathered, sequined costumes, the colors, and most especially the parade of nearly bare bodies. As we left the theater and walked out into the cold September night, I felt flushed beneath my sober black dress and pearl necklace. The finale of the vaudeville show had been Debussy's *Afternoon of a Faun:* a man and a woman, wearing nothing but tiny golden triangles in the appropriate spots, performed an exquisite, delicate dance, evoking the most erotic kind of lovemaking.

"What a marvelous sight!" exclaimed my mother, as she walked quickly in search of a taxi. "What perfection! That's exactly how beautiful and perfect Adam and Eve must have been in the Garden of Eden."

At some point during my adolescence, suspecting that the moon, the tides, and my hormones would soon reveal to me the secrets that Nature reserves for women, my mother invited me into her bedroom one afternoon when I returned home from school. Locking the door behind her, she walked over to her dressing table and sat me down in front of her to discuss, quite eloquently, the surprises and changes that my body held in store for me. Petite and slender, with short, dyed-blond hair, my mother was a refined woman, a great admirer of literature and theater. I can't remember her exact words, but I will never forget the powerful, thrilling feeling she imbued in me that day. Naturally, her intention was to inform me about motherhood and its myriad responsibilities, but the things she said about the power of femininity echoed far beyond the realm of the biological in my young, impressionable mind. I was a woman. Of the human race only we were endowed with the gift of life, the perpetuation of the species. The human body was Nature's most prized creation, a marvelous, intricate work of art—but the female body in particular was the most astonishing and beautiful of all. We were Nature's masterpieces. And as such a splendid creature, my body would soon be ready to receive the egg, nurture it, and allow it to blossom in the darkness of my womb. Naturally, I would not experience motherhood until I found someone worthy of "that most precious bond of communion," as she called it, and until then the egg would remained unfertilized and dissolve. The chrysalis that my womb would knit each month, ready to receive life, would be released in the form of menstrual blood. She led me into the bathroom, and showed me how sanitary napkins worked. Then she handed me, in a sealed box, the pink elastic band which I would tie around my waist to hold the napkins in place. (This was, of course, in the days before self-adhesive pads.) This event was a most solemn rite of passage, I was taking my place in a great relay race and my mother had passed me the centuries-old torch of femininity. I remember how sad I felt for my two brothers as I left her bedroom, for they would never be able to share in that wondrous experience. And when my first menstrual period arrived shortly after, I felt as though Nature had finally anointed me. I was glowing with pride.

Later on, my mother also told me about sex, though she didn't provide me with too many details about the mechanics of the sexual act. My introduction to the world of lovemaking was pure poetry. My mother illustrated her points with stories of myth and legend. From what she described, I surmised that sex was a most glorious act, a kind of majestic union born of two naked, intertwined bodies forging new life as well as eternal bonds of love and intimacy. "It is the most meaningful gesture of union and communication that two human beings can share," she said, punctuating her words with gestures made with her long, delicate hands, as her solitaire ring—a gift from my father—sparkled against her finger.

Once my marriage was consummated, I finally embarked upon my adult life. My husband and I rented an apartment. Our building was known as "the eagle's nest," because it had once housed the U.S. embassy, and there was, appropriately, a golden eagle perched upon the top story. The neighborhood was traditional and quiet, close to the shores of Lake Managua, at the foot of the city. Though smaller than the immense Lake Nicaragua in Granada, it is a spectacular expanse of water surrounded by mountains and volcanoes. On one side of our apartment building there was a cozy little park with a bubbling fountain. Yet, once I was settled into this new, independent existence, I began to wonder why married life wasn't anything like what my mother had described. I knew something wasn't right. My marriage wasn't anything close to the magnificent union, communion, or intimacy that was supposedly the cornerstone of conjugal life. My illusions of romance had begun to dissipate as early as my honeymoon, which we spent at my parents' beach cottage on the Pacific Ocean.

Despite my most persistent efforts, I couldn't entice him out of his melancholy. Like an ostrich, he would bury himself in his listlessness—pessimistic, apathetic, and impenetrable. The adventurous spirit he had managed to muster during our courtship had simply vanished. I tried lots of things—taking his hand, coaxing him into evening strolls on the beach, fantasizing about wild, pagan dances beneath the moonlight—but he wasn't up for that sort of thing. Too risky. You never knew who was out there, on that huge, deserted beach, where silvery crystals glittered in the leaden sand. We were better off inside, he said.

An entire week locked up inside, just the two of us, should have been the fulfillment of all my Hollywood-style honeymoon fantasies—the happy couple hanging a "Do Not Disturb" sign on their hotel room door, emerging five days later with rosy cheeks and Henry Mancini music playing in the background. But real life refused to lend itself to such excess. We grew so bored that we ended up driving into León, a nearby city, to buy cheap paperbacks and comic books for entertainment. When we returned to Managua, he would spend long, silent hours mesmerized by the television set. He had no desire to go out with me or his friends, not even to the movies. For him, it was enough to know that I was nearby—we didn't even have to talk, he said. I would go into the bathroom and cry. My illusions of changing him into a happy man quickly evaporated. I was furious at the trap I found myself in—all because I had been so innocent, so romantic. In my terrible hurry to get on with life, I had married a man who longed to hide from it.

When he suggested that I quit my job and stay at home, as most married women did, I flew into such an indignant rage that he realized he would have to resign himself to my independence. Ever since childhood, I had always felt that being a woman was an advantage, and perhaps that was why I considered myself free, master of my own domain. It had never crossed my mind that a man could think he had the right to stop me from being who I was. There was no way I would accept the kind of marriage or motherhood that would require me to relinquish the infinite possibilities that life had in store for me. And so I kept my job until the nausea and the fatigue of the first trimester of pregnancy took over.

I was nineteen when I gave birth to my daughter Maryam. From the private wing of the Baptist Hospital, I could look out the window of my room onto a rubber tree with shiny leaves of green and violet, fluttering in the wind beneath the afternoon sun. As I watched them sway to and fro, I imagined they were the ears of some prehistoric animal. Each time a contraction gripped my womb, I would try to relax by breathing slowly and counting those leaves. They said that trying to fight the pain was counterproductive, and I wanted to be stoic—like a tree holding out against violent gusts of wind and rain. After twelve hours of labor, though, I just wanted release, to escape my body altogether and end the suffering. Yet despite the pain, I was awed by how Mother Nature had taken over. It was as if She had made a pact with my body, and I was nothing more than an observer. There was no need for me to meddle with the birth process, for an age-old wisdom controlled everything with clocklike precision: the water breaking, the contractions coming, faster and faster, every five minutes, then every two minutes. My heart was the drum that kept the rhythm. There was no escape. The mechanism at work was not going to stop until the process reached its culminating moment. I gave in to the erotic pain of that powerful force pushing me open from inside.

Nothing existed but my pulsating womb.

The doctors and nurses who checked in on me from time to time kept commenting on how young I was. But I felt ancient, part of the female multitude that shared, in this rite of passage, the power from which the sea, the continents, and Life itself had come into existence.

Clinging to my epic musings about childbirth, I was able to endure the pain and the various indignities I was put through in the hospital. First, the nurse shaved my pubic hair. The most intimate part of my anatomy was at the mercy of a perfect stranger, a fact that was more than unpleasant—it was terrifying. She moved so swiftly and with such astonishing determination that I feared I was going to be the victim of an involuntary clitorectomy. I remained as still as I could, scarcely daring to breathe, my eyes glued shut. The same nurse then administered an enema that doubled me over in pain. I barely made it to the bathroom with my dignity intact, my hospital gown gaping open behind me and my enormous belly protruding out in front. Just when I thought the humiliation was over, I was then subjected to a constant parade of doctors intent upon monitoring the dilation of my cervix. One by one they would enter my room and without the slightest reservation they would pop their head between my legs to inspect my private parts, as if attending a gynecological open house. The doctors kept referring to my baby as "the product," as if I were an assembly-line machine preparing to churn out a piece of garden equipment.

Finally Dr. Abaunza arrived. Tall, with broad shoulders and a thick mustache, he wore an impeccable starched white robe and a smile that reassured me that everything would be all right. He was a god. I could trust his resounding voice, his strong hands. Just seeing him made me feel better. My parents, my mother-in-law, and my husband took turns at my bedside, occasionally going out to the balcony to speak with the doctor in hushed tones. As the contractions came faster and faster in the early dawn hours the distant cadence of their voices helped anchor me to a reality that seemed to be moving farther and farther away, part of a pain-free world that I no longer lived in. My body suddenly became a violent attacker, contracting and twisting me in knots. I begged Dr. Abaunza to call the anesthesiologist. The pain was unbearable.

At long last they brought me into the operating room, and injected me with an epidural that anesthetized me from the waist down. When the time came to push, I appealed to my instincts, for I felt nothing. The only thing I was aware of was the message I sent to my muscles. The anesthesiologist, a small, delicate man, climbed onto a step stool and pounded on my stomach. It was as though he were trying to give it CPR. The scene was so utterly ridiculous that I began giggling, and I had to force myself not to burst out in a genuine fit of laughter.

"It's time," the doctor said. It was then that I suddenly felt something watery, like a fish, slithering between my legs. The operating room, with its bright white neon lights bouncing off the chrome instruments, was instantly transformed, as if cast under a spell. The little man stopped pounding on my stomach and moved over to my feet, where the doctor and smiling nurses continued ministering to me, serene and relaxed now.

"It's a girl. She's perfect," said Dr. Abaunza, as the room was suddenly filled with the shrill cries of my daughter taking her first gulps of air.

From the distance that separated my head from my toes, I saw her, naked, coated with a thick white goo, her little arms and legs flailing around, her wet, black hair, her eyes tightly shut. They held her up for me, and she opened her hands. I counted her fingers and toes. I looked her over, sniffing her like any animal smelling her newborn. It seemed incredible that this creature had issued from me, from the darkness within me.

In my mind, I pictured the red light going off outside the operating room. A red light meant it was a girl; blue was for boys. My parents, my mother-in-law, and my husband would be so thrilled. We all wanted my first baby to be a girl.

I was proud, exhausted, shaking like a leaf.

That morning, bundled up in a blanket like a cigar, Maryam was brought to me by a nurse. I gathered her in my arms, speechless before her tiny, wrinkled face, so very *mine* it was like cradling myself in my own arms. I gave thanks for being a woman, who could experience—just like a mare, or a lioness, or any other female—that fierce primative instinct to protect and nurture another living creature. She was so fragile I was inundated with tenderness. I was a fountain bubbling over. The warmth of my belly traveled up through my chest, my arms. It was love.

For the first months of my daughter's life, I retreated into a private little world that the two of us shared, deliciously and exclusively alone with one another. I wanted to eat her up. I couldn't stop touching her, kissing her, savoring every little gesture she made. We had moved to a small, dark house across the street from my parents, but her room was the sunniest. I had painted the furniture myself, and had adorned the exquisite netting around her crib with little pink ribbons. After her father would leave for work, I would carry her into bed with me and we would sleep together until mid-morning. In the afternoon, I would put her in her baby carriage and walk down to a nearby park whose main attraction was a grove of leafy chilamate trees with their aerial roots. The other babies in the park were cared for by nannies, but I wanted my daughter all to myself. And anyway, without my salary, my husband and I had almost no money. We ate lunch and dinner at my parents' house every day.

My deep plunge into motherhood was so fulfilling that it even made up for my mediocre marriage. But after six or eight months I knew I had to return to work. We were in bad financial straits. It embarrassed me to be so dependent on my parents, and domestic life was beginning to bore me. The conversations with other recently married friends always revolved around contraceptives, interior decorating, and debating the competence or incompetence of nannies.

After Maryam was born, my husband came out of his shell for a while, and we started getting together more with friends, gatherings where the men would stand around talking business and the women would sit and discuss "female" things. At dinnertime, the topic was always politics. My generation was thoroughly disenchanted and felt there wasn't a real, viable alternative to Somoza. The most recent serious attempt to challenge the dictatorship had occurred following the campaigns for the 1967 elections. On January 22 of that year, a protest by the Conservative Party

had ended in a massacre. The leaders of the Conservative Party had organized a massive, peaceful protest rally to get the dauphin of the presidential dynasty to renounce his candidacy, but the National Guard had
opened fire on the crowd. More than three hundred people were killed
that day. Miraculously, my brothers, Humberto and Eduardo, made it out
alive, scurrying over the hundreds of shoes strewn across Managua's main
avenue. Eduardo arrived home with a wound from a bullet that had just
grazed his arm.

Thanks to the intervention of the U.S. embassy, the Conservatives
sealed an agreement with Anastasio Somoza Debayle, after a rigged election had made him president. The pact basically ruined the opposition,
destroying their credibility in the eyes of the public. From that point on,
young people like us felt trapped in a kind of uneasy resignation. The
only alternative seemed to be the Sandinistas, an underground group
known in the 1970s for a series of military operations in the mountains
of Nicaragua. The Sandinistas championed a particular ideology that
was a mélange of New Left socialism, cooperativism, and popular democracy, a movement that came to be known as Sandinismo. The Sandinistas
claimed to be the successors to General Sandino's nationalist legacy, but
they didn't seem like a real alternative for us. They were guerrillas. They
advocated armed struggle, violence, socialism. At times they openly
defied the government, and the dictatorship would crush them in the
most lopsided battles, deploying airplanes and tanks to attack kids with
handguns. The dead bodies, riddled with bullet holes, would then be
paraded before the press, and the photos regularly appeared on the front
page of the newspaper. The Sandinistas' courage and sacrifice commanded
our respect, but we still considered them dangerous, subversive communists. Their operations were shrouded in secrecy, and people avoided any
mention of *them*. We all feared *them*.

Domestic life was suffocating me, and I soon began to have nightmares
about it. Half of my body had become a household appliance and quivered
like a washing machine. I read a lot of feminist literature during that
time: Germaine Greer, Betty Friedan, Simone de Beauvoir. The more I
read, the less I was able to stomach the prospect of years and years discussing recipes, furniture, interior decorating, and the like. Saturdays at
the country club bored me to tears—we were turning into our parents:
husbands playing golf, kids in the swimming pool, and the women talking about all the same things—nannies, the Pill, the copper IUD, or the
gynecologists of the moment. About the only thing that caught my atten-

tion during that time was Neil Armstrong landing on the moon. And my daughter, of course, but talking to a baby had its limitations.

Through my father I got a job at Pepsi-Cola. I answered the telephone and acted as a liaison between the manager and Publisa, an advertising agency. It wasn't what I was looking for but I needed to work. But then Bosco, the head of Publisa, offered me a job as an account executive, which I accepted right away. That decision changed the course of my life.

CHAPTER FIVE

*Of how I stopped being a "perfect wife"
and started getting mixed up in illicit activities*

MANAGUA, 1970

MY DAUGHTER WAS just taking her first steps when I began to work at Publisa. I joined the team that handled the advertising accounts and the creative aspect of the campaigns, which consisted of Bosco the manager, a man I will call the Poet, and myself. The Poet's office was right next door to mine, two cubicles separated by thin plywood walls covered in burlap. Bosco, being the manager, had the only office with walls that went all the way to the ceiling. On our side of the building, big picture windows looked out over red zinc and tile roofs and the cathedral towers nearby. Off in the distance one could see the blue silhouette of volcanoes towering over the far end of Lake Managua. The city was a bustling town of sharp contrasts. In the 1950s, cotton exports produced an economic boom which modernized some areas of Managua. Most of the city, however, was still provincial and poor, with picturesque, brightly painted *taquezal* and adobe houses; most people lived in large barrios spread out along the main roads. The majority of these barrios had no public water system or paved roads. The gulf between rich and poor was abysmal, but it was accepted—as a natural fact of life, or with Christian resignation, as if it were part of a world order that wouldn't ever change. I remember visiting those slums as a child; the nuns from school would take us there to teach us about the importance of charity. One day we went to Pescadores, a lakeside shantytown. I will never forget the little old lady I saw eating paper, sopping it in dirty, coffee-colored water to satiate her hunger. She was a wrinkled, skeletal woman, with skin hanging off the bones of her arms and a toothless grin which, from that moment on, became my mental image of the word injustice. You didn't often see that kind of poverty in the center of Managua, where there were lots of buildings like the one I worked in, a modern five-story.

We worked hard at the agency but we also had a lot of fun. Even though advertising is essentially a business, it had the prestige of being a kind of art form. The atmosphere was informal, and schedules were flexible—it had to be creative, after all. Bosco, the Poet, and I were always laughing about something, and they seemed determined never to take work too seriously. According to them, formality and creativity were a terrible combination. Bank employees were supposed to be punctilious, not us. Madison Avenue was our point of reference, and we followed it closely, because we wanted to be as original as the creative directors who had designed the ad campaigns for the Volkswagen Beetle ("You can in a Volkswagen"), Avis ("We try harder"), and Alka-Seltzer.

Camaraderie and friendship came naturally in our line of work. The Poet quickly picked up on the various issues I had as a young wife, bored with the stilted, stifling atmosphere of my social circle. He laughed at my proper upbringing as a schoolgirl at La Asunción, my years as a society girl, belle of the country club. He was originally from Granada, and was proud of both his aristocratic lineage and the privileged, intellectual environment in which he grew up. At his father's house, he had rubbed shoulders with the country's most renowned poets, who regularly gathered there. His father was also a poet who wrote beautiful sonnets and owned a fabulous art collection from Nicaragua's colonial period. The Poet decided that he would become my intellectual tutor.

"Let's go and have a coffee at La India. Don't worry about being seen with me. Only artists go there. Painters. Poets. Friends of mine. Come on, let's go. I want you to get out and meet different people, the people who really matter in this country."

I took the plunge. It's just a cup of coffee, who could possibly object to that? I thought. His siren song was irresistible—even more so once I set foot in La India, an unpretentious, smoky café always filled to capacity. And on the other little outings we took—trips to home-grown art galleries in between our client visits—I met painters, writers, and all sorts of characters who flung me into a new dimension. Simple, convivial, and poor for the most part, they had cobbled together a little community in which they shared books, art materials, money. They read voraciously and talked passionately about what was happening in the world—the

Vietnam War, pop culture, the sexual revolution, the responsibilities of the intellectual elite, the 1968 rebellion. Their conversations were sprinkled with names like Sartre, Camus, Chomsky, Marx, and Giap, as well as topics like the literature of the "boom," Van Gogh's letters to Theo, Count Lautréamont's *Chants de Maldoror*, Japanese haiku, and Carlos Martínez Rivas, the favorite master of Nicaraguan poetry. They also drank like fish, smoked pot, tripped on acid, fell in love, and recounted their various agonies and ecstasies to one another. They were real hippies, filled with energy and boundless curiosity. The Poet introduced me to the intellectual space they inhabited, a place that made me feel like Alice in Wonderland. I didn't smoke, had never dared to sample drugs, nor did I care for alcohol. But they didn't give a damn. I was their audience and they had me riveted.

"You've never read Carlos Martínez? What about Cortázar, García Márquez? You're so behind. It's like you stopped after Shakespeare and Lope de Vega. Read, read," the Poet said. He began to lend me books, and occasionally would take me to a small, cramped little bookshop, where I would buy books and we would bump into other poets.

"Look, there's Carlitos Alemán Ocampo. Let's say hello."

Two minutes later and Carlitos and I were fast friends. He was a writer, slight of build, with a childlike grin and a passion for philology.

One day, a day like any other, the Poet closed the door behind him as we walked into his office, a conspiratorial look on his face. As soon as the door was shut, he kissed me. I slapped him across the face.

"How dare you! You know I'm a married woman!"

"But I'm in love with you. I was dying to kiss you," he said as he smiled playfully, unfazed by my reaction, which made me uneasy. He began to talk about my mouth, about how sensual and irresistible it was. He wouldn't back off, not an inch. He acted as though my slap had been a caress.

"Leave me alone," I said.

As time went on I got used to the Poet's advances but they still bothered me mainly because, despite my objections, I didn't want him to stop. They made me feel desirable, irresistible. The depth of sensuality I sensed in him was driving me mad with curiosity. And I didn't know what to think of myself—was this reaction evidence of some awful character flaw, perhaps? I didn't know, but something told me that if I denied this part of myself I would never learn the secrets of life, nor would I ever know the Love I had read so much about and which I certainly hadn't found with my husband. It didn't seem fair that a social contract like matrimony could condemn me forever to a situation that was simply the result of bad judgment, a mistake. But I also wanted to be a good wife. I tried to get my husband to react to me the way I thought a man in love should, but his listlessness was a constant barrier that blocked all my efforts. He said he loved me but he seemed to think there was no need to show it. He lived in his own world, far away from me. To simply talk to him I would have to wait for the commercials between TV programs because he got so annoyed when anyone interrupted. He acted like someone much older than his age, already plotting how to retire from a world he perceived as a dangerous place populated with unscrupulous people who were all too eager to hurt him. When I protested, he simply said nothing. His silence was exasperating, and I would break down in tears, not knowing what to do. We were as different as night and day.

The Poet continued his offensive. He just couldn't control his "wild exuberance," he would say, feigning remorse. That was what he called his joie de vivre, and it was the most attractive thing about him, the thing that most seduced me, especially given the person I was living with. The Poet wasn't good-looking but he acted like he was, and that was what made you notice his beautiful smile and sparkling eyes. I didn't give a damn if he wasn't an Adonis or if he was carrying a few extra pounds. All he had to do was passionately describe a poem, a bit of history, or a delicious meal and I would suddenly find him unbelievably attractive and seductive.

To challenge me, to get to me by probing into my self-awareness, the Poet would analyze my life—especially my resistance to him, and the choices laid out before me. He thought it was abundantly clear that I didn't know what love was—but he also said he sensed my "sensuality" from the minute he met me. I gave it off, he said. Even his friends had noticed.

"Do you know what they said to me the other day? Who is that sexy woman you were with?" How could I throw my life, my gifts, away? he asked, over and over, as he talked about literature, read me poetry, and imparted impassioned lessons about the dense, complicated history of our country. I will always have a debt of gratitude to the Poet for having brought me in touch with the soul of Nicaragua. I had always been enamored of its physical beauty, its wide lakes and tall volcanoes, its trees of abundant foliage like a wild woman's mane, its humid ravines filled with the pungent aroma of coffee plants, its voluptuous, Rubenesque clouds, its fantastic sunsets and torrential downpours. But it was the Poet who introduced me to the secrets and inner workings of the land where I had my roots. He helped me see how the past clarifies the present, how it reveals the origins of the political realities and the abject misery I was witnessing all around me. He inspired in me the passion to read history. So I read chronicles by the first Spanish explorers to set foot in Nicaragua describing how they were dazzled by its landscape and beauty, and books about General Sandino, his fight against U.S. intervention, and the series of events that gave rise to the Somoza dictatorship.

"I just want to be with you, alone, somewhere quiet," the Poet said one afternoon, pleading with me to come to the apartment of a friend of his. "Can't we talk somewhere other than this office?"

I suspected it was a ruse, but he swore up and down he only wanted to talk, and I decided to believe him because the temptation was as luscious as the apple on the tree of Good and Evil. He took me to a tiny studio which belonged to one of his writer friends, in an old, run-down building. The room was filled with books. There was a wide mattress laid out on the floor, a desk, and an old armoire. Through the windows you could see the spires of a nearby church. After we were alone together for a short while, he made his move. I resisted, but mostly because I was supposed to. I was afraid to take the bite that would expose me to him, but I also knew that I didn't have that much to lose—it wasn't as though I was going to be expelled from any earthly paradise. My marriage was a barren, hopeless desert which only held together because of my cowardice and my misplaced feeling of responsibility. To catch a glimpse of the possibilities—of the "other side"—was altogether irresistible, and in the end I gave in. When it was over, the thing that surprised me the most wasn't my audacity: it was my total lack of guilt. The afternoon rolled along, lazy and indulgent. The secrets of the flesh were revealed to me, amid smiles, tales, and the Poet's poems, which he read out loud to me. "I am going to read to you my definition of love," he said, and as he read a long poem about towering Nicaraguan mountains and dreams, I watched him in the yellowish glow of the afternoon. And I smiled, feeling that finally I had been granted not only sexual pleasures but those of real intimate, joyous communication with a man. I will never forget the tenderness with which we reveled in one another that afternoon. Neither my imagination nor the literature I had read nor my mother's stories had deceived me.

I was twenty-one. The Poet, twenty-six.

That transgression was my personal genesis. It made me question all my obligations, and I began to think seriously about my rights, about what my life was and what it could be. My desire for freedom grew as wide as the universe. What remained of my life as a young, upper-class wife was nothing but appearance. Volcanoes, cataclysms had begun inside of me.

CHAPTER SIX

Of how poetry and revolution surged into my life

MANAGUA, 1970–1971

I DON'T REMEMBER what came first—poetry or conspiracy. All my memories from that period are luminous, close-up images. Poetry was the result of that exuberant, life-giving spirit. Once I could assert my power and strength as a woman I felt able to shake the impotence our dictatorship made me feel, with all the misery it had sown. I could no longer believe that change was impossible. I had reached a boiling point, and my body celebrated this wonderful affirmation. The simple act of breathing was a thrill. I drank the world in, and I was possessed by such a feeling of plenitude that I wondered how my skin could contain me. Any day now, happiness, like an ectoplasm, was going to spill out of my pores, and I would float off, naked, dancing through the streets of Managua.

One day I walked into the Poet's office, and saw him with a lanky, wiry young man with a face like Don Quixote. He had teeny eyes hidden behind giant eyeglasses, and a long, thin mustache.

"Camilo Ortega," the Poet said to me. "Sit. Camilo just told me that they almost took him away yesterday."

"So," Camilo said, continuing his story as I sat down. "They were about to throw me in the back of their jeep, so I shouted as loud as I could. 'I'm Camilo Ortega and they're taking me away!' You know—the worst thing is for them to get you without anyone else knowing about it. So I yelled and yelled. People came out of their houses. The soldiers got nervous. They hadn't counted on my screaming like that. One of them walked over to me, kicked me from behind and then pushed me around—

not to force me into the jeep, just to kick me out of the way and get rid of his urge to beat me up. Then they got in the jeep and drove off."

"And your brother? How is he?"

"It's hopeless. They're not letting him go. In December we'll stage a protest. We'll do graffiti, take over a church, the usual. 'Christmas without political prisoners.' "

"Daniel is Camilo's brother. He's one of the Sandinistas in jail," the Poet explained to me.

I wondered if Camilo was a Sandinista too. He seemed different from the artists and dilettantes I knew. He was quiet but intense, as if he were concentrating hard on something, and he had an air of responsibility that made him seem far older than his years. He spoke softly, almost in a whisper. But what I noticed right away was the intangible power he held over the Poet, who now seemed placated and serious—something highly unusual for him. He gave Camilo a copy of *Praxis*, the magazine he edited, which served as a forum for the group of artists, writers, and painters who worked together under the same name. We discussed the magazine: the essay by Ricardo Morales Avilés about the responsibility of the intellectual, the recently debuted Praxis gallery, which held recitals and art exhibitions. We talked about the widespread anger at the recent price increases—transportation, milk, and bread had all just gone up. Before he left Camilo asked us if we had seen the movie *Woodstock*. The music was great, he said. Joe Cocker did a fantastic rendition of the Beatles song "With a Little Help from My Friends." And then there was Jimi Hendrix and his guitar. We had to see it.

Camilo came back to the office a few more times. We would go across the street to a juice stand where you could look out toward the Gran Hotel, the tropical hotel par excellence in those days, with a green awning and an entrance hall filled with palm trees and birdcages with parrots and macaws. The sidewalks, littered with potholes and loose bricks, bristled with activity—throngs of people bustling about, traffic jams in the streets, taxis honking like mad, as well as a few horse-driven carriages. Modernization had hit Managua like a steamroller, transforming the city into a crazy hybrid of tradition and progress.

Camilo asked me to join the Sandinistas. By then, I was pretty familiar with all the signs and symbols of the underground movement. In the artsy circles, the Sandinistas were regarded with admiration and respect. I had now read all the books I needed to convince me that armed struggle and revolution were Nicaragua's only chance. George Politzer's book, *The Fundamental Principles of Philosophy*, turned me into a philosophical materialist; Frantz Fanon, in *The Wretched of the Earth*, gave me a crash course in colonialism, neocolonialism, and the realities of the Third World. Eduardo Galeano, in *Open Veins of Latin America*, revealed to me the sad, bloody history of my part of the world, and taught me about Big Stick politics, the Alliance for Progress, and the loathsome consequences of the Monroe Doctrine, which declared that "America was for the Americans"— meaning that the American continent had to be considered the exclusive backyard of the United States. I had also read Marcuse, Chomsky, Ernst Fisher, and Che. Socialism had won me over. But joining the Sandinistas was a risky proposition. It meant putting my life in the line of fire. I had my doubts too: the theory known as the "guerrilla focus" had only worked in Cuba. And what kind of system were they proposing, exactly? The Soviet model, from my point of view, placed far too many restrictions on personal freedoms. And how would we foment a revolution without a proletariat? Camilo, who didn't have a car, would often ask me to drop him off at the university on my way home. During the ride, he'd lecture me on subjects ranging from the failed military tactics of the guerrilla focus, to the ideology sponsored by Sandinismo. The revolution would not be communist, he'd say, but Sandinista, which meant that it would incorporate various theories, including Marxism, but adapting them to our specific reality. He had an answer for everything, and boundless reserves of patience to respond to my many doubts. When he asked me whether I was ready to join the Sandinistas, to give him a straight yes or no answer, I confessed that fear prevented me from committing myself.

"All of us are afraid. That's normal."

"But I have a daughter . . ."

He didn't ask me to go underground. I could do little things. Nothing risky, but enough to make my own small contribution.

"Your daughter is precisely the reason you *should* do it," he said. "You should do it for her, so that she won't have to do the job you are not willing to do."

He was right. I couldn't choose to be a coward.

"All right," I said quickly, without flinching, thinking of the way one slips under a cold shower.

"Don't tell anyone," he said. "Not a word. Not even to the Poet. This has to be between you and me. It's a question of compartmentalizing, of minimizing the risks."

It was night by the time we reached the university, a series of simple, prefab structures connected by hallways and staircases, protected from the elements by corrugated tin roofs. I dropped him off at the parking lot, and watched him disappear into the corridors. My stomach churned as I drove toward my house. I passed through slums, I saw the dilapidated buses slow down to pick up the passengers who piled in, hanging off the doors even as the bus heaved onward. Somewhere within my anguish, a sudden sense of relief—maybe it was joy—washed over me. It was as if the guilt of privilege had suddenly been lifted from my shoulders. I was no longer another transient observer, contemplating the misery from the comfort of my car. I was now one of the people fighting it. I cared about how the people of Managua were suffering, day in and day out, and I would prove it by doing something to effect a change. And that made me feel less alone, for a reassuring voice inside me lifted my spirits and calmed my fears. I was so relieved to leave behind that paternalistic Christian-style charity that always brought me back to the convent school nuns who, each Christmas, asked us to bring gifts for the girls of lesser means who attended our school in a separate annex next door. According to the rules, all gifts had to be the same: a piece of fabric, candy, and a toy. When it was time to give them out, the nuns would line us up in pairs, one rich girl and one poor girl. One by one, in front of the Mother Superior, the gifts would be handed over. As I waited my turn in line, the heavy, shapeless present, wrapped by my mother in simple, plain paper, felt like such an obvious welfare package. I always felt so terrible for the other girl—for her, the ceremony must have seemed like a well-intentioned form of humiliation. Troubled by the role I was forced to play, I could barely look at her as I handed over the gift. Then, we would kiss each other on the cheek and go to the end of our respective lines. That was the only time of year we ever laid eyes on each other, and that was what charity meant to me.

But this was different. I was on the other side now.

At home, everything was the same. Caught up in his work and his depression, my husband barely noticed me. We did some things together, but of our daily life the things I remember most are his apathy, his lethargic gestures, and the television screen, like the glow of a life he could look at but never really touch or feel. I fulfilled my role as wife and mother, and played with Maryam in the garden amid the abundant foliage. Thoughts and verses would spring up in my mind like kernels of popcorn frying in the hot oil of my secret life. It occurred to me that the words were banging down my door, begging to be written down, yet I resisted committing them to paper. Somehow I felt as if the act of writing would ruin the charm and the emotion of the images I conjured up in my head. I was better off staying where I was, standing motionless by my daughter's swing, watching her romp around while words and phrases rolled before my eyes as if written on banners floating in the sky.

I described all this to the Poet.

"Write," he said. "Write about what you feel. You have a responsibility— a historic one." His eyes were intense, serious.

The next day I arrived at the office with six poems. Shyly, I placed them on his desk.

"I wrote them last night," I said. "They just came out, like rabbits."

He took the sheaf of papers. He lit a cigarette. He sat back in his chair. He propped his feet up on his desk. The Poet had a potbelly from all the rum and beer he loved to drink. He wore long-sleeved shirts. As he read the poems, he exhaled long curls of cigarette smoke.

"Very good," he said, as he went from one page to the next. His voice, deep and clear, sounded surprised. Years later he would confess how astonished he had been by what I, a relative novice, had written—he had been half joking when he made that "historical responsibility" comment. He finished reading, stood up, and walked around the desk to sit down next to me. I can't remember his exact words, but something in his voice told me that he meant what he said. That was when Carlitos Alemán Ocampo arrived. The Poet gave him my poems to read, and Carlos seconded his opinion.

"They need a little work," said the Poet. "Once you get to be like us"—he allowed himself a devilish grin at that—"all your writing will be grand, but in the beginning, you have to polish, edit. A poem should be like a tamale, closed up and tightly bound. Nothing extraneous, but nothing missing either. Take a look at this one, for example. Study it. Think about the words it doesn't need."

"I'm sure you can get Pablo to publish them," Carlitos said. "He'll love them."

I worked hard as I weighed each word, removing myself so that I could look at the poem objectively, without me in the middle. It was so hard. That lovely metaphor, for example, was unnecessary. I marked it. I was never able to be a very merciless surgeon, because I was so infatuated with words. Only with time has it become easier.

We went in to see Pablo Antonio Cuadra, the editor of *La Prensa*'s literary supplement. He had a proud bearing, like a Nahuatl prince. His dark skin was the color of cinnamon and his thicket of hair, pure white. He was a tall man, with an elongated body that could have walked right out of an El Greco painting. I felt as if I were in the presence of a living monument, for this was Nicaragua's most renowned poet. His office was packed with books, folders, papers. Just outside sat his chubby, long-haired, moon-faced secretary who pecked away frantically at her typewriter. Rosario Murillo. I would get to know her later on.

"I'd like to publish these poems. With a portrait of you next to them," said Pablo Antonio. "When would you be free for a sitting?"

Not long after, Róger Pérez de la Rocha arrived at my house to paint my portrait, which he did in black printer's ink. We ended up having a lot of fun. Even my husband laughed, watching us like someone studying exotic animals in an encyclopedia. Róger was another character from Managua's bohemian scene—a jovial young artist like all of us. He cursed nonstop and hummed ranchera music as he worked. He was a barrio kid, proudly so, but extremely well read, able to recite from memory entire poems by Carlos Martínez Rivas.

Barely fifteen days after I had written my first poems, *La Prensa Literaria* published them, devoting almost an entire page to me. "A new voice in Nicaraguan poetry," read the headline next to the portrait Róger had painted. I looked dark and mysterious.

"Your poor husband," one of my aunts commented the day after the poems appeared. "How could you write—and publish—those poems? What on earth would make you write about menstruation? How awful. How embarrassing."

"Embarrassing?" I retorted. "Why should I be embarrassed?"

My aunt looked at me, horrified. And with an *ay! hijita!*, she got up and left.

———

The publication of my poems was nothing less than a scandal which rocked the upper echelons of Managuan society.

"Vaginal poetry," declared the matrons. "Shameless pornography."

"It's a good thing you published them under your maiden name," remarked my mother-in-law. Men leered at me with hungry, knowing looks.

"You must be quite a passionate woman," they would say with glazed eyes.

It was 1970. I wasn't saying anything that had not been said before by men, but I was a woman. It was not done. Women were objects, not subjects of their own sex drive. I wrote joyfully about my body, my passion, my pleasure. The poems were not explicit—they weren't even remotely pornographic. They were simply a female celebration of her senses, the wonder of her body. But they created an uproar.

My husband then announced to me that he didn't want me publishing any more poems unless he read and edited them first. Absolutely not, I told him. Over my dead body. I would give up writing first. Fortunately the High Priests of Nicaraguan literature rallied to my defense. The great poets José Coronel, Pablo Antonio Cuadra, and Carlos Martínez Rivas championed my cause. And in Nicaragua, poets are venerated, celebrated figures. Our national hero, the most acclaimed Nicaraguan, is Rubén Darío, a poet who is considered the Father of Modernism in the Spanish language. To be known as a poet in my country is to enjoy one of the highest, most cherished status symbols in society. My husband and family, finally, were forced to surrender to the blessings of prestige.

The controversy didn't deter me—it inspired me. To upset the most conservative circles of Nicaraguan society made me realize there were more ways than one to subvert the establishment.

The Poet, meanwhile, was busy building fabulous castles in the air, fantasies in which he and I would live happily ever after, writing poems to each other on our naked bodies until the end of time. My love for him, though, was more like that of a playmate, a partner in crime. The Poet would have been a nightmare as a husband. I could never picture him sharing responsibilities—he would have dumped them all on me as he went on proclaiming his "wild exuberance."

It wasn't long before I realized that when you break certain societal rules there is always a price to pay. The rumors grew louder and louder, until they eventually reached my father's ears. Blissfully ignorant in the happy little bubble we had created for ourselves, the Poet and I acted as though we were invisible. Instead of treating one another as furtive lovers, we walked through the city streets smelling of sex, our hair tousled and our eyes aflame. Anyone could see that we were euphoric, possessed by both the passion and defiance we liked to think only a chosen few ever knew. Unfettered in our arrogant sense of freedom, we made love on mattresses surrounded by canvases and smelling of turpentine in the tiny, ramshackle studios of our artist friends or in borrowed apartments. We even made love on top of our desks at work, giggling as papers went flying in every direction, gasping for breath to muffle the sounds of our lovemaking as typewriters hummed and coworkers bustled about outside our office door. Our cheeky disregard for discretion made us the hot topic of local gossip. Even my absent, distracted husband began to sit up and take notice. Sooner or later someone was going to say something to him. There was no way on earth I could escape the obvious: I had to make a decision: stay with the Poet—and assume the corresponding risks—or return to the familiarity of my marriage. No matter what I chose, I knew that nothing would ever be the same. I had grown wings. I felt ready to take flight. But the Poet was like a hurricane, too turbulent for me to handle, and I was terrified at the prospect of making the wrong decision and dragging my daughter with me. When I saw how my father was suffering, I made up my mind.

I'll never forget the look on the Poet's face on the other side of the desk when I told him. I feel as though I can still see the landscape behind the window, hear the rumble of the air conditioner. We couldn't go on like this, I said. I couldn't go with him. He had figured as much, he said. He knew it would have been too hard on me, having to confront my entire family about it. The conversation was sad, but not tragic—I think we both understood that we had pushed things as far as they could go. At least we still had our friendship, our mutual affection. More than anything I felt relieved—I was worn out by the tension of the weeks that had led up to this, and all the subterfuge that went with it. And while the Poet may have sparked the revolution that now raged inside me, I knew that what I felt went far beyond him or any partner I would ever have.

"I would have made you happy," he said, wrapping his hands around mine.

"You *did* make me happy," I replied.

He smiled. He was never one for melodrama. He got what he could out of life but he also knew when to give in.

Not long afterward, I changed jobs, sometime in the middle of 1972, I think. I was really making an effort to extricate myself from that love affair, like a snake shedding a layer of skin. I returned to the regular, married life that I had been sleepwalking through during my affair. It was a shock to see my husband again as the man who shared my life, my bed, the morning bathroom rituals, when for many months I had dismissed him from my life. The payoff was slim: sure, I didn't have to worry about accusations—"I know you have a lover"—and I suppose I felt honorable again. In spite of myself, I was mortified by the malicious smiles of my mother's friends, as they elbowed one another whenever I walked by, and the men who would cluster around me murmuring all sorts of double entendres as if I were wearing some kind of sign inviting them to try their luck with me. Much later on I would stop caring about what they said, and even relish disturbing their hypocritical sense of decency. But I hadn't quite reached that point yet. At the time, my fear of ostracism, of being left out in the cold, won over the need I felt to get away, to leave that environment altogether.

Camilo Ortega was the person who helped me realize it was important to keep up the pretense of my bourgeois life. The more time I spent undercover, without raising any suspicion, the more useful I could be to the Sandinista movement. By maintaining a facade of innocence and continuing to do my rounds in the traditional social circles, I could keep my finger on the pulse of the bourgeoisie, and report their feelings and thoughts regarding the dictatorship. Being an upper-class woman was an ideal alibi for my subversive endeavors. I knew that I had to keep my position in that world in order to eventually blow it up from the inside.

Not long afterward, Camilo told me he was going away for a long while. Someone else would call me, he said, and through that person we would resume contact. We said goodbye on a street corner.

That was the last time I saw him.

CHAPTER SEVEN

Of the oath I took before a pregnant woman

MANAGUA, 1972

TWO OR THREE months later, I received the call Camilo said would come. By then, secretly relieved, I had assumed they wouldn't be calling me. My heart skipped. I arranged to meet the caller, but at the last minute I lost my nerve. As I sat there at my desk, I struggled in vain to banish the image of that man waiting impatiently for me to arrive. Later on, I chastised myself for my cowardice. I felt depressed. Yet when the man called me back, annoyed, I made up a lame excuse.

"Would you believe they called me in for a last-minute meeting," I lied. "I had no way to get in touch with you . . ."

"When can we do it, then?"

We arranged another day and time. Another meeting spot. Sometime in the afternoon. I left the office as planned, but just before I arrived at the agreed-upon location, I turned right around and walked straight in the opposite direction. I can't, I said to myself. I shouldn't. This is madness. In my mind's eye all I could see were newspaper photographs of dead guerrillas.

Several days passed before the man called again. Every time the phone rang a surge of adrenaline would rip through my heart. I would just say no, I said to myself. But in the end I couldn't. I was too ashamed of being a coward. What would Camilo think of me when they told him?

"Listen, sweetheart," the man said over the phone, obviously fed up with me by now, "if you don't want to keep the date, just say so and I'll stop calling. It's dangerous for me to be waiting around for you."

"No, no, please give me another chance," I begged.

All of a sudden, I realized I was on the verge of closing a door that was my only way into a more meaningful existence. And I would be doing it out of fear. If I didn't do this now, I would just get more and more comfortable in my inertia, and the false sense of security that surprisingly I wanted to cling to.

With my half of the bill that Camilo had given me as our secret identification (according to Camilo, the man I spoke to on the phone would have the other half), I dashed out of my office, feeling slightly nauseated, and hurried toward our meeting spot near the old cemetery in Managua. There he was, on the street corner we had agreed upon—tall, dark, thin, and with a saintly expression on his face. He got into my car and said hello. Thank goodness I hadn't stood him up again. From the back pocket of his pants, he produced the other half of the bill.

"I'm Martín," he said, as he joined the two halves in his lap. "Camilo sends his regards." Then he smiled. His teeth were bright white. His smile washed away all my fears.

A few weeks later I learned that I was the 1972 winner of the Mariano Fiallos Gil poetry prize, the most prestigious award given by the Universidad Nacional Autónoma de Nicaragua, the national university. The awards ceremony was held at the university's main campus in León, a colonial city less attractive and more run-down than Granada. I gave my very first reading there, and was overwhelmed by the audience's enthusiastic response to my poems.

As my husband and I drove back toward Managua, I reveled in my triumph, inspired by the feeling that there really was such a thing as happiness. Look, I said, we have to talk about our marriage. We can't go on living like this—your apathy is deadly. How can it be that nothing makes you happy? I asked. We're young. Why can't we be happy? He complained about life, about the monotony of his job, day in and day out. We talked about other options. Moving to a little house on one of the islands in Lake Nicaragua, a more simple life in a small community. He liked the idea of that fantasy, and gave serious thought to the things I said. We talked for the entire ride home. I began to think that maybe all hope wasn't lost after all, that some kind of miracle was still possible. I put my heart and soul into the possibility of a reconciliation. I tried with all my might to revive the spark of love that had so long since faded out.

A few weeks later, while traveling through Europe with my father and my sister Lavinia, I learned that I was pregnant with my second daughter. Despite the fact that my marriage was still an uphill battle, the news filled me with joy. For months now, a restless, fertile sensation had been brewing in my body. It felt as though that pregnancy belonged only to me—as if I alone was responsible for this creation.

Back in Nicaragua, I began to meet with Martín. He turned out to be far more consistent than Camilo in his desire to instruct me and make me feel like a real part of the cause. I liked his personality—he was reserved and serious, but with a discreet, guileless sense of humor. We would get together to study secret documents, things like the Sandinistas' political platform and the statutes of the Sandinista National Liberation Front (FSLN—Frente Sandinista Liberación Nacional), in a sprawling, shady, tree-filled park just outside Managua, where the fuselage of an old airplane and an abandoned locomotive were the main attractions for the few children at play. During the week, the park was relatively deserted, serving mainly as a meeting place for furtive lunchtime tête-à-têtes, with children, candy vendors, and unemployed people idling about here and there. Martín and I pretended to be students, carrying our mimeographed sheets of clandestine literature inside notebooks emblazoned with the university seal. Behind its tranquil exterior, Managua was fraught with all kinds of unexpected hazards. The city was swarming with police patrols. At any given moment one could find oneself face-to-face with the dictator's special forces, the so-called Anti-Subversive Brigades, riding in their military jeeps, with their murderous soldiers armed to the teeth. One could never be sure.

Just like Camilo, Martín captivated me with the secret, quixotic life of the guerrilla. He trusted me. He never showed any doubts regarding my determination or commitment to the cause. Such a degree of trust challenged me not to let him down. Maybe it was because of the beliefs we shared or the risks we took together, but a bond of real friendship and affection had formed between the two of us. It was a profound feeling, a kind of implicit, complicit pact, and Martín was the first of many people I felt this way about—to my amazement, this happened over and over again with almost all the other Sandinistas I would come to know. It was Martín who finally put my last reservations about the Sandinistas to rest. I was exhilarated by the vision of our country, transformed—into a land of harmony rather than great gulfs separating one man from the other. When I received the honorarium for my poetry prize, I gave it to Martín, to give to Camilo's family.

"Getting rid of the dictatorship is only one step toward achieving our goals. Clearly a critical step, but it won't do us any good if the country stays the same. We're not working to change a person"—said Martín—"we are working to change a system. A democracy where the people can really forge their own destinies. Not a democracy administered by the same power brokers who don't want people to learn how to read because they're afraid that knowledge will make them powerful. That's why one of the first jobs of the Revolution will be to teach the illiterate to read."

There would have to be a redistribution of land, he added. People need land to work, they need loans, and women had to be emancipated in order to work alongside their husbands so that together they might build a new, better future. He told me an anecdote about Carlos Fonseca, the founder of the FSLN, who would constantly badger the Sandinista women who lived in the safe houses not to wash the men's clothes without being asked. They should read, study, write, he said.

It was very important to Martín that I commit to memory a pamphlet that explained some basic security measures for living an underground existence.

"I want you to treat this like a lesson at school," he said. "These guidelines can make the difference between life and death."

I learned them, and he tested me as if quizzing me on my multiplication tables. The pamphlet was filled with tips: how to check your rearview mirror constantly to detect a tail; how to shake off a tail either on foot or in a car; how to act natural so as to blend into the urban environment; how to control one's nerves; how to deal with unforeseen events; how to recognize state security agents. According to Martín, these methods constituted a code of conduct that became second nature when you practiced them every day. The most dangerous thing of all was to be too trusting, to think you were safe. That was when you would run into trouble.

"For example," he said. "I think the two of us draw attention. It would be better if your contact was a woman. Now that you're past the first orientation phase, I'll put you to work with a *compañera*, my wife. You'll get along just fine with her," he said, with a slightly malicious smile.

Leana, his wife, was a very petite woman. When I saw her there, standing on the street corner where I first picked her up, I knew we would get along. She was also pregnant, though her pregnancy was much farther along than mine. Her belly seemed to have taken over her entire body. She had short hair, and was fair-skinned, with freckles on her cheeks. She was only a little bit older than me, but she had a very maternal quality which was a blessing—I've always needed mothering. We became fast friends, and during our meetings, the political analysis almost always gave way to personal conversations and shared confidences. We couldn't help but mix the political with the personal—I always thought you couldn't truly commit to the cause of freedom unless you freed yourself first. One couldn't give what one didn't have. One couldn't make others happy if one didn't know how to be happy in the first place. It just wasn't possible.

We talked about the concerns we had for our children. Leana had a little boy at home. "If something happens to us, they'll have their fathers, the rest of the family. We're not the only ones capable of raising them, you know," she reminded me. "If we thought like that, we would never be able to participate in anything. If we want to survive, we have to be careful, but we also can't waste our lives worrying about death. I could die in a car accident tomorrow. At least, if I die in the struggle, I'd know that I died doing something for them. And my children will know that."

Leana was the one who swore me in as a Sandinista. It was noon, in Las Piedrecitas park, beneath a giant chilamate tree whose roots dangled down like strands of golden hair. We were sitting inside the car, practically suffocating from the heat. "I swear before the Nation and before history," she said, and I repeated her words. There was a lot of rhetoric in the oath but it was beautiful nonetheless, with grandiose, heroic words. You committed yourself to the cause of liberty, and swore to fight for your country to your very last breath. I recited the words quickly, without much ceremony, trying to tone down a bit of the pomposity, but when Leana and I embraced to seal the declaration, I was moved to tears as I felt her enormous belly brush against mine; my witnesses were those two children waiting to be born.

CHAPTER EIGHT

Of how a cataclysm obliterated the landscape of my earliest memories

MANAGUA, 1972

THE BACKDROP FOR all these memories—my first house as a newlywed, the office where I worked, the spot where I had my first clandestine meeting, the hospital where Maryam was born, the streets I walked with the Poet, the apartment where we made love—disappeared on December 23, 1972.

In a matter of moments, the reference points for my entire lifetime were turned to rubble. The earthquake that destroyed Managua shook the earth at 12:28 a.m. on December 23. It measured 7.5 on the Richter scale. Because the epicenter was very close to the surface, the quake destroyed most of the city. Ninety percent of the houses and buildings crumbled. Six hundred city blocks were razed. Before the dust from the pulverized adobe houses had begun to settle, fires broke out. Nobody knows exactly how many people died. The figure varies between ten and twenty thousand. Without electricity or running water the hospitals were at a loss to care for the thousands of victims. That night, three hundred thousand families were left homeless.

Because it was right before Christmas, the tragedy felt like betrayal. During that time of the year one has the impression that the world is enveloped in an atmosphere of goodwill and benevolence. So much unexpected death and destruction felt like a low blow, the sadistic joke of an unmerciful God. Early that night, Managua had been bright with Christmas lights, the streets decorated with fat, happy Santas, the shop windows powdered with artificial snow, and the plastic Christmas trees blinking merrily. We went to sleep looking forward to family dinners, stuffed turkey, and gifts for the children, and woke up in the Apocalypse.

I can still recall the dense atmosphere that December afternoon. The sky was gray and it was unseasonably hot and windless. I had fled from the crowds that packed the stores downtown feeling I would suffocate. I left Maryam's presents to be gift-wrapped and went home, wondering whether I was catching a cold or feeling the effects of the first trimester of my pregnancy. I couldn't get into the Christmas spirit and was aware of the irony of the big, joyous Santas, dressed for the North Pole, who would find no chimneys in Nicaragua. The spray-painted snow, the alpine villages on shop windows, the plastic evergreens, all irritated me.

At home, I played with Maryam on my bed. I commented with Alicia, the nanny, about how still and heavy the air was. "Not a leaf has stirred," she said. "If it weren't December, I'd say a storm was rolling in."

Nature was too quiet, too expectant. My acute animal instinct told me something was wrong. That evening I moved Maryam's crib to my room so she could sleep near us, I left the house key next to the door, and moved fragile knickknacks from the tabletops. My husband told me to calm down, that nothing was going to happen, but I went to bed anxious, fearful. At ten o'clock we had heard a booming sound, a noise like an earth tremor, but nothing had moved. In spite of my premonitions, at some point I managed to fall asleep. When I woke up the world was coming to an end. The quake had thrown me from bed. The first image I remember is being on my knees on the floor. I grabbed the bars of my daughter's crib and pulled myself up; I could barely move because of the violent shaking. A thunderous, beastly roar came from the earth, and mixed with the crashing din of the house tearing from its foundations, objects breaking, furniture falling. In the pitch black, my husband was suddenly next to me. "Help me with the baby! Help me!" I yelled at him desperately, fighting to keep my balance and lift her out of the crib. He got hold of her and we ran to the door, zigzagging and stumbling, dodging pieces of pots and earth from the hanging planters in the garden which were launched like projectiles. The walls were creaking, the glass levers in the windows clattered like mad castanets, the hinges on the doors screeched as they were torn out. We ran barefoot over the dirt and broken objects. Alicia ran too, with a towel over her shoulders, shouting, "Blessed Virgin, holy Trinity, merciful God, save us!" I thanked God I had left the key by the door. I tried to open it. My hands were trembling. The earth kept shaking. It seemed impossible that the earthquake was lasting such an eternity. It felt like the house was a monster that would trap us. I cursed my husband's obsession with security. All the windows were barred, even the ones to the inside patio. We were in a prison and the door wouldn't open. I shouted that I couldn't open it. My husband handed me Maryam, who was still half asleep, and started to kick the door. Collapsed from the frame, it wouldn't budge. Finally, in desperation, he pulled on it with all his strength and we managed to get out to the street.

As we reached the sidewalk a long wall across the street crashed down in a billow of dust. The neighbors shouted. Everyone on the block was outside. Frightened women and men were holding each other, hugging their children. The pavement was undulating, as if riding on the back of a slithering serpent. Suddenly it stopped. Everyone was silent. Afraid of moving, afraid to believe that the monster had calmed down. Overhead, a sinister full moon shone, huge and orange in a sky that glowed red from the fires. It felt like the sun had plunged into the city. Slowly, people began to move on the sidewalk. Every few minutes, the earth shuddered slightly. I was cold. My body was shivering and my teeth chattering. I silently prayed to the earth, begging it to stay still, not to move. I remember wondering if this was the end of the world, if this was a planetary catastrophe. It felt like it. One of the neighbors obsessively tried to find a radio station, but all we could hear was static.

Less than half an hour went by. A group of us had just finished making sure that everyone on our block had all their family members accounted for, when another gigantic roar rose from the depths of the earth and hit with as much strength as the first earthquake. It was total panic. This time we didn't even have the comfort of being half asleep or the distraction of having to get out of our homes. We were exposed and utterly vulnerable. I have never felt so much like an animal, like prehistoric men and women must have felt on a young planet torn by nameless cataclysms. Houses jumped as if the cement had suddenly become soft and malleable. Electricity poles swayed like palm trees in a hurricane; their wires waved over our heads like gigantic jump ropes. We heard glass breaking. Sirens wailing in the distance. The city was sinking, bobbing like a boat on a wild sea. I hugged my daughter. I squeezed her to me so she wouldn't hear the frightening noise. I prayed. My husband shouted, "Let's go, Let's go!"

But there was nowhere to go, no refuge, no other ground to support us. It's the most disconcerting thing in an earthquake: there's no safe place, no foreknowledge, no certainty. The worst nightmares take hold of the imagination: the earth was going to open up and swallow us, a volcano was going to erupt in the middle of the street, the city was going to sink. By then, the worst was over but we couldn't know that yet.

The rest of that night my husband, Maryam, and I huddled inside our car, parked by an empty lot nearby so nothing could fall on us. We tried to find in sleep a way out of the nightmare, to no avail. I covered my daughter and myself with a crocheted tablecloth I had grabbed from my dining room and tried to control the chills of fear that made my teeth chatter.

I lost my city that night, but many others never saw the sun rise over the rubble. At least, we were alive.

Wide-eyed and filled with a morbid curiosity, my husband and I, like many others, drove around as soon as it became light, to see what was left of the city. I couldn't believe my eyes. Of the places where I had spent my childhood, my adolescence, and my adult life, nothing but ruins remained. Blurry images in the sunny December morning. Without reference points to guide us, we felt like sailors without a compass in a sea of ashes and rubble. Occasionally, when our eyes filled with tears we could make out the outline, like a mirage, of what had been a familiar place. We tried to go downtown, but it was closed off. The corpses of buildings lay in the streets, broken and smoldering. No one from my immediate family or my husband's family died, but it seemed little consolation when so many people had been killed. Terrible stories were shared in the long lines at gas stations, where the employees pumped the gas by hand because there was no electricity. Total strangers would tell of their tragedies, and cry on each other's shoulders. It was all part of the collective grief. We all knew we had lost something essential.

Nostalgia filled the city. We were shipwrecked. I clearly remember certain images: the five-story building where I had taken ballet classes as a little girl, collapsed on itself like a house of cards; my mother sitting in an aluminum beach chair in the vacant lot next to her house while the uniformed maid brought her breakfast on a silver tray complete with a white lace, impeccable cloth; the coffins lining the sidewalks; broken bridges; poor neighborhoods in ruins and the people with blank, crazed stares; the exodus as people desperately left in old pickups and trucks, piled high with belongings and furniture, as if someone had ordered the city to be evacuated. There was no water, no electricity. Rumors spread that hundreds of bodies were trapped in the ruins. People feared the outbreak of epidemics. There were also stories of looting throughout the city: soldiers from the National Guard had been the first looters.

The best and worst of human nature was coming afloat.

My husband and I joined the endless caravan of overloaded vehicles that clogged the highways as everyone left town. We quickly packed our things into a truck owned by one of my husband's uncles and set off for Granada, where my parents-in-law lived. We said goodbye to my parents, who would leave the following day for their house on the beach, near León. I would have preferred to have gone with them but I didn't dare suggest it. I knew exactly what my mother would say: that it was my duty to stay at my husband's side.

As we inched our way toward Granada, I felt a terrible urge to hurry up and get there, to get away from Managua, leave it behind, forget about it, never set foot again in that great festering wound of a city, escape. I didn't think I could live through one more tremor. My legs ached from the effort to hang on to the ground. Condemned by the force of gravity, what are human beings to do when the earth itself fails them? My husband's uncle talked incessantly, the drone of his voice intensely annoying. It seemed that after hearing the rumbling of hell, my ears had become hypersensitive. Maryam, snuggled up against me, still clung to the notion of Christmas. What would happen to Christmas? Would Baby Jesus still come bearing gifts?

That morning I had stolen a doll for her. My father and I had gone to the only branch of his store that survived the earthquake, to remove the remaining merchandise. As we passed by a mattress store advertising some kind of promotion which involved giant dolls, I grabbed one, telling myself it didn't matter. It would be looted anyway. My daughter would have one toy on Christmas. That night, I felt better thinking that at least she would have the doll. I wanted to protect my daughter's Christmas fantasy.

In the hours following the catastrophe, I scarcely gave a second thought to the other little girl, the one growing inside my womb.

"Don't exert yourself," my husband said over and over again as we loaded things into the truck. I shrugged; I believed in the tenacity of that tiny creature inside of me. The idea of a miscarriage was like imagining an arm or a leg suddenly disengaging from the rest of my body. Impossible.

Once we reached his uncle's farm near Granada, we unloaded the furniture. We left it in a covered shed, utterly unconcerned about material possessions, which, as we had just learned, could vanish so very quickly. They were a nuisance. We just wanted to forget about them.

My parents-in-law had a colonial-era house, spacious and sad, with high ceilings and somber rooms, caves filled with musty, ancient objects. Whenever I thought of my husband living in that house as a child, a tight, oppressive feeling would clutch my chest. Despite his youth, my husband seemed so exhausted by life, and that house seemed to explain why. The only sunny part of the entire place was an interior courtyard with a broken fishbowl in the shape of a Chinese pagoda, and a malinche tree with its fiery red-orange leaves, with pods that would explode like tiny dry, earthy firecrackers.

The electricity wasn't restored in Granada until the following day. I began to cry when the lights came back on, as if life was beginning again. Other relatives descended on the house as well—uncles, cousins, and my husband's grandmother Doña Antonina, a youthful octogenarian who was by far my favorite of my husband's relatives. In the evenings we would settle down onto mattresses laid out in the corridors. My mother-in-law supervised things, issuing orders like a regular field marshal, while the rest of us bewildered, shell-shocked disaster victims mechanically obeyed her as we wondered what would become of our lives.

The children were the only ones who reveled in this makeshift settlement. Maryam, with her giant doll, was thrilled that the earthquake hadn't destroyed Santa Claus's toy workshop.

CHAPTER NINE

*On how one continues to live after losing a city
and what I did in Granada*

GRANADA, 1973

LITERALLY TORN FROM our city and memories, we Managuans had descended on the elegant, sleepy city of Granada, arriving with wagons, pots, and pans, to shatter the calm of our reluctant hosts. Located on the eastern shore of the great Lake Nicaragua—the second largest lake in Latin America—Granada had been the stage of wars and conflicts ever since it was founded in 1598. When Managua became the country's capital, Granada retired like a lovely lady to live out a restful old age. In the shadows of graceful mansions, its inhabitants cultivated a kind of phlegmatic skepticism that made them immune to political enthusiasms and passions. The favorite pastime of Granadans was to sway on their rocking chairs at their front doors in the afternoons, to see who was going by, chat and watch the sunset. The influx of strangers in December 1972 gave them plenty to gossip about. It was remarkable how creative they were weaving stories on those long evenings about who did what, when, where, and with whom.

Shortly after arriving in Granada I ran into my artist friend Róger and the Poet, who had all sought refuge there as well. Neither the Poet nor I tried to relive the past. I was pregnant and he was in love again. He had finally found the woman of his dreams. He was living with her at his father's home, an old mansion with thick adobe walls and ocher-colored paint that had been slowly peeling away. Inside it was a labyrinth of rooms, hidden courtyards, and an oratory whose construction had been ordered by a saintly aunt whom the family hoped would be canonized, sooner or later, by the Vatican. Valuable eighteenth- and nineteenth-century paintings hung on the walls, and the rooms were dotted with dust-covered pedestals displaying colonial iconography. For the few months I lived in Granada, that house was the nerve center of all the earthquake-displaced bohemians, and I started dropping by more and more frequently in the hopes of reestablishing contact—exactly how, I wasn't quite sure—with FSLN members scattered throughout the country in the earthquake diaspora.

During my stay in Granada I became quite close with a woman I had met through my husband's family. The Poet, Róger, and I called her Justine because she had the same mysterious air as Durrell's Justine. She had big black eyes, and a refined, sensual air like a Siamese cat. Justine and I were confidantes, trading stories about love affairs, and confessing how uncomfortable and out of place we both felt in the conservative, complacent atmosphere of our upper-class world. Justine and Róger were in love. Together the three of us explored the narrow streets of Granada, looking for balconies and corners he would quickly sketch onto a notepad, stopping at fruit-juice stands, contemplating magnificent sunsets over the lake. We were enchanted by the city itself. No other city in Nicaragua has maintained so well its colonial splendor. It is an architectural showcase featuring traditional thick adobe walls and mysterious inner patios, narrow streets and balconies with ornate iron railings, old churches filled with the aroma of votive candles, raised sidewalks several feet above street level, and a quaint central park with a gazebo where bands play on Sundays.

The matrons of Granada would whisper furiously whenever they saw us walk by with the thin, bearded man with the wing-eared, black felt hat and rubber peasant's sandals. At twenty-something, Róger Pérez de la Rocha was a thin, almost fragile man, of medium height with long expressive hands. Olive-skinned with the face of a Bedouin, he moved with the pace of someone who knows the road is long and yet is in no hurry. Róger had no fear of words. He'd say whatever popped into his mind and, with incredible self-assurance, used popular expressions or ingenious, off-color terms he'd made up himself, sprinkled generously with street slang, as if to flaunt his working-class roots. A troublemaker and loudmouth who liked to get drunk, he became a mystical being when he spoke of painting or poetry. I enjoyed imagining what the Granada gossips would be saying as I walked next to him with my pregnant belly. It felt good to be pregnant, to carry a symbol of life after the devastation of the earthquake.

Róger said I glowed and he was always talking about painting me with a flower coming out of my stomach.

Thanks to an extraordinary coincidence, I ran into Martín and Leana the first time I went to visit my parents in León. I was at my aunt's house when I saw them walking down the street. Hardly able to believe my luck, I dashed out to them. We hugged, updated each other on our lives, and then Martín gave me the password for the person who was to establish contact with me in Granada.

"Who are they?" asked my mother suspiciously when I returned. "Where do you know them from?"

"They're friends from work," I replied.

"I've never seen you so excited to see anyone," she remarked, and watched me for a long while to see if I would offer any more information. I played dumb.

The person who contacted me, following Martin's instructions, was Andrea. I had met her a few weeks earlier in the Poet's house when we were helping organize volunteer groups to work with the earthquake refugees the government had relocated to Granada. Andrea had been my younger sister, Lucía's, classmate at the convent school in Managua. In London, where they both had been sent to learn English, they had lived at the same residence for girls. Thin, with very delicate, fair skin, Andrea did everything she could to dress as simply as possible. She used no makeup at all, and wore jeans, Lacoste shirts, and moccasins—the perfect preppy uniform. She wore her brown hair short and pulled back; there wasn't a trace of vanity about her.

"You should have seen me before, when I came back from London," she said. "I smoked with this long cigarette holder, and I had a feathered boa that I wrapped around my neck. In Managua! Can you picture it? In that heat? I don't know what I was thinking!"

Her transformation was nothing less than radical. And it wasn't just her wardrobe, it was her spirit too. She took life so seriously, as if she couldn't waste time on jokes or anything fun, giving the impression of an efficient Swiss woman trying to survive amid a pack of rowdy Latin Americans.

As daughters of the bourgeoisie, the two of us could spend time together without raising any eyebrows. Every day, my husband would leave for work in Managua, Maryam would go off to her little nursery school, and I would get together with Andrea. Whenever she appeared at our house, my mother-in-law would greet her warmly, invite her in for coffee or lunch, ask after her family. The two of us organized a humanitarian aid program for the earthquake victims, but our work was also political. We would go down to the Centroamérica school to recruit new members from among the refugees, and try to convince them to demand that the government deliver the aid they had been promised—the aid that Somoza was red-handedly robbing them of, before the exasperated eyes of the entire world. Early the morning after the catastrophe, planes loaded with supplies and aid began to fly into Managua. We had watched these huge cargo planes arrive, and had felt hopeful and relieved that the world hadn't forgotten us. That the tragedy happened during Christmas had moved people in many countries to help.

Very quickly, however, it became apparent that the aid wasn't reaching those who needed it and that the National Guard and the dictator were reaping immense benefits from the disaster. While refugees were forced to take shelter wherever they could and beg for food, the tents sent for the earthquake's victims were ending up in the backyards of military officers, whose families, fearful after the quake, preferred to sleep in tents in their gardens. Officers' wives and high-level government officials were selling the rations, the powdered milk, and the first-aid kits. While canned goods and urgently needed items ended up in the hands of merchants, the only things that made it to refugee camps were sacks of potatoes and small amounts of rice, beans, and sugar. The earthquake increased the dictatorship's greed and let loose the unbridled corruption of an already unscrupulous regime. The Somoza family owned the cement monopoly, the factory that made roofing materials, the wood distribution, the plywood factory. The reconstruction of the city meant an economic boom for its businesses. As if that were not enough, the family abused its power to take over lands, control loans, and monopolize insurance and financing transactions. Companies owned by the dictator's buddies were granted the contracts for cleaning up the rubble and rebuilding hospitals and public buildings, with no pretense of legality or fair competition. The government's abuse of power became intolerable for the Nicaraguan bourgeoisie, bringing the antagonism between them and Somoza to a head. For the first time, anger against the dictatorship crossed class lines, encompassing rich and poor.

After appointing himself president of the National Emergency Committee, the dictator declared a state of siege and martial law in the country. In Granada, signs of the pillaging were abundantly clear. It became a virtual cottage industry: tobacco shops and stores were suddenly selling flashlights, portable stoves, and many other items that had been donated to aid the disaster victims. The regime insiders showed off their new toys, distributing camping tents left and right to all their friends. All criticisms and accusations were silenced. Somoza forced all the radio stations to join the national broadcaster and harshly censored the media. But too many people had been witness to these abuses for which no one would forgive the dictator. This injustice was the last straw. The earthquake did much to nourish the nascent seeds of rebellion.

Every day, Andrea and I would go to the empty shell of a school that served as a shelter for two thousand people displaced by the earthquake. Perched upon a cliff that jutted out over the shores of Lake Nicaragua, the Colegio Centroamérica had been a white, graceful building, a prow upon the ship of knowledge, sprinkled with the foamy waters that blew in off the lake. I still remember the great anticipation I felt when, as a teenager, my family and I would go to visit my brothers, who were studying there. To go to the Centroamérica was a privilege; we would walk down the wide hallways teeming with the young men among whom my friends and I would choose a husband someday. It was a way of legally entering that mysterious, athletic, competitive world that was the exclusive domain of men: the classrooms where they studied, the Olympic-sized swimming pool where the Sharks—the school swim team—would practice and rehearse their aquatic exploits. The name itself—Centroamérica—was synonymous with strength and discipline, as the school was famous for its high academic standards. The professors were strict, highly educated Spanish Jesuits in black soutanes, young priests with clipped beards and expressive eyes, which I contemplated as I wondered how on earth they managed to be so calm and accepting of the fact that they were condemned to celibacy for life.

But when I returned so many years later to that mythical luxury liner where all those boys had set off on their voyage toward knowledge and wisdom, the place was in ruins. Dilapidated, dirty, the trees in the courtyards all dried up. Nothing was left of the school but a skeleton of spiderwebs and neglect. Up and down the hallways of this decrepit monument two thousand people lay piled on top of one another, like a giant nomadic tribe camped out, using the place as a rest stop on the road to nowhere.

The faces of the destitute men and women were like zombies, staking out their respective territories by piling up their few belongings in the hallways, where there was barely an inch to spare. Entire families camped out in dark classrooms with boarded-up windows. Here and there on the brick floors, people lit primitive bonfires to cook what little they had in dented black pots. Wet clothing hung from the slender pillars separating the wide hallways from the interior patio that ran down the length of the building. A team of little ragamuffins ran around, zigzagging through the famous statues in the Statues Courtyard, where the priests exhibited the excavations from years of archaeological labor on the islands in Lake Nicaragua.

Lean-tos either of black plastic or of olive green canvas sprouted up like mushrooms in the spacious patio where the boys once played baseball. Amid the cracked tiles of the dried-up swimming pool, a breeding ground of caterpillars and weeds had begun to flourish.

The earthquake victims were made to wait in line for several hours to receive the rations which an unpleasant relief worker doled out from the back of a truck. As they received meager amounts of rice, beans, potatoes, and sugar, the women placed their goods into bags, cardboard boxes, and plastic baskets and then moved on, dragging their heels as they shuffled off with their sad booty. The air was thick with the combined smell of food, humidity, and too many people piled into one space. "At least we have a roof over our head," said one lady, shrugging her shoulders philosophically as she observed the scene from a bench. People complained about being left there like cattle, but they bore up to it with stoic resignation.

Sad, listless, wandering through the hallways, the people seemed to be fading. Our visits brightened their day, and they opened up, telling us their stories. Andrea strode confidently through the hallways. She had quickly made several friends among the refugees, including a pregnant woman who, when Andrea asked about the father, cheekily replied: "What do you think I am, sweetheart, a psychic?"

I took care of some of the refugees' simpler requests. There was a little old lady to whom I brought cough medicine one day. Together with her rooster and hen, she was living in one of those dark, smelly classrooms with fifteen other people, maybe more. About a week after I brought her the medicine she needed, she called me over with a conspiratorial nod of the head. I walked to her side, and she handed me a wrinkled plastic bag with six pink eggs laid by her hen.

"You're pregnant, these eggs will do you a world of good," she said. "They're fertilized eggs, made with love."

I was all ready to say no—how could I accept such a gift from her, when she had practically nothing at all for herself? But the look on her face told me there was no way I could refuse. To do so would have been an offense. I've thought of that face, that giving, and that lesson in dignity many, many times over the years.

Shortly before leaving Granada I met Ricardo Morales Avilés at the Poet's house. We bumped into each other as he was entering and I was leaving. When the Poet introduced us and I heard his name, I recognized his familiar face. He had been in jail. A university professor. A top Sandinista leader, the only one who kept operating in the open thanks to his connection to the university. I figured he had to be about thirty-five. He was medium-sized, with wide shoulders. His long nose, slightly flattened near the top, was crowned by a pair of arresting green eyes that jumped out from beneath his broad temples, contrasting sharply against his dark skin. Those serene eyes had quite an impact on me. Ricardo radiated the rare energy of an absolutely centered person. We chatted briefly, leaning against the balustrade as the distant breeze blew across the lake, filtering through the streets in the late afternoon. I don't remember exactly what we talked about. Poetry maybe. He was also a poet.

Ricardo's eyes and the aura of his presence have always stayed with me. After hearing so many stories about his legendary courage, I was very honored to meet him.

Ricardo was killed a few months later. After he died, for reasons that I will explain, I became intimately familiar with the events of his life.

CHAPTER TEN

On how I returned to my broken city, to childbirth,
and an unexpected death

MANAGUA, 1973

JUST BEFORE I was due to give birth, we returned to Managua. Ruins and debris were piled up everywhere. Crude signs posted on top of crumbled houses alerted the passersby of the former occupants' whereabouts: "We're at Aunt Lola's house in Masaya." In this chaotic atmosphere of loss, the city had come back to life somewhat by migrating toward the outlying areas. We rented a house in Altamira, a new housing development, recently opened just when the earthquake hit. Many of the homes on its main avenue had suddenly transformed into stores and businesses, which had its advantages: to get groceries all one had to do was walk down the street. In the evenings, night watchmen guarded the streets, blowing into their whistles every now and again. I retrieved the furniture we had stored in the uncle's warehouse and had all the pieces painted bright, psychedelic colors. I wanted bright colors, not the darkness of colonial decor. The house was tiny but filled with light; it even had a little patio.

As my due date approached, Maryam and I went to León, to my parents' house. The hospitals in Managua were in shambles, and so I waited out my last days at my parents' house near the beach.

My daughter Melissa came into the world, calm and serene, on June 13, 1973. From the minute I laid eyes on her round face with those wide-open, inquisitive eyes, I felt as if that little girl were tickling my arms, ringing bells, or stirring up some deep joy untapped within me. She had such a friendly, sweet face that I chose her name because it means *miel*, honey.

A few days after birth, she turned as yellow as a canary. The pediatrician at the hospital in León, a young man with thick eyebrows, jet-black hair, and a deep sadness in his eyes (he had recently returned to medicine after having his leg amputated), ordered a blood analysis. They pricked her skin, and Melissa burst out crying. Right then, I hated that doctor.

"Her bilirubin level is high," he said. If it didn't go down they would have to replace her blood. We would know in a few days. The baby had ABO incompatibility, a condition similar to the one caused by a negative Rh factor in the mother. Her father's blood type and mine were incompatible and unless her blood stopped rejecting the mix, she would have to undergo a full transfusion.

Even our blood couldn't get along, I'd think, pondering how ill matched my husband and I were. The wait to decide whether or not to give the baby a transfusion was unbearable. I felt pain every single time they drew blood from her. Because she was so tiny they had to insert the needle in her groin to catch the femoral artery, or in her neck to get the jugular. And it had to be done every day. I growled like a lioness watching her cub in pain, while Melissa kept growing yellower and yellower.

Meanwhile my breasts were swollen with milk and terribly sore. Nursing her, for some reason, would only make matters worse, so on the same night Melissa would have the exchange transfusion, I was given an injection to dry the milk in my breasts. That shot hurt not only my body, but my soul.

Blood samples from an endless list of potential donors were taken, but none of them turned out to be an appropriate match. In León we were staying at my aunt's, a redheaded mother of ten whose sprawling colonial house was as friendly as she was. As I paced up and down the corridors with Melissa in my arms, cousins, nephews, and their friends kept coming by, offering to donate blood. Finally, at midnight, the donor was found: a volunteer firefighter who lived next door. Yader Avilés. I'll never forget his name, or that of the doctor, Carlos Icaza, who emerged from the operating room later that night, pale and sweaty, to tell me that everything was all right. Melissa had her new blood and she would recover just fine.

Exhausted yet electrified by the tidal force of my maternal instinct, I returned to Managua with my daughter in my arms, safe from harm.

———

I saw Justine frequently. Just seeing her appear at my doorstep in the afternoons made me happy, for me and for Melissa, who suffered from colic until she was about five months old. Justine and I would take her on rides in the car; the only thing that calmed her crying fits.

Then one day, Andrea turned up in Managua, transformed into a happy woman. She was still the same person who was perennially worried about all sorts of transcendental, mysterious issues, but the expression on her face and the gestures she used had softened considerably.

"I'm in love with a fellow Sandinista. I call him Andrés," she said. She couldn't tell me any more because she would be divulging "compartmentalized" information, but she did tell me how deeply in love they were, how wonderful and sweet he was, and how she had never loved anyone quite like this before. I got along much better with this new Andrea; I always felt somewhat put off by the old one, so absent and impenetrable. In reality, Andrea was very vulnerable, a woman hungry for affection. She had invented her personality, based on her image of a person who carried out secret, high-risk activities, but when she fell in love she finally dared to just be herself, and allowed her more playful, friendly side to emerge.

Our clandestine net expanded during those months. The dictatorship's voracious greed following the earthquake tipped the scales of a precarious equilibrium that until then had allowed the businessmen and the dictator to enrich themselves. As the opposition to Somoza grew, the more extreme proposals for overthrowing him—such as the armed struggle advocated by the Sandinistas—began to seem more and more legitimate. Secret networks were now being formed in neighborhoods all over the city, and we were constantly finding more and more sympathizers on every social stratum—some people offered money, others provided shelter for those in hiding, and others volunteered their cars for us to use.

Andrea would give me clandestine literature to read. I had trouble finding an appropriate hiding place for it until it occurred to me to unglue one of the Styrofoam ceiling panels in the bathroom from its aluminum frame and hide the papers behind it. I would lock the door, climb onto the toilet, lift the panel, and take out the papers to read them. Then I would put them back. My husband didn't notice a thing. He was so unobservant that he never stopped to think I was staying locked up longer than usual, that women are not in the habit of reading in the john like men do. Several years would go by before he realized what I was up to. And only because I volunteered the information.

Occasionally Andrea would use my car. The deal was that she would leave it in the driveway before my husband would arrive. Several times, however, unbeknownst to him, she would return it as the two of us were eating lunch. She was as silent as an alley cat.

Around that time I made my first recruit: Alfredo, my cousin Pía's husband, a serious, thoughtful economist who had studied in France. We spoke often about politics, and after testing the waters, I decided he would be a good candidate and proposed the idea to him. After some thought he agreed to join, and soon afterward Pía paid a visit to the house. She had been suspecting we were conspiring and wanted to be let in on the secret. I moved to recruit her also—to me it was a question of equal opportunity. Why him and not her? The two of us still laugh whenever we think back to that day. Pía was an unrepentant hedonist. She had a great big heart, but really didn't understand much about politics.

"So . . . when the revolution comes," she asked, "are we all going to be on the same level?"

"It will take a while," I said, smiling. "But yes, that's the idea. That nobody should be exploited and workers be treated fairly, that we build a society where people support each other and bridge that huge gap between rich and poor."

"Excuse the extremely bourgeois question," she said. "But will I still be able to buy scented soaps to use in the bath, or is that too bourgeois?"

I burst out laughing.

"I doubt anyone would try to stop you from using scented soaps in the bath," I said. "We're not saying that everyone should be poor, just that other people should have the things we have."

"It's just that, well, those things are important to me," she said. "But anyway, you can count on me. I want to help, too."

Justine also helped out by donating money, though she did so with reservations. She didn't want to deal with anyone but me, she said. She wanted to keep her distance. It was too scary for her.

Amid a world of soiled diapers, Melissa's colicky cries, and my daily struggles to placate Maryam's newfound jealousy of her baby sister, I assembled my first underground Sandinista network. Together we would read documents such as the ones I kept hidden above the bathroom ceiling. Reading and studying were duties of every Sandinista rank and file and I took them to heart. I devoured all the Latin American revolutionary literature that was coming out then: books on Che, the Uruguayan Tupamaros, Ruy Mauro Marini's theory of dependence, Lukács's thesis on ethics, debates about art and political commitment, Freire's education for liberation. Using Freire's method to teach adults to read, I worked on improving my daughters' nanny's reading skills, and also recruited her as a Sandinista collaborator. Anita was a thin young woman, my right hand around the house. Her cooking was a saving grace, since I couldn't cook at all; in that I was truly my mother's daughter. My mother hated domestic chores, she dreamt of the day when we could substitute meals with pills, just like—she said—astronauts did.

On the afternoon of September 18, 1973, Anita entered my room with the transistor radio she kept on at all times except when she slept. When she came in, I was reading in bed, and looked up, alarmed.

"Listen, listen," she said. "I think some Sandinistas have just been killed." Sitting on my bed, we listened to the news flash. With that typical radio announcer's tone of voice—the kind that registers the same emotion whatever the news—I heard the report about the shoot-out between the Sandinista guerrillas and the National Guard in Nandaime, a small town near Granada. My hands went ice cold. Four Sandinistas were dead. Only two had been identified: Ricardo Morales Avilés and Oscar Turcios.

I could still see Ricardo, resting against the balustrade in the Poet's house, the day I first met him. I thought of our brief, friendly exchange and in my mind's eye I could see his face, as clear as if he were right there in front of me. His deep green eyes. His smile. Like a shimmering mirage suddenly broken. So many things crossed through my mind right then: poems he had written, the huge university protests demanding his freedom when he was in jail, the Poet telling me what an extraordinary person he was, so centered, so intelligent, so noble. And so young, I thought, so young. His whole life before him. I didn't know Oscar Turcios very well. I only saw him once, from far away at the Centroamérica school while waiting for Andrea. They called him El Ronco—Gruff—and Andrea used to talk to me about him, his sense of humor, his endless jokes.

Anita was standing now, looking at me.

"I'll leave the radio with you," she said, and left the room. I wanted to thank her, but I couldn't even think straight. I wanted to do something. Turn time back. Do something to prevent what had just happened, erase the deaths altogether. Rewind, rewind, as if you could just hit a button and stop the inevitable. For the first time in my twenty-three years I felt the absolute impotence one feels at the violent, sudden death of someone dear. I didn't know what to do with myself. Giant waves were crashing inside me, but there was something else there too, something that was rising up slowly but surely through my veins. A great gust of wind suddenly put all the pieces together. Fragments of conversations. I didn't want to be right, and I felt like vomiting when I realized Ricardo was the man Andrea loved. Her Andrés.

At some point I fell apart, and began weeping in despair. The intensity of the pain startled me—it was as if one of my own brothers had died, someone close that I loved and not a person I barely knew. That was when I understood how strong the bond between those of us who were in the struggle was: we were a team, a unit. I also realized how much I cared about Camilo and Martín. The pain was like a violent amputation that left me incomplete—as if with him, all of us had died somewhat. I thought of the next day's newspapers. The photographs of the dead bodies splashed across the front pages. And Andrea. I couldn't stop thinking about Andrea.

She came looking for me that afternoon. She didn't have to say a thing; I knew my instinct hadn't been wrong. Fragile and trembling, she curled up in my arms. "Andrés," was all she could say as she sobbed inconsolably. I stroked her head, holding her for a long while. I cried too. Tears rolled down my cheeks, and I held her as the sobs shook through her body. I felt as if I were suffocating just thinking about what she was going through. My palms burned. Funny, I always seem to feel the agonies of the soul in the palms of my hands. After a while we sat up on the bed with a box of Kleenex.

"How did you know?" she asked.

"I don't know. Intuition."

"What am I going to do?" she wailed, rubbing her hands rhythmically against her jeans, in a mechanical, automatic movement. "They don't know anything at home. I'm going to have to pretend nothing's wrong. Oh my God! And today my mother asked me about Andrés. He called me every day. I told her he was a friend from the university—I'm going to have to pretend he's still alive—and I'm going to have to come here to cry. You don't mind, do you, if I have to come here to cry? They got him alive, you know. When they realized who he was they killed him. And then they hit the house. Two others, women, escaped. But they got the other two and killed them when they caught up with them. Poor Ronco. Juan José, whom you never met. He was a wonderful *compañero*. My God."

Andrea didn't refuse to look at the newspaper. I remember how she sat on my bed the following day with the newspaper in front of her. "Poor baby," she murmured, "look at what they did to his face, my poor Andrés." Her words tore my heart to shreds, but I knew that there was nothing I could do. Anything I said would be useless. Consolation just wasn't a possibility. Little by little, as the days and weeks passed, I came to know all the details of their courtship—racing together in the pouring rain, singing the song they loved sung by a Spanish band. Andrea took me with her on all their trips to their last goodbye. She had never imagined that it would be the last she would see of him. Over and over again she would describe the scenes like paintings, frozen in her memory. It was as if talking was the only way for her to hang on to the memories. As long as she could just talk about him, the images would remain fresh. The words would prevent them from dissolving into nothing. And so she repeated the same anecdotes over and over again, like a spell she cast to keep Ricardo alive. She was like that for months, and I watched her slowly fade away. She lost weight, stopped wearing makeup.

One day she came over and told me she was leaving. The Organization (as we often referred to the FSLN) had decided it was no longer safe for her to be working in Nicaragua, so she was going to Mexico to work with Sandinista supporters there.

"I told my father I want to study there. You'll get a new contact now," she said.

We said our goodbyes. It was sad. I wanted to think the time away would do her good, but I could only imagine her settling into Mexico, living alone, and meticulously, lovingly caring for her ghost.

CHAPTER ELEVEN

On how I met Roberto and Marcos, and became a courier
for the underground resistance

MANAGUA, 1973

MY NEW CONTACT was Roberto. He had a face like a bird, something I noticed the minute he took off his dark glasses as he sat down in front of my desk. His head was small, with rounded temples, huge, close-set eyes, a pointy nose that curled downward, and thin lips poised above a tiny jaw. My office at the advertising agency was small, with two leather chairs for guests. My desk took up almost the entire office.

"Cat got your tongue?" he asked, with a friendly, warm smile.

We instantly liked each other. It was nearly impossible to resist that expression, those gestures. I could just picture him as a little boy in the neighborhood, wiry and alert, trading toys, charming his teachers, leading his friends in their childish exploits. He had a special kind of magnetism that compensated for his short, stocky figure and that odd, birdlike face. He looked around—at the paintings on the wall, Róger's portrait of me, my diploma from the Charles Morris Price School in Philadelphia, the thick, peach-colored rug—and asked me what kind of "arrangement" I had in the office. Could he visit at any time of day? Did he have to make an appointment? Was I the boss or did I report to someone? I told him that I had just returned to work after giving birth to my daughter. How many children did I have? Two. I explained that my new job was to oversee an almost bankrupt billboard production company which two new partners had recently infused with a substantial amount of money. They hoped that the investment, along with my contacts and experience in public relations, could turn it into a small but profitable advertising agency.

How many people worked there? he asked. At the time there were four of us: the accountant, the art director, the secretary, and I. You live nearby, right? Yes, two blocks away, ideal for me—I could pop in to see my baby whenever I wanted. Perfect, he said. I get the picture. And your husband? he asked. He's an engineer. And he doesn't know a thing about this, I said. And I smiled.

"You and I are going to act as go-betweens for two *compañeros*," he explained. "One is Martín, whom you already know, and the other is Marcos, whom you'll meet soon. Marcos is not just undercover like us; he is a clandestine operative, so most contact with him is via letters. Martín will telephone you to pick up his letters for Marcos. Then you'll give them to me, and I will deliver them to Marcos. Martín will also be calling you to get whatever Marcos sends back with me. That's what the plan is for now. And if anyone catches either one of us with those letters . . ."

As his voice trailed off, he drew an imaginary line across his throat with his index finger.

Martín called me the next day. I was excited to hear his voice, but he said he couldn't talk; he was in his office. At five o'clock we were to meet on a street corner in Managua.

"Don't be late," he repeated. "Five on the dot. Go by the Radio Minuto clock."

Radio Minuto. How I grew to hate that radio station. "Your time, minute by minute." A mechanical female voice announced the hours, minutes, and seconds as they passed, with the constant tick-tock of a clock in the background of all their programming—music, news, everything. For us punctuality was paramount, and so I would always arrive early, and end up driving around to kill time. Minutes become an eternity when you have to count every second.

Martín was exactly the same, thin and lanky as ever. Leana had given birth to a boy, and they were doing fine, he said. He asked me if we could use my house as a daytime meeting place, while my husband was at work. Yes, of course, I said. He gave me a thick, heavy envelope to give to Roberto. Since we had to arrange our meetings via telephone, we invented names for our rendezvous points. One corner was named "Aunt Rosa," and a certain street became "the doctor's office." He gave me a list of several locations with their code names. You won't forget them, will you? No, I won't forget them, I promised, committing them to memory. Drop me off here, okay?

And we said goodbye.

Before leaving for Mexico, Andrea told me a story about a fellow Sandinista who, whenever he borrowed someone's house for a meeting, would send the hosts a list of the food he'd like to eat. She said it with a very straight face, although to me it sounded like a joke. I was reminded of this one day as Roberto and I were going over the details of a meeting to be held at my house.

"They told me to give you this—here, it's the breakfast menu," he said, pulling a wrinkled piece of paper out from his bag and handing it to me with a knowing smile.

He came to my office almost every day, in and out with the greatest of ease, pretending to be a potential client.

I read the menu. Fried eggs, ham, and pineapple over toast. I looked at him, amused.

"Only if you can," he assured me. "It's not an order. One of these men is always hungry—he's living with a couple that's on a macrobiotic diet. He dreams about food."

"Well, I'm no cook, but I'll do my best. But this dish sounds awful." We laughed.

Later on, Marcos would swear to me that he never sent in a menu, but I'm sure he did. It was his way of enjoying the sweet charms of the bourgeoisie. I met him in person for the first time at that meeting where I also discovered, as I saw them arrive, that Bayardo Arce, a journalist I knew, and Luis Carrión, a society kid like me, were Sandinistas as well.

After the meeting, I had to drive Marcos somewhere in Managua, navigating through the hectic midday traffic in the most infernal heat. He was a bit taller than average, with green eyes, which made me suspect he was from Matagalpa, a region in the north of Nicaragua. At the beginning of the twentieth century, there was a wave of German immigration to Matagalpa, spawning a generation of tall, blond children, a highly uncommon phenotype in Nicaragua. I remember studying his nose that turned up ever so slightly at the end, with elongated, oval-shaped nostrils. For most of the ride he was silent, and we drove farther and farther into crowded neighborhoods, dodging the taxis that stopped wherever they felt like it, never bothering to signal.

"Never tailgate when you're driving with a clandestine operative," he suddenly said as I inched closer to the vehicle in front of us. "You have to leave enough space to maneuver in case there's trouble. And did you look in the rearview mirror? Don't ever forget about that. You know, it would be a good idea for you to explore the city—you need to know all the streets, the dead ends, the traffic circles—plus any paths that can help you shake off anyone tailing you. All of this is extremely important for anyone driving people like me around the city."

He wasn't like the others. It was easy to see he was used to being in charge.

I drove with extreme caution. Then, as if suddenly aware of my existence, he broke away from his thoughts for a moment, turning around in his seat. He looked at me, and began to talk about artists. I had belonged to the Grupo Gradas, hadn't I? I nodded. The group had broken up after the earthquake, I explained, because public meetings were prohibited under martial law. Then he asked me about Praxis, the Poet's group. The gallery space had tumbled down, and there wasn't enough money to keep the magazine going, I told him. But artists had to become active again, he exclaimed. Art was key to mobilizing and motivating people.

I dropped him off in the western part of the city, near a large cemetery mostly used by low-income residents, which was enclosed by crude cement planks. He stepped out of the car, and rapidly disappeared down the street, hunching his shoulders as if to hide his height. I wondered how he managed to get around unnoticed. Who was he? His only disguise was a baseball cap. According to Roberto, he was extremely well educated, and spoke four languages.

As I drove away, looking for the way back home, I had to navigate through the labyrinth of narrow streets of that crowded, lower-middle-class barrio, which still bore the effects of the earthquake. It was an area I didn't frequent, but I had gone to a church there once with the Grupo Gradas, a group of singers, poets, and painters, led by the poet Rosario Murillo, whom I had met at the *La Prensa* offices when she was secretary to the editor Pedro Joaquín Chamorro. The Grupo Gradas organized readings and concerts in various neighborhood churches around the city, and people would attend in droves, mainly to hear the protest music of Carlos Mejía Godoy, one of Nicaragua's most talented songwriters. They knew the choruses to all his songs by heart. "Yo no puedo callar. No puedo quedar indiferente. Ante el dolor de tanta gente, yo no puedo callar." ("I cannot remain silent. I cannot remain indifferent. In the face of so many people's pain, I cannot remain silent.") The group became so popular that the National Guard began showing up at the meetings, to intimidate the public and get them to disperse. The more progressive priests, inspired by the tenets of Liberation Theology, gave the artists a place to play, and what started out on the church steps eventually found its way inside. I only participated in a few concerts—before the earthquake—but I never forgot the image of those little churches, packed to capacity, the faces of all those people singing out loud, their fists raised high in the sweltering heat.

Ahead of me, on the road, I noticed one of the National Guard jeeps that patrolled the city streets day and night. There were two soldiers in front and two in the back. The men in back carried rifles, which they would carelessly point at passersby or at other cars on the road. I thanked God that Marcos was no longer with me.

CHAPTER TWELVE

On how I got my first book of poetry published,
and on how the dictatorship's secret police began tailing me

MANAGUA, 1974

AFTER POETRY CAME into my life and I gave it free rein to move through me, I often experienced lightning storms of poetic inspiration. Poems would bolt out of me like high-voltage discharges. Pages of verse began to accumulate. Before long I was ready to publish my first book. There were no publishing houses to speak of in Nicaragua, and so Jaime Morales Carazo, one of my advertising clients and a patron of the arts, struck a deal with me: he would put up the money to publish it if, in exchange, I would allow him to keep a large portion of the books to give as Christmas gifts from his company. That was how *Sobre la grama* (On the Grass) was published. Róger designed the cover. The title was my way of paying homage to Walt Whitman's celebration of the human body, the landscape and the multitudes of his homeland. The great Nicaraguan poet José Coronel Urtecho, my mentor and friend, wrote a long, lauda-tory introduction to my book. "The woman who reveals herself is a rebel," he said, referring to my celebration of the erotic. It couldn't have been more appropriate, given the far more secret dimension of my rebel-lious activities—though he knew nothing about them.

The book party was held at the Tague Gallery, run by Mercedes Gordillo, a true pioneer committed to putting Nicaraguan painting on the cultural map of Latin America. Held in a covered terrace next to a garden filled with rosebushes, the party and reading was attended by my friends from the art world as well as other guests. I still remember the aroma of damp earth that permeated the evening, the rapt faces of my audience, and the great joy I felt at holding at last a copy of my book. It had a simple blue cover. It was like a child I had just brought into the world. Like I had done with my children, I also wanted to smell it and hug it close to me when going to sleep.

At twenty-four, I was a citizen of a terrible, destitute country, but no misfortune seemed eternal to me. I was sure we could change everything and build a bright future. Meanwhile, I enjoyed my freedom, my friends, my job, my small office, and my colleagues, who managed a sense of humor while fulfilling their obligations; I enjoyed my daughters, my small universe where I was a woman and acclaimed poet. I would drive around Managua, often in a state of euphoria, with the wind blowing in my hair and the music of Carole King, the Mamas and the Papas, and Mocedades blasting from my car's radio.

Nothing could have prepared me for the afternoon when I returned from a quiet lunch with my daughters to find two of the ad agency's three partners waiting for me. What a surprise, I said, as I rushed in, flinging myself into a chair. What had happened to siesta? What was this impromptu visit all about? One of the partners, the most outspoken, smiled thinly as if trying to lighten the gravity of the moment and said that unfortunately they had something serious to discuss with me.

"I'm going to tell this to you straight," he said. "Samuel Genie called us." Samuel Genie, the chief of Somoza's State Security Office—the dictator's brutally repressive apparatus. "He told us that you're in with the Sandinistas, that we shouldn't keep you here. Well, he clearly 'recommended' that we fire you."

I experienced an instant unfolding of my self. I became two people. A cold, rational Gioconda took control of the situation while the other one trembled, curled up in a corner somewhere inside of me. I knew who had been the informant too—it was that man, that Somoza supporter who came around to see the agency's accountant. It was he, I knew it. He must have picked up on something.

"Me?" said the woman standing there, with the most genuine look of shock on her face. "That I'm with the Sandinistas? Me? 'Tania, the guerrilla?' I said, laughing, bringing up the title of a well-known book about a woman who had been Che's companion in Bolivia. "Are you crazy? Just look at me, please, look who you're talking to!" They surveyed my tight blouse, faded jeans, and the flirty blue cap perched just so on the right side of my head, allowing a little ponytail to peep out from the left side. I knew they would see me for what I appeared to be: a bourgeois young woman dressed like a hippie.

"Genie is the one who says so. Not us. We believe you, but I don't have to tell you what a warning from Genie means," one of them said.

No. They didn't have to tell me. It was my luck that both partners were on good terms with the regime. "Warnings" were not common. Naturally, since I was a public figure, from the upper class on top of it, the dictatorship had chosen to intimidate me rather than move in to capture me. To detain someone like me would have been an acknowledgment that the Sandinista movement was something other than just an obscure group of subversive "bandidos."

"But it's not true. It's totally false," I said with a shocked, pained expression on my face. "This is a mistake. You must tell Genie that he's made a terrible mistake. Wait a minute . . . I know!" I suddenly exclaimed, in a moment of inspiration. "I'm sure it's because I am a poet. Because I run around with people with long hair, painters, hippies. Artists are always suspect. We have a bad reputation. You know perfectly well that I'm anti-Somoza, but honestly, a Sandinista . . . ?" I kept my tone of voice light and amused, self-confidently laughing at myself. "God forbid—I'm such a coward, I am even afraid of firecrackers!"

What am I going to do? I was asking myself the whole time. That afternoon, Marcos, Martín, Bayardo, and Luis would be meeting at my house. I had no way of communicating with them. No way to warn them.

I noticed that one of the partners was smiling. Relaxed now, he looked over at the other one. I could tell he was already considering his alternatives. He would talk to Genie, ask him to reconsider, offer him my explanations.

"All right," he said. "Let's just leave it at that. To do this has been quite uncomfortable for us, something we would rather have avoided. So in any event, whatever you do be careful. Don't go and get involved with the Sandinistas. It's very dangerous. And make no mistake—you're being watched, your telephone is tapped. State Security doesn't mess around."

"Believe me, I feel terrible—worse than you do about this," I said, genuinely chagrined. "But please make sure that that man understands he's got the wrong idea about me."

I saw them to the door.

The girl I once was, the one who had been the product of a Catholic school education, was always astonished at the way the woman I had

become told lies with the aplomb of someone asserting the most unequivocal truth. My imagination had turned out to be an asset. I was a natural
conspirator from the start. But that incident was my trial by fire. I was
sure I had thrown them off my trail just as I had learned to do with my
husband. When I did it with him my nose did not grow, my face did not
turn red, nor did I avoid his gaze whenever I invented false obligations or
lied about my whereabouts. But that day after the men left my office, my
habitual cool melted into a panic. I had to think of a solution, and fast.

It had been one or two weeks since I had separated from my husband. All
the constant juggling acts I had to perform to keep him believing I still
was someone I had ceased to be drove me, one day, to finally ask myself
what was the point of holding on to the dead corpse of our relationship. I
had been married for six years already. And why, for whom? My daughters? My parents? A man that in any case only inspired fraternal feelings
in me, whose life was just the daily routine of home and work, work and
home? Was I afraid that his terrible melancholy would devour him if I left
him alone? I can't be sure what it was that he or I said when, at last, we
decided to part. All I remember is how relieved I felt. He gathered his
things and left. He rented an apartment and I stayed in our house with
my daughters. I explained to them that love does not always last forever.
They would always have their father, but from now on he and I wouldn't
be living together. Maryam, my older daughter, was six years old and
took the separation harder. Melissa had just celebrated her first birthday
and didn't understand much. My mother took the news better than my
father did, who warned me it was hard to be a divorcée in a society like
ours. But in the end he accepted it. I think he almost felt as if he had me
back, that now he could be the one to take care of me again.

But I couldn't turn to my father in my present predicament. As I
racked my brain, beating back the terrible images that flew through my
mind (my house surrounded by cold-blooded soldiers opening fire, killing
us all), I came up with a plan. I called Justine. When she arrived, I told her
what was going on. She and I would take the *muchachos* out in our cars, I
told her. We would divide the group and drive away in different direc-
tions. Just her presence calmed me: she didn't seem agitated or frightened
at all. Justine had an inner strength she wasn't fully aware of. Together,
we drove my girls and Anita to my brother Humberto's house.

"Don't you move from here," I said to Anita. "Not until I come back for you. Under no circumstances are you to go back home without me."

The men arrived at five o'clock on the dot. Bayardo, Luis, Marcos, and Martín. No Roberto. I filled them in. Slightly put off by Justine's presence at first, Bayardo and Luis sat down in the living room and began to talk to her. Marcos and Martín called me into the bedroom. Sitting on the bed, Marcos looked undisturbed. He had taken his baseball cap off and was running a hand through his hair. I didn't know what they were waiting for. And it made me nervous that I seemed more alarmed than they did. I almost got the feeling that Marcos was still considering staying at my house all night according to the original plan. He looked at Martín.

"What do you think?" he asked.

"Well, man, I think the *compañera*'s right. The sooner we get out of here the better. If they have her under surveillance . . ."

"How do you feel?" Marcos asked me.

Fine, I replied. A little nervous but fine. It was them I was worried about. That was why I had called Justine, so that we had two cars to get them all out of there. "All right," said Marcos, standing up. "Better safe than sorry. We'll leave in the two cars as if we were going to a party. You," he said, turning to me, "go on with your life as usual. We'll see what happens. Roberto will call you. For the moment we will suspend all direct contact."

I didn't calm down until I returned home and had made sure that Justine had made it back safely. It was comforting to prove that I did, in fact, have the presence of mind to face the unexpected.

I recalled the fortune-teller Justine had brought me to as a distraction, shortly after my husband and I had separated. It was my first experience in the realm of magic—trying to glimpse at the future to better deal with the present. In the penumbra of that modest room, the woman prophesied for me great love, a son, and trouble with the law. After turning over the cards, she turned to me and declared, "With struggle, there will be triumph," just as I was asking myself if the Revolution could ever succeed. These were the "troubles with the law" she had predicted, I thought to myself, astonished.

I had not missed a male presence in my house since the emptiness I experienced the first days after my husband left. On the contrary—I had enjoyed reading without the constant background noise of the television. I had felt like a mare set loose from the corral, running through a field of green grass just after a rainfall. I went out whenever I wanted; I could get Martín's or Roberto's phone calls at home. I could go about my work with artists and Sandinista sympathizers, attend meetings at nighttime, see my friends. Even life with my daughters had become more pleasant. On weekends we went to the beach with my brothers and their children. I had fun with my brothers. Humberto, especially, had interesting friends, people who were riding the wave of those times, exploring things like Zen Buddhism, Carlos Castañeda. But now I hadn't the slightest idea of what awaited us, of the dangers my daughters and I would have to face alone.

That night I had tickets for the theater, where I had agreed to meet my brother and his wife. I barely remember what we saw. I surrendered to the darkness, hoping that its protection and comfort would calm the paranoia that gripped me. One of the privileges of my social class, I had recently realized, was the unspoken feeling that we were immune. Bad things happened to other people. We, instead, imagined the world as a cozier place and trusted our good fortune. Changing sides meant giving up that internalized sense of security. Those class privileges would never be wiped out entirely—another person wouldn't have been warned as I was, for example—but they would wane as time went by. Deep inside, I was happy to become just another person, to be stripped of the advantages that separated me from everyone else, advantages that plagued me and made me question whether the others really considered me one of them, as I so badly wanted to be.

The performance was over. The lights went up. Walking toward the exit, looking at all the people in their formal clothes, I felt a visceral revulsion for such collective exhibitionism. People went to the theater not just to see, but to be seen. It was a veritable parade of fashionable clothes, shoes. As they got dressed, these people surely relished the comments their outfits would inspire: look how elegant so-and-so looks tonight, how thin she is, how shiny her hair is. I distanced myself, thinking I was fooling them. They would never, ever suspect that I no longer belonged to their circle, that I no longer cared about any of that. They have no idea how I despise them, I thought, how I despise this empty, vain ostentation, this sense of superiority that comes from possessions or a prominent last name.

I said goodbye to my brothers in the parking lot. The theater, with a white marble facade, had survived the earthquake. It rose from the shores of Lake Managua, trapped in the darkened area that was once the center of the city. To get home I had to drive through the devastation. I always felt a certain apprehension when I passed through the wreckage—block after block of gutted buildings, hulking giants, their windows like hollow sockets of a monster with many eyes. Gusts of wind ripped through this wasteland like the mournful cries of those buried alive. I drove down an avenue where, here and there, streetlights were still working. I stopped at a red light at the intersection next to the spectral remains of the Supreme Court building. I looked in my rearview mirror. It took me a few seconds to come to grips with the shape I saw in the darkness, behind my car. Like the enemy spaceships in a science fiction movie that materialize out of nowhere, a military jeep was following me camouflaged in the shadows, its headlights turned off. I made out the silhouette of two men, the driver and someone in the passenger seat. I felt my blood turn to water and as it slid silently down to my feet, I became a rag doll, weak, almost unable to move. My heart pounded wildly, desperately trying to retrieve the life flow that had emptied out of my chest.

The light turned green. I accelerated past the equestrian statue of Somoza in front of the stadium. The jeep kept following me. Without headlights. I continued on. I needed to return as fast as possible to the area where there was some kind of life, where I would find neighborhoods, the neon lights of the bars, bakeries. I went by my parents' house. I had the fleeting impulse to stop there—I wanted to run to my father's bed, bury my head beneath the pillows, and beg him to protect me. Over and over again my eyes darted up to the rearview mirror, praying that it wasn't true, that it was just another product of my paranoia. I went around and around aimlessly, changing my path home to convince myself that this was just a coincidence, but no. The jeep followed me like a shadow tenacious and menacing, mimicking my every move, turning everywhere I turned. I decided to drive toward my house. When I turned onto my street to park, the jeep continued on down the avenue, but I heard the engine go off as it stopped at the corner. I got out as quickly as I could. I entered my house, closing the door behind me and silently, without turning on the lights, I peered out the dining room window: the jeep was parked on the other side of the street. Now there was no doubt in my mind: I was being followed.

As I trembled inside my small house, the bright colors of the furniture seemed to be mocking me. I stole across the room to the open door of my daughters' room. I stood there for what must have been a long time, watching their peaceful faces as they slept in their orange-colored beds. Melissa with her pacifier and Maryam with her arms wide open. If only I could take them back into my womb to shelter them. I wanted a womb to hide in with them, the warm safety of the amniotic fluid. At least Nicaragua wasn't like Argentina, or Chile, where the dictatorships tortured and killed children along with their parents. I didn't fear for their lives—what I feared was the idea of them being left all alone. Did I have any right, as a mother, to take such risks? That question gnawed away at me for years, like an accusatory finger, the gesture with which my mother always scolded me. But my fate was already sealed. Inside of me there wasn't the slightest impulse to turn back. A threat like this, in fact, had the opposite effect: it fed the rage I felt for the dictatorship, for a system against which we, the citizens, had no form of defense. Ever since the earthquake the country had been placed under a state of siege. Our constitutional rights were suspended. Nobody protested, mainly because we had already been living like that long before it was officially declared. Then and there, I vowed to myself that I wouldn't allow fear to turn me into a passive observer of all the ills and injustices that surrounded me. It would do me good, I thought, to experience in my own flesh and blood the kind of vulnerability my fellow countrymen lived with every day. It was essential in any struggle to withstand the obstacles, to persevere. Otherwise we would never be able to realize our dreams. If I gave in to fear, I would end up killing my soul to save my body. I barely slept that night, not even taking my clothes off. I was afraid of knocks at the door. Of the men, and the thought that they could drag me outside, beat me in front of my daughters.

In the morning I went to my brother Humberto's house for breakfast. I could trust him. For my daughters' sake, I thought, someone in the family should know what was happening. Humberto had a long history of political involvement. A former student activist, he had led a number of protests during his university years. Toward the end of the 1960s, he and other students made history by breaking onto the playing field of the baseball stadium during the opening game of the National League, and right in front of the president's special grandstand where the dictator stood, they unfurled a huge banner that read "Basta ya. No más Somoza." That is, Enough is enough. No more Somoza. As I drove to Humberto's house, I didn't notice the jeep. Humberto wasn't very surprised at my

revelations, nor did he do anything to dissuade me from my collaboration with the guerrillas. From time to time, he too collaborated with the
Sandinistas.

"Let's go to Las Colinas," he said. "I want to test something." Las Colinas was an exclusive residential community on the outskirts of Managua.

"The jeep is not following you anymore," he announced as we drove
around. "But, do you see those two men in that Chevy?"

I had seen them, but hadn't paid much attention, obsessed as I was by
the jeep from the night before.

"Those men don't have any business being here," he said. "They don't
fit into the scene, can you tell?"

He was right. They were totally out of their element.

"Try not to go out by yourself," Humberto said. "I think they're following you just to scare you, but anyway, make sure you're with somebody else when you go out."

From that day onward, the brown Chevy Nova, the two men dressed
in their loose white guayabera shirts, wearing dark glasses, were like a
giant insect hovering behind me, stinging my back with their two pairs
of eyes. One was stocky, the other, skinny. They didn't even bother not to
be seen. They parked their car in front of my house and strolled along the
sidewalk waiting for me to emerge. I ignored them, pretending to be
unruffled, going on with my life as if this were nothing at all, but the uncertainty consumed me. I was left to speculate about what their intentions
might be. Each time I hugged my daughters goodbye I was racked with
the anguish that it could be our last hug. What if those men were just
waiting for the right moment to snatch me away and make me disappear?
No longer able to endure the uncertainty, I got into my car one day at
noon, and drove to an outlying area of Managua where a residential complex was under construction. I entered the labyrinth of deserted streets,
giving them the perfect opportunity. By exposing myself like that, I was
able to ascertain that, at least for the time being, General Genie and his
thugs were only trying to frighten me out of my dangerous liaisons.

Although I had to make them think I had seen the error of my ways,
the infringement of my freedom, my space, my safety only helped to
strengthen my resolve.

They tailed me for two months. Creature of habit, I grew accustomed to
being shadowed and actually became quite adept at evading them. End-

lessly inventive, Roberto would come up with ingenious ways we could keep in touch. He had no trouble understanding what was happening when I tried to dodge his questions the first time he called. "I'm just so busy these days," I would say to him. "I've got these two clients chasing me all day long for this advertising campaign. I just can't get away from the office . . ."

"What you need is to have fun," he said. "You work too much. Why don't you go to the movies tonight? They're showing a very good film at Teatro Cabrera."

"Are you going?" I asked.

"No. Not me. I saw it already. I'm going to go see one of those Chinese martial arts movies. Kung Fu. That's what I like."

So that night, I convinced my husband, who had come over to see the girls, to take me to the movies. Just as I suspected, at the Cabrera— a new cinema with a luminous marquee flashing over an aquamarine background—I spotted Roberto in the foyer as we paid for our tickets. My shadows had gotten out of their car and were leaning against the posters, which announced the coming attractions, close to the box office. They looked at me, chuckling sardonically. Don't come inside, please God, don't let them come inside, I prayed. I walked past them, but they didn't follow me into the theater. Halfway through the movie I stood up to go to the bathroom. I was carrying a letter for Roberto, whom I spotted the minute I got up, sitting in a seat along the aisle. As I walked by him, I dropped the little square of folded paper into his lap. When I returned to my seat, he walked over and pretended to trip, leaving a tiny ball of paper on the floor by my feet that I surreptitiously scooped up and stuck in my handbag.

My husband didn't notice a thing. He didn't even realize we had been followed.

Later on, alone in my room, I read the message. It was from Marcos. He congratulated me for being brave and gave me encouragement. He had no doubt that I would remain committed, he said. I got teary-eyed. He trusted me and that made me very happy.

With Justine's help I managed to rendezvous with Roberto several times. The tail became a challenge to be addressed with a sense of humor and a variety of creative ploys, such as disguises and wigs. I would sneak out of my house through a side door and get into Justine's car. She would take me to the place where Roberto would pick me up. I would hide crouching between the seats as the car headed toward a highway famous for its many motels. In Nicaragua, motels rent by the hour and are hide-aways for secret lovers. Roberto laughed, saying that the highway was better known as the Road of the Locos. Given that many of the female passengers were out of view, one frequently saw excited, happy drivers chatting away like crazies to themselves. The motels, in general, were crude places, a series of rooms set around a central yard, each one with its own enclosed parking space. Guests came in, parked, and then closed a canvas curtain to hide the vehicle from view. Once inside the room, fur-nished with a bed, a table, and a chair, the occupants waited for the motel employee to come and collect the rate. The money was slipped to him through a sort of cat door. That way everybody remained anonymous. In exchange for the money, the motel employee handed over a roll of toilet paper, a towel, and a small soap. They were sordid places but perfect hide-outs. I remember one motel where even the bed was bolted to the floor with a lock and chain. Roberto told me that in the past the Organization had taken furniture from those places to furnish their safe houses.

We had Cokes to drink while Roberto updated me on the political situation, and gave me the most recent Sandinista publications. We talked a lot and laughed. I don't remember ever being sad during that time. Even within my isolation I didn't feel alone. I was happy to have pushed beyond fear. I finally felt I had become part of the group. I belonged. Marcos would write to me. His letters were sweet, full of determination and pur-pose. He had a ceremonious way of referring to the "motherland," his-tory, justice. In one of his letters he informed me that because of my courage and perseverance the Organization was promoting me from "col-laborator" to "militant" (which meant I had earned my full rights and responsibilities within the Organization). I read it many times. I was deeply moved. I thought it was an honor. To this day I don't recall any prize giving me as much satisfaction as I felt for being promoted in those circumstances.

During that time my job as a courier was put on hold, but I continued my fund-raising efforts, expanding our network of sympathizers, securing medicine to send to the guerrillas in the mountains. I also wrote opinion pieces, which were published in *La Prensa*. I had come up with a pen name: Eva Salvatierra. Pretending to sound like the original Eve, I would subtly criticize and ridicule the political situation in the country. To keep myself busy in the evenings, I accepted Justine's invitation to attend a

"Parent Effectiveness Training" seminar at the university organized by a group of friends, all young, upper-class mothers. The instructor—a woman—had come from the United States. I will never forget the surreal experience of participating in elaborate discussions on how to handle temper tantrums, time constraints, and children's difficult questions, and this, while being watched by the secret police. I tried hard to concentrate. I tried to pretend I was just another one of those elegant women concerned about being good mothers, but I was painfully aware of the two men pacing outside, glancing at me through the window—everyone but me oblivious to their presence.

To feel shadowed like that brought home to me the meaning of hate. Until they showed up to circle my days and nights like a pair of bloodhounds, I never thought I could ever feel the impulse to kill another human being. I had learned to use a gun shortly before they appeared in my life, just after my husband and I separated. On August 10, 1971, Managua was busy celebrating its patron saint, Santo Domingo de Guzmán, and Roberto suggested we go to the beach. We would be the only ones there.

"I'm going to start your military training," he announced.

We pulled up to one of the beaches on the Pacific coast. It was deserted, the shiny steel of the ocean surface melting and rising in high white-capped waves that crashed against the lead-colored sand. Above, the sun, perpendicular, beat down on our heads mercilessly. We parked next to a broken-down palm hut with its fork poles crooked and its leafy roof dried and brittle. Roberto lifted up his shirt and took out a very large gun from the back of his belt just above his hip.

"You can't tell, can you? I bet you never noticed." He smiled at my surprise. He told me it was a P-38. He would show me its assembly and disassembly, its safe handling and operation.

He deftly field-stripped the gun. He placed all the components over a large piece of driftwood that he had carefully cleaned and covered with his shirt. His short, chubby fingers when handling slide, barrel, spring, firing pin, the cocking mechanism seemed light and dainty. Disassembling and assembling the gun looked simple enough, but when it was my turn to try, it wasn't so easy. Especially pulling back the slide so that the hammer would be in firing position.

"It won't bite you," he said. Guns cast such a strange spell upon men, I thought to myself. His eyes glittered. I, on the other hand, had to overcome my instinctive rejection. To me the gun was a tiger, a snake. Later, I trained with more sophisticated weapons, but I never overcame my original apprehension. Roberto placed a couple of old tin cans on the sand. He showed me how to hold the weapon in a two-hand grip, how to get into a balanced stance so that I wouldn't lose my footing from the recoil. Instinctively, I shut my eyes when I squeezed the trigger. I was totally unprepared for the sharp ringing that pierced through my brain after the detonation. I thought it would render me deaf forever.

"Happens every time," he said, matter of fact. "You'll recover your hearing in a bit." He had good aim. I missed every time. Only years later did my marksmanship improve, and I even came in second place in a shooting contest. It turned out, according to my military instructor in Cuba, that I use the left eye to aim even though I am right-handed. I had to factor this in. That day at the beach, however, I registered not only my body's reaction at each detonation, but the unsettling vibration shaking my soul. How could anyone in his or her right mind enjoy this kind of thing? How could anyone have a fascination for weapons and forget they were meant to kill? We, for example, did not learn to shoot for sport but for war, which in Nicaragua had become the only alternative left to us by the dictatorship. As I held the weapon in my hand, I understood I would have to transform my belief in our struggle into the more practical decision to use force if need be. That was the whole point of military training. While I took aim and shot over and over that day, I gained an understanding of the power of life and death one feels when pulling the trigger. However, it was not until my persecution began that I knew within myself that I could kill. I came to feel such hatred for those malevolent men constantly watching me. More than once I felt that, had it been necessary, I wouldn't have had any qualms wringing their necks with my bare hands.

On the way back from my lesson at the beach, I asked Roberto if he'd ever had to kill someone. He said no. According to those who had, he added, the first time was the worst. Nightmares inevitably plagued them. They just couldn't erase from their minds the bullet impact, the sight of the body collapsing.

"One *compañero* told me that the finger he used to pull the trigger went numb and stayed like that, in a constant cramp, for days. Just moving it was excruciating."

If he ever had to, said Roberto, he'd rather do it in combat. At least then you were never too sure who had hit whom.

———

Around the middle of October 1974, my shadows suddenly disappeared. For almost two months I had felt like an animal in a zoo, trapped by those two pairs of eyes. It was hard to believe that when I looked into the rearview mirror, I no longer had to see that ubiquitous Chevy Nova, those faces hidden behind dark sunglasses. For days I held my breath, waiting for another car to appear. I drove all over the city to make sure that I wasn't under a more sophisticated surveillance system, one which used several different cars, perhaps. But there was nobody. Neither they, nor any other men tailing me. I was clean. Clean. But the sensation of being shadowed became part of me. I suffer from a state of chronic alertness since then; I obsessively check my rearview mirror.

CHAPTER THIRTEEN

*On how I reconnected with Marcos and participated
in the preparation of a commando operation*

Managua, 1974

THE MANAGUA SIERRA is a mountain ridge that rises south of the city. A few kilometers outside Managua, the temperature drops and the foliage becomes lush and thick. The road twists and turns, climbing higher and higher between deep ravines. Monumental trees emerge from these depths shaking their green manes. Dirt roads that deviate off the Pan-American Highway descend into coffee plantations secluded among the shady and humid landscape. Ever since I was a little girl, entering those pathways always transported me to a primitive world of natural, unspoiled, indomitable beauty.

My cousins Pía and Alfredo lived in Mazatlán, my grandfather's coffee plantation. To get there, you had to travel through a road cut into a rift. It was an exuberantly green realm permeated by the scent of roasted coffee and humus. A cutting wind blew sharp among the sword-shaped leaves of *espadillo* trees.

My first meeting with Marcos, after the secret police finally stopped tailing me, took place in this hacienda. Before heading for Mazatlán, I followed Roberto's instructions, and drove around the city for two hours to make sure I wasn't being followed.

Our meeting location could hardly have been a more beautiful, more romantic place. The eaves of the picture-perfect wooden, Caribbean-style house were carved as finely as lace. The screens on doors and windows lent it a timeworn, welcoming feel. It was set on a slope over the driveway, so it seemed to float in a garden enveloped by the balmy, light, clean air, and the huge tree trunks that sprouted up from amid the thousands of hibiscus flowers down below. I envied my cousin. She had been lucky enough that our paternal grandfather, a stern and distant man, had allowed her to live there.

I arrived on time, bored and impatient after two hours of driving around. I wasn't expecting him, so it was a surprise to see Marcos emerge, hugging me as if I were an old friend returning from a long, perilous sojourn somewhere. He seemed even more beautiful than before, perhaps because now he looked at me with a more intimate and affectionate gaze. I was a bit flustered. In spite of myself, the air of authority Marcos exuded inhibited me. I somehow couldn't find my spontaneity when I was near him. I thought of his letters, those sweet letters filled with words of encouragement. With his arm around my shoulders, we entered the house. I laughed and made jokes, pretending that it was so easy to just slide right into that happy atmosphere of old friends reuniting. But each time I looked up and our eyes met, I would turn the other way, uneasy. I think that was the night I fell in love with him. I don't know if he felt it too, but he looked at me as if really seeing me for the very first time. He was another person. Nothing, not even the baseball cap, was left of the distracted, almost surly person I had known. Over dinner he laughed, lively and extroverted.

Pía was an excellent cook. Working dinners with Marcos in Mazatlán eventually became a weekly event, and she hosted them with all the "discreet charms" her social status had bequeathed her. I can't recall when it was that Marcos first mentioned the time he spent in Paris, but as soon as she discovered his penchant for French cuisine, she began preparing French meals and would serve appetizers such as steamed artichokes with homemade mayonnaise, and bake *pain d'epices* to accompany our coffee breaks. She even managed to find Gitanes cigarettes for him. She doted on Marcos with a dedication that I admired and secretly envied. That feminine side, that celebration of all things related to the home, the kitchen, the attention to little details, was foreign to me. I never thought much of it—to me, it was a symbol of female servitude. Seeing my cousin, however, I understood how seductive those arts could be, how pleasant they made others' lives, and the satisfaction that one could derive from the pleasure of others.

Marcos was a man of many passions; history, for one. He had an in-depth knowledge of Nicaraguan history. If we read it thoroughly and interpreted it correctly, we would find that it would unlock for us the path to understanding. He insisted that we had to dive deeper into our own experience. (I can still see his long fingers flipping through the yellowing pages of a book.) Important as it was to learn about Marxism, philosophy, etc. (he, in fact, had learned German just so he could read *Das Kapital* in the original), we would never get a grip on our own reality much less bring about a revolution if we didn't know our own history backward and forward. Equipped with an understanding of the dynamics between social forces and the economy, I was able to profit from our study sessions with Marcos, which were inspired and passionate, and helped me develop quite an accurate political intuition.

Every week, Marcos would assign Alfredo and me a variety of tasks. My job in the advertising agency granted me access to valuable information regarding the dictatorship's dealings with economic powerhouses in the country. I even happened to handle the advertising accounts for some companies that were part of the Somoza family's economic empire: a meatpacking and export plant, a shipping company, the Mercedes-Benz distributor, insurance and financial firms. From all these clients of mine I would surreptitiously snatch company documents that I thought might be relevant to us—information on their transactions, balance sheets, dealings abroad or with local businesses. I also drew up elaborate profiles of their top executives, their salaries, and their bodyguards or security apparatus. This kind of information served the Organization to document the government's corruption, to find out who was involved with whom and how deep, to keep track of the power struggles within the tyrant's circle. For several years now I had slowly and patiently accumulated important data, but what Marcos wanted now was on a different scale in terms of details and precision, and to gain access to it implied bigger risks. At some point during those months he came up with a list of things Alfredo and I were supposed to get: fifteen wristwatches, men's and women's evening wear, first-aid supplies, water-purifying tablets. He even asked us to find him gas masks—a task we were unable to perform. No gas masks anywhere. You didn't have to be a genius to figure out that the Organization was planning something big.

More and more often, during our weekly meetings, while Pía cooked dinner and he happily chewed on artichoke leaves dipped in mayonnaise,

Marcos would drop hints about a large-scale operation. Would we agree with the idea that it was time to do something "big"? Alfredo and I exchanged looks. What could we say if we didn't have any idea what he meant? It was hard to offer any kind of opinion, and we didn't dare ask him to tell us more, so we answered in general terms, as vaguely as was expected. Alfredo would touch his beard pensively. Big like what? I would ask.

"Like an unequivocal blow, something that would make it to the international news, something everyone in the country would know about. The time is coming for us to break our silence, and prove that Somoza was lying when he swore he had done away with Sandinismo after he defeated us in the mountains of Pancasan in 1970."

"Sure," I said. "It would be swell if people realized Sandinismo is very much alive."

"I'll give you more details later on," he said, smiling good-naturedly at the noncommittal answers we gave him. "Don't worry. I'm only thinking out loud."

Late into the night I used to drive Marcos to his safe house. It was a short trip. I would drop him off in no particular place, just on the side of the Las Nubes road, near El Crucero, a little hamlet at the highest point of the Managua Sierra. It was usually blustery, foggy, and cold on that road. On both sides, separated by vast empty lots, there were large country houses, most of them dark and empty, some even boarded up. The place reminded me of the English moors in *Wuthering Heights*. It was desolate and barren and there was a constant biting wind whipping the trees and loosening the old wooden bones of the houses.

Only much, much later would I learn that near the place where I would leave Marcos, there was a house (whose precise location I never guessed), which already then sheltered thirteen members of the commando unit that would participate in the operation he had been talking about and which took place in December of that year.

He asked me the oddest questions, regardless. One day, there were pictures in the newspaper of Bianca and Mick Jagger arriving in Nicaragua to visit her family and bring donations to earthquake victims. That night he turned to me in the car. "Don't you think Bianca might let herself be

kidnapped?" he asked. "It would be publicity for her. We could even ask
her to let us kidnap her, to get her husband to give us a little money . . ."
He fell silent for a moment. "No. People would look down on us if we kidnapped a woman."

I laughed at such traditional notions. People no longer thought of
women as delicate flowers or helpless beings, I told him. Women's lib at
least had given us adult status. Bianca was no fragile sixteen-year-old.

"Our people are still very traditional," he said to me. "No. Let's just
forget it."

Marcos inhabited a cenote—a water hole, a deep, submerged world where
no one was allowed. Occasionally he would emerge to walk along the
edges, never straying too far from the distant realm where he had his
refuge. When he broke through to the surface, he would see me and become
aware of my presence as if suddenly he noticed a brilliantly colored bird
and reached out to touch it carefully, full of curiosity. That was how it
was the first time he took my hand in the car. As if he had seen my hand
resting on the gearshift and suddenly it seemed like an intriguing object.
The gesture took me by surprise. We were driving down the road. He
closed his two hands around my right hand and began to examine it, finger by finger, like a blind person learning a shape in the darkness.

"I like you, you know?" he said. I nodded. My mouth went dry. The
car, the night itself entered a space where gravity became as heavy as it is
on Jupiter. He was a mythical figure to me, distant and close at the same
time. The usual social formulas that worked with other mortals didn't
work with him. He would emerge from his world, his eyes devouring me,
looking for something beyond my skin, and I could do nothing more than
open my doors, allow him in, let him look at me, try to see through him. I
don't recall what words if any we said to each other, or if it all was one
long wordless ceremony, but a few days later, on our way to his house,
driving through the foggy moors where the wind blew, he told me to turn
onto a narrow street hidden in the tall grass, an odd little street that led
nowhere. First I turned off the motor, then the headlights. There we
were, hidden in the darkness, the gusts of wind blowing the high weeds in
a whirlwind against the car. I felt as though we were standing on a platform, waiting to be launched into the starry night. The howling wind and
the long, sustained shrill of the crickets echoed inside the car like sounds
from an astral realm. Marcos would take me to his world, and I would

never return. Day would never be day again. Marcos moved in his seat. He reached beneath his shirt and removed his gun, placing it between us, in the space between the two front seats.

"And what's that, what do you have there?" I asked, trying to stay in contact with reality, as I pointed to a small black leather case that he never let out of his sight.

"A hand grenade," he said, laying the case at his feet. "The day I go I don't want to go alone. They'll have to pay."

I swallowed hard. I had had that bag so close to me, so many times—in the car, on the table—I had never imagined what was inside.

"It can't go off on its own, don't worry," he said, smiling. His sweet, tranquil face, far from the cenote. He gazed at me. We touched each other's face, hair. I closed my eyes and placed my ear against his chest. I wanted to cry. It was so easy to stop a heart from beating. The pistol. The grenade. Marcos kissed me. He drank my soul through my teeth. His hands, slightly clumsy, searched for the buttons of my blouse. In the cramped space of my tiny Alfa Sud—nipple color, as Róger always said— we bumped against the steering wheel, the security brake, all the damned accessories and gadgets of auto mechanics. I hunted for the lever to move the seats back. It had to be operated manually. Slow. Laborious. I cursed the Italians. Marcos cranked it around and around for what seemed like an eternity. Half naked, tentatively in that confined space, we made love. Maybe it was the danger, the eternal risk, the not knowing if this would be the last time, but it was beautiful, with the intensity of a passion that was beyond words, something that had no other way of expressing itself. We didn't talk much afterward, but from that moment on, whenever we separated at night, the narrow street, our moans in the darkness served as a farewell ritual.

The one night we went down to the city, we went to a middle-class neighborhood. We parked the car and walked through the streets lined with short almond trees. It was dinnertime. Families were together. We could see them through the brightly lit windows: a woman cradling her baby, a man in a T-shirt and slippers watching television.

"I have to admit that at times I envy their lives," Marcos said, in a melancholy voice.

The house he was to sleep in that night was waiting for renters to arrive, an empty shell. No furniture, no electricity. A tiny house, like a

small, barren, deserted island. We sat down on the floor. Marcos placed
the gun and the case with the hand grenade against the wall. We snuggled
up against one another.

"Don't go," he whispered. "Stay with me."

"I can't. The girls . . ."

The cold, hard floor was far more uncomfortable and hostile than the
gearshift or the steering wheel. When I said goodbye to Marcos at the
door, I felt like a mother leaving her son in a dank, grim boarding school.
He didn't have a blanket. He was used to it, he said. Underground one
always slept with the shoes on. I had no reason to worry, he insisted.

Back home, in the solitude of my bed, I remembered bits and pieces of
one of the Poet's poems:

> *What makes a man leave his wife?*
> *All that is cuddling and warmth*

Were we all mad? What mystery in human genes accounted for the
fact that men and women could override their personal survival instincts
when the fate of the tribe or the collective was at stake? What was it that
enabled people to give their lives for an idea, for the freedom of others?
Why was the heroic impulse so strong? What I found most bewilder-
ing and extraordinary was the real happiness and fulfillment that came
along with commitment. Life acquired unequivocal meaning, purpose,
and direction. It was a sensation of complete, utter complicity, a visceral,
emotional bond with hundreds of anonymous faces, an intimacy of multitudes in which any feeling of loneliness or isolation simply evaporated. In
the struggle for everyone's happiness, the first happiness one found was
one's own.

At the beginning of November, Marcos gave Alfredo and me the basic
details of the operation they had planned. The commando group would
break into one of the Christmas parties to be attended by some of the
most prominent figures in the Somoza regime. They would then be taken
as hostages until the dictatorship agreed to negotiate their release. That
was all we needed to know. From that moment on, he said, we were part of
the commandos' information and logistical team.

"We need to get as much intelligence information as possible on
Christmas parties held at embassies, and at the homes of people like

bankers and government ministers. We can't know exactly when or where the operation will take place until we have that information."

How could he possibly not know, I thought. He had to be trying to throw us off track; it had to be that for sure. But Marcos insisted. Every day he would ask me the same question: "You haven't heard about any parties?" Later on I found out that the entire commando unit had prepared for the operation without knowing exactly where it would be carried out. They found out at nine in the morning of the very day. Pretending to be air-conditioning repairmen, Roberto and another *compañero* had entered the house and sketched a floor plan only a few hours earlier.

At a loss for more detailed information, Marcos decided, in characteristically Latin American style, to send us around drawing up floor plans of every possible location where that kind of Christmas party might be held.

The notion of entering an embassy to surreptitiously sketch its floor plan immediately brought to mind images and the soundtrack from *Mission: Impossible*, which, along with *Star Trek*, was my favorite TV show. Since there was no way I could count on Martin Landau or any other member of his team for help, I turned to poetry. To avoid feeling any kind of moral scruples I chose Pinochet's government, that is, the Chilean embassy.

I requested an appointment with the cultural attaché to talk about publishing houses in Chile. I was hoping to find an editor for my poetry book, I said. I made my appearance dressed in a white linen pantsuit, Barbara Bain style. Welcoming me effusively, the functionary let me into his office. Of his features I only remember his bushy eyebrows and thick mustache. An indistinct man, he suffered from the servile, pusillanimous nature that is endemic among civil servants in dictatorial regimes. Framed on the wall, General Pinochet struck a napoleonic pose as he looked to the future. The cultural attaché, meanwhile, stroked the ends of his long mustache, observing me with a viscous look in his eyes that made me want to clean up my clothes and take off in a run. The embassy was an old mansion that had been adapted for use as an office building. I began making mental notes of every door and window as we discussed the terrible lack of publishing houses in Nicaragua. Flipping back my hair and sipping my coffee, I played my role—the refined woman, the poet who saw her horizons limited by the backwardness of her country. Chile, instead, Chile! What an intellectual giant it was, I sighed. Why, it was no surprise at all that Rubén Darío had written there his best book, *Azul*. I waited for an appropriate moment of silence to lower my eyes—timidly, modestly—and ask if he would be so kind as to show me the way to the ladies' room. With a benevolent, mischievous smile, he led me to a door that opened onto a corridor and pointed the way. I walked in and then walked straight out of the bathroom, turning in the opposite direction of his office. I moved quickly, trying to cover as much terrain as my legs would allow. I passed through an interior patio and continued down another hallway until I reached another room, opening the door and apologizing for the intrusion as someone jumped up and offered to escort me back to the cultural attaché's.

"It's so easy to get lost in this maze. How many rooms are there in this house? It seems enormous," I commented to my guide.

I left the embassy. Mission accomplished. I got into my car, drove a few blocks, and then parked under the shade of some trees. There I sketched the floor plan.

"Magnificent," Marcos said with a broad smile when I handed it to him. That was his highest compliment, the one he used whenever he wanted to sound overly impressed. I took advantage of my poetry book to do the same ruse in other embassies.

One afternoon, early in November, Marcos asked me to take him on a reconnaissance mission. He wanted to explore potential escape routes for the Operation's commandos. We traveled from the Managua Sierra down several rustic trails until we finally came out at the back end of a giant shantytown people called the Open. It was around five in the afternoon. Dusk in the tropics. After a midday downpour, the air felt crisp and carried the pungent smell of damp earth. We emerged from a clump of stout trees into a clearing. In the distance we could see the last row of houses in the neighborhood, the simple constructions of cement bricks and tin roofs, the smoke from wood-burning stoves. Marcos pointed to a road that went down in the direction of Managua, parallel but far away from the highway. On the shoulders, there were huge piles of freshly shoveled earth, giant dump trucks, and the metal skeleton of a very large building, rising up alone in the middle of the farmlands. An odd sight. What were they building there? A factory warehouse? The twilight, yellowing and tenuous, outlined the image with strokes of the surreal. Suddenly, out of nowhere, a National Guard soldier appeared carrying a standard-issue Garand rifle. My heart fell heavily in my chest like a ripe fruit dropping from a branch. I pushed on the gas pedal instinctively, gaining some speed and pretending I had not seen him raise his arm, signaling for us to stop. I just wanted to take off.

"The gun, hide it, hide the gun," I managed to tell Marcos, choking with fear.

"What is it? What's going on?"

The soldier was running with his Garand cocked. I let him out of my sight for an instant to make sure Marcos was putting the gun away. At that very moment, the air shattered into a million pieces with the sound of a shot.

"Stop, stop!" Marcos hollered. The soldier fired again. We heard the bullet whiz just millimeters over the hood of the car. I slammed on the brake as hard as I could, and the car screeched to a stop in a cloud of dust. I gripped the steering wheel. The only clear thought in my mind was that Marcos must not die, not then.

The soldier stopped firing. He came running toward us.

"When he comes tell him we are just cruising around," Marcos said. "Calm down now and just tell him we are out cruising."

I pulled myself together. I ran my hand across my hair. The National Guard soldier, in his combat helmet, stuck his head through the window and looked at us.

"Didn't you see the signal to halt?" he shouted. "What are you doing around here? This is General Somoza's property."

"We were just taking a drive," I said meekly, with my most innocent face. In Nicaragua you didn't argue with armed soldiers. "You scared us," I said, smiling demurely.

"Go drive around somewhere else," he said, raising his arm, pointing angrily toward the highway. I started the car and slowly took off. I saw that Marcos was holding tightly to the black leather case where he kept the hand grenade.

"Did you pull the pin?" I gasped.

"No. I didn't do a thing, don't worry," he said, stroking my arm, over and over as if soothing a child or a cat. "Are you all right? Do you feel all right? Are you okay to drive?" We reached the intersection. Nearby a new luxury building complex was going up, Residencial Satélite Asososca. A blinking yellow traffic light signaled the turn, a few meters beyond.

I'm fine, I said, amazed that I could feel all right just moments after we were so close to getting killed. Only my heart was drumming like crazy and my hands were clammy. As we approached a middle-class residential neighborhood, Marcos insisted I pull over. There, we waited for my legs to stop shaking. He held me. He seemed unperturbed. Even his heartbeat was steady.

"That was close," he said, and smiled as he ran his hand through my hair.

Two years later, on November 7, 1976, right under the traffic light at the entrance to Residencial Asososca, a combat unit from the infamous Anti-Subversive Brigades intercepted the car carrying Marcos and two other *compañeros* who were being chased by the dictator's secret police. The soldiers opened fire and killed the first two men the instant they stepped out of the car. From the back seat, Marcos fired at the soldiers until he too was gunned down. The soldiers pulled him out of the car and although he was already dead, they unloaded their weapons in him. His body dead and bloody jumped and quivered as it was riddled with bullets. My friend Fernando Cardenal, a Jesuit priest, saw the entire thing. He described it to me afterward. He told me how the blinking yellow light illuminated Marcos's body. How he had seen the reflection of that amber yellow traffic light on his blood. "It seemed they feared him even after he was dead," he said.

I thought about death, lurking there, waiting for him at that intersection where we had almost died together. And perhaps that first time she spared him by chance, just because I was with him and it wasn't yet my turn. Every time I go by that place, my sorrow pairs up with a profound terror at the puzzling circles of destiny and the fragility of human existence. I wonder if this coincidence crossed through Marcos's mind. For a long time afterward, I obsessively tried reconstructing his last moment. Was he scared? What happened to the grenade he always carried with him? Such a solitary thing, death. The dead are not granted the consolation of journeying with others. For the living, there is only the anguish of imagining that final, utter helplessness.

CHAPTER FOURTEEN

On how I found out—while I was in Europe—
that the foretold Operation was underway

MANAGUA–EUROPE, 1974

MY HUSBAND AND I had been apart for six months. Autonomous and free in my small home, I came and went juggling my secret and my regular life. However, being a single mother in my traditional milieu was proving to be harder than I thought. My parents were troubled by my situation, and I could tell my daughters felt the absence of a father figure. My husband had vowed to shake off his indifference and come out of the cave. When I decided to give my marriage a second chance, I didn't feel I had to put into question either my covert occupations or my love for Marcos. By then I had mastered my split existence and managed each of my lives as if they were separate realities, parallel universes, which were filed in different areas of my brain. I guess I had enabled myself to do what men did in my country—who had lovers yet held on to the convenience of their married lives. I suppose I used a similar kind of logic when I decided to give my marriage another try. Marcos and my other concerns were something else for me. Part of a world ruled by its own laws of physics and its unique table of chemical elements.

My timing couldn't have been better. No sooner had the underwear, shirts, and men's socks reappeared in my dresser drawers, than Marcos suggested that I leave Nicaragua and stay in another country for a few months. They expected that the dictatorship would launch a wave of sweeping, nasty repression following the Operation.

"Those they have labeled as Sandinista supporters will be the first to fall," he said. "They'll get you in the first roundup. It would be better for you to weather the storm someplace else. As soon as we can assess the situation, we'll let you know when it's safe to come back. We need to make sure that they haven't got anybody who might give them your name."

I don't recall whether or not I let my husband know that the trip to Europe I suggested—which to everyone else should appear as a second honeymoon after our reconciliation—was also intended to get me out of a political emergency whose exact nature I couldn't disclose. I must have told him something to justify leaving our two daughters at my parents' home at Christmastime. In any event, the full revelation of my dangerous liaisons came later, when I announced that instead of returning home with him, I would have to wait at my sister Lucía's home in Barcelona for the signal that the coast was clear, that it was safe for me to go back to Nicaragua.

I said goodbye to Marcos on the misty familiar road. "Forward on to victory," he said, quoting Che. My smile, light and cheerful, was meant to convey to him my certainty that things would work out all right. Neither of us had to be reminded that this could very well be the last time we would see each other. We eluded any sense of drama, as if it were a bad omen. He got out of the car, walked around to my window, and kissed me again.

"Don't do anything I wouldn't do," he said with a wink.

I watched him as he walked away receding into the distance. Several times he turned back to look at me, smiling and waving his hand up high. The lines of a poem came to me. The poem was from one of my favorite poets, Joaquín Pasos: "Es preciso que levantes la mano para llevarme de tí un recuerdo de árbol." ("You must raise your hand when we part/For I want to keep of you a memory of trees.") I felt no bad premonition. That made me feel better. I'm rarely wrong when dark forebodings seize me. I had asked him how I would learn about the outcome of the Operation.

"You'll read about it in the newspapers," he said.

My memories of that trip are a collage of blurry images, tourist activities, and tours on tall buses with big windows down shady avenues. The canals in Amsterdam. Crowds on the Gran Vía in Madrid. A dinner at La Coupole with his cousin Bernard, who lived in Paris. Christmas with my sister Lucía and her husband, Antonio, in their small apartment. Our departure for Italy. My husband, the eternal pessimist, was certain that this would be his first and last trip to Europe. He wanted to see everything, as if he had an unavoidable obligation to do so, even though at a certain point our saturated minds could no longer distinguish the nationalities of the various landscapes, museums, street scenes, and airports we passed through. With my broken French and rudimentary Italian, I scanned the newspapers looking for the magic word "Nicaragua," despairing that the *compañeros* hadn't been able to come across the "right" Christmas party, or that the plan had failed because New Year's Day was coming up and still no news.

We were on our way back from Pompeii, the imposing Vesuvius towering over the road where remnants of the lava flow reminded me of the barren landscape that surrounds the Santiago volcano in Nicaragua. The tourist bus made a rest stop at a nondescript bar along the road. We had fifteen minutes to run to the bathroom and have a cup of coffee.

Standing at the counter, I sipped a cappuccino, idly watching the news on the television set, the ubiquitous fixture in those roadside bars. Suddenly, the map of Nicaragua flashed across the screen. The announcer said *guerriglieri sandinisti*, and suddenly time stopped. I felt as though my life was hanging from the thread of the newscaster's words, which I tried desperately to understand. That was when the tour guide called us back to the bus. It was time to leave. My husband stood silently beside me, as transfixed as I was by the news report. It ended too soon, just when the tour guide came looking for us. We were the last ones.

"What happened? Did you understand anything?" my husband asked me as we boarded the bus. "What did the guerrillas do?"

"Something big, it seems," I said. "But I didn't really understand. We'll have to wait and read the newspapers when we get back to the hotel."

From that point on, I had trouble speaking. A glacial chill came over my body, starting at my spine and traveling out to my limbs. My hands and feet were freezing, and my teeth chattered uncontrollably. I must have caught a cold, I said to my husband, as I curled up in my seat, hugging my knees to my chest, instinctively searching for the fetal position. With my eyes shut, all I could do was recite the prayers of my childhood: "Guardian angel, sweet companion, don't forsake me, day or night; Our father, who art in heaven . . . deliver us from evil. Amen." I repeated these words over and over again the entire way back, trying to force my imagination from going wild, trying not to think of any fatality. Marcos, Marquitos, please be safe, for the love of God, I whispered between prayers, asking myself how on earth I was going to be able to visit the Pantheon, the Vatican, the Roman Forum, when all I wanted to do was to find shelter and stay there, curled up with my eyes shut, like someone waiting for the end of an air raid.

I prayed in every single church that I visited the four days the Operation lasted. I felt God had to be on our side, not Somoza's, although I couldn't help recognizing the irony of praying in the Vatican for the success of a guerrilla operation. My husband seemed moved by the bravery of the Sandinistas. "Who could they be?" he asked, speculating as to the identities of the guerrillas, as we tore through the newspapers, intent on deciphering the news reports in Italian. Only when we returned to Spain were we finally able to get all the details.

On December 27, 1974, the commando unit Juan José Quezada, named after a fallen comrade,[*] broke into the home of the president of the Banco Central de Nicaragua, José María (Chema) Castillo, while a party was underway. The commando unit was comprised of five women and eight men, numbered from zero to thirteen. Zero was chief commander. The guerrillas released women, musicians, and waiters, and kept everyone else hostage. Among them were Somoza's brother-in-law and one of his cousins, several ambassadors, the manager of the Esso oil company, and other leading political and business figures.

Managua's archbishop, Monsignor Obando y Bravo, was chosen as an intermediary in the negotiations between President Somoza and the guerrilla's chief commander, Zero. The people who had been released described Zero as a tall, light-skinned, good-looking man (even though he wore a nylon stocking over his head to erase his features). Almost a year later Marcos told me the story in detail: how they heard about the party that morning on *El Clarín*, the political gossip radio program. He told me about the unexpected trouble they had encountered when the *compañeros* who were assigned to "borrow" some taxicabs to take the commandos to the party realized that, even though they were disguised as National Guardsmen, they couldn't get taxi drivers to stop until they donned

---

[*] Juan José Quezada was a Sandinista fighter fallen in combat in 1973. We used to name commando units after fallen comrades.

civilian clothes. He told me they had only tested the weapons for the Operation once, at midnight on Christmas Eve, when fireworks were booming all over Managua and the city was enveloped in a gunpowder haze. And he talked about the only fatality, the fight put up by Mr. Castillo, the host of the party and owner of the house, who tried barricading himself in his bedroom, where he kept his arsenal, and died in the ensuing shootout in the hallway.

"If it hadn't been for that, nobody would have died. The Operation would have been perfect," he said.

I reminded him that the hostages even praised the "courtesy" of the guerrillas.

"One of the ladies," Marcos said, smiling, "thought that we were thieves and swallowed the diamond ring she was wearing. Can you imagine thinking of such a thing at a moment like that?"

Throngs of people had gathered at the roads to see the guerrillas go by in the buses that carried them to the airport, when Somoza complied with their demands three days later.

"In the negotiations we requested that the army withdraw from the streets, so people came out unafraid and cheered us, waving handkerchiefs and bandannas. It was so moving to see the hundreds and hundreds of people lined up on the side of the road the entire way."

The demands met by the dictatorship included the release of the prisoners, a payout of one million dollars, and the uncensored publication of a series of communiqués about the general situation in the country and the goals of the FSLN.

At the airport, the commandos joined the political prisoners. "To see our *compañeros* free, to hug them, to be with them again was the best part," Marcos said. "We counted the money in the plane on the flight to Cuba. After we arrived, this Commander Zero slept for three days straight."

Nothing like success, the feeling of triumph, to make you feel you can conquer anything. Basking in the splendor of my *compañeros'* valor, I told my husband about the role I had played in the December 27 Operation. That was the reason I couldn't return to Nicaragua yet, I explained. I had to spend a few weeks with my sister. Fly to Barcelona and wait there for the go-ahead. All these years, and you never said a word? he asked reproachfully. He always knew I would end up getting myself in some kind of trouble. But this, my God! Nevertheless, it was clear that a part of him admired and respected me for what I had done. I dare say he even felt proud of me because he offered to come with me to Barcelona to see me arrive safely at my sister's house, and that's what he did, acting the whole time like it was his duty to protect me, as if by doing so he too was participating in the guerrilla glory of the Sandinista cause.

My sister Lucía just stared at me, her dark brown eyes open wide in astonishment. Petite, with the same slender, delicate frame as my mother, Lucía had also married young, to her first boyfriend. In her sheltered world, innocent and good, my behavior seemed incomprehensible and reckless, but tactful as she was she kept her opinions to herself. I was her sister and if I needed sanctuary, she would provide it. I entered her domestic life, but I felt like a caged lion pacing around her apartment or aimlessly wandering the dull streets of the small industrial town where she lived on the periphery of the great Catalan metropolis. After the life I had led during the past few years, I felt out of place among the docility of the women in Martorell, who spent their days in a bustle of activity, mopping the floors, preparing baby food, getting dinner ready, while their husbands vanished during the day, swallowed by another life elsewhere. I remember scanning the newspapers, searching for news about Nicaragua, to no avail.

When Antonio, my brother-in-law, returned from work, the pent-up energy brewing inside of me during the day would bubble to the surface and infuse our conversation. He loved to provoke me, and enjoyed contradicting my opinions whatever the subject. We'd break into heated arguments, which, by the time dinner came, had become a duel. While he and I unsheathed our sharpest verbal daggers upon one another, Lucía would get more and more anxious. She despaired trying to mediate between us while I delivered diatribes against the barbaric Spanish conquest, while Antonio made fun of what he liked to call my "revolutionary delusions," my romanticism. Usually after we managed to upset Lucía to the point of tears, we would declare a truce. Like headstrong children, we would retreat to our bedrooms to sleep, silently despising each other. With time, Antonio and I have learned to respect and even love each other, but in those days we were bitter antagonists, though I think that underneath it all, we actually enjoyed the intellectual passion of our verbal encounters punctuating the otherwise unbroken routine of everyday life.

After two months of this exercise, however, I was desperately concerned about my daughters, and still hadn't heard from Marcos, and so I decided it was time for me to act on my own. I called Alfredo. Unfortunately, he wasn't as quick as Roberto had been at deciphering the hidden meaning of my apparently inane words. Nevertheless, I inferred that even though he didn't have precise instructions for me, he felt it was safe for me to return home. It seemed none of the people who could turn me in had been captured in the sweeping raids carried out by the regime after the Operation.

I left Barcelona and flew to Panama, where my mother was waiting to escort me back to Nicaragua.

CHAPTER FIFTEEN

*On how my mother helped me prepare for an interrogatory
and what happened upon my return to Nicaragua*

PANAMA–NICARAGUA, 1975

WHEN I ARRIVED in Panama, I wished that my mother could have been a plump, big-breasted woman so that I could plunge into her bosom—I yearned for an aroma, a memory of being nursed, something that would transport me to the safe, placid days of my childhood. But my mother was neither plump, nor big-breasted, nor was she prone to big hugs, cuddling, or pampering. Her love was prudent, concerned. From the minute I spotted her in the airport I knew she was having a hard time forgiving me for the anguish I had put her through, that she was not about to approve of my entanglements, but that she would have never forgiven herself for abandoning me when I most needed her.

Panama was the connecting point for flights between Europe and Nicaragua. My mother knew the place, she had it all under control: taxis, hotels, shops. Panama City is something of a hybrid of Miami, Central America, and the Caribbean, a city of banks, large stores, luxury hotels, ancient ruins along the seashore, and a densely populated downtown area where Asians, blacks, and native Panamanians peacefully coexist in a noisy, colorful cultural mix. Ever since my days in boarding school in Spain, returning to Panama from Madrid was always a special treat. Not because I liked the city, but because of its luminosity, the intense green of its vegetation, the sight of the Pacific Ocean. As soon as I stepped off the plane I would feel the energy of the New World, the youthfulness of the country, the flamboyant, baroque style of its people sporting brightly colored clothes, displaying a mix of races and speaking Spanish with a soft, musical accent. Panamanians suffered from a confused national identity, their fate marked by a canal that not only split their geography but that opened them up to all sorts of influences, peoples from all latitudes, exotic goods coming from India, China, Indonesia, a bustling duty-free industry and widely spread contraband trade.

We stayed in the Hotel Continental, in the area known as La Cresta. The way my mother settled into the room and unpacked her suitcase, her perfect posture when she finally sat on a chair, were clearly intended to make me feel that she did not approve of what I had chosen to do. My poor mother, I thought. She was worlds away from guerrilla embroil-ments and political persecutions—this elegant woman, dressed in a tai-lored summer suit, her short blond hair carefully coiffed, her perfectly manicured hands, a soft tone on her nails, her legs with the nylon stock-ings. My husband had explained my troubles to her. She wanted details. Despite her frown, I think she actually enjoyed being in the position to extend the rope that would save me from falling into the precipice. Softly, slowly, she voiced her questions and gave me a brief report of what was going on in Nicaragua. She didn't miss the opportunity to lay her blame and make me feel guilty. Ah, my poor daughters, how they had missed me, how Melissa had cried for me; my father had had so many sleepless nights, my husband had become a shadow of himself, consumed by worry.

"You are guilty too, Mom," I snapped. "You taught me to feel respon-sible, to care about others."

She hadn't come to Panama to argue with me, she said, but to help me. Obviously there were many ways to interpret what being responsible meant. I kept quiet. I couldn't deprive her of speaking her mind.

What hurt me most was seeing how aloof she was. She knew how to be distant, and I could rarely reach out to her unless I accepted her rules and refrained from emotion. No impassioned arguments, no insults, and no loss of composure. I knew what she wanted. As soon as I agreed to go by her rules, my mother loosened up and became a formidable ally. In the end, I always gave in.

The next morning after a room service breakfast—one of the things my mother most loved about hotels—we got to work over coffee cups, toast and butter, and tiny jars of marmalade. I wanted her to help me prepare for the very real possibility that I might be detained and ques-tioned at the airport in Managua by the regime's secret police. If that happened, I had to make sure to misinform them and lead them off my track. I needed to construct a perfectly plausible, tight story—what

we referred to as a "legend" in guerrilla lingo—that would give them reason to believe that whatever I had done before and after the December
Operation—even meeting Marcos and Roberto, if it were to come up—
had a simple explanation and in no way indicated an involvement with
the guerrillas that they should worry about or that would merit torturing
me or putting me in prison. First I wrote a draft. Reading it one could
easily see me as a romantic, naive young woman who had barely flirted
with political rebellion. Then we went over it making sure that every
date, every motivation for going here or there made sense and agreed
with the spin we were giving to what was mostly factual truth. Then I
memorized the whole thing. And then my mother, who loved the theater
and had acted in more than one play staged in Managua, decided to take
on the role of the interrogator so that I could rehearse my part. She must
have relived every espionage scene, every torture and brainwashing session in the many movies she had seen in her life, because by the time she
was through I was out of breath. Over and over again she tried to get me
to contradict myself. She tried cornering me. She tried provoking me.

Despite the incredible stress of the situation, we managed a few
laughs. Her love for me probably made her leap across boundaries she
never thought she would have to cross in her life as a mother. But she did
it with enormous grace. My mother was a petite, delicate, and difficult
woman. She denied herself the intensity of her feelings but, in hard times,
she always rose to the occasion, revealing herself as the extraordinary
woman she was. Sometimes I see so many similarities between her and
me. We both wanted to push the limits, and I think she resented me for
being the one to dare. She had chosen obligation. And I had chosen my
dreams. The ebb and flow of her love wavered between pushing me away
or drawing me close. She wanted me to keep afloat until I reached port,
nurtured by the primeval waters of her womb, but I knew that her waters
would engulf me. I needed to swim far away. I wanted to be another ocean.
I don't think she ever understood, she never knew what to make of me.

I can only imagine how dreadful it must have been for her—the entire
flight back to Nicaragua, she sat stiff and upright in her seat, her eyes
shut, silently praying, the rosary beads in her hands moving to the
cadence of the Ave Marias—yet that she wouldn't try to stop me, that
she would accept my decision to return, to go and face danger, was a sign
to me that she was letting me do it because she believed I would have the
wherewithal and the strength to get through it.

CHAPTER SIXTEEN

*On how I survived another year of brutal dictatorship
and how it was that the Sandinista movement multiplied and divided*

MANAGUA, 1975

I DON'T KNOW what twist of fate saved me from being captured. Privilege, perhaps. Either the Security Office had more important things to do or my dossier got lost somewhere. I got off the plane, and went through immigration and customs feeling as if my life were hanging from a thread. Only after we left the airport and got on the road that crosses the sprawling, ugly industrial part of Managua, en route to my parents' house, did we feel it was time to breathe with relief, utter a Thank God! My mother didn't allow herself but a stern glance in my direction. Dread and danger behind her, she reverted to reproach. At home, sitting on my parents' bed—parents, husband, siblings, children crowded in the large bedroom with its picture windows and wooden blinds—my daughters climbing on top of me, I quickly went through the pile of newspapers my father had kept for me. As soon as I began to read the news, the relief I felt at being back with my family, in my childhood home, vanished. I became convinced that the secret police had knowingly let me through to use me as some kind of decoy because there in front of me in the newspapers, one issue after another, were pictures of Roberto, Martín, and that mysterious house near El Crucero that I had never seen before—so close to the path hidden in that pasture where Marcos and I would hide away together. The joy I felt upon returning to Nicaragua quickly turned to panic. My father saw the alarm and fear come over me. He ordered my daughters and my younger sister out of the bedroom.

"They're going to capture me. Now I am sure of it. I know these people," I said, pointing at the newspaper, "and I am sure Somoza's secret police know I do. I shouldn't have come back! What am I going to do now?"

The expressions on my father's, my mother's, and my husband's faces were grim, circumspect. They knew even less than I did about what to do in those circumstances.

"Maybe I should seek political asylum," I said. "Slip into an embassy." I was appalled by what I read in the newspapers. From the telephone calls to my family and the reports I had read in the Spanish newspapers, I couldn't have guessed how fierce the repression had been in the wake of the December Operation. But now the evidence was right before my eyes. Raids. Jails filled to capacity with every last person they suspected of being connected to the Sandinistas. Somoza had created a special court— unconstitutional—made up of military officers to try civilians accused of conspiracy. The trials had just begun and the court was starting to hear the prisoners' depositions.

How is it that you didn't let me know what was happening? How come you didn't warn me! You should have written, said something! I was so ignorant to walk into this trap! I ranted and raved at my parents and my husband. If I thought asylum was my best option, said my father, he would take me to an embassy. But he suggested going to talk first to Dr. Carlos Baez, a family friend who had also been our pediatrician. He had been there. He had done it. He could tell us what to do, how asylum worked, what embassy I should go to.

Dr. Baez, the same man who had given me my vaccinations, who had nursed my childhood illnesses, falls, and scratches, and who was now my daughters' pediatrician, finally managed to calm us all down. He advised me against seeking asylum, saying I should just wait. It was a good sign that I hadn't been stopped at the airport. To seek asylum was to enter a realm of uncertainty. Years could go by before the request was processed and all that time I would be living in a no-man's-land, unable to leave the embassy grounds.

I returned to my home. For the first two weeks I barely went out. I got so seriously paranoid that I feared the cars parked on the street— expecting them to morph into live, dangerous creatures at any moment. I only wanted to stay in bed, curl up in the fetal position, and suck my thumb. I was overcome by the strong and inexplicable urge to have my father carry me in his arms and rock me on a rocking chair while he sang lullabies and hushed me: there, there, my little girl. All through my childhood, my father's arms were the circles, the walled-in enclosure where fear could not penetrate. When I was a teenager, we became buddies the day I vowed not to be afraid of him anymore, not to view him as the judgmental, omnipotent figure that my mother invoked whenever we misbehaved. It took me a while to feel comfortable joking around with him and speaking my mind, but my change of attitude worked like magic. We became dear friends. No one else in my life has been as supportive or trusting as my father. His faith in me allowed me to be true to myself. Since my earliest memories I have always associated him with light. I remember, for example, his hands pulling the cord to start the diesel engine that supplied electricity to the house on the beach where we spent our summers; or seeing him, in the dark, during Managua's frequent power outages, lighting a Coleman lamp so that we could do our homework. My father always illuminating my shadows.

I would have given anything to get him to hold me close to him until danger had passed, but I was a grown-up woman now and I had to live with the consequences of my actions.

Fortunately, real life wasn't going to let me hide. My daughters needed their mother. My household financial needs forced me to look for a new job because I had quit my last one before leaving for Europe. Worried about my state of mind, Justine would take me out for coffee, lunch. I saw Róger again.

My brother Humberto was also a great help in restoring my spirits and my optimism. When we were children he had been a master at inventing games that blended seamlessly with our everyday lives. He created the fantasy of a very large country where he was the president-for-life. He wrote its constitution, mapped out its territory and bodies of water, and created its ethnic makeup, carefully recording everything in the blank accounting ledgers my father gave him. My siblings and I inhabited that country and obeyed its laws, each of us assigned a different name. Mine was María Elena Shirley. Even after we became adults he would often break into the game and pretend he was president, ordering us around. During that trying time, he made me laugh like an idiot at the ridiculous guilty sentences he decreed, at the way he poked fun at my fears, surreptitiously breaking into my house as if leading a surprise attack. He knew I hated that my husband watched so much television, so one day, when there was no one in my house, he jumped over the gate and staged a robbery. We arrived home to find clothing strewn across the floors, the drawers open wide, and the television gone. We stood around pondering what to do. My husband was grumbling, upset by the loss of his TV. And then Humberto began laughing hysterically and gave himself away. We found the TV in the garden.

In time, my brother and I found ourselves holding radically different political views, especially since he experienced a religious conversion and became a born-again Catholic. Yet, mainly because of our happy childhood, we managed to remain on friendly terms. Whenever we're together, we try to be children again. If we let ourselves be adults, we begin to argue, the contradictions emerge. Inevitably we lash out at each other. Luckily, the wounds have never been deep enough to totally throw us asunder.

Soon after I returned to Managua, I met with Pedro Araúz Palacios in Mazatlán, at Alfredo and Pía's house. Marcos had gone with the commandos to Cuba and Pedro had taken his place as head of the urban resistance. The tenor of that meeting was so removed from the study sessions and dinners with Marcos that I couldn't help feeling overwhelmed by nostalgia. Pedro, whose nom de guerre was Federico, was a tough, coarse man whose prominent jaw gave his face an authoritarian, unfriendly edge. He wore mirrored sunglasses the whole time, which prevented me from making eye contact with him. He harshly reprimanded me for returning to Nicaragua without waiting for instructions. "You, *compañera*, were scheduled to go to Cuba. You shouldn't have come back. You disobeyed your orders." I brought up the issue of my daughters, the fact that I had waited for two months and never heard a word, but to no avail. He kept admonishing me. "But I would happily have gone to Cuba," I repeated. On one hand I was glad to imagine it had been Marcos who had wanted me there, but on the other hand I was quite relieved that I had not left my little girls. Federico, however, had no patience for my justifications. Because I was a militant and was subject to disciplinary measures, he decided to put me in the cold. I would not be given any responsibilities to speak of until he thought I had learned my lesson. I would just do menial jobs, like translating long and boring weapons manuals. I lucked out though, because he gave me a new contact person to work with who turned out to be one of the sweetest, most gentle men I have ever known. Jacobo Marcos, a psychiatrist of Palestinian descent, a mild-mannered person, with a well-rounded education, who looked at the world with a very healthy mix of tolerance and skepticism and who laughed under his breath with the expression of an old child whose innate wisdom prevented him from taking anything too seriously. Jacobo played a key role for me in that dreadful year. We pretended to be therapist and patient. It was the perfect cover. Every week, I visited his office, which has stayed in my memory as a dimly lit place furnished with heavy, dark Spanish-style pieces upholstered red to match the curtains. There, we had all the privacy we needed. He won me over with his utter lack of ceremony, his irony. He had good coffee in his office too. Tiny porcelain cups. The immediate sympathy I had felt for him rapidly increased when he told me he had been the person who had recruited Marcos for the Sandinista cause, in Paris. It was because of him, in fact, that Marcos had chosen that name as his pseudonym. Jacobo understood the inner workings of the Sandinista movement infinitely better than I; he understood its leaders and their limitations— a knowledge that was very handy particularly toward the end of 1975, when the FSLN went through a political crisis which, in 1976, splintered the Organization into three separate factions.

Paradoxically, the crisis occurred precisely because of the vigorous expansion of the Sandinista movement following the December 27 Operation. New people brought new ideas and proposals on how to spread the anti-Somoza struggle and reach out to the masses more effectively. They clashed with the traditional views held by Federico and Tomás Borge, who had been left in charge of the movement in Nicaragua, while Marcos, Carlos Fonseca, and other leaders planned strategy and trained in Cuba. The crisis marked the moment in which three distinct concepts of Sandinismo came to a head: Federico and Tomás maintained that the indefatigable guerrilla columns operating in the mountains in northern Nicaragua were the real backbone of the movement. According to them the military defeat of the regime would take place when rural guerrilla warfare became widespread and people rose in the cities to give the final blow to the dictatorship. However, the undeniable success of the December 27 Operation, especially when it came to the number of people that had since joined the resistance, favored Marcos's strategy, which called for military operations in the cities. He had concluded that popular urban uprisings had been the method of choice through Nicaraguan history. To overthrow the dictatorship, he believed we needed to set in motion a widespread insurrection. The other splinter group, which had led the split, argued that the movement could only expand by mobilizing the agricultural and industrial proletariat and making them the driving force of the resistance.

In time, these three different approaches manifested themselves in three different groups, which came to be known as "tendencies": the GPP (Prolonged People's War) was for the guerrillas in the mountains, the Terceristas were for the war in the cities, the Proletariats were for organizing workers. During the first few months of the crisis, however, the differences were not completely clear, the battle of ideas was raging, and there were a lot of accusations—one accused the other of betraying principles, selling out to bourgeois ideas. It was a very confusing time and many of us suddenly found ourselves in a kind of no-man's-land.

By October of 1975, I was back from the "cold." I never saw Federico again. Instead I began to have regular contact with Tomás Borge. Tomás's personality encompassed the most exalted heroism with the most frivolous human indulgence, especially vanity and gossip. He was short (a physical trait that tormented him), with the face of a Mongol warrior, and the bearing of a man given to imagining himself leading an army of soldiers. Unsophisticated but extremely seductive, he was a sensitive soul who was easily moved by emotion. If something particularly touched him he could come up with a dazzling display of goodwill and generosity; he also had a penchant for words. He could blend beauty and simplicity in powerful sentences. As the only survivor of the FSLN's "founding fathers," he was somewhat of a legend and lived up to his image. He loved to amaze; yet one never knew if what he was saying was the truth or something he had concocted given his fertile imagination. I was in awe of his having survived so many years of a clandestine existence, of his vast experience as a conspiratorial old devil, and admired the nobility of heart I could sense underneath his taste for theatrics. To me, he was like an overgrown little boy I had to protect from his tendency to carelessly and defiantly wander the streets.

I was assigned to drive Tomás to his meetings with contacts in the city. With him, the simplest operations were often nerve-racking for he seemed intent on courting danger. He would get out of the car to buy a lottery ticket on a random street corner, for example, or else he would sit upright in the car completely unconcerned about hiding, acting as though he actually wanted people to notice him. He was high on the dictatorship's list of most wanted Sandinistas and so his audacity didn't just make me nervous, it infuriated me. It didn't make any sense to me that we would run risks only so that he could feel like a macho man. Ironically, that's how we became friends—I would object to his orders or simply disobey them if I felt they were reckless or impulsive. He liked the fact that I talked back to him. He accepted my criticism, making fun of himself and confessing it was very hard for him to adjust to a way of life that so little agreed with his personality.

The day Tomás told me that Roberto might be calling me, I immediately knew something was amiss. He said that if Roberto called, I was to contact him right away. "Roberto has not returned to his safe house," he explained. The use of the paternal patronizing tone he affected with me sometimes, "pay heed, my child," seemed to me like a dark omen. I realized he was trying hard to give me the impression that it was nothing of concern, so that I wouldn't catch on to the fact that he was asking me to turn my friend in, to put my loyalty to the Organization before my loyalty to Roberto. I played the game and acted natural, as though it was all perfectly normal. Of course, I said. If Roberto called me I would let him know. I was quite puzzled as to why Roberto would have left his safe house, especially since he was one of the most publicized fugitives from the recent December Operation.

It made me happy to hear Roberto at the other end of the line. It had been a long time. I pictured his birdlike face, the glasses on top of his head. Yet, the urgency in his voice alarmed me.

"Listen," he said. "I've got serious skirt problems. I got involved with a woman and her husband is after me. He's seriously trying to kill me. I am not kidding. So I need your help but you can't tell anyone, nobody, that you are going to see me or that I called. Do you understand what I mean?"

I picked him up on a street corner and we talked for several hours while we drove around the outskirts of the city in the car. He told me about the problems that had caused the split in the Organization, he said that Tomás and Federico had taken Luis Carrión and Jaime Wheelock (the leaders of the dissident faction) at gunpoint to an embassy to force them to seek asylum and leave the country. Luis and Jaime had managed to get out of the embassy, Roberto had gotten out of the safe house, and now their group—of dissident fugitives—needed help so they could leave the country and contact Marcos and the other party leaders, to let them know what had happened and to tell them their side of the story. Conflicts of opinion had to be resolved through discussion, not with loaded guns and coercion. I agreed with him entirely—they deserved to be heard, to voice their disagreements.

For the next two weeks I found myself caught in a double bind. I had to pay attention to Somoza's secret police but also make sure that Tomás would not suspect I was working for the dissidents—the "split-offs," as he called them. I contacted Rosario Murillo, the poet who had organized the cultural group Gradas. She lived in one of Managua's crowded barrios and she agreed to shelter Roberto and the others for a few days. Rosario and I were on pins and needles, aware of the double-sided risk we were running.

At the university, among the student arm of the FSLN, people hotly debated the issue, calling into question the methods of the Sandinistas' most hard-line leaders. The rift began to grow wider. Rosario would bite her nails as we talked in her house, decorated with posters of rock groups, beanbag pillows, and bead curtains. With her eyes open wide like a hunted animal, jiggling the many bracelets and rings she wore, her flowing tunics and long hair wrapping up her hippie look, Rosario would bring me up to date on the details of the dispute. Together we discussed our disenchantment, our astonishment at how messed up things had become inside the Organization. We drank herb tea with honey, comparing notes on what each of us felt at the sight of the Organization crumbling before our eyes as if hit by an earthquake. We couldn't believe that such an idealized image as we had of the Sandinista National Liberation Front, the Frente as we often referred to it, could be wrecked so easily. How could it be that the *compañeros* weren't being allowed to express their opinions freely? How could we think of seizing political power in the country if all we would expect people to do was to support the struggle of small guerrilla groups holed up in the mountains? That was it, Rosario would say, if the Frente couldn't solve the split it would self-destruct. We would have to get out, resign. Yes, I would agree, it would be better to forget about it before it suffered the same fate that had befallen so many other Latin American liberation movements that split up into a thousand pieces and ended up killing one another within their own ranks. One only had to see what had happened to Roque Dalton in El Salvador. Killed by his own people.

Rosario soon cut her ties to Tomás, who, according to her, had the bizarre habit of simply appearing at her house unannounced. My relationship with Tomás, however, remained more or less the same as always—he would still call me to meetings, come to my house, ask me to drive him to and from various places in and around Managua. One of those afternoons when I went to pick him up, I found him with a small, pretty woman in a low-cut top, with a look that was somewhere between sensual and innocent, like an actress from a Roger Vadim film. I recognized her from the photographs I had seen in the newspaper. Her name was Charlotte Baltodano. Another high-profile fugitive. She and her husband had rented the famous house used by the commandos in the December 27 Operation.

"Do you think she could spend the night at your house?" Tomás asked me.

I said yes, but I also warned him of the risks. My house was not the safest place to be.

"I know, I know. It's just for tonight."

Upon my return from Europe, to ingratiate himself with me, my husband had given me a gun, money, and even agreed to meet Tomás on one occasion. This, their one and only meeting, was enough to dissuade him from his timid intentions, and effectively eliminated any desire he might have had to be involved with the Sandinistas. Unfortunately, before the meeting, I tried to show Tomás what I considered were the best routes out of my house in case of an emergency. My husband overheard him say "Don't worry about that, dear, if the National Guard comes, we'll all die here anyway." Tomás's histrionic disregard for human life was too much for my husband. And so when he saw me enter the house with Charlotte, whose fugitive photo was frequently splashed across the newspapers, his face turned white.

"It's just for today," I said to placate him. Charlotte disappeared into her bedroom and stayed there until it was time to leave the following day. At dusk the two of us took off for Managua.

Raised in California, Charlotte spoke Spanish with a slight accent. She had a daughter who had been living with her grandparents ever since she had gone underground. She only saw her now and again, she told me, sad. We turned a curve. A small red car, parked on the side of the road, began moving as soon as we passed by, tailing us. In the rearview mirror, I could see four passengers. Earlier that day I had seen the same red car, two or three times in the surrounding traffic, but after making a few detours to see if it was following me, I dismissed it. Now I knew it was too late.

"They're following us," I told my passenger.

She took a second to check. Then she leaned over her backpack, removed a pair of sneakers, and changed out of her heels. She went back into her backpack and produced two guns.

"Do you know how to use this?"

I nodded, and she placed one of the guns on my lap, a bullet in the chamber, and the safety lock already released. At five in the afternoon the traffic was heavy on the narrow, two-lane road. As the car slowly inched forward, I quickly weighed our options. If there were a confrontation, both of us would be killed. It would be four against two and they surely had more experience and better aim. There was no way we could shake them. In a way, the dense traffic protected us, but at any moment the men could simply get out of the car, cut us off, and open fire.

"They won't catch us alive, do you agree?" Charlotte asked.

I nodded.

A cold determination took hold of me right then. I considered the possibility that military jeeps could intercept us farther ahead. How many soldiers could we eliminate before they got to us? I pictured the jeeps surrounding us. I felt no fear, only a rush of adrenaline. Time was moving in slow motion but my mind was working with astonishing speed and precision. A few meters ahead I could make out the entrance to a residential complex whose streets were a labyrinth of corners, traffic circles, and narrow alleys that gave way to a maze of local roads.

Impulsively, without gauging the distance between the formulation and the execution of the plan, I stepped on the gas of my Alfa Sud. Suddenly I veered to the left, speeding down the middle of the lane and heading into the oncoming traffic. Drivers yelled out at me and swerved, unable to react any other way. Parting the waters of that automotive Red Sea, I reached the turn I wanted, veered right, and plunged into the maze of streets until I reached a dirt road that led to the other side of the Ticomo valley and came out at the back of a densely populated working-class barrio. It was a bold maneuver. I didn't have time to weigh the risks but it worked. We got away, lost sight of the red car, and I was able to deliver Charlotte, safe and sound, to her destination. On the way back to my house, my legs shook uncontrollably. I didn't say a word to my husband. I was very frightened. I thought I was going to be captured that day. But nothing came of that chase. To this day that incident is still a mystery to me. Apparently they kept hoping they would catch me with a bigger fish.

My apprehension and dread grew as the days went by. The situation within the Organization was growing more and more confusing. I didn't know whom to trust. I wanted to believe that the movement couldn't fall apart, that the negotiations in which Roberto and the others were involved would succeed, but it terrified me to think what would happen if I were captured or had to face some serious risk at a moment when my faith in the cause had weakened and I had begun to fear that so many dreams and efforts might be wasted. The dictatorship's net was closing in on me. Jacobo was captured in December. I had spotted the car with four agents from the secret police standing watch outside his clinic a few days before. When I saw them I decided to just drive by and skip the meeting we had scheduled for that day. I sent him a warning message, pleading with him to be careful. But Jacobo didn't heed my advice.

Alfredo got in touch with me to pass on Federico's instructions: I was to leave the country immediately. As stipulated by a Sandinista code of honor, it was expected that, at least for a week, Jacobo would remain silent even if he were tortured. That was the allotted time those who had been in contact with him had to get cover. We knew that after a week he would have to talk and reveal some names in order to save his life. There was no doubt in my mind that I had to follow the order, even if it came from Federico. I had less than a week to get ready to leave the country. Once again, December brought farewells and disasters. My poor daughters and all our Christmas plans. That year I had even bought the famous Christmas tree and decorated it with bright, colored little lights.

Despondent and frightened, I wandered through the streets of my city. Managua was like a young girl disfigured by a terrible accident. Burned, broken, but a survivor. The tenacity of its inhabitants bestowed on it a beauty that was beyond aesthetic considerations. I went to my favorite lookouts, like the place on the highway where the majestic Momotombo volcano seems to be a giant walking ahead, its neck wrapped in white wisps of cloud. I visited my favorite trees, to make sure I would remember their trunks and the brilliance of their leaves. I filled my lungs with the many smells carried by the wind. Amid the traffic and the din of the markets I focused my eyes on the dark, round, noble faces, some rough, some delicate, of the many long-suffering people who refused to give up hope. I silently prayed that the Sandinista movement would deliver what it had promised them. I ardently wished we would not fail them.

On December 20, 1975, I boarded a plane for Mexico, alone, on the pretext of taking a vacation. At the airport, fearing the worst, I cradled my daughters as I waited for my flight to be called, hoping the heat from their little bodies might warm the icy chill traveling up and down my spine. I felt like a hunted animal.

"They just called you on the loudspeakers," my husband said as he leaned toward me. I went white and sprung up seized by panic, uncontrollable panic.

"Sit down, sit down. I was only joking," my husband said, a mocking smile on his lips, tugging at my dress. This was not one of the many things I eventually forgave him for.

The week after I left, the agents from Somoza's secret police came to my office at the advertising agency and confiscated all my papers. A few months later, my name was added to the list of the hundreds of people who were tried by the Military Tribunal. My parents hired a defense lawyer who read some of my poems in his opening remarks to prove I did love my country. I was given a seven-year prison sentence in absentia.

Later I found out what the dictatorship's secret police thugs did to Jacobo. He was buried in a standing position up to his neck and left for a week in an outdoor courtyard under the scalding sun. His captors kicked him and poured garbage and urine on him. But he kept his word and remained silent. Because of him I was able to flee and avoid my prison sentence.

EXILE

Vientos del pueblo me llevan
Vientos del pueblo me arrastran
Me esparcen mi corazón
Y me aventan la garganta

—Miguel Hernández

People's breaths, like wind, sweep me along/They scatter my heart/They fill my throat with voices

CHAPTER SEVENTEEN

On what happened after I fled to Mexico City
and started my life in exile by getting together with old friends

MEXICO, 1975

I ARRIVED IN MEXICO disoriented and breathless, feeling as though I had run all the way from Nicaragua taking giant leaps over the clouds. Fear kept me from grieving for what I had left behind, and from worrying about the future. The experience felt like a replay of my trip the previous year: fleeing the country at Christmastime to wait for events to unfold, and then, possibly, go back home. My friend Róger, who was in Mexico City doing a workshop at the Taller de Gráfica Popular (a famous graphic arts atelier), had reserved a hotel for me and I went there straight from the airport. The cab cruised through the streets of the dense, interminable metropolis illuminated for the holiday festivities, its avenues swarming with people rushing along with bags—from the big department stores, Liverpool, El Palacio de Hierro—overflowing with gifts, the red Christmas bows peeping out.

I settled into my room, a sober affair furnished in Art Deco style, and lay down on the bed. I tried to relax, following the exercises Jacobo had taught me in his office and breathing deeply. Poor Jacobo. What he must have gone through. Whenever I complained to him about my paranoia, he always said that in our profession, it was a good thing.

At ten in the evening, Róger came to the hotel—jeans jacket, beard, mustache. We had a beer. He must have sensed despondency in the faraway look on my face, because he suddenly announced he was taking me to his studio. It was close by, he said the stroll would suit me. We walked down the street until we came to the building which housed both the studios and a printing press. Outside it had the same antique, run-down, colonial feel of so many houses in Granada, Nicaragua. Inside, the presses churned, with a loud, monotonous noise. Róger introduced me to the workers, declaring proudly that because I had just escaped from the clutches of Somoza, they had to cheer me up. After half an hour, the men stopped the machines printing Christmas cards, and improvised a special welcome in an attic that reeked of ink. We ended up drinking tequila and singing Mexican ranchera songs—the best cultural pretext I have ever known for letting out one's woes, a free, friendly therapy that, in the company of those workers, was the best gift I received that day. I returned to the hotel content and touched.

"You're not alone, love. Don't worry. I'll tell the other *compañeros* that you're here. I'll come and have breakfast with you tomorrow," Róger said.

I presumed that through Róger I would contact the network of Sandinista exiles in Mexico, which included Andrea and the Poet, because for safety reasons I hadn't brought a single telephone number with me. I was right. From the next morning on, through the time I stayed in that hotel, the phone didn't stop ringing. By noon, my room was filled with people. Róger and the Poet came with two other friends. There were great big hugs, laughter, lots of vitality—"lively exuberance," as the Poet liked to call it. They ordered Tecates and Coronas from room service, chatting nonstop, anxious to know the goings-on in the FSLN and "the country." I realized that the split within the Organization had thrown all caution to the wind, they didn't seem worried about keeping information from one another. Their excitement and optimism revived my flagging spirits and made me reconsider my despair. They were of the opinion that, in the end, the crisis would have a healthy effect because it would force the leaders to openly discuss strategy and other issues with the rank and file. Up until then, inner consensus had been built mainly around anti-Somoza sentiments plus some very basic objectives stated in the FSLN's political program, but that wasn't enough anymore. We needed to discuss different military options and guerrilla tactics and also possible alliances with other political forces and groups. I said I was convinced that the dissidents' resolve to remain within the movement and insist on the right they had to question the leadership and be heard had shattered the notion of absolute authority held by the more dogmatic and orthodox leaders, who refused to consider the alternatives and possibilities that had been opened up by the December Operation. The Poet turned out to be the only one of the group who offered a sound defense of the GPP's strategy. He dismissed the dissidents, calling them pseudo-intellectuals, which only fired up the debate. Someone mentioned a book's title. "Let's go to the bookstore," somebody else called out. Afterward we could have lunch.

The Mexican bookstores were heaven on earth to me. The banned books that were inaccessible in Nicaragua were all there, but they were expensive and I had to be extremely careful with the thousand dollars I had brought with me. I didn't know how long I would have to live on that money.

"Don't worry," one of them said, casting a sidelong glance at my handbag. After a few minutes I felt one, two, three books slide their way inside. I looked at the face of the culprit, playing innocent as he leaned against a bookshelf. I got nervous. I didn't know what to do. They started motioning for me to leave the bookstore. As I approached the sidewalk, my purse weighed heavy in my arms. My face was burning up. I searched their faces, but they just played cool. We crossed the street. After a few blocks, we reached a park. Nearly collapsing in laughter, they pulled out the books. Three or four.

"Revolutionary law number one," someone said. "Capitalism has cheated us. Books are not to be bought, they are to be repossessed."

"This is robbery," I said. "Let's not kid ourselves. And don't do that to me again. You scared me to death."

"It's not robbery. Books are ideas. They should be able to circulate freely within society. At no price at all, or for pennies. It's outrageous to think that knowledge is only for those who can pay for it. Knowledge is universal. It belongs to all of us."

They were really convinced by their arguments. There was no way to dissuade them. But if it upset me, they said, I didn't have to do it. To "repossess" books one needed presence of mind, otherwise the game was up. But for the time being, I had books to read.

Later that afternoon, Andrea arrived with Felipe, waving excitedly. She was glad to see me, but she wasn't happy herself. I could see in her eyes that she had reverted to her secretive, aloof countenance. As was characteristic of her she tried to compensate for her lackluster eyes with expansive gestures and words. Felipe looked like a college student. Simply dressed, serious, with the grin of a child determined to act like an adult. I knew his family. He and Andrea were full-time political cadres working for the FSLN in Mexico. Through them I learned that Marcos and the other members of the Directorate did not approve of Federico and Tomás's actions in Nicaragua, and that they were trying to negotiate with them for the return of the dissidents back into the Organization. Avoiding a division was important, but not at the price of the FSLN's advancement. Sandinista tactics and strategy needed to adapt, to modernize. I agreed to join the group that was intent on mediating a compromise. In time after these efforts failed, the group would become another faction, the third tendency, the one that sparked and carried out localized popular uprisings which, eventually, culminated in a general insurrection. Andrea left and Felipe stayed on a while longer, talking with me in the hotel coffee shop. My fears of foundering in a foreign city had evaporated. This was more like arriving home into the bosom of a family that loved me and worried about my welfare: the fraternity, the warmth of my *compañeros* brought me back to the uncanny elation I was seized with so often and so unexpectedly during those years of struggle. I often felt I was standing at the edge of a precipice, yet I experienced a profound and tangible happiness nevertheless.

"Tonight someone you know is going to come and pick you up here," Felipe said, lowering his voice, leaning toward me conspiratorially. "You don't need a password. Just be down in the lobby at eight on the dot. This person can explain what's going on better. After you talk, we'll figure out the rest, where you're going to live, all that."

Then he left. I went up to my room like a robot following an order. Who else but Marcos would announce himself like that? To send such an obscure message was so much like him. Who else could it be? But wait— he's in Cuba, I reminded myself. Well, what did I know? He could be anywhere; after all, stealth was his business.

My heart was pounding. I had trouble breathing. My palms were sweating. I need one of those pills I take before flying, I said to myself. If not, I wouldn't be able to get dressed, or even move around my room. I took a bath. Combed my hair. At eight o'clock sharp I went down to the lobby. I didn't see him. I peered through the glass. A tall, dark-haired man in a gray jacket rushed toward the hotel. When he approached the entrance he looked inside. Those green eyes. I raced outside. A minute later my face was buried in his chest. He hugged me so tight and then he loosened me up to look at me, only to embrace me again. He did this several times. I teased him about his very dark hair to hide the turmoil I felt inside. Together, we walked away from the hotel.

"I knew it was you," I said. "I suspected it from the start."

He laughed. His dark hair brought out the intense green of his eyes, a lush green like the Nicaraguan countryside just after the dry season when the torrential rains begin to fall. Even his drab, worn clothing couldn't detract from his good looks. I marveled at the confidence with which he walked through the city. It was cold. The December evening, illuminated by the reflection of countless lights, vibrant and alive, unfolded, ignoring us. We were just another couple. Here, death wasn't hunting us down. It was like walking out into the open air after living in catacombs for years and years. In that great metropolis we were invisible, and the streets offered us warm, protective shelter. I grabbed hold of his arm, emboldened by the anonymity. I don't know how many streetlights we passed through, how many streets, it was as if we had no other task in the world except to walk. I told him about everything I assumed he wanted to know. I let him lead the way wholly absorbed by his mere presence. Just by being there he filled so much space inside of me that it was hard to believe that a year had gone by since I had last seen him; it was as if that void in time had simply closed, swallowing up every last trace of his absence.

A month later, the sweet gentleness of that night would make me cry.

We went to the Sanborn's on Reforma for coffee and cake.

"You should eat, you're very thin," he said. "And you look like a fugitive. It's over, you're here now. You have nothing to fear."

He kept holding my hands and stroking them. We talked for a long while about the crisis within the Organization. He believed his mediation would solve the problems. Soon he would travel to a meeting that would bring together all the members of the Directorate. In the meantime our work had to go on. He was relieved that he wouldn't have to worry about my safety anymore, he said. He had been convinced long ago that I was running too many risks by staying in Nicaragua.

"But maybe I can go back," I said. "If Jacobo didn't give them my name . . ."

"Jacobo will assume you left the country. He'll assume you're out of danger. He has to say something for them to stop torturing him. I don't think you should even consider going back. I would rather see you transferred to Costa Rica. We already have enough people here. We need people in Costa Rica."

We talked about Jacobo. He was very fond of him.

"Did I ever tell you? When I was seventeen years old I went to Europe on a merchant ship. I lived in Germany, France. It was in Paris where I met Jacobo. He was the person who made the contacts which allowed several Sandinistas to train with the Palestinians. I was among them."

Jacobo had let his guard down. He had been too confident, Marcos said. No doubt they would put him through a lot of pain and suffering, and Jacobo was such a gentle, sensitive person.

On the way back to the hotel, he told me stories about the December Operation. He was amazed that Somoza's secret police didn't have a clue about his identity still. For them he remained the mysterious Commander Zero.

That night, Marcos stayed with me at the hotel. Sheltered and safe, we lingered on each other's flesh like explorers who are, at last, allowed to see by daylight the island they had only traversed by night. I marveled at the sight of his strong, lean, perfectly chiseled body, the soft downy hair that covered it. He made me think of a beautiful Greek sculpture: Myron's Discus Thrower. He murmured that I was more beautiful than he had imagined. So was he, I said. That night I felt as if we were performing a solemn, joyful ritual, tenderly and delicately, like if we were touching images in a mirror, scared that they might suddenly dissolve. Or like if we had been two blind people whose vision has suddenly been restored and who anxiously memorize one another's faces for fear the blindness will return. I was unable to sleep the whole night. Occasionally I lifted myself up from the bed and leaned on my elbow to look at him. He was so handsome, like a beautiful Spartan warrior, yet so vulnerable and finite. Sadness overwhelmed me. I began to cry softly because I had the unequivocal certainty, the strong premonition of his death, and knew that I could do nothing to protect him. This terrible certainty stayed with me from that moment on. I tried to stunt my foreboding, to scare it away by flinging my hands, my love, against it, but every time Marcos slept next to me, I'd get bleary-eyed.

We saw each other several times in the weeks that followed. I rented a room in a somber, gray apartment building close to Insurgentes, the great boulevard that bisects the city. It was a simple room, like a hotel bedroom, furnished with a bed, dresser, and chair. There was a bathroom and a closet, and the windows opened out onto the building's internal courtyard. I had no telephone, only a public phone in the hallway. Marcos ordered me not to give that number to anyone. Even in Mexico the dictatorship had us under surveillance, he said. It wasn't safe to give it to anyone, not even my family.

In my absence, my parents were taking care of my daughters because my husband felt he couldn't care for them alone. In the dank, humid hallway of that building, my hands trembled every time I called my parents' home. Are the girls all right? I would ask. After my mother or father assured me that yes, they were fine, I'd feel my blood warm up again. I suffered tremendously thinking of my daughters. To listen to their small voices eagerly asking me when I was coming back and to be unable to console their dismay made me feel nauseated. Every breath burned as if my lungs were on fire. I'd try to explain to my kids what I was doing, telling them about poverty, needy children, and the obligation to be responsible to other people. I think I sounded like some missionary nun as I tried to explain the scope of a commitment that went beyond our individual happiness. For the love of the many, for a future where things could be fair for everyone, I had to temporarily sacrifice being with them. Even though I was aware they were still far from understanding me, I thought that someday they would understand. A poem by Edwin Castro, a patriot assassinated by the dictatorship, came to mind: "A day will come, my son, when everything will be different." But this was the kind of solace that could soothe me. For them there was no other palpable reality than their mother's absence. "Are you my mommy from the airplane?" Melissa would ask me. Maryam, who unwittingly had turned into my mother's spokesperson, would exacerbate my guilt with her reproachful, pained tone. In her childish handwriting, my poor little girl even wrote me a letter declaring that maybe there were poor children in the world, but at least they had their mothers. When I was done talking with my daughters, my father would get on the phone and the conversation would inevitably end in tears. My mother, on the other hand, focused on practical things—was I eating, was I safe, that sort of thing.

After a month in Mexico, I was indicted by the Military Tribunal. Now there was no way I could go back to my country until the dictatorship fell. The Poet showed me the article in the Nicaraguan newspaper where the news appeared. It wasn't a surprise, but I remember well the abyss that opened up beneath my feet, the vertigo of losing the last hope I had been clinging to. I would have to start my life over again somewhere else, earn a living so I could see my daughters again, decide a million things, including the fate of my marriage. A black hole of uncertainty loomed before me. My only anchors were my *compañeros*, my convictions.

Ever the optimist, the Poet hugged me, encouraged me. His energy, his vitality had miraculously remained whole, untouched. He had married the woman he had been with in Granada, a wonderful woman whom I grew to love and respect, and they had a baby. The Poet was friends with the most important poets and painters in Mexico, and I saw him frequently at Solidarity Committee meetings or at friends' houses.

Paradoxically, my geographic exile marked the end of my own personal exile. Living in exile freed me from the disguises and subterfuge I had needed to create a false image of myself, and allowed me to express what until then had been walled within me. During my first three months in Mexico I wrote the book of poems *Línea de fuego* (Line of Fire), which won the Casa de las Américas prize in Cuba in 1978. No longer did I have to worry about disclosing my political beliefs. Poems besieged me and I wrote every day. Once I opened the dikes, emotions that I had lost touch with arose again from my very depths. Nostalgia infused the maelstrom of words that poured out of me. Verses turned into buoys to keep my memories afloat without drifting away. Wrested from Nicaragua, I wrote of its monumental clouds marching in a formation of graceful, wispy towers billowing in the blue sky; of its blushful, breathtaking crepuscules, of its rain-drenched aromas and its verdant sprawls. The love of that landscape bound me to my diminutive country as much as ideas, honor, and the quest for freedom.

In my room, curled up in bed for warmth, I read and I wrote. Never before in my adult life did I have so much free time to write without interruptions. There were days when I didn't even go out to eat. On my room's windowsill, using the outside temperature for refrigeration, I kept butter, milk, jam, and bread. It was my regular diet.

Some nights Marcos's arrival broke my solitude. He would call beforehand or just show up. My ears were attuned to the sound of his footsteps advancing first toward the elevator in the lobby of the building and then from the elevator to the door of my room. Listening to the sounds of that edifice for his approach became my nocturnal obsession. It was during those months that Marcos fully developed the political and military strategy that would culminate in a popular insurrection. By then he had arrived at the absolute certainty that for the people to get involved en masse in the struggle to overthrow the dictatorship, the Sandinista movement had to make its military presence felt in the cities. It had to plan to take over urban military installations. Rebel attacks against military quarters had been a constant in Nicaragua's history of resistance.

Another issue he painstakingly grappled with was the need to forge alliances with other political tendencies. The FSLN couldn't go on acting like a sectarian guerrilla movement, he said. The Organization had to dare to open up and enter into talks and negotiations with other political forces; it had to abandon an ideological dogmatism that was anchored in the childish attitudes typical of left-wing movements. He talked about these things until the wee hours of the night, illustrating this or that issue with passages from history books he would read aloud to me. It was fascinating to watch his unrelenting passion as he came up with different scenarios, and tossed out hypotheses to hear my opinion or just to gauge my reaction to his words. I think he used me as a sounding board because he valued my insistence that we spell out all the foreseeable consequences of each of his ideas, and he appreciated a certain level of skepticism on my part. I enjoyed taking part in these long disquisitions. At times I thought he was just thinking aloud or listening to the sound of his own words to see whether they made or didn't make sense. Moreover, I got the sense that he was making sure his ideas would come across and be properly understood. I think he was well aware that in a political organization such as ours—whose leaders died unexpectedly and suddenly—it was essential to pass the ideas on to other cadres that could reproduce them. My conversations with Marcos, and the freedom to engage in political activities that I found in exile, strengthened my sense of belonging to the Sandinista movement.

The months that followed were hectic. We met several times a week to discuss our growing network of contacts in Mexico, but our main concern was to achieve a consensus among us to bring to the raging debate on the future of the Sandinista movement. As a poet and an intellectual, my job was to act as liaison with the Mexican artists, writers, and journalists to enlist their support in our efforts. Since the media in Nicaragua were strictly censored, we depended on the international media and the prestige of writers and other personalities to bring to light and denounce the atrocities and human rights violations perpetrated by the Somoza regime. Mexican artists and intellectuals opened doors for us to many important cultural institutions, universities, and think tanks, which enabled us to draw attention to the situation in Nicaragua. This was how we generated a broad base of support for the Sandinistas and fomented opposition to the Somoza dictatorship. José Emilio Pacheco, Jaime Labastida, Pablo González Casanova, Elena Poniatowska, and Efraín Huerta were among the many highly prominent Mexicans who rallied to our defense, and I was moved by the tremendous generosity and determination they displayed on our behalf. Carlos Pellicer was the honorary president of the Solidarity Committee for Nicaragua, and Thelma Nava, Efraín Huerta's wife and also a poet, was the tireless acting president. Painters like Arnold Belkin and José Luis Cuevas also supported us. Cuevas gave us one of his paintings, so we could auction it and raise money for the cause.

On Sundays, Andrea and I would sell copies of the *Gaceta Sandinista* newsletter in Chapultepec Park. We would set up a table and walk through the tree-lined paths and the open-air concerts with piles of newsletters under our arms. "The *Gaceta Sandinista, compañero*, solidarity with Nicaragua," we would call out. There was always someone to buy the magazine. Mexico City was the preferred sanctuary for the diaspora forced on a great number of Latin Americans by the many military dictatorships in the region. Idealists and dreamers from all over the continent ended up there. Each one of them managed to turn the hard reality and hopelessness of his or her country of origin into a springboard to soar and dream up the most romantic utopias. Singing, talking, writing, painting, we surrendered fully to the mystique of heroism. Come what may we had to usher in a new way of life that would be better than the one we were forced to live. There were too many of us harboring the same wish. Our illusions felt like tangible realities when we shared them with each other.

"When are you going to go to Costa Rica?" Marcos asked me.

"Don't you think I could sneak back into Nicaragua and do covert work? I'd rather go back with you."

He smiled. He touched my hair.

"One has to be where one can be most useful. It would be almost impossible for you to remain underground. You are too visible. People would notice you. No, no. Your place is abroad. The work abroad is very important and it will be more so as we proceed with our plans back home."

After I was indicted by the Military Tribunal, my husband announced that he was coming to Mexico to talk. I knew what I had to tell him. There was to be no more duplicity for me, no more yielding, no more allowing anybody to pull me back and prevent me from joining the forces of history galloping full speed. My daughters and I would manage. After all, I had been earning a living since I was seventeen. I would find work in Costa Rica.

My husband arrived and for three days we barely left his hotel room. He struggled with my decision, imploring me to change my mind, offering to move to Costa Rica with me, to change. We both cried so much I felt as if my tears would run out. His suffering filled me with sorrow but I knew that even if he could change, it wouldn't do us any good now. I had no love left for him. It was hard to believe that I had ever loved him, that he had fathered my two daughters. Besides, I was no longer the same. In my flight to escape the pull of his devouring melancholy, his lack of vitality, the dread life inspired in him, I had become someone else. He was not a bad person. It distressed me to know that now he would have to come to terms with himself, but I was also aware of the limits of my compassion. Eight years was the sum of so many days together, however. To part ways with all of that was to suffer the loss of the part of each of us that made up the couple, and even if one willingly submitted to the amputation, the pain was intense. So intense, in fact, that during those three days, there were several moments when I thought I would relent just to save myself from his grief, but I stood my ground because there was no point in delaying an end foretold. I remained firm in my assessment that we couldn't go on. When he finally understood that my decision was final, he flew into a rage. I forget what he said but to see him unleash his anger freed me from the lingering pity I felt. I remember welcoming his anger, thinking it would help him rebuild his life, it would allow him to face the fury that had burned inside him for so long, fueling his bitter melancholy. I walked with him to the hotel lobby. He got into a taxi and headed for the airport without a goodbye, without even a backward glance.

Crestfallen but relieved, I started walking toward Andrea's apartment, pondering whether or not there existed an ethical frontier between aspirations and duties. Was I destroying my home in pursuit of my dreams? Would my husband recover? What effect would the divorce have on my daughters? I didn't have any answers. All I knew was that it couldn't be any other way. I felt emotionally drained, exhausted, but I was convinced that life's events had their own mysterious reasons. Exile, for one, had forced me to make the decision I had delayed for so long.

When a *compañero* carrying the addresses of many of us in the Mexican network was arrested, Marcos advised me to move. I went from my grim, sad little room to a students' residence in Coyoacán. My window looked out on the central plaza and the aroma of freshly baked bread wafted up from the bakery on the ground floor. In Mexico, I was often touched and amazed by the warmth and solidarity of the people I met. I used to hitchhike most of the time, to avoid piling into crowded city buses—back then, it was still safe. I was astonished to realize that most of the people who picked me up, people from all walks of life, knew who Sandino was. The great Mexican muralists and intellectuals of the day had done their part in leaving behind their visual and literary testimonies, but the December Operation was also still fresh in their minds. Andrea and I visited schools and universities. We were constantly together during those months and took every opportunity to gain access to any forum where we could talk about the Nicaraguan struggle for national liberation and rally support.

Although sadness was very much with her still, Andrea's spirits had improved in Mexico and she was giving love another try. She had found in her tireless dedication to the revolutionary cause a source of inexhaustible strength which kept her energized and cheerful, infused with that inner happiness that could withstand misfortune and that seemed to be the vital primeval substance which fed us all. We were like a small community bound together by the dreams we shared, a tight fraternity where solitude, despondency, or futility had no place. When Andrea's family came from Nicaragua to visit, they would "adopt" me as if I were another one of their daughters. Their only son, whom we all called by his pseudonym, "Rodrigo" (and who later became commander in chief of Nicaragua's National Armed Forces), had taken part in the December Operation. Through him I would send messages to Marcos, who had practically disappeared from my life after returning from a mysterious trip he had taken.

I was weary from the nights I had waited for him in vain, strained because I never knew when to expect him, afraid that he would come just when I had gone out. I was sure something was wrong. At long last I wrote him a doleful letter where I complained that he who was so keen on ending people's sufferings didn't care about the pain I—a comrade— was going through. I quoted Sartre: "I have no faith in the revolutionary who claims to love 'the people' yet is incapable of loving those who are close to him." I wrote that I just wanted to know what was going on and understand his prolonged absence. He came to see me a few days later and sat me down on his lap. Taking a deep breath, he confessed he was involved with somebody else, a woman who was a very good person, loved him very much, and had recently joined him in Mexico. His tone seemed to suggest that his dedication, his decision to leave me for her, was based not on whom he loved the most, but on compassion, as if between the two of us, I would be better able to survive without him. "You know I'll always love you," he said, downcast, silently asking me to understand, to still be his friend—Sandinista allegiance, above everything else. "You're strong," he said. "You'll get over it." I pretended to agree. I hugged him, pressed my head against his chest, and thanked him for being honest. Yes, I could live with it, I said. I preferred to deal with the truth rather than keep on wondering and waiting for him. And of course I would be his friend, I would always be his friend.

Sorrow hit me like a ton of bricks, but I was rescued from this gloom by the poet Efraín Huerta. Efraín had offered me a job. He was in his sixties and had lost his vocal chords to cancer of the larynx. He was able to communicate by talking with the stomach like a ventriloquist. Most people had trouble understanding him, but I didn't. We clicked from the start. "You look like Sophia Loren," he said to me. How could I not love him after such a compliment? I was to discover in time that he was a fan of Sophia Loren's. She was for him what Superman was for a small child. He was really and truly head over heels for her. He even dreamed about her all the time. I found this odd bit of celebrity worship endearing, because he wasn't a man who was easily impressed. In fact, he was rather skeptical and reserved, even acerbic at times. His poetry of urban life was piercing, biting, lacerated; an implacable indictment of modernity's alienation and lack of humanity, yet it was infused with a unique sensitivity and tenderness for the human condition. Even though his illness was a terrible burden, Efraín grabbed on to life belligerently and fiercely.

He was known in literary circles by his sign, the crocodile. He was a tame, loving crocodile, who instead of making me work—he hired me to type up a book of his poems—gave me many happy moments: he paid for me to take a taxi to and from his house; when I sat down to work I'd find cigarettes and candy next to the typewriter; at mid-morning, arm in arm, we would take a stroll down Polanco and have coffee; I'd leave his house in the afternoon carrying books and magazines he gave to me. It didn't take long for me to realize that he had offered me the job, not so much to help me, but so that together, like survivors in a shipwreck, we could ease our mutual loneliness and nostalgia. We both dreamed of a place that only lived in our hearts, yet lured us with the intensity of its own reality. It was perhaps the place where poets come from and want to go back to, a land of balance and harmony. Maybe it was just that place where he got back his voice and his strength, and where I saw my daughters grow safely and happily. We never talked about it. It was not necessary. We wrote poems.

Marcos's confession plunged me into a deep sorrow. My love for him was an obsession that stayed with me a very long time. To this day I cannot conjure his image without tears welling in my eyes. The golden light that shines on idealized heroes shrouds my memory of him and blinds me to his more human and fallible side. I think I was never able to reach his core, the inner sanctum beneath his all-encompassing love for the revolutionary cause. I had the feeling I had managed to slip in through a crack and capture his attention for an instant. But maybe every woman who loved him felt the same. As I found out much later, we were many.

I saw him for the last time before I left for Costa Rica. He invited me to lunch at an old Spanish restaurant on the second floor of a run-down building near the Zócalo in Mexico City. It was a meeting place of old republicans and anarchists, veterans of the Spanish Civil War. They were gaunt, somber men, figures out of a Goya painting, wearing a look of determination under black Basque berets. Sitting at tables covered with white tablecloths, they smoked and drank wine from short glasses.

Marcos, who seemed more absent than usual, acted as if I were an old, dear friend, but every so often his gaze would settle on me, peering into the depths of my eyes with loving concern. We talked about the work waiting for me in Costa Rica, a country he felt was of strategic importance given that its proximity to Nicaragua made it the most logical backstage for our struggle. He gave me the names of the people to contact there. Toward the end of the meal, over coffee, his eyes surveyed the room.

"They're so determined," he said, gazing affectionately at the old men at the tables around us. "They're still waiting, hope against hope, that Fascism will finally come to an end in Spain."

Keeping his eyes on them, he continued talking. They were a testament to perseverance, he said. Other popular struggles should serve as a source for our own inspiration and strength. To have convictions and to keep them come hell or high water was what forced the impossible to give birth to the possible.

"If you ever go to Paris, look in the bookseller stalls along the Seine for books on the Maquis, the French freedom fighters who led the resistance against the Nazis, and think of me," he said, smiling mischievously. He kissed me softly on the lips as we said goodbye on the sidewalk. I turned around to walk away, but after a few paces I turned again to look at him one more time. His broad shoulders, his gray jacket were still visible in the crowd's milling. I felt heavyhearted and forlorn, and I had to fight back the urge to race after him. It didn't matter that he no longer loved me. What I wanted was to beg him to beware of the risks and not let death catch up with him. I was certain I would never see him again.

The next time I saw him, he stared at me with fixed, lifeless eyes. His bullet-riddled body was displayed on the front pages of Nicaraguan newspapers. The dictatorship flaunted the corpse before the media like a trophy in their manhunt.

But I can barely remember him dead.

I see him walk away into the crowd, I see his broad shoulders, his dark chestnut hair. I see him fading slowly in the distance under the opaque luminosity of a hazy Mexican noon.

CHAPTER EIGHTEEN

On how I embarked on a new life in Costa Rica and on the difficulties
I encountered in my efforts to reunite with my daughters

COSTA RICA, 1976

THE ABANDONED TRACKS of an old railroad line ran up the street in front of the house where I lived during my first months in Costa Rica. It moves me to remember how it was that I ended up in that place, my parents' love and their efforts to make me backtrack to a time that was already long gone for me. To them I was still their little girl mixed up in things way above her head. That was why, when I arrived in San José that April of 1976, they were there waiting for me, solicitous as always, with a room already rented and paid for in a hostel for female university students, run by a very proper lady, a widow from a well-known Costa Rican family, a "good" family, as they said. And so it was that, even though my life had traversed through marriage, motherhood, and conspiracy, I landed in a kind of sorority house. I think my room must have been the reading corner of that old colonial mansion, which Doña Luisa transformed into a bedroom by hanging a curtain to block it off from the corridor that led to the bathroom. My bed and dresser just barely fit into the cramped quarters, creating a rather dubious kind of privacy. The atmosphere of the house, the meals with all the other girls together in the dining room, reminded me of my years with the nuns in Spain. I felt like the storybook Madeline. But my parents were quite proud of their discovery, and since I was virtually out of money all I could do was thank them and hope to find a job that would allow me to rent an apartment where I and, eventually, my daughters could live.

After Mexico City, San José seemed small enough to fit inside a hand-

kerchief. It was a small, green, picturesque city surrounded by mountains, floating in the mist of its humid, temperate air. Long, melancholic
walks permeate the memory of my first few weeks there. I would walk
along the old railway line beneath the constant drizzle, thinking I could
hear the echo of trains in the fog. Like a dull rain, the meaning of exile
slowly penetrated my bones, inundating me with a profound sense of loss:
my country, my daughters, Marcos. But my convictions overpowered my
gloom, and situated my own hardships in perspective, transforming them
into something temporary, manageable. That was the price of freedom.
Who was I to try and escape from the thing that no one else in my country could escape? After all, my troubles were nothing compared to prison,
death, torture—I was one of the lucky ones. Still, so many days misted
over with rain. Not the torrential downpours of Nicaragua, but the light,
constant Costa Rican drizzle. As if it were attuned to my tears, nature
had submerged me in a world of water. It didn't seem improbable to imagine that moss was soon going to grow under my fingernails.

The "Ticos," as the Costa Ricans are known in Central America, were
friendly. Instead of rolling their r's, they softened them, mixing in a hiss-
ing sound. Traditionally, Ticos have mocked Nicaraguans'—"Nicas"—
lack of sophistication while we have teased them for their affectation.

The day I arrived in San José, Julio Cortázar was giving a presentation
in the Teatro Nacional. I took this as a good omen. He was one of my very
favorite writers. I don't know how many times I read *Hopscotch*, his better
known novel. The Poet even used to call me "La Maga"—a character in
this book—because I identified so strongly with her. Right there in the
theater I ran into Sergio Ramírez, one of the contacts Marcos had given
me, and we agreed that I would visit his office the following week. Sergio
then introduced me to Julio. He was very tall, an overgrown boy with
piercing blue eyes, and a noticeable French accent mixed in with his
unhurried Argentinian Spanish. I liked the way Cortázar, the man, resembled the things he wrote about; he was unassuming and accessible. I
couldn't have guessed then that life would regale me with the good fortune of getting to know this immensely lovable human being up close.
After the success of the Revolution, I saw him many times in Managua
and once, on a trip to Paris, after I told him that ever since reading *Hopscotch* I had harbored the fantasy of walking with him through the landscapes of his fictional world, he took me on a walk along the banks of the
Seine.

After a few days in Costa Rica I found a job at an advertising agency whose owners were two brothers: one who looked like an actor in a second-rate soap opera, and the other, a lackluster creature with the soul of a bureaucrat. Both of them harassed me constantly, the first with sexual innuendos and the second by keeping constant tabs on my movements. I didn't even last a month there. I summarily quit in a fit of rage when the actor tried to get physical with me. That same day, I found out through a colleague that Garnier, another highly prestigious agency, was in a rush to fill a spot in their creative department. I arrived at the interview and was extremely clear about my political situation—I considered it a matter of principle. Fortunately for me, the Costa Ricans—champions of democracy that they are—viewed refugees of the Somoza regime as people of valor and integrity. The following day they told me I had the job. I had a wonderful time working at Garnier. The owners, Arnaldo and Alberto Garnier, and Luis and Hernán, my supervisors, were kindhearted people who welcomed me into the company with warmth and grace, earning my lasting gratitude. They stood by me above and beyond the call of duty. At that agency I came to know the friendliest, jolliest side of the Costa Rican character, the key factor, I believe, that has made that country an oasis of peace amid the drama and torment of Central America. Hernán, the creative director, was in his thirties, a good-looking, witty, intelligent man who was self-confident enough to allow his staff to let their imaginations take flight. We got along famously from the start, and in less than three months I was given a substantial raise. At last I was ready to move and send for my daughters.

In Costa Rica, the Sandinista network was still in formation, as Marcos had warned me. After my arrival I met with Jaime Wheelock, the leader of the dissidents, in the restaurant Los Antojitos. Young and handsome, he had a way of absently looking into the distance as he talked; one felt transparent as he gazed at the utopias he outlined with his words. Educated in Chile, Jaime had done a great deal of detailed, careful research on Nicaraguan history. I had been particularly taken by one of his books which dealt with the indigenous resistance in Nicaragua during the Conquest, because ever since I was a child my maternal grandfather, Francisco Pereira, would tell me stories of what tough warriors the Nicaraguan Indians had been. I could still remember the passion in his voice when he related to me the story of Princess Xotchitl A Catalt, Flor de Caña (Sugarcane Flower). She was the daughter of Agateyte, the great chief of one of the most important Nicaraguan tribes, the Subtiavas. A group of Spaniards had asked and been granted permission to settle in their lands. Flor de Caña and the Spanish captain in charge of the settlement fell in love. He gave her a horse and taught her how to ride. The lovers would take long strolls galloping joyfully until sunset. One day, however, the Spaniards decided to take over all the land of the Subtiavas and attacked Agateyte and his people. When the battle was raging, Flor de Caña mounted her horse and went to look for her lover. When she found him, she took her bow and without hesitation shot an arrow that pierced his heart while she shouted: "Die, you who betrayed my people, killed my father, and stole my honor, die!" After her deed was done, she took her horse and galloped straight into the flames of her father's dwellings which the Spaniards had set on fire.

Jaime's book, *Indigenous Roots of Anti-Colonial Resistance in Nicaragua*, presented historical facts that refuted the fallacies of the "official history," which maintained that the Indians had coexisted peacefully with the Spanish. His information, along with my grandfather Pancho's memories, inspired the character of Itzá in my novel *La mujer habitada* (The Inhabited Woman).

Jaime also wrote the book *Imperialismo y dictadura* (Imperialism and Dictatorship), which Somoza banned in Nicaragua and which was one of the things that the secret police found inside my desk when they raided my office. The fact that I had a copy of this book was later used by the prosecutor in the trial to prove my "illicit association" with the Sandinista National Liberation Front.

From our conversation, I gathered that Jaime did not share Marcos's optimism regarding the possibilities of reunification among Sandinistas. He doubted that the more dogmatic leaders would ever budge, and he turned out to be right. We left the restaurant and headed for Sergio Ramírez's office. My first job, Jaime said, would be to help Sergio edit *Solidaridad*, a weekly insert with news from Nicaragua that was distributed in the newspaper *Pueblo*. I would be given other tasks later on.

I recall that Vanessa, his girlfriend, picked the two of us up at the restaurant's parking lot.

"Will she see you?" I asked him, since we were partially hidden by some tree branches.

"Of course," he said, with a mischievous gleam in his eyes. " 'Because the eye of a woman recognizes her king/even when nations tremble/and fire rains down from the heavens.' " The quote was from a famous Carlos

Martínez Rivas poem. What self-confidence, I thought, he is very lucky to think he's loved like that.

Sergio Ramírez, a writer and lawyer, eventually became vice president of Nicaragua. I didn't know him very well, but I did know his books— original, acerbic, and constructed with the precision of finely calibrated works of architecture. As a writer, I liked him. Besides, he was married to Tulita, a beauty with jet-black hair who for me was inextricably linked with the magic of my teenage summers at the beach. At nighttime in Poneloya, my brothers and I used to walk on the sand near the water's edge. Off in the distance we could see Tulita's family's house, standing off by itself over a rock formation. It was a big, permanently unfinished house, that looked like a haunted mansion because the gray cement had never been painted, and some walls and window frames were missing. Nevertheless, the family settled there every summer and from the beach one could see them inside, as if they were living in a doll house. We nick-named it the Sinister Mansion. Every evening, out of their enchanted home came Tulita and her sisters, one of them a fiery redhead, beautiful and resplendent on their way to the club, where they danced the night away, and where they inevitably won every beauty contest. By associa-tion, then, I felt close to Sergio from the start. We were like old friends rediscovering one another after a long time apart. Inside of Sergio's tall, large frame, which at times seems to get in his way and burden him, lives the soul of a romantic poet. Often absorbed by his musings, he is, never-theless, a generous and loyal friend. He took me under his wing and offered his steady support those first few days in Costa Rica, when I felt so alone and lost. At the time he was collaborating with a Puerto Rican filmmaker, developing a screenplay about Sandino. To give me something to do, he brought me to these meetings, which were always entertaining, full of anecdotes about the days when Sandino was just a little man with a big Stetson hat, fighting in the mountains of Nicaragua, with an army of peasants, against the U.S. Marines who had occupied the country. His had been the first guerrilla war on the American continent.

After I started to work in the advertising agency, I would come to Ser-gio's office late in the afternoon. He was the director of the Central American University Council, an institution that hosted the most presti-gious social studies program in the region. After his staff left, he and I worked side by side, writing, designing, cutting and pasting the insert that we were responsible to deliver to the publisher every week. It was hard work, before computers and desktop publishing.

In Sergio's house I met Armando Morales, who is to Nicaraguan painting what Rubén Darío is to Nicaraguan poetry. His works hang in the great museums of the world, including the Museum of Modern Art in New York. Armando asked me to be his model, and in exchange he would do my portrait and give me drawings. I posed for him in his San Pedro studio, a haven of tranquillity animated by the artist's musings spoken softly as he sketched. He would digress on subjects like watercolors, pigments, his thematic obsessions, the reservoir of images his memory held. With textures and hues he gained the kind of insights writers hope to achieve with words. His carbon sketches of my naked body were remarkable, as was, for me, the peculiar experience of that place. It seemed to exist outside time; quiet, introspective, smelling of oil and acrylic paint, where nudity was innocent and served art. I used those sessions as active meditation. I was sad to give them up when other responsibilities began to encroach upon my time.

It must have been May, or June. I was out shopping one day in the center of San José, getting ready to move to the apartment I had finally rented, when I heard someone calling after me: "Gío, Gío." Only one person called me "Gío." Jimmy, my teenage boyfriend, my first boyfriend. My mother had detested him. He was my brother Humberto's best friend at school, a precocious biologist with a fascination for reptiles. He used to show up at my house with boa constrictors or other types of snakes wrapped around his neck. My mother would refuse to leave her bedroom.

"Jimmy!" I cried out in delight, thrilled to see him all grown up, and looking like Jean Paul Belmondo. His face, crafted with sweeping brushstrokes, was just the right complement to his athletic body. I had a vivid recollection of him jumping on the diving board at the country club's swimming pool, wearing the tiniest swimming trunks, and executing his flawless, effortless dives.

We hugged for a long time, affectionately, tightly. We had loved one another with unique adolescent intensity when I was fourteen and he sixteen years old. My parents' disapproval made us feel like Romeo and Juliet, and I always suspected that he was one of the reasons my parents deported me to boarding school in Spain. During a summer vacation in England, away from the nuns' watchful eyes, we wrote to each other, long, passionate letters that eventually became less and less frequent until we finally fell out of touch. Both of us had gotten married. He was now living in the United States, divorced.

"Have you had lunch?" he asked.

It was Saturday, so our lunch lasted several hours in a restaurant that looked like a barn out of the American West. Jimmy was in Costa Rica doing research on the symbiotic relationship of a fly that deposited its eggs in those of a frog. I credited his sudden appearance to a miracle of Divine Providence. Ever since Marcos's rejection, I had been mortified by self-doubts—that terrible female affliction. As soon as I left the office, I would be seized by loneliness. Jimmy's presence brought back my spark. I could sense that he saw me anew, as a woman, my pubescent awkwardness long gone. By the time dessert came, we were holding hands. We were eager to embrace and continue where we had left off so many years ago.

That night, after a romantic dinner, we checked into a hotel. I clung to Jimmy as if his body were about to issue forth a time of innocence, the blank page of adolescence. He held me, pressing his body against mine for a long time, stroking my hair, rocking me softly. I curled up in his arms seeking shelter like a turtle hiding in her comfortable shell.

The following day, Sunday, he helped me move into my new apartment. We loaded what little I had into his car and I said goodbye to Doña Luisa. The move, which I had thought would be a burden, turned festive. There he was, making sure the gas, the lights, the telephone all worked. Nothing like having a man to banish the musty, moldy smell of an uninhabited house. He stayed with me that night. The apartment was inaugurated amid the giggles, murmurs, and moans of our unexpected romance.

Jimmy stayed for two weeks. With him I felt renewed, and awed by the beauty of the country that would be my home for several years. Together, in shady riverbeds and lush, tropical woodlands, we would hunt for tiny green frogs with translucent stomachs. I saw iridescent geometric insects, aerial swamps, and cloud patches trapped in misty tunnels of pure green. Back in the university laboratory, beneath the stereoscopic microscope, Jimmy introduced me to the marvelous, diminutive world of moss, mold, and the circulatory system of the minuscule frogs.

Later on, it would occur to me that he had been sent by some angel to strengthen me. He left, but promised to come back, to call me. I busied myself putting the finishing touches on my apartment. At last, I had the nest ready and was fully prepared to receive my daughters. But I was growing impatient, because every day I had to listen to another explanation about why their arrival was delayed. On one of those nights—unforgettable—my father broke the news to me.

"Sweetheart, your husband is refusing to send the girls over to you. He says he's keeping them and will sue you for abandonment."

To this day I get dizzy when I relive the sensation of the ground beneath my feet sinking, pulling my body down. My father went on to tell me that, according to my husband, I would be unable to care for my daughters in a responsible manner, that any day I could just take off and desert them.

"But he was the one who brought them to your house when I left! He's the one who hasn't been responsible!" I exclaimed.

"I know, sweetheart, I know. What can I say?"

I called my husband. I tried to stay calm but it was impossible. How could he do this to me? He knew better than anyone the reasons why I left, and why I couldn't go back. His replies were arrogant, defiant. Motherhood wasn't for me, he said. I had other priorities. He wasn't interested in my feelings. His mind was made up, he said, and he hung up on me.

Alone in the apartment, with nobody to talk to, I thought I was going mad. I felt my heart would explode from the rage building up in my chest. I had never expected something like this from my husband. I never thought he was the kind of man who did such a thing. Especially because he had no idea how to take care of the children by himself. All this time they had been at my parents' house, for crying out loud! Vengeance was the only reason to tear my children away from me! Meanwhile what was I to do; I who was sentenced to jail and was far from Nicaragua? There had to be a way out. Think, I said to myself, think. I had to get a lawyer.

The lawyer confirmed my worst fears. It was a lost cause. I was a fugitive. I had no rights. I could kiss my daughters goodbye. He didn't use those words exactly; he tried to be diplomatic. He handed me some Kleenex and drove me home.

Filled with blind and impotent fury, I was in agony. Everyone—my boss, the secretary, Sergio—looked at me with compassion. They wanted to help, but what could they do?

I couldn't accept the finality of the case. Giving up is not in my nature. Whenever I have faced difficult problems I have gone at them like a boxer calculating her punches. Something was telling me I would not have to lose my daughters. Somewhere there was a solution. I just had to find it.

And I did find it. One weekday at lunchtime. I still remember the exact moment, precisely which rooftops I was seeing from my window. In an instant I fully understood why Archimedes ran naked out of his bathroom into the street, shouting "Eureka!" the moment his mind grasped the concept of buoyancy. I wanted to do exactly the same thing. I had suddenly remembered the time when my husband, trying to ingratiate himself with me, gave me a pistol and money for the Sandinistas. With that memory in hand, I planned my strategy. I tried to contain my excitement so that I could be totally calm when I telephoned him. I walked to the phone company. I didn't mean to challenge him, exactly, but my voice sounded angry and defiant.

"I'm calling you to let you know that I'm coming back to Nicaragua," I said. "I'd rather my daughters see me in jail than have them think I've abandoned them."

"You're crazy . . ."

"From this point I hold you responsible for whatever happens to me. And I want you to know that I will talk. I'll tell State Security about the money and the gun you gave me." I could hear him trying to speak, nearly choking. I hung up the receiver.

When I went out to the street I was powerful, like a vengeful goddess ready to defend her children with whatever weapons were necessary. I felt happy to be a woman, to have my instinct, to be who I was.

The following week, on a Saturday afternoon in July of 1976, after seven months apart, my two beautiful daughters arrived. Maryam clung to me, thrilled. My brother Eduardo, smiling broadly, told me she had driven him crazy asking how many more hours, how many more minutes it would be before they arrived. Melissa, only two years old, asked if I was her mommy from the airplane as she clambered through the apartment. I had bought them a bunk bed with a ladder they climbed up and down over and over again, fascinated by the idea of actually sleeping in such a bed. By nighttime, after the cakes and candy they'd clamored for, I tucked them in and told them bedtime stories. Once they were finally asleep, I fell into bed, exhausted, though I barely slept. I kept getting up to look at them, to make sure I wasn't dreaming: my two little girls were actually sleeping close to me. Finally.

CHAPTER NINETEEN

On how I reconciled politics and motherhood; love and disenchantment; and how a bad premonition came to be fulfilled

SAN JOSÉ, 1976

OVERNIGHT THE BUSTLE of children broke through my solitude. The girls ran up and down the stairs, like little colts, their sounds reverberating through the house and into the small paved courtyard/parking lot at the center of the apartment complex where we lived. Sabanilla was a safe, quiet neighborhood that began near the university and extended into a suburban area higher up with lots of trees and well-tended gardens. Cristina, a good-looking brunette woman, came from Nicaragua to be the children's nanny. I enrolled Maryam at the local school, and she took the school bus to and fro. Ours was a house filled with women, and in it my daughters and I were a close-knit family once again, making up for all our lost time. With that special ability only children have, they enthusiastically adapted to their new life. We didn't have a car, but to them, even the hassle of riding on public buses was a great adventure. I marveled at them, touched by how quickly they forgave me for being away, by the intensity of their love. Snuggling in bed with them, a cat and her kittens, I explained to them why we had been separated for so long, and told them how much I had missed them while we were apart. I didn't know if they understood any of what I was saying, and I wasn't sure whether I was saying it for their sake or for mine, but in any event I felt I owed them an explanation. I am convinced that I did the right thing by including them in the difficult realities of my life at that time, although I had my doubts as to whether they should know the political nature of my problems. Nevertheless I couldn't come up with sound reasons to hide the truth

145

from them, and I refused to force them to live in a fantasy world. To be trusted by others had made me grow as a person, and I felt my trust would do the same for them. They knew that we were living in exile, that their mother was wanted by the authorities, that I and many others like me were fighting so they could grow up in a country where all children would have food to eat, clothes to wear, a school to go to. A country without dictators, without Somoza.

They developed an astonishing talent for discretion. They never put me in compromising situations. They became my tiniest and most loyal *compañeras*.

Living in the United States, I can't help but contrast my experience in Costa Rica with that of some mothers who agonize over the small challenges life sets before their kids. Even something as simple as the start of kindergarten turns into a carefully planned enterprise fraught with danger, requiring the most sophisticated strategies of maternal engineering. They seem to see their children as fragile, vulnerable creatures; unintentionally, they end up overprotecting them, denying them the space they need to discover their own strength, and to develop the common sense that will serve them later on in life.

Finally, when I was happily ensconced with my daughters, when the gnawing anxiety of having them so far away had lifted from my sternum, when I was able to breathe freely once again, another terrible tidal wave crashed over me. I don't know if I have a need to find things to be miserable about—more than once I have been known to run from happiness—but the huge, idealized image of Marcos suddenly crashed down on the shores of my soul, blasting ships, bridges, entire populations in my psyche. Around that time Jimmy returned—sweet, wonderful Jimmy, who gave me nothing but tenderness and affection. He even suggested I move with him to the United States. How could we let another opportunity slip through our hands? he asked. From somewhere deep inside of me a furious Medusa emerged. I was cruel. I lashed out. How could he even dare suggest I abandon my principles? Did he not realize how essential, how irrevocable they were to me? Go to the United States? The *United States*, of all places? Leave the things that made me who I was, to become the obscure, faceless, insipid wife of a university professor? Not on his life. I felt the same pressing commitment to my cause as he felt to his science. I vividly remember that afterward, alone in my room, I searched the depths of my breast, looking for my heart, asking myself if it hadn't disintegrated altogether. I felt no pain rejecting Jimmy. Had I just been looking to him for consolation, for solace? I asked myself. Maybe that was it. Perhaps the fury I felt was the irrefutable proof that consolation simply wasn't possible, that Marcos was still lodged in a deep furrow within me.

Work was my salvation. In between advertising campaigns, I organized Sandinista support networks over the phone, drafted press releases to keep the news media informed as to what was going on in Nicaragua, and wrote articles for *Solidaridad*. Fernando Cardenal, the Jesuit priest, came to Costa Rica around that time, en route to Washington, where he was to deliver a report on the human rights violations in Nicaragua to the House Subcommittee on International Operations, presided over by Donald M. Fraser. For several nights, we worked from dusk to dawn in Sergio's office, organizing the many testimonies Fernando had managed to secure and smuggle out of Nicaragua in his briefcase. The accusations were spine-chilling: peasants thrown from helicopters by the National Guard, summary executions, rapes, huts burned to the ground. The dictatorship was implacable. In the country, in the city, it stifled any kind of resistance or dissent. The United States Congress was investigating the issue. Fernando would present his case before them.

During that period I felt the need to prove to myself that I could still wield the seductive, ancestral powers of my gender. It was my way to deal with Marcos's loss and what it had done to my sense of self, my own validation as a woman. A desire to seduce, to conquer, that felt almost masculine in its determination, arose within me. Men ceased to surprise me. All that was needed were certain gestures, the right degree of dare or demureness in a wide-eyed look, to reveal my sensuality, for them to follow me as if I were the Pied Piper of Hamelin. I learned what subtle seams to undo in order to render them pliable and docile. I decided to probe into the myths that declared my gender capable of provoking chaos, irrationality, wars, and universal cataclysms by biting into an apple or untying a sandal. This exploration chased away any doubts I may have had about my womanly powers, but it couldn't chase away the sadness I felt.

As time passed and Nicaragua grew distant, poetry abandoned me. I only wrote an occasional verse every now and then. My well seemed to dry up. Costa Rica's beauty didn't awaken my muse. It was too calm. Even the cows seemed purposely placed in that bucolic, tranquil countryside. I missed my raging sunsets, the green entanglement of treetops, the verdant ravines, and the furious downpours. Costa Rica seemed too shallow and tame: like the light interminable rain that kept falling over San José.

In the morning of one of those placid, cloudy days—November 8, 1976, to be exact—Alfredo, my cousin's Pía's husband, whom I had last seen in 1975, called me from Nicaragua. His voice had not changed. "How are you?" he asked. I was delighted to hear him.

"What is the occasion? I haven't heard from you in so long!" I exclaimed.

I heard him hesitate, and remain silent.

"What is it?" I asked. "Is something wrong?"

"Yes, Chichí," he said, using the affectionate nickname he gave me. "Rafael was in a serious accident yesterday. He died. He's dead. I just wanted to let you know."

I needed no more explanation. Rafael, Marcos, these names were pseudonyms used by the man I had loved. His real name was Eduardo Contreras and now he was dead. I remember that Sergio Ramírez came over to my house shortly afterward. He hugged me, and was so gentle and sweet to insist that I should go with him to his office, he didn't want me to be alone; like a zombie, I got into his car. All morning I sat on a sofa watching him work, wondering how it was that life could continue as if nothing had happened, that the day would keep on going with people coming in and out of the office and the phone ringing. Sergio talked to me about what he had learned; about the jeep that intercepted them, about the two *compañeros* who were also killed. Without drama he gave me the consolation of his company, his empathy and support. I will always be grateful to him for that.

I kept thinking about that afternoon, about the Nicaraguan newspaper *La Prensa* that the delivery man would bring like he did every day, except that this one would have the picture of Eduardo, dead, on the front page. It had been eight months since our lunch in Mexico City, and then a few more after he went back to Nicaragua and failed in his attempts to reunite the movement. Nevertheless, he had left a legacy. His idea of an insurrectional strategy to topple the dictatorship was carried on by what became the third faction within the FSLN, the Insurrectional tendency, the Terceristas. As it usually happens, however, others took all the credit. Eduardo's crucial role was never sufficiently recognized by the leaders of this group. Neither Daniel Ortega, who became Nicaragua's president, nor Humberto Ortega, his brother and chief of the armed forces, made any effort to honor Eduardo's memory once the Revolution came to power. His name was just added to the list of many hundreds of men and women who fell during the struggle, our many heroes. A market in Managua was named after him: Eduardo Contreras. It was a humble homage to this exceptional man.

Marcos's death (I never thought of him as Eduardo) opened a season of rains in my heart; for several months, night after night, I went to sleep drenched in tears. I couldn't close my eyes without seeing him, without my memory bringing me back minute details of every moment we had shared. I couldn't accept the enormity of his death.

On the same day Marcos was killed, the National Guard announced the death of Carlos Fonseca, the founder of the FSLN, in an ambush in the mountains of northern Nicaragua; and reported another fallen Sandinista in Managua, Roberto Huembes, one of the principal leaders of the Proletarian tendency. I had to write the press releases and distribute them to the media. It seemed it would never stop. Every day the newspapers brought more photographs of dead bodies, bloody Sandinista bodies, their open eyes staring at us.

CHAPTER TWENTY

On how the insurrection was set in motion

San José, 1977

WITH MARCOS and Carlos Fonseca gone, there were no more attempts to unify the FSLN. I continued working for the Tercerista tendency, also known as Insurrectional Tendency. Soon after Marcos's death I met Humberto Ortega. He introduced himself as Alberto but I recognized him because of the resemblance he bore to his brother Camilo. His right hand was deformed as a result of a gun wound he received as he escaped from the jail where he had been locked up after his failed attempt to liberate Carlos Fonseca, the chief of the FSLN, who had been languishing in the same jail. So he extended his long and thin left hand to me. His angular face, penetrating eyes, straight nose butting up against a tiny mouth, and the black hair parted on the side, brought to mind the caricaturesque image of Peter Sellers in *The Pink Panther*. The combination of his physical traits, his nervous tics, and his fast-talking manner (his favorite filler was "get it?") made me realize that I would have to make a real effort to take him seriously. But I forced myself to put aside my initial mistrust because I had fully expected to respect and admire him, not only because I was so fond of his brother but because of his long history in the resistance.

In one of our first meetings I picked him up in the secondhand Volkswagen Beetle I had just bought. After months battling the public transit system, I felt as if I was in my own little Pegasus.

"One of your front lights is busted," he said as he got into the car.

"But I just drove the car from the dealer!" I said, annoyed as we crept up a narrow street in the middle of San José, headed for the wide avenue we would have to cross to get to where we were going. We merged into the heavy five o'clock traffic. Once on the avenue, in the middle of the inevitable gridlock that paralyzed the streets whenever there was a soccer game in the stadium, the car suddenly thumped and then stalled. Over and over again I tried to restart it. I was getting nervous now, because the drivers around me were starting to honk, sticking their heads out the window and yelling at me to get out of the way. Humberto, meanwhile, kept turning his head, looking around in every direction, not knowing what to do, because he wasn't just a fugitive in Nicaragua, he was wanted in Costa Rica as well. If someone recognized him, he could end up in jail. I couldn't believe my terrible luck, that my rotten Beetle had decided to conk out at that very moment. The sound of the horns and the traffic jam only got worse. It was madness.

"I better get out," Humberto suddenly said. "If the police come, that's it for me."

He got out, dodging the cars like a matador, taking giant leaps until he reached the other side of the street and disappeared into the mob of pedestrians. Now I had to get out of the car and look for someone to help me push it, one or two good Samaritans among all those drivers who had suddenly made me the target of all their frustrations. The whole episode was a nightmare, but once we reached the curb at the other side and I calmed down, I was seized by an uncontrollable fit of laughter, which brought tears to my eyes. What a scene, my God. I had been so proud of my new little car, and look what a mess it had gotten me into!

Humberto and I laughed about it together when we found each other later on. Our little misfortune quickly broke the ice between us. Soon I began working closely with him, organizing underground networks in Costa Rica. Humberto was in command, and was preparing to set in motion the military actions and political alliances that would lead to a popular insurrection against Somoza. He sent me as his emissary to reactivate the Costa Rican Committee for Solidarity with Nicaragua, which consisted of representatives from political parties as well as various intellectuals and other prominent figures. This committee would be key in enlisting the Costa Ricans' support for the Sandinista cause. We had to be able to count on solid support networks, especially since Costa Rica was the rear guard for the struggle in Nicaragua. The Honduran and Salvadoran governments were military regimes allied with Somoza, and it was far riskier to try to operate in those countries. Around that time, Humberto asked me to arrange a meeting with Sergio Ramírez. At the home of a filmmaker friend, I organized the meeting where the two men first met. With Sergio's help, Humberto began to carry out another one of Marcos's ideas, which involved organizing a group of prominent Nicaraguans, people known for their honesty or for their opposition to the dictatorship. The plan was that when Sandinista guerrillas achieved military control of some territory, they would become the figureheads of an alternative government, which would function inside or outside of Nicaragua. The point was to create the core group of what would be a great anti-Somoza coalition, bringing together political parties, grass-roots organizations, unions, and whoever wanted to join forces against the dictator. The Sandinista movement would cease to be just a guerrilla group to become the leading force in a national effort to depose the tyrant.

Sergio proposed a number of people, including Fernando and Ernesto Cardenal, brothers and Catholic priests. To meet with them and invite them to participate in the provisional government, I joined César, Marcos's brother, on a trip to Los Chiles, a tiny town on the Nicaraguan border. The meeting took place in the Las Brisas hacienda, a bucolic enclave on the banks of the Frío River, a small tributary of the great San Juan River. My friend, the poet José Coronel Urtecho, lived there with his wife, María.

César, my travel companion, had neither the air of authority nor the presence of his late brother. He was more down-to-earth, more accessible. He smoked a pipe and wore tight Lacoste shirts. He was a doctor. Good-looking. Plus, he made me laugh—I've always had a weakness for men who can make me laugh. I was afraid that I might fall in love with him as a way of hanging on to the ghost of his brother, but I was saved from that fate because he followed in his brother's footsteps. Not long afterward, he married María Isabel, the woman who, not so long before, had become his sister-in-law: Marcos's widow.

The plane we took to Los Chiles was an ancient DC-3. It looked like an old public bus, with fraying upholstery and beer and soap advertisements on the passenger seat headrests. In the back of the cabin, a giant pig locked in a cage sat next to a couple of traveling businessmen.

César and I were cracking up, wondering where we would end up in that joke of a plane: "Hold on tight, girl," he said, holding back laughter when the propellers began to spin, making an infernal whirring noise.

It was a terrifying flight. I left César's arm covered with scratch marks. The plane kept making wild leaps, occasionally diving hundreds of meters, due to the air pockets the pilot didn't seem able—or willing—to avoid. The pig snorted and growled the entire flight, while my eyes felt as if they would pop out of their sockets from fear that I might be taking my last good look at earth. At least, I thought, my last vision of the planet would be the silhouette of the Nicaraguan border, the grayish reflection of Lake Nicaragua on the horizon.

It seemed the entire population of Los Chiles jostled against one another alongside the landing strip, awaiting our arrival. Never in my life had I been in such an impoverished, remote part of the world. I felt as if we had been transported to a village in the thick of the Amazon. The airport consisted of a dirt road, and we had to remove our bags from the bowels of the plane ourselves. Little, unpainted wooden houses lined the perimeter of the four-sided plaza of Los Chiles, which seemed suspended in a cloud of dust. There, the hacienda jeep came to pick us up, and once the village was behind us, we began to penetrate the lush foliage of the countryside. At the entrance to the hacienda, the driver stopped the jeep in front of a small group of people. We surely wanted to say hello to Doña María, he said. In Nicaragua, Doña María was a larger-than-life figure. Her husband had immortalized her in an extraordinary poem called "Pequeña biografía de mi mujer" (A brief biography of my wife). In those verses, the poet sang of his wife's strength and independence: she had given birth to and raised their ten children and was the sole manager of the hacienda. She worked the tractor, the boat, and supervised crops and cattle while he led a life of contemplation, dedicated to his literature.

When I saw her that day I recognized her by her green eyes and freckles, but there she was, just another worker, dressed in khaki shirt and pants, short hair tucked under her baseball cap, cigarette stuck between her lips. Up to her knees in mud, she was inspecting an irrigation tube. Her handshake was strong and manly, and after greeting us she sent us up to the house. With time, Doña María and I grew to love each other, but that day I felt her looking at me with hostility, as if she resented my long hair and my youth, aspects of herself that she had shed so many years before.

Don José welcomed us into Las Brisas wearing dark pants, a long-sleeve white shirt, and a black beret. I recognized the landscape of his prose and poems: the house with yellow balustrades, pitched roof, quaint Caribbean architecture, amidst the exuberant vegetation, the small dock jutting out into the river and herons on the shore. Countless travelers

had passed through this place, their tales bringing life to Coronel's stories. The hacienda had an aura of legend which remained etched in my
memory and also found its way into my own writing. For *Waslala*,
my third novel, I re-created that house along the river, and the poet and
his wife became characters in my fictional saga. While we waited for
Ernesto to arrive, César talked with Fernando, and Coronel showed me
his library, a great room with big windows, and crude bookshelves piled
high with double rows of books. The floors were littered with newspapers
and magazines, and the desk was covered with papers. Just as I had imagined, Don José was a man very much at peace with himself. You could see
it in the glint of his inquisitive blue eyes. His friendly face was a rosy hue,
his nose slightly curved. His white hair, thin at the top, was abundant
and long. Always fond of visitors and good conversation, he showed me
his studio and talked to me excitedly about Anna Akhmatova, the Russian poet.

"You must read her," he said. "She has the same passion you have, but
hers is turned inward. She's tormented but she's extraordinary."

Ernesto Cardenal arrived from Solentiname in a *panga* with a young
man from the island. Gliding noiselessly over the water, the wooden
canoe pulled up to the dock. I'll never forget the scene. Ernesto wore
jeans, a loose white cotton shirt, and sandals. He was, already, one of
Nicaragua's most renowned and most translated poets. He had been a
Trappist monk in Kentucky, a disciple of Thomas Merton, but he had left
the monastery and returned to Nicaragua to establish a utopian community on an island in Lake Nicaragua. In Solentiname, Ernesto preached
the gospel and also taught the peasants to write poetry and to express
themselves through exquisite, naïf paintings.

The meeting with Ernesto and Fernando gave us what we were hoping
for. Both of them agreed to be members of the provisional government
whenever it materialized. Ernesto was a quiet man, but when he spoke he
did so with conviction. From the day I met him, I knew that he was the
kind of person who would never flinch or waver once he'd decided where
his loyalties lay. Fernando was gentle and easygoing, but with the same
determination. These were not men of half measures, and in that they
were clearly brothers.

I remember the humid night, the scent of the jungle, the river
water, the call of the night hawks, the clouds of fireflies, the squawking
of the herons in the morning. Ernesto left early with Laureano Mairena,

the young man driving the boat, who wrote poetry and whose face has remained vividly etched in my mind the way it often happens with people who die young. He was killed in the war against the Contras. Ernesto wrote a beautiful poem in his honor. Every time I hear it, it makes me cry.

César and I returned from Los Chiles in a ten-seater plane that made me yearn for that old DC-3. The pilot had long hair and wore a Hawaiian shirt printed with flowers and parrots. After a very bumpy ride we made it back to San José.

Trouble began when I finally found out the details of the definitive plan to set the insurrection in motion. The way I saw it, the insurrection had to be the culmination of a gradual process in which military action would go hand in hand with grassroots efforts to organize people in the cities and towns to join the armed struggle. As far as Humberto Ortega saw it, however, the insurrection was to be the product of one masterful military operation. His plan consisted of launching a series of simultaneous attacks against National Guard quarters in different cities and towns across the country. After these attacks, the citizenry would rise up en masse, and we would take control. This was what he presented, one night in San José, to the Sandinista cell that met in my house every week to study and follow up on our networking efforts. All around the table, the faces registered shock and skepticism. There were six of us, three of whom were sociology students: Oscar Pérez Cassar, Marcos Valle, and Blas Real. The other two, Arnoldo Quant and Rafael Rueda, had been, like me, forced into exile by the dictatorship.

"So you're saying that you think once the attacks are launched, the people will spontaneously rise up?" asked Oscar, whose code name was Pin. His eyes, pitch-black beneath his thick lashes, looked alarmed.

"We are talking about crippling attacks, get it? Simultaneous. In several cities. The army will have to disperse. The people will join up and take over the cities. We will broadcast a call to arms, for everybody to join in the general insurrection, get it?" said Humberto.

"But there's no basic layer of work with the masses," said Blas, gesturing with his long hands.

"The Socialist Party will take care of the masses. We're already in contact with them. The masses will unite. When they see the insurrection has a military force behind it, they will take to the streets. Plus, we'll have the provisional government inside Nicaragua appealing to the people as a whole, asking them not to give up the resistance until the tyrant is out, appealing to every sector of society."

I don't remember all the details of that argument, but it was long and heated. We told him that we didn't agree with him, that we weren't so optimistic. I was furious. His plan seemed to reduce the entire insurrectional strategy to a military adventure. I thought Marcos would never have agreed with this. Launching a general insurrection required a long process of preparation. It was absurd to think that victory could be achieved with one sweeping maneuver.

Humberto dodged the controversial questions like a boxer, answering with evasive remarks. His basic rationale was that, since it was a secret plan, the rest of us didn't have the information necessary to fully understand it. Since that was, in effect, our specific occupational hazard, it was ultimately a question of trust. We had to believe that the leadership had weighed the risks and understood what had to be done. And since we weren't in Nicaragua, there was no way for us to keep our finger on the pulse of the political climate inside the country. According to Humberto, the consensus was that the ground was ripe for action.

After Humberto left, the rest of us stayed around talking. We were flabbergasted and we knew we could not stop what we thought was a completely irrational plan.

"Let's write something," I suggested. "At least we can make our position clear."

"You write it, Melissita," said Pin, using my code name. "And the rest of us will sign it."

Surrounded by books by Clausewitz, Giap, and Lenin, I quoted entire paragraphs from their works stating that unless popular support was certain, no insurrection could be successful. I stayed up that night, typing on my portable Smith-Corona until dawn.

Of all the Sandinista leaders I had met, Humberto Ortega was the first who really troubled me. Without blinking an eye, he manipulated reality to suit his needs. And he did it with such conviction that sometimes I wondered if he actually believed what he was saying, or if he just underestimated my intelligence. He could justify anything. As time went on I realized that what he cared about were the ends. As far as the means to achieve those ends, he was utterly without scruples. I remember complaining once about a *compañero* whose constant lies and bad judgment were giving the Organization a bad name. How could we give responsibility to such a person? I demanded.

"I know he's a piece of shit," Humberto replied. "But if shit is what we have to make the Revolution happen, shit is what we'll use."

I fell silent, feeling terrible. I wondered if I was clinging excessively to my principles, to the vestiges of my Christian education. I even toyed with the idea that his tolerance was the sign of a political wisdom that I lacked. Later on, however, the person he defended was eventually forced out of the Organization for being dishonest.

That experience taught me, in no uncertain terms, that a war can be won with any class of people, but a fair, ethical system of government cannot be put in place if the people who take it upon themselves to do it lack those qualities, or sacrifice those values along the way.

I don't think Humberto ever stopped to think about those things. The triumphs he achieved and the adulation they brought him led him to fancy himself a great strategist, and they also reinforced his tendency to never think beyond short-term results. Perhaps the most disappointing thing was to see him act like any other politician, instead of like the revolutionary I expected him to be.

When I recall the countless letters I wrote during those years, I am always amazed at the faith I had in the power of my words, in the power of well-founded arguments and thoughtful reflection. I didn't think my words would fall on deaf ears, but I can't be sure that Humberto ever read what I wrote. In those days I felt strongly that we were a collective, that we shared responsibilities. I believed the idiosyncrasies of certain leaders and their decisions didn't necessarily have to affect the entire movement. This is why I didn't even consider abandoning it.

In the end things didn't happen the way Humberto wanted, but it paid off to be audacious. The method chosen was costly, chaotic, and bloody, but the surprise attacks set the country on fire. We didn't take power but the fight for national liberation acquired irrevocable momentum. Perhaps if the process had involved more careful deliberation we would have advanced more slowly, with fewer casualties. On the other hand, it could have prevented the offensive from reaching critical mass. But history is written about what is, not about what could have been.

CHAPTER TWENTY-ONE

On how samba music brought solace to my grieving heart

San José, 1976–1977

"WHEN A HEART is broken by a man, only another man can mend it," a Nicaraguan witch doctor once proclaimed to me, responding to my request for a magic potion that would cure my heartbreak. I thought I would spend New Year's Eve of 1976 crying over Marcos in my house, but my friend Toño Jarquín decided to save me from myself, and insisted I go with him and his wife, Luisa, to a party.

Life went on. I was young. It would do me good.

At that party I met Sergio De Castro. He asked me to dance. At first I said no, thank you, but he wasn't the kind of man who took no for an answer. He took me by the hand, making me get up from the cushion I was sitting on. He was a tall man, nice-looking, and his premature baldness made him rather intriguing. Plus, he moved like only Brazilians know how to move. Samba, I soon learned, has the power to banish sadness, especially if you dance it with someone who carries it in his blood. The apartment was tiny but the party spilled out onto the parking lot of the building complex. It was a merry group, full of nice people, with the abundant joy that the Amazon spreads across those vast lands. One could hear the melodious sounds of Brazilian Portuguese being spoken all around. I danced. Dancing is great medicine, but when midnight brought hugs and kisses, all I wanted to do was cry, go home and cry.

Sergio offered to drive me to my house, but first he wanted to take me to another party for a minute. A short while later, I was in a great big house filled with strangers all gathered around a pool, and my companion suddenly flung himself in, clothes and all. He was wearing jeans, and now they clung tightly to his body. The body of a Carioca: well-rounded butt.

From that first night I noticed the intensity with which he approached nearly everything he did—even having fun. A take-charge attitude that told me he was the kind that wouldn't relent until he got what he wanted.

When he brought me home, he insisted I invite him up for coffee. My daughters were away visiting their father for Christmas. My house felt empty and sad. He stayed with me that night.

Sergio established himself in my life with an iron sweetness. His persistence was admirable. He lived close by, and he often came looking for me. "Let's go to the movies." "Let's go have dinner." "Let's go dancing." When my daughters returned, he became their friend. On weekends he would invite us out. Maryam was in heaven. Melissa called him a "silly bald man" and regarded him with that refreshing skepticism of small children who mince no words. Maryam wanted a daddy. She wanted to feel that she had a family. He would come over and we would carry a picnic lunch to La Hoja forest, La Cruz mountain, beautiful, green spots near San José. If on the road we passed people with car trouble—a couple with a flat tire, or a car that wouldn't start—Sergio would always stop to help. He was a compulsively good person. Often those Sunday excursions turned into rescue operations. I would lose my patience, but Sergio always had a political response for me. The redemption of the world was a daily obligation for him, part of the Revolution. When he was fourteen, Sergio was detained for being a Trotskyite in Brazil. Then he moved to Chile where he lived under Allende until he was forced out when Pinochet took over in 1973. He was a militant member of Costa Rica's Socialist Party, and he took politics and militancy very seriously—nothing like the Nicaraguan way, which was full of jokes, improvisation, and irreverence, even in the most dire circumstances. But I also had my serious side, the side that felt compulsively responsible for the rest of humanity, and in that we were alike.

Grief-stricken and bruised, I let him lick my heart's wounds. But he turned out to be a lover with a firm vocation for marriage, and I often felt myself fenced in, desperately looking for an escape, though I never knew why. I began to say no to his invitations, alleging political meetings, work. He didn't get upset. He never got upset. When it came to politics he had more theoretical knowledge than I did. He had read more. He was constantly giving me lectures, helping me comprehend this or that issue, broadening my understanding of politics, applying his great insight to the Sandinista movement, and the situation in Nicaragua, and the entire continent. And he made love to me with the same militant dedication, exploring me from head to toe, inside and out, with the charms of a native son of the sensuous Ipanema beach. But he was also the kind of man who knew when it was time to call the exterminator because there were ants in the house, or who reminded me that the girls needed to see the dentist. He began to take me to meet his friends. Before I could even tell them my name he would introduce me as his girlfriend.

But I was still crying at night. I would talk to him about Marcos. I would tell him about my love for him, how much I had loved him. Sergio would console me and be understanding. He didn't get jealous. It didn't bother him that the ghost of another man slept between us.

When my sixth sense alerted me that this man had invaded my life, my practical side would spring into action, arguing that I would never find another man who was so good, so perfect: father, lover, *compañero*, dedicated professor. I could tell he was driven by the certitude that, in the long run, I would give in. Patiently, he waited for me to let down my defenses.

After two months of going out together, he asked me to marry him. We were in the elevator at Garnier. He was taking me back to the office after lunch. I made fun of his hurry. I told him he was crazy, that I had only just finished signing the papers for my divorce, and that it hadn't even occurred to me to get married again.

It must have been February or March of 1977. The advertising agency was giving me more responsibilities and a better salary. After my latest raise, I moved into a bigger house and bought a new car. The house was an architectural dream of white walls, clay bricks, wood, built-in furniture, different levels, with giant round lamps covered in brightly colored canvas shades. I fell in love with it. It had been empty for several months because it was too modern for Costa Rican tastes, at least that's what the real estate agent told me. I even got it at a discount. Sergio helped me move, and after a few days he announced he was moving in. I could take my time thinking about marriage but meanwhile why couldn't we at least live in the same house? I didn't react with much enthusiasm, but he didn't seem to mind. He brought his things over and made himself at home. I let him do it because the truth was, what more could I ask of life than a man like Sergio?

Around then, I went to Mexico to do a job concerning the Sandinista support network. I went to stay in Andrea's place. She was out of town, but she had a Frenchwoman guest in her house. In a political rally I attended, a painter and Sandinista sympathizer gave me a charcoal drawing based on a photograph of Marcos, and I put it on my bedside table in Andrea's apartment. The Frenchwoman looked at it. That night, while we drank coffee, the two of us in our pajamas, sitting on the rug in the bedroom, we engaged in a heart-to-heart woman's talk which lasted until the wee hours of the morning.

I confessed to her that coming back to Mexico brought up lots of memories. As we smoked a cigarette, I told her about my love affair with Marcos. She listened in silence. When I was finished, she leaned against the wall, and shook her head side to side in a gesture that was both despondent and incredulous. The Frenchwoman was older than me, with ebony hair and eyes. She might not have been beautiful but she had a way about her that made her very attractive.

"I don't believe it," she suddenly said. "My God, I just don't believe it!"

And she told me her story. She had met Marcos in Paris many years earlier. They had fallen in love. He went back to Nicaragua but kept writing to her, asking her to wait for him, promising he would return. Then his letters stopped. A year went by, two years. Twice she had been on the verge of getting married, but both times, just before the wedding day, she had received letters from Marcos, begging her not to marry, swearing he loved her and would return to marry her someday. Because he had been the love of her life, those letters would drive her mad with indecision. In each case, she had ended up breaking off her engagements only to have Marcos disappear as suddenly as he had appeared. Eventually she too found out—through the testimony of various *compañeros* who appeared before the Military Tribunal—about the woman he finally married. At last, she realized that Marcos would never return, that she was not his cherished Parisian girlfriend, the woman he loved and to whom he would return once his obligations to homeland and history were fulfilled.

The Frenchwoman was an embittered soul. She never forgave herself for her naïveté, for the lost years, for her betrayed trust. Her tale left me stunned. I couldn't comprehend it. What could possibly explain Marcos's behavior? Why would he do such a thing? Was she really telling the truth? But then, why would someone invent something like that?

For the entire trip back to San José, to Sergio, to my daughters, I was submerged in a long soliloquy trying to tame the feelings that like wild animals seemed to have escaped from their cages to run loose within me. Did Marcos, my heroic guerrilla, love all of us? Or did he think he loved us? Did the clandestine life imply a kind of splintering, the development of an emotional capacity to live several parallel lives all at once? I myself had come to realize that once you begin to break societal norms, the line between right or wrong blurs. Eventually, each person invented his or her own compass and ethical standard, which could become a slippery slope when life and the future were so uncertain. What you wanted was to take everything in, drink from every glass. "Eat today, because you never know what tomorrow will bring," the Sandinistas jokingly said. That philosophy extended into other areas as well. In the end Marcos decided on one person alone. And he married her. His moment came when he had to decide. Perhaps he realized that he couldn't keep up that juggling act. Looking out the window at the clouds, watching them advance above the blue, crystalline water of the Caribbean, I felt terribly sad for him. I could almost justify what he had done. After all, he was dead now. Good for him that he had tasted the fruits of so many women ready to fall in love with him. His time had ended far too soon.

Sergio was waiting for me at the airport with my girls. I landed straight into his arms. After that trip I surrendered to him, to his loving care, to his way of taking charge of everything. I curled up like a cat. Why was I going to refuse his love, the nourishment he gave me while I purred, slept, and licked my wounds, the little saucer with milk and water he set for me at the foot of the bed? Marcos haunted me for a long time. I still don't understand the full, undecipherable meaning of that love, a love that so clearly devastated me. But, during that period of my life, I didn't allow myself to mourn. I buried my pain, trying to distance myself from it so that it wouldn't drain me of all my energy. I worked tirelessly to keep afloat and cover up everything that made me grieve. I patched up my heart. And I no longer cried at night.

CHAPTER TWENTY-TWO

On the hectic preparations for the attacks
and on how I was unexpectedly called to perform a dangerous mission

COSTA RICA, 1977

TO QUELL THE various doubts and anxieties, Humberto Ortega sent Marvin to our cell. He was a veteran of the guerrilla combat in the mountains, older than the rest of us, quiet and taciturn, but with a special revolutionary mystique. Tall, rail-thin, with a soft, calm voice, he inspired respect. It was easy to believe him, to trust the things he said. His presence, and especially his belief that the audacious military plan would very likely succeed, helped to appease us somewhat. We knew it would be useless and even presumptuous to keep on resisting the idea. Given that Costa Rica would be vitally important as a fallback country, it was time to prepare the political terrain. We had to ensure that the Costa Ricans would support us and pressure their government to condemn Somoza and recognize the legitimacy of the provisional government.

We also needed to organize the military schools to train the *compañeros* who would be entering into combat in Nicaragua via the southern border. One of these schools took place on a Sunday at my house. When Marvin proposed the idea to me, I didn't understand exactly how a suburban house could be used as the site of a military training session. Don't worry, he said, you'll see. There were sixteen men and women in all. I didn't know anyone except the *compañeros* in my cell. Very early in the morning we started by going over different military units: squad, platoon, squadron, company; the number of soldiers in each, the differences between vanguard, center, rear guard; the chain of command, and the types of orders. In the afternoon we assembled and disassembled several types of rifles, among them an M-16, a Garand, a Galil, the weapons used by the Nicaraguan army. We learned their properties: calibers, range, firepower, and we studied different types of grenades. The most interesting part for me was when Marvin taught us marksmanship. We lay on the floor in the living room as if in a shooting range aiming at a piece of paper. We took the rifles and triangulated. That is, we fired imaginary shots which we marked on the paper until we had made a triangle. I no longer remember the theoretical basis for this, but the exercise allows one to calculate the trajectory of a projectile quite accurately—as if by magic. All the students were transfixed. We worked together closely and bonded as the day went on, calling each other by the number Marvin assigned to each of us at the beginning of the training.

I assumed that those designated for combat would be attending a proper military school. It was inconceivable to me that anybody could participate in a military attack just with this kind of theoretical knowledge. Throughout the day I kept looking around and asking myself if I would ever see those faces again.

By the time Sergio returned with the girls in late afternoon, the students were gone. All that was left in the kitchen were the leftovers from lunch: empty boxes of Kentucky Fried Chicken, with Colonel Sanders's smiling face.

None of us knew when or how the projected attacks would take place. On October 12, around nine in the evening, Sergio Ramírez and a *compañero* I knew as Mauricio—his real name was Herty Lewites—appeared at my house unexpectedly.

"We need you to take some weapons to the border," one of them said. "It's extremely important. We are missing one person and you are the only one we can turn to."

"The attack is tomorrow," said Sergio, his face reflecting the urgent situation. "Those of us who are part of the provisional government are going in to Rivas later tonight. The moment has arrived," he said, nervous but excited. "If everything goes well, we'll all be in Managua by tomorrow." I was surprised that Sergio Ramírez, the thoughtful, rational Balthazar (his pseudonym), was so optimistic.

"Do you think Sergio can go with you so you don't have to go alone?" he asked.

My Sergio agreed when I asked him. Of course he would go with me, he said. I was upset. I didn't understand why, only at the last minute, they had decided to use me. It seemed like a lack of foresight, a troubling symptom of their tendency to improvise.

"I would have preferred to have been told about this before," I said. "But if you think it's necessary I'll do it. I just wonder what you'd have done if Sergio and I had been at the movies," I asked, insistent. A Byzantine question. I always have trouble keeping my mouth shut.

They gave us the instructions. A jeep would be waiting for us in Liberia, Costa Rica. It would lead us to the place at the Nicaraguan border where the weapons would be delivered. Once we were done, we were to return to San José. It sounded easy enough—that is, until I got a look at the pile of weapons we were supposed to load in my tiny, canary-yellow Toyota. At least three or four suitcases, plus three or four army duffel bags, filled with weapons.

"If the Costa Rican Rural Guard stops you and asks what you're carrying tell them that it's your luggage, that you're on your way to your honeymoon in Nicaragua."

"The spare tire doesn't fit," Sergio announced, sticking his head out of the trunk. "We'll have to put it in the back seat."

By the time they were finished loading the weapons there wasn't an inch of room left in the trunk or the back seat, and there was still one overnight bag left to put in.

"Put it by your feet," Mauricio said. "But don't smoke, whatever you do. A precaution. It's full of grenades."

I thought about traveling four or five hours in a car packed with explosives but it was pointless to worry, to be scared about it. I am still astonished when I think back at how coolheaded I was, but the truth is that after a while I was energized by a sense of excitement. After all, since 1970, I had been preparing myself for this sort of thing.

Carried away by the gravity of the moment, we said a solemn goodbye.

"We'll meet in Managua tomorrow," said Sergio—Balthazar, that is.

Maybe, I thought. Maybe I'm the one who's mistaken. I hope so.

Sergio and I entered the house to say goodbye to the girls and to ask Cristina to sleep in the room with them because we wouldn't be returning until the following day.

It was a clear night as we began our journey. Signs marked the way: Peñas Blancas, Nicaraguan Border. I was overcome by a sense of optimism. I told Sergio that perhaps we had been kept in the dark to keep the operation compartmentalized. Surely something so big had not been planned carelessly. "Can you imagine if it all works out?" I said. "I think Sergio Ramírez has to know what he's doing." "Let's hope he does," said my Sergio, "but I can't envision taking power so rapidly. It would be a first."

But rather defensively I argued that the Frente had been at this for years: the guerrillas in the mountains, the work in the barrios. I didn't want his skepticism at that moment.

"Come on, don't be pessimistic," I said. "You just don't know what we Nicas are made of. The people are amazing. And they're sick of Somoza. It's been more than forty years, don't forget."

Sergio worked as a journalist for one of Costa Rica's most important radio stations. He said it would have been a good idea to leak some information to the executive editor, without revealing any details, of course. It was going to be a huge story. They would need all their people to cover it.

"Do you realize that if we're caught with this arsenal we'll get deported?" he asked.

"Don't even think about it," I said. "We can't afford negative thoughts now."

Nevertheless, I couldn't help worry that our grossly overloaded car would break down on us. The slightest incline slowed it to a crawl.

"It will be a real feat if this little car makes it," Sergio said. I, meanwhile, was dying for a cigarette but the bag of grenades, lying at my feet like a coiled snake, dissuaded me.

As we approached the Nicaraguan border, where the road ran along the Pacific coastline, the climate changed and became warmer. It was that particular heat that only rises out of my land. It expanded me, unfolded sensations within me as if my body were blooming, and able to encompass feelings that the rainy oppression of San José had dampened. I began to hum. "You look like you're on a vacation trip," Sergio observed.

It was two in the morning when we arrived in the border town of Liberia. The meeting place was empty. No jeep, nobody in sight. I began to fume. "Now what are we supposed to do with all these guns?" I complained loudly, cursing my compatriots under my breath. I was embarrassed that Sergio had to witness such an appalling lack of organization. We waited silently for a while parked at the appointed spot.

"We can't stay here like this," I said, finally. "There's more surveillance here than in San José."

In a truck stop—open twenty-four hours—we sat outside drinking Cokes and looking at the highway. We didn't have a contingency plan. We hadn't even considered the possibility that our contact wouldn't show. A Rural Guard patrol car approached us. I smiled at Sergio, took his hand, leaned over to kiss him. The patrol car slid into a spot near ours. The officers got out. My heart was in my throat. I was afraid they would see inside our car but our little romantic scene had managed to distract them. They glanced at us and went inside. After a while they emerged and took off, never noticing a thing.

We sat there for a seemingly endless hour and a half. Nervously, I kept swinging my leg back and forth, sliding my foot in and out of my sandal just avoiding having it come off, a mindless pastime.

The jeep finally appeared on the road. We got into our car. They signaled and we followed. They got off the main road and drove for a long while along a dark, narrow lane before eventually coming to a stop.

"We got held up, brother," said one of them apologetically. We barely spoke. We were all tense.

We did the transfer hurriedly under the weak light of the quarter moon. Free of our cargo, we took the road back.

CHAPTER TWENTY-THREE

Of how a military failure turned into a political victory

SAN JOSÉ, 1977

SERGIO AND I had assumed that we would hear news of the attack on the radio as we drove back from the border, but by nine in the morning there was still no word. Anxious and worried, I went over to Tito Castillo's house to see what was going on. Tito was a member of the provisional government. Ernesto, one of his sons, opened the door. He would die later, in combat, in the September 1978 offensive, but then he was a tall, lanky young man who wrote poetry and whose white, quasi-translucent skin gave him the aura of an angel. As soon as I crossed the threshold I knew the attacks had failed. There, sitting in the living room, were most of the members of what would have been the provisional government. They looked weary and disappointed. Humberto Ortega gesticulated wildly while speaking into the telephone in a corner of the room.

I found out from Sergio Ramírez and Tito that the general plan had to be aborted. The supposedly synchronized military operations didn't even come close to being simultaneous. A mechanical failure in one of the vehicles had prevented them from even making it across the border. Of all the planned attacks, only three were actually executed. One of them, led by combatants from the Solentiname community—disciples of Ernesto Cardenal—struck the army outpost in San Carlos, a small lakeside port near the mouth of the San Juan River. Another unit hit the army headquarters in the city of Rivas on the southern border, and another attack was made on a military patrol near the small community of Mozonte, in the north of Nicaragua. All the other operations got tangled up in a web of commands that were issued too late, weapons that never arrived at their destinations, and general miscommunication. Amid the chaos of that morning, I heard incredible tales of dozens of rifles that were damaged because someone had the bright idea of hiding them in the bottom of a riverbed; of commanders whose courage failed them at the last minute; and of others who exposed themselves to danger too soon, like Marvin, and were wounded just as combat began. The level of improvisation was truly reckless, and casualties were already being reported: Elvis Chavarría, Ernesto Medrano.

Tito's house, with its big picture windows overlooking the garden, was teeming with people walking in and out, unable to decide what to do with the energy they had stored up for the victory they had hoped to savor that day. We had lost communication with several units that were preparing to attack inside the country, and we were growing alarmed. They had to abort their missions, but we had no idea how to warn them. Seeing no better alternative, we composed messages disguised as press releases and distributed them to the Costa Rican press. We prayed that our Sandinista fighters would hear them over their shortwave radios, and understand they were supposed to hold off the attacks. On October 17, however, a military unit did attack the army headquarters in Masaya, a densely populated city thirty kilometers from Managua. We learned about the disaster over the radio. More Sandinistas were killed. Among them Federico—head of the GPP (Prolonged People's War tendency). He had no idea about the attack and had the misfortune of arriving at a military checkpoint near Masaya just as the attacks were taking place. He was detained and assassinated by the National Guard. Every day the army published more and more names of dead, wounded, and captured Sandinistas. All of my worst fears had come true, among them the conspicuous absence of the masses who were expected to spontaneously rise up and join the insurrection. Overall it looked like a monumental failure, but out of the debacle came some ideas that would reverse the course of events. The members of the provisional government, for example, became what was known as the Group of Twelve, when they issued a statement in support of the FSLN. That twelve prestigious Nicaraguan citizens would publicly side with the Sandinistas against the dictatorship made headlines both in Nicaragua and around the world. As events unfolded, Humberto Ortega, like a Houdini, spun his version of what had occurred. Unabashed, he began to assert that the October plan had never been to seize power, but rather to ignite the flame of rebellion in the cities. In the end, he convinced himself of this and that was how history would remember it because—just as Marcos had assumed—the attacks did have an enormous impact, not just on the dictatorship but on the Nicaraguan people. They marked the start of a rising tide of rebellion which, ultimately, justified the loss of lives and excused the improvisation. "All's well that ends well." Unfortunately, such is life. Mistakes along the way are forgotten, nobody is held accountable. The dead cannot get up to voice their claims.

My house was soon filled with guerrillas who had been in combat in the outposts near the Costa Rican border. The stories they told were bone-chilling. Many of them barely even knew how to use their weapons. Though flabbergasted at the lack of preparation, they were remarkably good-humored about it, joking about how they had been sent out to do a "live" practice. They brought with them more army bags filled with weapons—including bazookas—which we hid in a small, protected space in our roof. My daughters were fascinated by these tired, dirty men dressed in olive drab who smiled and played with them. After two or three days they were gone.

It was around that time that Rosario Murillo, her children, Zoilamérica, Rafael, and Tino, and her then-companion, Quincho Ibarra, lived in my house for a couple of months. I watched, amazed, at the maternal devotion with which Zoilamérica looked after her little brother Tino, who was only a few months old. Rosario and Quincho were adrift, caught in a sea of confusion, and were talking about going to Paris to study film. A few months later, Rosario met Daniel Ortega and they soon became a couple.

The people in my cell decided to call a meeting with Humberto to let him know our opinions and critique his poor judgment. The facts spoke for themselves, but in addition we felt it was important to review the entire episode so as to avoid a similar fiasco in the future. The meeting took place in Blas's dining room, and it was a tense scene, filled with recriminations. Marvin's arm was in a plaster cast, the result of a bullet wound, and he glared at Humberto, who defended himself tooth and nail. According to him, we owed the political effervescence that had taken hold throughout Nicaragua to his decision to launch the attacks at exactly the right moment.

Humberto had a point. Only a month before the attacks, on September 17, 1977, Somoza finally lifted the censorship of the press imposed after the 1972 earthquake. In addition, the dictator was now in Miami, recovering from a heart attack. People were beginning to whisper that he might have to resign for health reasons, which generated another flurry of internal conflict among the various men now vying to be his successor. Plus, the reins of the government were in the hands of an ineffective Parliament. The military actions coincided precisely with the void in the power structure and the removal of press restrictions. The threat of armed conflict, along with the communiqué issued by the Group of Twelve, caused a chain reaction. Businessmen, the church, and the parties were now clamoring for a National Dialogue in which the dictatorship would commit to respecting democracy. The wave of protests gained momentum, especially after the veil of censorship was lifted and people became aware of the many atrocities that had been covered up by the dictatorship. The families of political prisoners exhumed cadavers to disprove the causes of death recorded in the National Guard's forensic reports. People ostensibly killed by bullet wounds emerged from their graves with broken bones and smashed skulls, their bodies mutilated by torture. The country was like a powder keg.

"What were we objecting to?" asked Humberto. "Mistakes were to be expected in undertakings as risky as those we had attempted."

Reluctantly, we accepted his arguments.

Ernesto Medrano, a Costa Rican who joined the Sandinistas, died in those attacks, and the Costa Rican people responded to his death by closing ranks with the Sandinistas. People came to the Nicaraguan solidarity demonstrations in droves. I was amazed to witness the mobilizing, electrifying effect of armed struggle even in such a peaceful country. Thousands of Costa Ricans gathered in San José's Central Park to condemn the Somoza dictatorship and to pay tribute to the dead. The poets read their fiercest poems. Many Nicaraguan intellectuals who, until then, were only lukewarm supporters of our cause passionately joined our ranks upon seeing how we had inspired such solidarity among the Costa Ricans.

The contradictions and conflicts with the other Sandinista groups became more and more problematic. Those who supported the Prolonged People's War tendency—Federico's group—blamed the Terceristas for his death. Those within the Proletarian tendency argued that people weren't sufficiently prepared yet to back up military strikes.

But the groundswell of patriotism was in full force. Our fellow Sandinistas had not died in vain. Their deaths could not be blamed on mistakes or considered an unnecessary sacrifice. In spite of the reticence some of us had shown, we found ourselves riding a wave of grandiloquence that portrayed the October attacks as Sandinismo's masterful blow, the beginning of the end of the dictatorship. I wanted to believe it with all my heart. I chastised myself for my doubts, my anxiety. For the first time in my life I saw fists raised high in the plazas, people shouting "Long live Sandino!" and "Long live the FSLN!" at the top of their lungs. All the solidarity and enthusiasm that I had dreamed of for so long suddenly materialized precisely when I felt most distant and critical, when I had the greatest misgivings about the methods used to organize the rebellion.

Years later, in a most solemn ceremony, Humberto Ortega, commander in chief of the Sandinista People's Army, decorated me for my participation in the October attacks. I waited in line with my fellow Sandinistas for the commander, decked out in full regalia, to pin the medal on me. I smiled inwardly at the irony of being decorated for participating in a mission with which I had been in disagreement.

CHAPTER TWENTY-FOUR

Of the progress of love and the instinct to multiply

SAN JOSÉ, 1977

TIRED OF MY FATHER'S refusal to visit because I was living with a man who was not my lawfully wedded husband, I decided it was time to marry. Just as the wedding ceremony was about to begin in Sergio's parents' house in San José, Otto Castro, a lawyer friend who was to officiate, called us aside to tell us he couldn't go through with it. A document was missing. He stood there, incongruously dressed in his ever present black motorcycle leathers, his helmet still in his hand. In the living room, everything and everyone was waiting for us: my daughters, dressed up as little maids of honor, my parents-in-law, as well as my parents and my best friend, who had flown in from Nicaragua for the occasion, the buffet. "I'm sorry, Otto, but we can't cancel this now," I said. "Let's just go ahead with the ceremony, even if it's only symbolic, and then Sergio and I will go to your office and make everything legal." I refused to take no for an answer. The three of us walked into the living room and Otto married us.

We never took care of the legal formalities. We felt married, and time just slipped by. When we separated several years later, and my mother found out the truth, she was furious, and reproached me harshly, as if we had deceived everyone on purpose. But we hadn't. It was just something we forgot to do.

Once married, I settled into Sergio's placid love, which was like a cozy nutshell floating in the turbulent waters rushing through my life. We would sleep snuggled up against one another and our lovemaking was playful and filled with erotic fantasies and explorations. My daughters warmly welcomed Sergio's paternal presence in the house, and he assumed his role so responsibly, so affectionately, that I was the envy of all my friends. "What did you do to find such a good man who loves your daughters so much? Give us the recipe," they would say to me.

Compulsively didactic, my new husband decided it was his job to instruct me on how to view the world around me. But I didn't need instruction; I understood the world well enough, and his efforts irritated me. At times ironic, at times sweetly reproachful, his criticisms always managed to make me feel guilty, activating some obscure mechanisms hidden deep in my psyche. To defend myself I would uncage my lioness and lash out at him with fully extended claws. I have never been able to tolerate the macho tendency of "adopting" women, as if by marriage the man acquires a child or some helpless creature in need of guidance. Sergio may have been among the more enlightened of his gender, and he certainly used more sophisticated methods, but the paternalism inherent in his attitude infuriated me nonetheless.

It seems that every five years I was overcome by uncontrollable maternal instincts. My body called out to me, imploring me to use its fertile gifts. An unbridled, carnal energy took possession of my whole being. A gentle breeze against my skin, a sudden moment of joy, even an ice-cream cone would send me in search of fusion, of pandemonium, as if my womb wanted to absorb the world and bring new life to it. When Melissa was four and a half years old, I began to experience all these things and realized I was ready for motherhood again. The year before, after a slightly abnormal Pap smear, I had undergone a supposedly routine medical procedure, and the doctor had assured me that it absolutely wouldn't have any effect on future pregnancies or births. With his blessing, Sergio and I devoted ourselves to the task of laying siege to the first errant egg that would venture out of my ovaries.

During several months other, perhaps more patriotic, duties vied for our attention. Tasks that couldn't be postponed, rebel attacks that needed our support seemed always to coincide with my ovulation. Finally, we took advantage of a relatively calm period in December to storm my reluctant egg. I took my temperature morning, noon, and night. If I felt flushed at work and thought it could mean I was ovulating, I would call Sergio. Citing urgent, unexpected errands, we would both leave our offices, rush home and make love, determined not to let the moment pass us by.

At least this war would be carefully and scientifically planned, I'd tell myself. My strategy eventually bore fruit: Camilo was conceived in December. My daughters were thrilled at the news that they would soon have a little brother. My pregnant body made me feel whole, inhabited, beautiful. For the first time since 1972, my daughters and I had a family Christmas.

CHAPTER TWENTY-FIVE

Of a Nicaraguan El Cid and of how I lost Camilo and Arnoldo

MANAGUA–SAN JOSÉ, 1978

DURING THE CRUSADES El Cid, the legendary Spanish warrior, already dead from a mortal wound, was placed by his men on his horse Babieca to lead them into battle. Something similar happened to Pedro Joaquín Chamorro, the editor in chief of the newspaper *La Prensa*, when the dictatorship had him assassinated.

Pedro Joaquín had devoted his life to the politics of opposition. When I was a little girl we lived in a house adjacent to his in the Colonia Mántica neighborhood, in Managua. He was a pensive man with a slightly curved back, and he walked with a slow, deliberate stride. In my young eyes he was a hero: he was forever being thrown in jail, and no sooner had he been released than he would lash out once more against Somoza in blazing, fearless editorials. His daughters were my playmates, and my parents were close friends with him and his wife, Violeta. When Anastasio Somoza García, the first Somoza in the dynasty, was shot on September 21, 1956, in León, I silently crept down the stairs in my pajamas to where his wife, Violeta Chamorro, was telling my parents that the National Guard had seized him at their front door. Anastasio Somoza García had been killed by a poet and Pedro Joaquín had been arrested on suspicion. He was later released.

The Sandinista movement saw a potential ally in Pedro Joaquín. But what separated us from him were his objections to armed struggle. Nevertheless, after the October attacks, rumors spread that he might become the thirteenth member of the Group of Twelve and a supporter of the FSLN.

But on January 10, 1978, assassins intercepted him somewhere in the ruins of Managua when he was on his way to *La Prensa*, and gunned him down mercilessly with a shotgun.

In my office at Garnier, I was racking my brains to come up with an advertising slogan for a product, when Sergio called to tell me the news. Sergio Ramírez called a few minutes later. I hung up the phone and, not knowing what to do, I sat staring out my office window at the shimmering light of the morning sun. This was an incalculable loss. Nicaragua has produced few men of his caliber. Pedro Joaquín was the symbol of a personal and intellectual freedom which he had defended at all cost. That Somoza had him killed—a generally held suspicion at first, eventually proven without a doubt—showed that, out of desperation, the dictator had launched an all-out war. I thought of Doña Violeta, of their children, Pedro, Cristiana, Carlos Fernando, my friend Claudia Lucía. I called my parents and I could hear the shock in their voices. Everyone was stunned, they said. The atmosphere in Managua was very tense. Something had to give.

All expectations were exceeded by what happened next. Pedro Joaquín Chamorro became a warrior after his death: as his body was carried through Managua, Nicaraguans everywhere took to the streets, driven by forty-three years of suppressed rage. They mourned his assassination not only with tears but with stones and rioting, and everywhere symbols of the dictatorship were set ablaze. Along the Carretera Norte, the highway that went by the industrial area that housed the newspaper offices as well as various businesses belonging to Somoza's family and friends, the Nicaraguan people staged a protest the likes of which the country had never seen. They were especially merciless in their attack against Plasmaféresis, Somoza's plasma business. Every day, the poorest of the poor, those who had no other recourse, would line up in front of Plasmaféresis to sell their blood for two dollars a quart. *La Prensa* had published terrible photographs of famished, desperate donors waiting in line. People charged the compound, pelting it with Molotov cocktails to burn it down to the ground. The assault reached such frightening proportions that the National Guard was forced to retreat in the face of the anguished citizenry's unbridled fury. Protests led by students and factory workers soon followed, all calling for Somoza's resignation. The private sector called a general strike to protest Chamorro's assassination. On January 22, 1978, the anniversary of a massacre that took place in 1967, Managua was paralyzed.

In San José, the level of solidarity was so great we could scarcely deal with it. Journalists from all over the world flooded the city to interview Sandinistas. Revolutionaries from across the continent joined the Nicaraguan struggle: Chileans, Spaniards, Argentineans, Colombians, North Americans. The heightened intensity of the struggle minimized the differences between the three tendencies within the Sandinista movement. Unity was on everyone's lips. No longer was there any doubt that it would be the key to toppling the dictatorship. I learned that Camilo Ortega was sharing whatever weapons he obtained with members of the GPP, the tendency that had a broader and better organized support base. I was thrilled to hear it. Camilo was still being Camilo. The Insurrectional tendency had the best supplies because the Group of Twelve, thanks to their personal, professional, and intellectual prestige, had been able to secure resources from various governments, grassroots organizations, and political parties. The other two tendencies, more purist and suspicious of alliances, had to go to great pains to obtain weapons and money.

Forging alliances, obtaining the support of prominent figures and of people with economic means, was critical. This, however, not only required us to modify the revolutionary discourse, but to approach people who frequently agreed to collaborate because of their own shady economic or political interests. Humberto Ortega's tactic to insure their continued support was to give them a surprising amount of political responsibilities. Often, Sandinistas were put in the difficult position of having to accept orders from people who were clearly opportunist. This unscrupulous approach was based on Humberto's assumption that in the end we would be holding the reins. He maintained that it was necessary, if we wanted to achieve success, to move ahead and open new avenues in a society where so much had been off-limits to us. But I hadn't joined a revolution to play by the very rules we were trying to change. For me, the end did not justify the means. The Revolution sought not only to bring about political change, but also to instill ethical values.

My mistrust of the tactics undertaken by the Tercerista leadership only grew as time went by. Humberto Ortega may have been astute, but as far as I saw it, he was getting himself caught in a web that would be difficult to untangle without losing his humanity and his principles, even if it did help bring the Sandinistas to victory. I wore myself ragged writing impassioned letters of protest, venting all my concerns about the kind of revolution we would be making if we kept altering the truth and pretending we were other than what we were in the interests of "selling" the cause. He silenced my criticism, invoking the revolutionary fervor that had taken hold of the country. Remembering these events after twenty years, I realize those were the first signs of the unscrupulous political methods that later on damaged the ideals and mystique of the Sandinista cause and, in the end, led the Ortega brothers—who usurped the legacy of our brave liberation struggle—not only to political but to moral defeat.

I continued with my underground work despite the misgivings that gnawed at me. I was beginning to think seriously about leaving the Tercerista tendency. Not every Sandinista group operated the same way. Joining one of the other splinter groups might allow me to make a more meaningful contribution, one with fewer conflicts. I felt that strengthening other positions within the FSLN was critical to insure balance once the end finally came. After all, by then every one of the Sandinista tendencies was working toward the same goal. The disagreements were mainly political and in some way reflected my own preoccupations.

In those days, the one thing that continued to inspire me and prevent me from giving up was the courage of regular folks who joined the struggle with such admirable faith and determination. A few questionable acts could never diminish the heroism of someone like Elías, an underground courier who lost his eyesight building a homemade antitank bomb. When he returned from Nicaragua, he turned up at my house with a cane, and asserted that this misfortune would actually help his work since the National Guard would never suspect a blind man of any wrongdoing. And how could I ever forget Ismael, who lost his arm in combat? Ismael would call me incessantly, day in and day out, until I finally managed to get him a prosthesis. As soon as he was able to use it properly, he returned to the line of fire. *Compañeros* like them filled me with an energy that inspired my efforts to maintain and broaden our Costa Rican network, all the while continuing to work at the advertising agency.

Pregnant and exhausted, I would often fall asleep at my desk in the afternoons while trying to come up with advertising jingles or scripts for commercials. I would wake up with a jolt, embarrassed that my boss might have seen me through the glass walls that separated us. Since my previous pregnancies had been relatively free of problems, I assumed that the same would be true this time around. My womb had harbored a pregnancy during an earthquake, and surely it could deal with another during this turbulent period of clandestine activity. But my gynecologist failed to warn me of the risks involved now that my cervix had been debilitated by the recent operation. All too often, doctors decide that women are too ignorant to understand certain physiological processes, and so give vague recommendations and warnings. "Don't go driving down bumpy roads. Take care of yourself," he said.

I had already made contact with the GPP, the Prolonged People's War tendency, when, in February of 1978, another series of attacks were planned and launched from San José. Once again, at night, at the last minute, and for reasons I never understood, I had to go to the Nicaraguan border. When I returned to San José, I found out that the previous night, Sandinista units had attacked the city of Rivas as well as another National Guard outpost near the Costa Rican–Nicaraguan border.

"Once again the so-called practice run turned out to be the real thing. I don't understand why they can't train us properly," complained Arnoldo, a *compañero* in my cell who sought shelter in my house when he returned from the front, tired and dirty. Like so many others, he was one of the Sandinistas' "commuter" soldiers. He would cross into Nicaragua to fight and then retreat to San José.

That evening I discovered I was spotting, the first sign that my pregnancy might be in trouble. I got very scared. I couldn't bear to lose that baby, conceived with such dedication and love. My doctor simply advised me to remain in bed, once again without explaining anything, neither the reason nor the potential problems that might lie ahead.

Friendly, soothing Arnoldo became my de facto nurse, taking care of me when Sergio would go off to work. Together we would have breakfast. I was in bed and Arnoldo sat in a rocking chair by my side. His eyes were deep black and narrow because he was part Chinese, part mestizo. He had large, very white teeth, and there was always a tinge of melancholy in his quiet, shy laughter. I can still picture him, delicately balancing on the rocking chair in the lotus position, wearing a pair of blue-and-white-striped pajamas that looked like a prison uniform.

"What are you going to call the baby?" he asked me one day.

"I will give him the name of the *compañero* who performs the most heroic deed over these few months," I answered.

Arnoldo was with me the afternoon Sergio returned from work with news that the mestizo Indians from the Monimbó tribe in Masaya were up in arms. The National Guard had tear-gassed a church, killing a small child. The people of Monimbó donned their traditional masks and, beating their drums, barricaded themselves in their skimpy barrio: a few small buildings and houses mixed in with adobe and palm-roofed huts. This indeed was a spontaneous, popular uprising. The Monimbó artisans, who crafted fireworks and hammocks, faced the soldiers armed with Molotov cocktails, homemade bombs, and a meager assortment of other firearms. Women threw boiling water at the soldiers from balconies. A few weeks later, Somoza would crush the uprising using tanks and airplanes.

But that weekend, Arnoldo received instructions to prepare himself to go back to Nicaragua covertly. Normally reserved, he was jubilant at the idea that he would join the fight inside the country. With a small black knapsack slung over his shoulder, he hugged me at my doorstep, where Sergio, Cristina, my daughters, and I saw him off, wishing him luck.

"You'll do fine, you're too much of a badass for anything to happen to you," I joked.

He smiled. His shining eyes and the glimmer of his white teeth were the last I ever saw of him. That day was a Friday. On Sunday, just two days later, the National Guard got tipped off about a Sandinista hideout. They surrounded the house, located in a barrio just outside Masaya, and shot everyone in it. Arnoldo had just arrived there to meet with Camilo Ortega and join the Sandinista units that would participate in the uprising. My two beloved friends were gunned down together. It was a truly sinister coincidence.

CHAPTER TWENTY-SIX

On how a literary prize prompted me to reflect upon poetry

SAN JOSÉ, 1978

IN FEBRUARY, shortly before Arnoldo's death, I won the Casa de las Américas poetry prize. It was the most prestigious honor of its kind in Latin America, with a jury made up of the crème de la crème of Spanish and Latin American literature. When the competition for the prize was first announced in the newspapers, I had sent a collection of poems written since leaving Nicaragua. Sergio Ramírez suggested the title: *Línea de fuego*. Line of Fire. What with all the drama in my life at the time, I forgot about the contest, and the award was a welcome surprise. It was also extremely convenient, I thought. That kind of notoriety would be useful to me: it would open doors, give me access, and help me get the word out about the struggle in Nicaragua.

To me, poetry was a gift. It was water flowing from a spring within me, that I channeled onto the page, effortlessly. I also thought of it as energy produced by an unseen organ in my body—a sensory antenna, perhaps, that would capture aromas, feelings, sensations, and every so often would release a flash of illumination. If I had paper, pen, and silence at hand when the first verse broke into my consciousness, that thunderbolt would ignite a poem. All I had to do was let myself get carried off into that first bit of intuition, knowing that the full poem existed in that peculiar state of mind, in that single moment of inspiration. If I couldn't write it at that very moment, if I was driving or otherwise occupied, the poem would be lost. It would fly out the window. The electricity from that lightning bolt would disperse, no matter how hard I might try to recapture it later. Even if I remembered the first line, I could never reproduce the totality of that poem. Once that state of grace had dissipated, I could never experience it again. Because of the spontaneous, almost magical quality with which poetry came to me, it never felt like hard work. I never suffered the anguish of the blank page. I simply allowed myself to be a celestial lightning rod. Only years later, when I embraced poetry as a vocation, did I understand the relationship between inspiration and craft.

Up to that point, politics, not poetry, was my central preoccupation. My basic identity was that of a Sandinista; being a poet was a convenient addition, a valuable talent that was useful to the political cause. My poems then were a mixture—often chaotic—of the erotic and the patriotic, two things that reflected the experiences of my everyday life.

I wrote very little poetry in Costa Rica. Despite being in Central America, despite the fact that my life and my passion revolved around Nicaragua, being in exile affected my poetic sensibility. I realized then there was an inherent symbiosis between my poetry and my land. I needed to smell it, to experience the wind, the energy, the density of those clouds, the shapes of rising volcanoes, for my poetic juices to flow. The few poems I did write were triggered by some memory, the rain, an aroma, that would besiege me and send me back to the land I held within.

My poetry continues to be the expression of the body I regain when my soul returns to its roots. It is in my country where my poetry comes to life. A few days after I go back there I hear the poems swishing around me. My language, Spanish, is my home when I am abroad. Prose is my refuge, but my poetic breath is inextricably, intimately linked to the Nicaraguan landscape.

The Casa de las Américas prize had the merit of making me take my craft seriously. But several years went by before I would give much attention to my literary vocation. Reading the interviews I gave after I received the award, I see that I barely said anything about literature. I talked about politics.

CHAPTER TWENTY-SEVEN

On how I resolved my political anxieties and contradictions

PANAMA–SAN JOSÉ, 1978

I FINALLY DECIDED to break from the Tercerista tendency after a meeting in Panama with José Benito Escobar, one of the leaders of the GPP. We talked for an entire afternoon in my hotel room. José Benito was a man with a face out of a Mayan carving, but his easygoing personality, and the ancient wisdom he exuded, had softened the angles of his face. His impeccable white shirt and well-shined shoes reflected the values of a man from humble beginnings (he had been a bricklayer) for whom carelessness in personal grooming signified a lack of consideration for others.

I liked José Benito. He answered my questions clearly and simply, and I quickly understood how he had gotten his reputation as a man of moral integrity. It was easy to believe in his sincerity.

It didn't take long to see that we agreed on basic principles. After so many months battling my conscience, questioning whether my views were excessively romantic, and whether my ethical concerns had any place in a struggle such as ours, it was comforting to see that someone like him worried about the same things. He briefly explained the work that the GPP needed to organize in Costa Rica. Their efforts with the masses in Nicaragua were already well organized, but they had barely any support base in the neighboring country. They had to assemble a supply of arms and munitions for all the fronts, raise money to buy them through various political contacts, organize training centers for guerrillas, and recruit people from within the enormous Nicaraguan community in Costa Rica. An information system would have to be set up as well, to disseminate the group's political stance, so as to build a critical mass of

184

sympathizers who would support the struggle inside Nicaragua. It was basically the same thing I was doing for the Terceristas, the only difference being that now I was given more responsibility and a clearer picture of the strategy. The GPP did not function like the Terceristas, "commuting" to and from Costa Rica. He mentioned one other GPP person in San José, a woman named Dora.

By the time we said goodbye toward the end of the afternoon, he felt like an old friend. Without a doubt, he would have become a formidable leader, but he didn't survive. A few months later, in northern Nicaragua, he too was assassinated. His death and that of so many others robbed us of years of experience, of people of integrity. The Sandinista movement survived, but each one of those deaths was aimed directly at its heart. We lost so many good men and women. That endless bloodbath seriously compromised the wealth of experience and leadership that would be needed once we came to power.

So many hundreds of lives were cut short. In these pages, I can only write about those closest to me; the list, otherwise, would be too long. Pin, Blas, Arnoldo, Ricardo, Gaspar García Laviana, a Spanish priest, and two *compañeros*, all dead. All members of my Sandinista cell. I couldn't even cry over them anymore. By then I couldn't process so many deaths. They ceased to be real for me. They became myth, offerings made to a voracious sun god that demanded blood before it would cast sunlight once again on our darkened nation. Like the Aztec legend in which fallen warriors turn into hummingbirds, I imagined my friends inhabiting my garden, drinking nectar from flowers, armed solely with their great, pointed beaks. I only cried for my dead friends the day the Revolution triumphed. I wept thinking of their desolate bones, the hollow cavities of their eyes, the unmerciful slumber from which we could no longer awaken them.

After my meeting with José Benito, I returned to San José, to my typewriter to write another impassioned letter to Humberto explaining why I had decided to leave the Terceristas. I think he had gotten used to my letters by now. He didn't even bother to respond.

It wasn't easy to start all over again. Dora was a cinnamon-colored woman, with delicate, perfectly chiseled features who could be beautiful when she smiled, but who was generally somber, quiet, and hard to read. She had a cerebral aneurysm and lived with the constant threat of sudden death. I had no idea how just the two of us could set up a support network. Fortunately, we weren't alone for very long. First Alfredo and then Sabino arrived from Nicaragua, and we all busied ourselves with the frantic task of preparing for the arrival of a third person: Modesto, the GPP's top leader, a Nicaraguan version of Che Guevara, who had been commander of the Sandinista guerrillas in the mountains of northern Nicaragua for seven years. Judging by the planning that was done and the precautions that were taken, it felt as if we were getting ready to smuggle a cargo of diamonds. Such a careful way to work was a world apart from what I had been used to and it suited me far better. It also impressed upon me the importance of that mysterious figure. I would have given anything to drive the car that was going to fetch the guerrilla commander but the complications with my pregnancy continued to plague me. Not a week went by when I wasn't condemned to bed rest for a few days. When our awaited guest finally arrived, I had been stuck at home and I stayed up until Alfredo and Sergio De Castro, who by now had joined the Frente fully, returned. Modesto had crossed the border through the jungle, on foot, with Sabino, a young *campesino* who had been his guide and escort in the mountains. Sergio and Alfredo had waited at a designated place on the road on the Costa Rican side.

"What's he like?" I asked Sergio once we were alone, dying of curiosity.

"Tired," said Sergio. "He slept the whole way back."

Dora telephoned me early the next day. We left my house in the morning and drove around incessantly, going from one place to another, taking care of details and trying to secure a safe house in San José for Modesto— who, meanwhile, was staying in a small town half an hour outside of the city.

By the time I got out of the car at five o'clock in the afternoon to meet with Modesto, I had been at the wheel so long I could barely walk. Driving so many hours in my condition would prove a costly mistake.

I remember little from that first meeting. Perhaps because of the legend that preceded him, I had envisioned myself coming face-to-face with another Marcos, but Modesto hardly possessed a memorable physique: average height, sallow skin, not particularly athletic. His penetrating black eyes and well-defined mouth were his best features. It didn't take long to see that he was intelligent and thoughtful. There was something to the way he spoke, the way he constructed complex sentences and pursued an idea in spite of constant digressions. It must have been the mathematics. I knew that he had studied math at Patrice Lumumba University in Moscow. I also noticed that his hands weren't rough at all, they hardly seemed like the hands of someone who had lived in the jungle. Clearly this was a man who savored knowledge, and who had obtained it at great cost in hostile and unforgiving conditions. He told us that he would be leaving for Cuba in a few days to meet with the leaders of the other Sandinista tendencies, in the hopes of achieving more unity. Fidel Castro had agreed to act as the mediator in the negotiations and to serve as a witness to whatever agreement was reached.

When I returned home, I was in pain and beginning to feel sharp contractions.

I was barely five and a half months into my pregnancy.

CHAPTER TWENTY-EIGHT

Of how I landed in the hospital and was informed that my son had died

SAN JOSÉ, 1978

LYING DOWN WAS USELESS. My overwrought belly kept contracting. It became drum-tight. The doctor ordered me to spend a night in the hospital so I could be administered a solution to stop the contractions. The following day I was getting ready to go home when the doctor who came to discharge me brusquely placed his stethoscope on my belly. A torrent of liquid came rushing down my legs. The amniotic sac had ruptured.

Instead of one night, I spent ten infernal days in that room, sharing the heat, the indifference of the nurses, and the disdain of the doctors with my fellow expectant mothers. The ward for high-risk pregnancies had twenty beds, maybe more, separated only by metal bedside tables. Above the beds were big, gaping windows with dismal aluminum and glass shutters.

Good revolutionaries that we were, Sergio and I had decided that private clinics were for the bourgeoisie. So we went to the Hospital México, which was part of the Social Security system. They ordered me to remain immobile and administered massive doses of antibiotics to control the infection. They also gave me injections to stimulate lung development of "the product," as they so callously referred to the fetus. Accustomed to having my own doctor and a private room whenever I had been hospitalized, the experience in that institution was difficult but instructive. I was appalled at the way doctors treated us, as if we were whiny, spoiled brats, scarcely giving us any information, and simply failing to provide appropriate care.

One day, the woman in the bed next to mine began to complain that she couldn't feel her baby's movements. The doctor examined her and confirmed that there was no fetal heartbeat. Her child had died. She cried long and hard. They carted her off to the operating room, and that was the last we saw of her. After that, I became obsessed with my own baby's movements. I felt him fluttering inside of me like a little bird trapped in a cage. When he would quiet down, I would wake him up, gently tapping my belly, praying to all the saints to save me from the fate of that other woman, praying that my baby wouldn't die too. My saints were Camilo and Arnoldo, my two dead friends. "Guys, please help me keep this tiny creature alive. Wherever you are, please help me." I talked to the baby too. I kept talking to him. I encouraged him. I told him not to give up, to please keep on living. After eight days they made me get out of bed to examine me in another room. I fainted as soon as I sat up.

"You mean to say that you haven't moved in this entire time?" asked the doctor on call once I was lucid enough to respond.

"Yes. That's what they told me," I said. "Not to move at all."

"Oh, dear," he sighed. "That's what we tell all the women in that ward so they don't move around. They never listen, anyway."

"Well, if you gave them credit for a little more intelligence, maybe you'd have better luck," I retorted, furious.

That afternoon I had a long conversation with the doctor in charge of the ward.

"Please, do me the favor of treating me like a human being," I said. "I'm not stupid. I went to school. I know my body. I don't need you to simplify things. The way you treat women here is an insult."

The news of my protest spread from bed to bed. As soon as the doctor and the nurses left, everyone began talking at once, in loud, angry voices. I was right, they said. What they were doing was offensive. All the women complained that they treated us like spoiled girls, that the doctors refused to explain our own medical problems to us, as if we were too stupid to understand.

During the one-hour visiting period the hospital allowed, Sergio stared at me, incredulous, as I described the incompetence of the staff. He didn't believe me. He thought I was exaggerating, acting like a finicky, bourgeois woman. He managed to make me feel guilty, spoiled. He insisted that the doctors were good, that they were doing the right thing. The other women accepted them, why couldn't I do the same? I resented the way he dismissed my claims, my desire for more humane medical attention. I didn't just want it for myself. I wanted it for all women, I said.

Sergio's attitude was typical of the left. He believed that the true revolutionary should endure the same injustices the masses had to cope with. It was a quasi-religious morality that I didn't share. For me, the Revolution sought to end mistreatment, not to democratize it.

I never had a chance to start the upheaval I wanted to organize. Ten days after I was admitted, I went into labor. The antibiotics hadn't stopped the infection from spreading, and I was trembling and feverish by the time they wheeled me out on the stretcher. The women said goodbye. I still remember them so clearly. Long-suffering, stoic women, raising their hands, calling out their farewells.

In the company of a midwife who was more like a drill sergeant, I spent that night in labor, listening to the moans and wails of other women, conscious that since I was in a public hospital, under normal circumstances I wouldn't have the benefit of anesthesia. A doctor arrived at seven in the morning. He examined me.

"I detect fetal distress. We have to perform a C-section immediately," he said.

I had a high fever and was feeling quite ill. Suddenly, the long, lonely, and frightening night gave way to a frenzy of activity swirling all around me. The orderlies soon appeared, and they ran down the hallway pushing the gurney toward the operating room.

I was soon under the neon lamp. A doctor peered down at me, with the face of an airplane pilot—middle-aged, tanned, bright blue eyes. I closed my eyes as I struggled to raise my knees to my forehead so they could administer an epidural. I recognized the sensation, the needle between my vertebrae, the three movements: inside, higher, higher still. "Good job," I said to the anesthesiologist, feeling like an old pro. A light green curtain covered me from the chest down, my body divided in two like in a magic show, Houdini making my bottom half disappear. An unusually friendly and sweet nurse sat by my side, speaking to me in a hushed, calm voice. My only concern was to get to the end of that long ordeal. If I had to die, so be it, I just wanted it to be over. I was so exhausted and feverish. Somewhere far away I could hear the doctors. They were saying that the infection was serious, that it had spread. I felt the emptiness in my womb when they finally pulled the baby out, I felt the bond break. There was a long silence, no sound from the baby. Nothing. Just silence.

"He's dead," said the doctor. "At least we saved the mother." He said it to the others in an anatomy-lesson tone of voice, as if I wasn't there at all.

"He's dead?" I asked the nurse. "Was it a boy or a girl?"

"I'm sorry," she said, squeezing my hand. "But it was so small. There was no way it could survive."

"But what was it?" I insisted. "Boy or girl?"

"A little boy." She looked at me pityingly. "But he was so small. Do you have other children?"

"Two daughters," I responded.

"I'm so sorry," she said, squeezing my hand once again.

It doesn't matter, I thought, there will be others. Tears spilled down my cheeks, and the nurse dried them, looking at me sadly. I thought about how nice it would have been to have a boy; I had had a feeling it was a boy.

Suddenly there was a commotion on the other side of the curtain. The nurse stood up. A voice loudly exclaimed, "He's alive, he's alive!" as one of the surgical assistants ran with the little package in his arms.

The woman at my side smiled. The doctor, whose hands I had felt a moment before inside my belly as if I were a rag doll filled with straw, began to suture the incision. I prayed that my son would survive.

In the intensive care unit, writhing in excruciating pain, the likes of which I pray to God I will never feel again, I asked my private doctor, who had come to check on me, about my son. He looked at me, clearly upset. Hadn't I been told? He was so sorry, but my son hadn't made it. By my side, Ana Quiroz, my Florence Nightingale in that moment of agony, ran her hand across my head.

"No. No," I said, clenching my teeth, summoning all my strength to talk. "That's what they initially thought, but then they said he was alive."

"No, Gioconda. He is not alive. He didn't survive," the doctor said. "I'm so sorry."

My grief and disappointment made me hurt even more. I didn't even want to see Sergio when they moved me into a two-bed isolation room. Next to me was a woman whose baby had also died. I remember she tried to console me, in a tender, resigned tone.

It must have been around four in the afternoon when a nurse stood at the door and said cheerfully: "I just saw your baby! If you could only see how active he is."

I was appalled this was happening. It was a nightmare. Alive, dead, what? I begged the nurse to please stop saying that my baby was alive, don't be cruel, I implored. Enough is enough.

"My baby is dead," I said, lashing at her.

"But I'm telling you, I saw him," she said. "De Castro–Belli is your son, right? He's in critical condition. But he's alive."

I told her to summon the head nurse. This had to stop. Immediately. She appeared, her white nurse's bonnet had a black band across it.

"Your son is alive," she explained. "But he's in critical condition, so don't get your hopes up. The next twenty-four hours will be decisive. But for now he's alive."

"You have to let my husband know," I said.

"It was a mistake. I'm sorry. We'll tell him."

On my bed, I sat still, silent. I didn't know what to do. I didn't know what to say to the other woman in the room. Maybe her son was alive too. We lay there in silence. She began to cry softly. So did I. We both wept for a long, long time. We could hear each other, sobbing. Time passed and then I heard her voice, thin, still choked, asking me not to cry anymore. Now that my son was alive, I had to keep my strength, she said. I had to be strong for him. I closed my eyes. Women, my God, how resilient we are! What incredible, goddamned resilience we possess!

Three days later my fever began to rise. Neither the doctors nor the nurses would answer my questions. It was normal, they said. But I felt sicker every day. I asked my mother, who had come from Nicaragua to be with me, to get me out of there. I didn't care what Sergio said, I told her. I was going to die if I stayed in that hospital. The negotiations to get me out were endless. God only knows how many papers I had to sign, releasing the hospital from all responsibility. Sergio was against it, and apologized over and over again to the doctors. He glared at me reproachfully, but I couldn't have cared less. I wasn't going to spend one more day there. I wanted my doctor. I knew something was wrong. Very wrong. My mother and my parents-in-law, Valdecir and Celeste, moved me to a private clinic. The trip there, in Valdecir's station wagon, was excruciating, the IV bag swinging from one of the hooks above the car door. I lay on the back seat, and every time the car halted I thought I would die.

My doctor quickly assessed the situation. The infection was serious. Extremely serious. The following week they had to operate on me again. I was in the clinic for almost a month, hanging by a thread between life and death. Sergio was still angry at me. Visiting me only a few times, grudgingly.

After that month, I was finally able to see my son, in the nursery for premature babies. I saw him through the glass wall. A fragile, transparent baby, with a lovely mat of red hair on his head. "He's a survivor," my mother remarked. "He's destined for great things." He was beautiful, my baby boy. Strong. Absolutely determined to live. I gave silent thanks to Camilo and Arnoldo, convinced that their aid, their invisible energy, their young lives summoned in my hour of need, were the mysterious reason behind my tiny son's will to live.

"It's a miracle he's alive," said the ward's head nurse. "Here we all call him the Little Miracle. What will you call him?"

"Camilo Arnoldo," I replied. "After two friends I loved very, very much."

CHAPTER TWENTY-NINE

Of how the war spread throughout Nicaragua, and of the many dangers that came into my life when Modesto arrived

SAN JOSÉ, 1978

THE SITUATION IN NICARAGUA was growing more explosive every day. On August 22, a Sandinista—a Tercerista—commando unit broke into the National Palace during a session of Congress, and took all the representatives hostage until the Somoza regime agreed to free the hundreds of political prisoners that had been in jail since December of 1974. That was how Jacobo and Martín obtained their freedom. The commando team was very young. Number two, Dora María Tellez, in charge of negotiating with Somoza—a different Dora from the one I mentioned before—was twenty-two years old. She was a delicate, small woman, a medical student, who proved herself to be one of the fiercest guerrillas during the final offensive. She eventually led the troops that took control of the first city liberated in Nicaragua in 1979. Her military staff were all women.

On September 9, shortly after the assault on the palace, amid the silence of another general strike, a series of insurrectional uprisings was launched in several major Nicaraguan cities. Suddenly abandoning their fear—and caution—the people went head-to-head with the dictatorship's tanks and artillery, attacking with Molotov cocktails, homemade bombs, revolvers, and hunting rifles. Those who didn't fight distributed coffee and food to those in the trenches. People everywhere pried paving stones from the streets and built barricades in their neighborhoods. Their faces covered with bandannas, young boys laid ambushes that caused numerous casualties in the dictator's army. It was a people's war, with poorly armed civilians fighting against a highly trained army that had been generously outfitted with brand-new weapons, tanks, and planes, courtesy of the United States and Israel. Somoza and his son, who at twenty-something was the commander of the dictator's special forces, led the counterattack. Five-hundred-pound bombs, white phosphorus, and napalm were dropped, on their orders, onto the rebel cities. Then they laid siege with tanks and artillery fire until they successfully crushed the uprising in what amounted to a brutal massacre. But by now, the cruelty of the dictatorship couldn't stop the constant uprisings. Somoza knew he would have to destroy the country in order to stay in power. Businessmen, political parties, and the people of Nicaragua were all on the same side now. Popular organizations banded together to form the Movimiento Pueblo Unido, the United People's Movement. Everyone else joined the wave in the Frente Patriótico Nacional, the National Patriotic Front. Repudiation of the Somoza regime also spread internationally. Inside the United States, the pressure was mounting on Jimmy Carter's government to stop supporting Somoza, to suspend military aid, and to condemn the Nicaraguan government for its repeated human rights violations.

By September, I was feeling much better physically. After two months in an incubator, Camilo was released from the hospital. When we brought him home, he weighed little more than five pounds, a miniature, fragile baby. I left my job at Garnier to take care of him. I think that I have imbued in my children, from a very young age, a sense of confidence in their own abilities. That is the only way I can explain how they have all managed to survive the turbulent circumstances of their childhood without irreparable trauma. I was an optimist, always believing they would adjust to the world around them and appreciate it in their own way. I tried to be sincere, to never underestimate their intelligence, to trust that one day they would have the wisdom to understand the complicated circumstances of our lives. I firmly believed they would develop the ability to be happy and that they wouldn't think their happiness depended solely on me. Otherwise, I would have never considered motherhood compatible with the kind of life I led. Just like my girls, Camilo was a gentle, happy baby. He recovered in no time, growing healthy and strong.

———

Modesto returned from Cuba with good news regarding the preliminary agreement among the three Sandinista tendencies. I remember the meeting, in a small room with a low ceiling, in a house I'd never been in before. It was Modesto, Dora, Paco, and I. That was the day I first met Paco— older than the rest of us, blue eyes, good-natured, uncomplicated.

Modesto spoke softly but one could hear the passion in his voice. Looking at him made me feel close to the Nicaraguan jungles somehow. I think he still smelled of trees. He told us about the meeting, his impressions of the other Sandinista leaders, what he expected from them, the possible obstacles that could get in the way. Modesto looked at me—all of me, not just my eyes. His gaze, like a stream, flowed over me, over my denim overalls, over my thick mane, my shoulders, the curve of my neck. As if his eyes could touch me. I wanted to concentrate on what he was saying, but shivers were running through my body, as if my flesh could perceive some undisclosed danger. My stomach felt warm and was starting to get upset, the blood rushing to my belly. I began to feel as if a sleeping woman hidden somewhere in my gut was about to wake up. I couldn't identify the feeling but its intensity was enough to tell me that whatever it was, flowing between us, invisible and magnetic, was threatening and full of risks for me. Good lord! And I was still so weak, still convalescing, still trying to make sense of the void Sergio's behavior in the hospital had left inside of me. Even at the clinic, later on, it had been my mother, not he, who had been at my side while I struggled to find my way out of an endless labyrinth of pain. And now, this man's gaze, like thick honey, was oozing through the cracks opened by my distress.

I dashed home looking for cover in the safety of the nursery, among clean diapers, the smell of talcum powder, and children's storybooks. At the time I was also conducting a poetry workshop in my daughters' school. Beneath one of the great trees in the schoolyard, we would sit in a circle, playing word games, writing group poems transforming ourselves into rain, air, and metaphor. Maryam and Melissa were so proud and happy that their mother was the teacher, and it was a chance for me to be near them. But on the day of the meeting with Modesto, I felt a dark fear that all my efforts to create a normal family environment would come apart if I didn't suppress that migratory reflex stirring inside me.

From the minute he arrived, the work took on a frantic pace. The rebellion in Nicaragua advanced like a hurricane that builds spirals of clouds and wind far out at sea before hitting land with colossal force. For that reason, the pressure on the rearguard support network had increased tenfold. A large group of the Sandinistas liberated in August by the commando operation in the National Palace had come to San José—Paco was among them—and our team had grown enough to make full use of the clandestine network we had hurriedly assembled. The first, difficult months with the GPP quickly slipped from my mind, and I now felt in complete harmony with my new *compañeros*. From the beginning, Modesto entrusted me with a number of crucial tasks. I was the GPP's public relations person in Costa Rica. I dealt with political parties, international organizations, NGOs (nongovernmental organizations), and directed our work with the solidarity network and individual supporters. I was also constantly giving interviews to European and American journalists who arrived in droves in San José. Paco, Dora, and Alfredo, instead, looked after the clandestine operations to gather and send supplies to the combatants in Nicaragua.

I saw Modesto practically every day, there were always issues to be discussed, meetings to drive him to. Securing funds to buy arms and ammunition on the black market was one of our network's most important tasks. Paco would then oversee the smuggling of the weapons into Nicaragua, either in vehicles with false bottoms or with the collaboration of truckers who delivered goods throughout Central America. But Modesto felt I was the best person to deliver money, messages, and sensitive documents between Costa Rica, Honduras, and Panama, because he thought my upper-class looks would protect me from the usual scrutiny at airports. So, besides doing everything else I did, I began to go on missions transporting secret documents, forged passports, guerrilla correspondence. I usually carried these things hidden in my luggage. There was an elaborate technique, which we called "stuffing," to disguise these documents. I suppose some of these tricks were similar to those used to smuggle drugs in and out of countries. I would carry toys, for example, with tiny cassettes hidden inside, containing instructions for the guerrillas in Nicaragua or information to be read by the various Sandinista leaders abroad. The memos, handwritten in minuscule calligraphy, were rolled up in tubes and placed inside the legs of dolls or in stuffed animals that we would rip open and then resew. Sometimes, particularly when I traveled to Honduras, I carried a double-bottomed briefcase which contained forged passports that were used by guerrillas to reenter Nicaragua under cover.

I remember the time when I was given a large doll with rolls of letters stuffed in her legs. Only when I arrived at the security checkpoint in the airport did I realize that if I laid it on the conveyer belt and it went through the X-ray machine, the airport officials would see the tubes and think I was carrying drugs. Lightning-fast, I grabbed the doll and hugged it against me as I walked through the metal detector, without a problem. I became an expert at smiling in airports, at dressing just the right way so as not to raise any suspicion. These courier jobs often made me feel as if I were inside a spy movie. At times, I would be instructed just to wait at the gate of the flight I was going to take. I would open a magazine, start reading, and suddenly someone would appear by my side—generally someone I might have seen before but who showed up wearing on his shirt the plastic ID tags worn by airport personnel. The person would exchange a few words with me, leave a briefcase at my feet, and depart. Then I would get on the flight and deliver the briefcase to whoever came to get me at my destination. It never even crossed my mind to be afraid that I might be carrying a bomb, or to fear that my comrades in arms would spend my life like that. We, Sandinistas, were a national liberation movement, not terrorists. We were always against those methods that make innocent people pay for things that are not their responsibility. The FSLN never bombed civilian targets, cars, or airplanes, and in the two hostage-taking operations that we did, the hostages were always Somoza's cronies. The most dangerous moment of my courier missions was going through customs. Although I may have appeared calm and collected, my stomach was racked with much more than butterflies—a swarm of raging insects devoured my insides whenever I would step off a plane, and wouldn't abate until I finally emerged from the airport with my luggage.

Only once did I get into trouble. One day, Paco appeared at my house with a giant package wrapped in kraft paper. He put it on the table and told me he was sorry, but the money I was to deliver the following day had been issued in small bills. I looked at the package, which contained at least a hundred thousand dollars. Impossible, I thought. Where would I hide it all? It was almost five in the afternoon, we didn't have a double-bottomed suitcase, and the flight to Panama was scheduled for seven in the morning. I sat at the round dining-room table in the small house Sergio and I had moved to after our previous home was robbed, shortly after Camilo was born. Paco stood there watching me, waiting for me to emerge from the trance I had suddenly fallen into. He looked at me remorsefully. He knew the risks as well as I did. Finally, an idea flashed in my mind. I hurried out of the house with Sergio and went to buy a new dress, a big box, a huge bow, and wrapping paper with the classic wedding bells motif. Back at home, I packed each wad in white tissue paper, and carefully arranged them in the box, which I then gift-wrapped neatly, and tied with the large silver bow.

The next day I boarded the airplane all dressed up, as if I was going from the airport in Panama straight to the wedding reception. I had washed and blow-dried my hair, made myself up, and I looked all dolled up for the party. I talked to everyone within earshot about how excited I was to be going to my best friend's wedding. And nobody found anything odd about the gift I carried in my arms—a gift I never let out of my sight.

All my confidence evaporated when I arrived in Panama. An immigration official asked all the Nicaraguans to form a separate line. My eyes darted about in every direction as I tried to think of a plan, imagining the scene if they opened the gift, and fearing I could be held in jail. Lucky for me, however, I suddenly spotted a man walking down the hallway, an adviser of Panamanian leader General Torrijos, whom I knew because he was a Sandinista sympathizer. I stepped out of the line and walked over to say hello, smiling as if he were an old friend.

"Hello! How wonderful to see you!" I greeted him.

As I leaned forward to kiss him on the cheek, I whispered urgently in his ear: "I need you to get me out of here without passing through customs, please. I'm carrying money."

He looked at me—surprised at first, but he made a quick recovery. It wasn't too hard for him to guess what this was about.

"How much is in there?" he asked.

"Ten thousand dollars," I said, not missing a beat.

He took me by the arm. I don't know what he said to the immigration officer, but he stamped my passport without a glance. Then, arm in arm with my convenient friend, I walked through like a regular VIP.

When we got outside, I thanked him profusely.

"Be more careful next time," he chided me, winking. "You were fortunate to find me. Those guys in there wouldn't have let you go so easily."

I gave Modesto the money when I arrived at the safe house, in the outskirts of the city, where he was staying. His host was an engineer who lived there alone. The house was spacious and there was something forlorn, empty about it, as if its occupant had never finished settling in. There were boxes piled up in some of the rooms, and the furniture was simple and officelike. Sitting in a leather chair, Modesto watched me, amused, as I paced up and down, reviewing the incident, pondering on my good fortune. I was excited at having accomplished my mission and

happy to be there with him. Lighthearted, I sat on the couch and took
off my high heels; the skirt of my new dress, which was billowy, ankle-
length, and with a flower print, settled around me like a fan. At some
point, unexpectedly, Modesto got up and came toward me moving swiftly,
like a feline, to prey on my lips and plant a kiss on my mouth. I put my
hands on his chest as if to push him back but it was useless. That moment
had been building since the day at the meeting. So we kissed, gasping
with so much want as we had been painfully holding up. But when he
tried to go after my shirt, my skirt, I stopped his hands. I buried my head
on his chest, hushing him, telling him it would be better if we tried to
stay put. Let's not go any further, I said. You better talk to me, talk to me
about what you've been doing.

My heart was beating fast and hard, and a fire from hell was burning
my cheeks. He proceeded to stroke my hair for a long, long while.

When I was a teenager, my father used to joke about how easily I fell in
love. Because of my romantic nature and my desire to find the "perfect
man," I was easily swept off my feet, seduced by the intensity of unbridled passions. It was a perilous trait to have in an atmosphere of death
and danger, where regular codes of conduct didn't seem to apply, and I
paid a price.

On the trips I took as a courier—usually when I went to Honduras
and Panama—it was Modesto who would send or receive the packages I
delivered. He would put me up for one or two days, wherever he was staying, usually in the homes of Sandinista supporters. Though we slept in
separate bedrooms, we spent a lot of time together. Looking back, I think
what seduced me most about him was the faith he had in me. Sergio was
always criticizing what I did, while Modesto praised me and made me feel
valued. I could never move Sergio from the subject of politics. Modesto,
on the other hand, talked to me about opera, which he had learned to love
in Russia, of literature, physics, and mathematics, and gave me glimpses
of his personal history, of when he was a boy selling tortillas or newspapers in the streets of Jinotepe, his birthplace. And of his mother, who
worked ironing clothes by the load, to provide for their family, and of his
father, who was mostly away, disappearing for months at a time as he
traveled the world working on merchant ships. Modesto also told me
about his long years with the guerrillas: how he spent some time with just
two bullets in his rifle, how he shot a jaguar once and saved its tooth as a

memento. Or he would talk about the eternal hunger of the guerrillas, and their despair whenever letters arrived from the city in which their wives bemoaned their loneliness, or confessed that they had fallen in love with someone else. I would listen to him, captivated.

That man was getting under my skin and I just didn't know how to flee. In my mind, Sergio's flaws began to overshadow his strengths. It was as if the beams which held up our marriage were suddenly termite-ridden, crumbling slowly, inexorably. Sergio sensed the threat and ironically, as seems to be the case when one is facing loss, he began smothering me with criticisms and recriminations. In struggling to keep me, he widened the rift between us.

CHAPTER THIRTY

Of clandestine flights and a bizarre meeting
with Panamanian General Omar Torrijos

COSTA RICA–PANAMA, 1978

I DIDN'T ALWAYS take commercial flights when I traveled from Costa Rica to Panama, sometimes I flew on *Antoine,* a single-propeller Cessna piloted by Chuchú Martínez. Chuchú was straight out of a novel, a man of fervent political and literary passions—poet, mathematician, philosopher, and staunch defender of heroic causes, for which he was willing to risk almost anything. Chuchú would take off from Panama, and after successfully dodging air traffic control, he would land the plane at abandoned airstrips in Costa Rica, to pick up and drop off clandestine guerrilla passengers. That was how Modesto traveled and so did I on several occasions.

The first time I laid eyes on the landing strip where Chuchú was to pick me up, I thought it was a mistake. The strip was near Quepos, on the Costa Rican Pacific coast. I traveled four hours by jeep to get there from San José with Chepito, who worked in Paco's unit. Eventually we came to a dirt road between African palm plantations and open fields. I didn't see any landing strip, but Chepito stopped the jeep and announced that we had arrived.

"But this is a pasture," I exclaimed, looking out at the waist-high grasses beyond the fence where a rough-hewn wooden sign bore the words "Managua Airstrip."

"Let's get out, you'll see," Chepito said.

I laughed at the irony of the sign while we braved the shoulder-high grass of the field like hunters entering a jungle. It was hot as hell but, sure enough, if you used your imagination you could make out a landing strip, a thin band of well-trodden earth in the middle of this pasture where, at the moment, several cows were idly grazing.

"Help me get rid of these cows," said Chepito, dead serious. "This is the most dangerous thing about this place. The cows. We better hurry, it won't be long before Chuchú gets here."

I'm always amazed when I remember how daring I used to be then— especially since I'm so scared of flying now and agonize through each takeoff and landing, imagining every possible thing that can go wrong.

"Post-traumatic stress syndrome," declared the psycho-pharmacologist my therapist sent me to when, after moving to the United States, I found myself seized by uncontrollable fears that, among other things, turned flying into a veritable nightmare for me. The doctor had to be right, because that day on the Managua airstrip, I remember laughing out loud at the Chaplinesque scene: Chepito and I running through the pasture, slapping the cows' behinds with wooden sticks to get them to move. Already we could hear Chuchú's plane rumbling in the distance.

"You see? I'm a better poet than you," Chuchú said, hugging me. This was the way he liked to greet me. He was a dark-skinned man with gray hair who seldom smiled but whose voice and ironic turn of phrase seemed filled with laughter. He was always affectionately baiting me to compete with him as a poet.

"We should take off now," he said. The cows had wandered away. I said goodbye to Chepito and climbed into the plane.

Antoine moved like a paper airplane at the mercy of every gust of wind. The propeller's throbbing was overwhelming and we had to shout in order to hear each other. Chuchú said that wind was the plane's element. He adored Antoine de Saint-Exupéry, and thought that by flying, perhaps he too would write an immortal tale like *The Little Prince*. I will never forget that old, rusty Cessna with its well-worn seats, or Chuchú talking to me about his great friend Graham Greene, who spent long stretches of time in Panama as the guest of General Torrijos.

The flight was uneventful until we began our descent toward the airstrip where I was to get out. The North American controller in the Canal Zone came on the radio, asking Chuchú for explanations, in a none-too-friendly tone. What was he doing outside the flight path? Where was he going? Why was he initiating his descent? "Do you copy? Do you copy?" he insisted.

"I'm barely going to touch down," Chuchú shouted to me. "I have to get out of here, if not I'm in trouble. You're going to have to jump out."

That was what I did. Literally. The wheels barely brushed the ground when I opened the door and jumped. I was wearing shoes with heels, one of which broke off when I hit the ground. Chuchú managed to toss me my overnight bag, and took off. Only when I got up and brushed myself off did I realize that I hadn't the slightest idea where in Panama I had landed. The area surrounding the airstrip was completely barren. It was situated on a plateau at the bottom of a dry ravine of red earth, with no vegetation other than a few squat, prickly bushes. Looking south, I spotted a dirt path, and off in the distance, rising up in the east, I could see the silhouette of some buildings. Supposedly someone would be arriving to pick me up, but there was no one in sight. All I could do was wait. I walked over to some rocks, dragging the shoe with the missing heel, and sat down. In no time I was sweating in the humid, stifling Panamanian heat. I wouldn't have been particularly bothered by the wait if, an hour later, two threatening-looking characters hadn't appeared in the distance, advancing toward me. The only thing I had to defend myself with was a Swiss army knife that Modesto had given me. I hid behind the rocks, feeling like a cornered animal. Who knows what would have happened if a little airplane hadn't swooped down out of the clear blue sky, circling above the landing strip. I ran to the clearing, waving gaily to the pilot as if I knew him and had come to watch him practice. But the two men were coming closer now, leering at me with clearly sinister intentions. The taller one smiled diabolically. I knew I had to get out of there, find the road, start walking. It was too risky to stay where I was.

Hobbling and overheated, I reached the main road. After only a few minutes' walk, I finally caught sight of a car with the *compañero* assigned to pick me up.

But that wasn't the only surprise in store for me on that trip.

From September 28 to October 1, 1978, the Continental Congress for Nicaraguan Solidarity was held in Panama, endorsed by General Torrijos, Carlos Andrés Pérez (Venezuela's president), and other major Latin

American politicians who supported the Sandinistas. The halls of the University of Panama, where the congress was being held, were filled with enthusiastic sympathizers. It was their chance to catch a glimpse of some of the Sandinista guerrillas who had taken the National Palace in August. Torrijos had granted them political asylum, and so they were the heroes of the moment in Panama City. I attended the conference as a representative of the GPP. There were still divisions within the movement, but by that point they were more symbolic than practical. In those days we moved as a group: Dora María Tellez, Javier Carrión, Edgard Lang (who was later assassinated), and his wife, Marisol Castillo. Marisol was the daughter of Chema Castillo, whose house had been the site of the December 1974 operation in which he also perished. Like many other young people whose parents were supporters of Somoza, Marisol forged her own path and joined the Sandinistas. I could only imagine her inner struggle.

Modesto thought that during the conference I would have a good chance of getting to speak personally with General Torrijos. If so, he told me, I was to request passports for some *compañeros*, financial support, and an appointment for the two of them to talk without intermediaries.

Chuchú knew Torrijos well. Almost in jest, the general made him a sergeant in the Panamanian army. Chuchú was Torrijos's sometimes go-between with figures like Graham Greene, and he also occasionally represented the general's interests in clandestine talks with Latin American guerrilla movements. Torrijos had begun to suspect the possibility of future problems with the United States regarding the fulfillment of the Torrijos-Carter Panama Canal treaties, and that was the reason he wanted to cultivate the support of the region's guerrilla armies. But to make those contacts he had to operate in total secrecy. And Chuchú was his trusted operative for those missions. Back then, I never had any idea as to what Chuchú was really up to. All I knew was that he helped us, that Modesto regarded him very highly, and that he was the person through whom I might approach Torrijos.

I was sitting in the spacious hall of the University of Panama, listening to the speeches of various political figures at the conference, when Chuchú appeared at the door and called me over.

"Come over here. The general wants to meet with a group from the conference. We're going to his house," he said, direct as always.

I followed him out to a minibus where a few other people were waiting: my friend the Mexican poet Efraín Huerta and his wife, Thelma

Nava; Rodolfo Puiggross, an old exile and former leader of the Montoneros guerrillas in Argentina; and Jorge Turner, a Panamanian intellectual.

I don't really remember the exterior of Torrijos's house, more of a compound surrounded by a wall crowned with barbed wire. Inside, we walked into a large, one-story house with wide spaces sectioned off by mirrors and folding screens, a strange mix of bedroom, office, living room, and library. I remember seeing a blond woman with heavy makeup and tight pants walk back and forth with clothing in her arms, as if packing for a trip, as men in military uniforms looked at her.

Torrijos was a celebrated figure in Latin America. His nationalist politics had elevated Panama out of a kind of semicolonial interregnum, establishing it squarely on the Latin American map as a country to be reckoned with. He was a striking, charismatic man. His dark face was lit up by honey-green eyes. We entered a room and sat down next to a big picture window. At first, conversation was a little strained. Meeting a head of state is like being an actor without a script, on a set with a strange director whose instructions you have to guess at. Luckily, there is usually some professional around, someone who can improvise on behalf of those who are less self-possessed. In this case that person was eighty-year-old Puiggross, whose commanding age, countless dangerous exploits, added to the fact that he was Argentinean, made him a great raconteur. Torrijos was spellbound by his erudition and charm. Chuchú hovered nearby, whispering to other military officials. Drinks were served. The conversation flowed more easily now. At one point, as Torrijos led us into another room to show us his medals, I edged over to him and said I needed to talk to him, to give him a message from Modesto.

"Of course," he said, looking me up and down.

I didn't think our visit would last more than an hour, but it went on thanks to Puiggross's wit and endless political commentary. Torrijos talked about the Panama Canal treaties and their ramifications for Panama and the entire region. Sitting back in his easy chair, he smoked a Cuban cigar and laughed heartily at his guests' jokes and snappy comments. The sun went down. More cocktails were served. Suddenly the general stood up, and announced that he would be taking us to Farallones, his house on the beach. We would all have dinner there, he said. It was an order.

His aides began moving around in a frenzy of activity. A little while later, they announced that everything was arranged for the trip, and we left the house, once again climbing into the minibus. That was when I found out that we would be flying in the general's private jet. In the days of Torrijos, Farallones was part of the general's legend, his Camp David. The jet was small and comfortable—the same one, I assume, in which he died several years later while flying to another one of his hideaways, Coclecito. The general made jokes, pointing to a petite but well-proportioned young woman who acted as the plane's stewardess.

"She was made to size for the plane," he said, laughing mischievously. "She can walk down the aisle without having to hunch over like we do."

We were his guests, so we laughed along with him. Then, the blond woman we had seen packing clothes earlier entered the plane and went to sit in the back, separate from the rest of us. I realized that we were supposed to pretend she was invisible. Evidently, she was the girlfriend of the moment. Later on in life, I would eventually spend enough time in the proximity of power—generals, presidents, *comandantes*—to understand that their entourages often include elements that are hidden in plain view, things that happen before everyone's eyes, but which everyone pretends not to see. One goes on talking, laughing, behaving politely, no matter how uncomfortable the situation may be.

Of the house in Farallones, I remember the enormous covered terrace with its lustrous stone floor, brick column pillars, and a low wall beyond which the ocean roared. A light breeze carried the scent of brine. We sat down in rocking chairs set in a circle, to continue our conversation, but we couldn't quite re-create the previous ambiance. Maybe it was the place. Maybe it was the girls. More of them appeared. All very attractive, flitting about the general, leaning down to whisper secrets in his ear with a familiarity that was slightly disconcerting. You couldn't tell whether they were kissing his neck or his ears as he stroked their hair, drawing them closer. This must be his harem, I thought. The woman who had traveled with us on the plane was probably his favorite. For that night, at least. It didn't escape any of us that the comings and goings of these lovelies was part of a larger sexual game. But what was the game, exactly? An unspoken competition for the general's affections? It was hard to tell, but as a woman it bothered me. People thought of Torrijos as a man of the people, and the Panamanians adored him. I could picture the magnetism he exuded as he walked through the crowds. Beyond his imposing presence and his *caudillo* airs, he was a courageous nationalist, and committed to Latin American autonomy. Yet on a personal level, his brusque, imperious manner disturbed me. Chuchú told me that Torrijos had been all set to blow up the Panama Canal if Carter refused to sign the accords restoring Panama's sovereignty. The explosives had even been put in place. All the general had to do was issue the order. "He was going to do it, I'm telling you. We were completely ready for it. The tension was unbearable during those few days." I still don't know if what he said was really true, but back then I believed him, and I was awed by the notion that Torrijos would be willing to carry out such a self-destructive act, the ultimate act of rebellion, mad but courageous.

In Latin America, especially during those years, opposing Washington's politics was a matter of principle. We felt that we could never achieve dignity, or progress, as long as the United States insisted on imposing its will on us. We were a generation born and raised beneath the despicable dictatorships that Washington so unscrupulously supported: Papa Doc, Stroessner, Batista, Somoza, Ubico, the Brazilian military. The United States was the oversized bully of the neighborhood. One dreamed of defying its power, even if only for a moment, even at the risk of getting beaten up. The moment of defiance, the affirmation of our own independence, was incentive enough to risk the injuries.

It was about ten at night. I went to the bathroom and when I returned, the guests were all saying goodbye. I was disappointed that I hadn't had the chance to deliver Modesto's message to the general. Another time, I thought. I was tired, and anxious to leave.

Torrijos then caught my eye. He raised his voice: "You stay," he said. It was an order.

When all the others had gone, the general eased himself into a hammock with a glass of whiskey in one hand, and signaled for me to sit down in the rocking chair next to him. I did so, agreeably, as I mentally prepared the words that would begin our political dialogue, trying to anticipate the questions he would ask me. I was happy to finally have a chance at a long, private conversation with the general.

"I have a message from Modesto, General," I started, slightly inhibited at this unexpected opportunity.

The general lifted his gaze from the hammock. He looked at me. With his hand, he indicated that the matter could wait. He was dressed from head to toe in khaki. He had taken off his shoes, revealing his white socks.

At Chuchú's suggestion, I had sent him a copy of my book of poems a few days earlier, the one that had been awarded the Casa de las Américas prize. He asked one of his girls to bring it to him.

"I want you to read a poem that you wrote, one I liked very much," he said.

My heart still hadn't picked up on the danger. Each time I think back to the scenario, I am shocked at my innocence. What world did I think I was living in? I ask myself now. But at the time it never occurred to me that he could want yet another woman to add to his sultan's seraglio. I assumed the blonde who had come in the plane was on deck waiting for the night shift. So, naively, I was flattered that the general had read my book and wanted me to read a poem. Maybe he just wanted to rest. We could talk afterward. He opened the book and selected a poem.

"This poem could be a guerrilla anthem," he said. "Read it. Go on."

I read it.

"What a good poet you are, goddamn it! I want you to write a poem for one of my daughters," he said.

"But, I can't just write a poem on the spot," I stammered. "I've never sat down purposely to write a poem. They just come to me."

"I'm sure something will come to you if I tell you about her," he said.

Now I was really uncomfortable. It was hot in Farallones. The wind had died down. Stopped altogether. I tried another tack but he insisted. I wondered if he was drunk. I couldn't believe he was in his right mind, making such a ridiculous request. But the General stubbornly pressed on. He wasn't going to take no for an answer. I saw his eyes light up with that steely military determination, flinty and imperative. He called one of the girls over again.

"Bring her paper," he ordered.

It was useless to protest. This capriciousness demanded a sense of humor. "All right," I said. "You win. I'll do what I can."

He sent me to a table at the far end of the terrace. Having some space to myself made me feel better. The General remained in his hammock. The girls were still hovering around him. Every so often one of them would sit in his lap. It was late. I wanted to leave. I was tired and incredibly annoyed. How could I convince someone accustomed to snapping his fingers and getting whatever he wanted to leave me be? What would become of my political mission if he got angry with me? To what extent did I have to play his game? I wrote a few lines. I turned the absurd request into a little juggling act; writing verses about someone I didn't know wasn't such a big deal. I finished the poem, and approached him to read it. He smiled, satisfied. He showed it to one of the girls, who went off after a little while, leaving us alone. I made another attempt at conversation, telling him that I had a few concrete requests to make.

"I'd love to have a child with you," he said, peering at me from his hammock.

I laughed. I couldn't help it. Why was I laughing? he asked, serious. Any child of ours would be beautiful. Fierce, but sensitive.

"You don't know the solitude of power," he said. "You never know what to expect of all the people that surround you. But you're different," he said, and then fell silent, pensive.

"Well, I'm not available," I said. "I'm sorry."

From that moment on, all attempts to disguise his designs on me evaporated. He assaulted me with an avalanche of promises and flattery: that he would make me happy, take me with him everywhere, reveal all the secrets of Panama to me, the San Blas Islands, Coclecito. I didn't know what Torrijos was capable of. For all intents and purposes, I was his prisoner. He could rape me and there was nobody to defend me. He was the absolute sovereign of his domain.

I got up and walked inside the house. I tried to enlist the solidarity of the other women but they just eyed me suspiciously, their rival. I approached the woman who was the General's most frequent attendant and asked her about the plane. I told her that the General had offered to send me back to Panama City that night.

"The plane comes back tomorrow," she said, expressionless.

Finally Torrijos rose from his hammock with the help of one of the girls. He went inside the house. Consumed with rage, I stayed where I was, out on the terrace. I hated the general and his retinue, those women, belittled by the miserable servitude imposed on them by that boorish, primitive, powerful man. Looking out from the terrace, I saw a high wall and a security guard. Would he let me out? Maybe there was a town nearby, somewhere I could make a telephone call.

That was what I was thinking, inventing possible escape routes, when the girl appeared again.

"Come with me," she said. "The General wants to see you."

It was another order. I followed her. I thought that maybe Torrijos had come to his senses. That he would call me into his office to talk. We walked up a set of stairs. She opened a door and practically shoved me inside. I was in Torrijos's bedroom. Dressed in dark orange pajamas, he waited for me at the foot of the bed. He pointed to a tacky negligee spread out on the sheets.

"You can sleep here next to me. I won't touch you if you don't want me to. I promise. You have my word."

"No, thank you, General," I said, and bolted out of the bedroom, slamming the door behind me. I raced down the stairs, gasping for breath.

When I reached the bottom of the stairs, I was furious, and unable to contain myself any longer, I snapped at the girl: "I'm not going to sleep with the General, get it? And please, do me the favor of telling me where I can spend the night. There has to be a bedroom somewhere around here."

She shrugged her shoulders. Then she took a set of keys out of a desk, and told me to follow her. She brought me to an adjacent house and opened the door to a room that smelled of dust and mildew.

I locked the door behind me. I grabbed a desk and shoved it against the door to make sure no one could try to force his way in. I was so agitated and angry I couldn't sleep. I spent the entire night wide awake, cursing myself for being so stupid. Fleetingly I wondered if sleeping with the general was the kind of sacrifice that another woman in my place would have made for her country. But no way was I going to sleep with the General, not even for my country. Just thinking about it made me sick.

The next day when I went out onto the terrace, I found Torrijos in a room with big glass windows, sitting at a long table, eating breakfast with a group of people who seemed to have appeared, like magic, out of nowhere. I felt like a ghost, an invisible being nobody saw. Nobody said a word to me.

I sat on the terrace to look out at the ocean and wait. I was Gregor Samsa, and soon I would turn into a cockroach. I kept thinking of Kafka. It was all so absolutely bizarre. Suddenly I heard Torrijos's voice calling out to me. His expression was totally different. More lucid, but just as impenetrable as before.

"What was it that you wanted to say to me?" he asked.

Without mincing any words, I said my piece about the passports, about the meeting with Modesto. He nodded.

"Are you sure you don't want to stay with me? I'd take you to Coclecito. I'm going there this afternoon. I was just having breakfast with my brothers and sisters. I do that every Sunday."

"I just want you to send me back to the city, please," I said, trying to hide my anxiety. "I need to go back. I have to catch the flight to San José this afternoon."

He snapped his fingers. A soldier appeared. Finally, they took me to the blessed plane.

When I finally made it back to the house where I was staying in Panama City—the home of Mercedes and Will Graham, who always welcomed me with warmth and hospitality—I found Danilo, the head of Sandinista operations in Panama, waiting for me. He had handsome features that seemed sculpted in mahogany. He was strong and affectionate. As I hugged him, I burst into tears. He did his best to calm me down. In a voice choked up with anxiety and relief, I told him what had happened.

"That's an outrage!" he exclaimed. "Torrijos has no excuse for such boorishness! Damn! The things people do . . ."

Months later, Modesto had his meeting with Torrijos, who apologized for the "discomfort" he had put me through. I was surprised that he would even mention it. It was an apology from one leader to another, about the mistreatment of a subordinate, but it was an apology nonetheless. Chuchú assured me that the general was truly ashamed of how he had acted. Once again, I was amazed. It was far more than I expected of him.

That was my first brush with that explosive mix of power and sex that goes right to men's heads. Power gives them a sense of entitlement. They surrender to this heady feeling and, with their chests puffed out, pounce on the tribe and its women. That is how they avenge sad childhood or adolescent memories of rejection by demure schoolgirls on playgrounds. That is how they fight back the fear their mothers inspired in them.

"As a child I was no rebel. My parents would never have guessed that their demure, sweet, proper little girl would turn into the defiant woman who caused them so many sleepless nights."

"Petite and slender, with short, dyed-blond hair, my mother was a refined woman, a great admirer of literature and theater."

"At the Debutantes Ball, I flouted the unwritten dress code of pastels, designing my own gown which included a bold swath of red."

With my father on the Baile Terraza

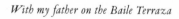

"I was quite pleased with the way I looked—that is, until my mother arranged the cap and veil upon my head, and guided each of my hands inside a long, kidskin glove. At that moment, all of a sudden, a sense of ridicule came over me, I felt I was being packaged up like a gift."

"While traveling through Europe with my father and my sister Lavinia, I learned that I was pregnant with my second daughter."

With Sergio and Camilo in Costa Rica, 1978

With the people of Mongallo during the National Literacy Campaign in 1980. I am second from left, at the school.

Flanked during a reception at the Cuban embassy in Managua, 1982, by the vice president of Nicaragua, Sergio Ramírez, left, and Commander Tomás Borge. Extreme left, in uniform, Commander Carlos Núñez, president of the National Assembly.

With Commander of the Revolution and Minister of Home Affairs Tomás Borge in Paris during a meeting with the press, 1983

With Charlie in Managua, 1988

CHAPTER THIRTY-ONE

Of how the walls of my Jericho came tumbling down

SAN JOSÉ, 1978

ON ONE OF HIS many trips to San José, Modesto was staying in a small, cozy, book-filled apartment that belonged to a professor, a Sandinista sympathizer. When I went to see him he was alone, listening to a tape he had received from René Vivas, who had replaced him as the commander of the columns in the Nicaraguan mountains. René's hushed voice could be heard above the shrill songs of innumerable jungle insects. He was telling of the damage to the radio equipment which, at great cost and difficulty, had been sent to his unit. In an effort to creatively hide the equipment in order to smuggle it into the country, someone came up with the idea of wrapping the components in plastic and placing them in cans of Sherwin-Williams house paint. By the time Modesto found out and realized what would happen, it was already too late. The paint had eaten through the plastic, and when it reached our *compañeros* in the mountains, the equipment, which René referred to as "parrots," was nothing but a useless mess. We couldn't help laughing at René's grim description of the unlucky "parrots" drowned in house paint.

It was a serious setback, because radio communication was critical for the success of Operation Eureka, which Modesto had been planning for months. It involved sending a plane with arms, ammunitions, and fresh combatants to reinforce the guerrilla columns in the mountains. The operation, which he would lead, would provide enough manpower and firearms for the guerrillas to make their way from the northern Atlantic region of the country to the Pacific coast. The plane, a DC-3, the weapons, and combatants were already secured, but the radio equipment was key to having ground forces take over the airport at the appointed time. Modesto finished listening to the tape and shrugged his shoulders. Setbacks were nothing new to him. We would just have to try again.

Above all else, I admired Modesto's tenacity. We shared a similar kind of naïveté. Both of us held on to a fervent belief in the inherent nobleness of the human species. Both perhaps were too quick to grant people the benefit of the doubt, which can sometimes be a fatal flaw in politics. Optimists to a fault, we were never afraid to dream and we had little respect for cynicism. Even after all that has been said and done, I don't think either of us has changed much. Even now, when I see him, he is still busily searching for solutions for our country. I, meanwhile, have chosen to believe the future is filled with possibility simply because believing makes me happier than not believing. History is a long process, and if one can muster the patience to understand it, one can derive satisfaction from the small battles that drive it forward. A cause isn't hopeless just because its objectives aren't reached in one's lifetime.

I couldn't go on living if I didn't believe in the creative powers of the human imagination.

Upon these convictions, upon the many utopias we dreamed and whispered about, a strong bond developed between Modesto and me. Those shared ideals that brought us close also nourished our need and fascination for each other. We grew blind to everything else. I had the most to wager and the most to lose, but I did not see it. After months vacillating between my impulses and my family obligations, I found myself succumbing.

"Come here. I've got something for you," Modesto said, taking my hand and leading me to the apartment upstairs, to the bedroom with pine furniture and a window from which we could see the mist hovering over the distant mountains.

I sat down on the bed while he rummaged through his suitcase. Despite the setback with the radio equipment, he seemed remarkably upbeat. A tendril of straight, black hair fell over his temples. Long gone were the curls and hair color of the disguise he used when I first met him. Finally he produced a slip of paper. He handed it to me.

"This is for you," he said. It was a poem.

To read it while sitting on the bed with his expectant eyes fixed on me made me come apart. All my doors, windows, hinges rattled loose. In the poem, he wrote that the image of me would be as inseparable from him as his carabine, or the maps that guided him in the jungle; he wrote that his love was as true as the certitude of victory. It was a beautiful poem, and it revealed a wealth of tenderness within him. I read it two or three times, not knowing what to say, feeling like I wanted to weep. My eyes conveyed everything he needed to softly push me back on the bed. While the afternoon slowly waned, we wandered the unexplored roads of the flesh, celebrating the ritual of a man and a woman fusing, daggers in a common sheath. Once I came to my senses, however, and regained my speech, I broke down and began to cry, racked with guilt. What was I going to do now? What would happen? I was suddenly swept by an awful sense of foreboding as if I could see what would unravel. Later on I would dry my tears and scold myself for making such a scene, for regretting something when it was already too late. Gently, Modesto did his best to soothe me. I think he said he would soon go back to his mountains; he said it had just been a parenthesis, a way to seek refuge from the war raining down upon us. He said I didn't have to worry that what we had done would threaten the stability of my marriage. Maybe he was right. But, despite my problems with Sergio, despite that my love for him was far less passionate, I was distraught at the idea of repeating the past. Before, marital infidelity had seemed like a necessary, justifiable evil. This time I found it despicable. I didn't want to hurt Sergio, he didn't deserve that.

As the days went by, however, as intimacy grew between Modesto and me, my resistance faltered. I turned a deaf ear to the recriminations of my conscience. I sought shelter in the transience of our lives, in the unpredictable nature of it all. How could I deny him a tenderness that could so easily disappear from his life forever? It was my gift to a man condemned to death. That was how I chose to look at it. But, in fact, I was gripped by a devastating love which shattered the compass that guided my life.

CHAPTER THIRTY-TWO

---

*Of the first time I traveled to Cuba and the unusual
meetings I had with Fidel Castro*

PANAMA–HAVANA, 1978–1979

"WOULD YOU LIKE to go to Cuba?" Modesto asked me one afternoon
with a seductive smile, like the genie just before granting Aladdin's wish.
The Cubans had invited a representative of the GPP to the celebration of
the twentieth anniversary of the Revolution. If I could take two weeks off,
he said, I would be the ideal person to travel to the island at the end of
December.

Generally I tried not to be away from home for more than two or three
days at a time. My children suffered from my absences, so my trips were
short but frequent. Even though I would be away for longer than usual,
I accepted Modesto's offer. Back then, Cuba was a beacon of revolution
in Latin America. What more could I ask than to be offered such an
opportunity?

I returned to Panama near the end of December to take the flight to
Havana. At the last minute, Modesto, who was planning to go with me,
decided against it. I never knew why. I imagined it had something to do
with the explosive argument we had shortly after I arrived, a heated
exchange where he reproached me for my lasting loyalty to some of
Marcos's ideas. Some irrational, unfounded grudge. He retreated into a
menacing silence after announcing I would be going alone to Havana.

Downhearted, I took off on the Cubana flight. From the minute I
boarded the plane I felt as if I had entered a different world. One of the
stewardesses had platinum-blond hair, and the other's was jet-black
(Cubans seem to have a real affinity for hair dye), and they moved about

the cabin with friendly insouciance. The flight, which was scheduled to take off at nine in the evening, took off at five in the morning. For breakfast they served us the beer and the dinner that we should have been served the night before.

The discolored and run-down landscape of Havana and the impeccable punctuality of the Party functionaries, hotel staff, drivers, and everyone who attended to us were my first impressions of socialism. I arrived in Cuba ready to replace sinister images (informed by an adolescence filled by anticommunist myths) with images of the splendid utopia I wanted to find in Cuban socialism. I saw the city through the rose-colored glasses of my hopes. The United States's economic embargo explained the broken-down buildings and everything that didn't work. I admired the dignity and indefatigable good humor of the Cubans, who piled into packed buses that never arrived on time and dressed in clothing reminiscent of the fashions of the 1950s and 1960s.

I stayed at the Hotel Capri. Its restored Art Deco design reminded me of the old hotels on Miami Beach. I soon discovered it was a fallacy that one could not move around Havana without the ubiquitous Party functionary tagging close behind. I wandered down its avenues, visited bookstores where books cost pennies, and talked to a lone fisherman on the Malecón. I was impressed by how even the youngest, simplest people were so well versed in politics. There was a special quality about those people, separated from consumerism, forced by their circumstances to focus their lives on different values, spiritual values like education, solidarity, love of country and community. The Cubans bemoaned all the hardships, but they got by cheerfully, with an epic sense of who they were.

The nationalization of all services and the absence of market forces were palpable—in the endless paperwork, bureaucracy, delays, and confusion you always ran into the minute you stepped outside your hotel and tried to buy an ice cream, or sit down to order a coffee. The hotel, nevertheless, operated like a dream. The food was excellent, especially the yogurt, and room service was fast and efficient.

In the midst of the anniversary celebration's festive mood, I was amazed to come face-to-face with guerrillas from all over Latin America. Leaders of socialist countries like Vietnam, as well as ambassadors of various liberation movements—Palestinians, Polisarios, South Africans. It was like a revolutionary fairy tale. I attended a military parade where thousands of soldiers, in chorus, saluted the memory of Che Guevara. Squadrons of MiGs zipped overhead, leaving bright trails of colored smoke, in open defiance of the United States and its opposition to Cuba having those planes. I visited museums with photos of Fidel and his bearded comrades in the Sierra Maestra. I met Gabriel García Márquez when we both got caught in a downpour, and we became inseparable bus companions as our hosts shuttled us from place to place. In the Casa de las Américas I met the friendly, unassuming Uruguayan poet Mario Benedetti, and the Cuban Roberto Fernández Retamar.

The days leading up to the anniversary were filled with official receptions. At the first one, a huge party in Havana's imposing, modern Conventions Palace, I shook Fidel Castro's hand.

"Where have the Sandinistas been hiding you?" he asked, looking me up and down.

I was standing next to Doris Tijerino, a legendary woman within the Sandinista ranks, who was living in Cuba at the time. She bantered easily with Fidel, and while their conversation went on, he kept looking at me, while I stood there in starstruck silence.

Fidel is a physically imposing man. The material of his formal, impeccable olive green uniform looked brand-new. His shoes gleamed. Everything about him exuded an air of authority, confidence, awareness that he was the most important person in the room. His face had very Spanish features, though the expressiveness of his eyes was purely Caribbean. Not a single detail of the surrounding scene eluded him, even though his attention was focused on us. After a little while, people began to gather around to hear him talk. He would ask questions and pontificate on the current situation of one country or another.

I imagined him as a kind of secular Moses, keeper of the Stone Tablets, leading his people on their journey to the Promised Land. Finally, he disappeared into the crowd. I was flattered that he had taken special notice of me.

The following evening, at a smaller reception for the Latin American delegations, I was talking to Mario Benedetti when Fidel came over to say hello. A handful of guests and Cuban Communist Party officials hovered around him. I found myself surrounded by a circle of men all casting devilish, conspiratorial smiles at me, acknowledging the attention their leader was lavishing on me. Mario told Fidel I was a poet, a recent winner of the Casa de las Américas prize.

"And what do I have to do to read your book?" he asked, as the smiles grew wider around us. I laughed. That was no problem, I said. I would make sure he got a copy.

"But I want you to write me a dedication," he added.

"Of course, Comandante, I'd be happy to," I said.

Fidel continued talking, but his eyes remained riveted on me. I tried to stay confident, impassive, under his scrutiny.

"And how can I get to see you?" he asked. "Going to your hotel would be difficult. I'm too well known around here."

I looked at him, flabbergasted. Everyone else laughed. I figured it was a joke.

"You're seeing me now, Comandante," I said, playing the game, hiding my discomfort. After a while Fidel left us, continuing his tour of the party, greeting old and new faces. The party was held in a house used for official guests. The garden, filled with exuberant tropical vegetation, was set up with tables that were spread about beneath the trees. Leaders of the most important Latin American guerrilla movements were everywhere, chatting pleasantly among themselves. They were members of the Chilean MIR, the Argentinean ERP, the Uruguayan Tupamaros, or Salvadorans from the FMLN, Guatemalans. In their own countries, each one was probably a fugitive with a price on his head. They all led struggles against military regimes or the status quo. I circulated among the guests, saying hello to people I knew, stopping to talk now and then. Amused, I realized that Fidel was making repeated attempts to get closer to me. He would make his way, and then, inevitably, we would be surrounded once again. He couldn't make a move without a big group of people following him or someone interrupting him to talk.

"You see, they're not letting me talk to you," he said with resignation during one of those moments.

I, meanwhile, was fully enjoying the scene. How could I not enjoy Fidel Castro's attention?

When it was time for dinner, Fidel sat down at a table at the far end of the garden. Shortly afterward, a flurry of men and a caravan of cars taking off announced the departure of the *comandante*. The atmosphere loosened up considerably. The other Sandinistas at my table teased me about Fidel.

We all laughed. They were serving dessert when Ulises, a top official of the Cuban Communist Party's Americas Department, whom I knew from Panama, sat down next to me.

"Please come with me," he said. "Fidel wants to talk to you."

Not knowing what else to do, I got up and followed him out to his car, intrigued and uneasy at the same time.

Fidel was waiting for me at a house that had the cold atmosphere of a place that rarely saw many people. The softly lit living room was like a theatrical setting, with walls covered in green wallpaper and gold-framed paintings with hunting scenes. The episode with Torrijos flashed d through my mind and I prayed that my much admired Fidel wouldn't do the same thing. I was reassured when I saw he was with Manuel "Barbarroja" (Redbeard) Piñeiro, one of his comrades from the Sierra Maestra, and now the head of the Americas Department. Piñeiro was a tough man to read. His coffee-colored eyes were intense, mischievous, vaguely threatening. He seemed to know it all, or at least he acted as though he did. I sat down next to Fidel on a long sofa, while Piñeiro, sitting in an armchair, observed the scene.

"I hope you forgive me for taking you away," Fidel said, smiling. "But otherwise I wouldn't have been able to talk to you."

I vaguely recall that Fidel occupied the first part of our conversation to ask me lots of personal questions: my social background, my parents, when I became a Sandinista, a poet. As long as we were conversing, I would be safe, I thought, so I talked to my heart's content. I told him about Marcos, Sergio, my children. We began disagreeing when the conversation veered to the subject of politics and the situation in Nicaragua. I couldn't resist mentioning that I had a hard time understanding why they in Cuba favored the Tercerista tendency and the Ortega brothers. I told him that I thought their politics were unscrupulous and would be dangerous to the Sandinista cause in the long run. Fidel grew agitated and raised his index finger, waving it around. He raised and then lowered his voice until it was almost a whisper.

"How can you doubt my intentions? I have been a staunch advocate of Sandinista unity. I have spent entire nights with your leaders, trying to get them to agree." And he stared at me with those penetrating eyes.

"But then why do you support some more than others?" I insisted, knowing full well that Fidel gave preference to the Terceristas, sending them more arms and equipment than the other groups.

"Where did you get that idea?" And he reiterated that he supported unity, and that he trusted the GPP leaders implicitly. He had no doubt that Modesto, Tomás, and Bayardo were men of principle. He suggested that perhaps the misgivings I expressed regarding the Ortega brothers were the very reason he was courting them, to help redirect their efforts.

"But you're only strengthening their position," I insisted. I wasn't going to let slip the opportunity to tell Fidel what many of us thought. I believed frankness was a way to show respect for his intelligence.

As so often happened during my life, when dealing with men in positions of power, it began to dawn on me that he wasn't there to listen, but to be heard. His voice was growing louder and angrier. He clearly thought I was being defiant and wanted to convince me I was wrong. When I realized I wasn't getting anywhere, that the conversation had degenerated into a confrontation of his truth versus mine, I stopped trying.

"You know more than I do, Comandante," I said. "Since my opinion is not as informed as yours, I am probably wrong. I have no doubt of your good intentions. I know how hard you have tried to bring us all back together. As a Sandinista, I am very grateful to you." I said a few more things to placate him. Slowly, he regained his composure. Piñeiro watched us from his chair, with those knowing, impenetrable eyes. The bizarre meeting came to a close. A bit flustered, I said goodbye to Fidel at the door, not knowing exactly what to think of that peculiar encounter.

Modesto arrived in Havana around that time, and sent for me. I went to see him. He was staying alone in the outskirts of Havana, in an empty, large house. I chattered incessantly about my impressions of Cuba, fearing he might occupy a silence to tell me he didn't love me anymore. But not an hour had gone by before we kissed passionately, with sudden intensity, as if we'd both been living in dread of having lost each other.

The party on December 31 was unforgettable. Hundreds of tables were packed into the small cobblestone Plaza de la Catedral in Old Havana, one of the most beautiful and intimate of Latin America's historic sights. The colonial buildings that line the four sides of the plaza, magnificently lit up, were the backdrop for the party, which was brought to life by a concert of Afro-Caribbean rhythms: *danzón, guaracha, guantanamera*. At midnight, the plaza exploded with cheers. I clinked glasses with revolutionaries from all over the world, even those whose causes I didn't know much about. And of course, with my fellow Sandinistas, we toasted to the end of tyranny, to the triumph of the people, to revolution. We Nicaraguans were especially emotional that night. Nineteen seventy-nine would be a critical year for us. We all knew it.

My return to capitalism and exile was fast approaching. One afternoon, while I was reading in my hotel room, I received a phone call from a Cuban Communist Party functionary asking me to please stay put. It was an odd request. I assumed it had to do with Modesto, whom the Cubans regarded with the utmost deference. The man called me again at eight in the evening, instructing me to go down to the hotel lobby. He would be waiting for me, he said. Clandestine life and its riddles were familiar to me and so I didn't ask him what it was about. When we got in the car, my escort didn't tell me where we were going, and I didn't guess our destination even when I saw we were approaching the headquarters of the Cuban Communist Party, a tall, modern building in the Plaza de la Revolución.

I think we were inside the building when I was finally told that Fidel wanted to see me again.

I took the elevator up to his office, and remembered that Fidel's work schedule went from four in the afternoon to four in the morning. As soon as the doors opened I saw him. We walked into his spacious, inviting office, simply furnished and filled with plants, a space suffused with the air of accumulated history. We spoke for almost four hours, until midnight. Once again, Piñeiro hovered around us, coming in and out of the room. Fidel had on his *comandante*'s uniform (which our Nicaraguan *comandantes* would later copy). I was still wearing my day clothes: jeans and a white blouse. He thanked me for the book I had sent him, complete with a dedication. We sat and talked on a white sofa near his desk.

"I've never met with anyone from the Sandinista rank and file before," he said. "I usually meet with the leadership, you know. I do hope you make it all the way to the end. I've seen so many people die in these attempts. So many *compañeros*. You can't imagine what it was like for me when Camilo, when Che died. I led the group that went out to search for Camilo's plane. There wasn't a single sign of life, nothing on the sea. We lost Camilo. Never found him. Despite all our efforts. And Che. We have his hands, right here. You know? Can you imagine? His hands. Che was like my brother."

I could hear the emotion in his faint voice. I had to lean closer to hear him. Later on we got on the subject of politics. I asked him if he had already become a socialist when the Revolution triumphed, thinking of the big crucifix he wore around his neck after coming down from the Sierra Maestra.

"I had been formulating a similar system, on my own," he said. "The distribution of wealth. I was surprised at the coincidences when I read Marx for the first time. I converted to Marxism very quickly."

He told me the story of the Cuban Revolution, and of how he wrote his speeches.

"I always read Martí," he said. "He is my source of inspiration."

Then he took out José Martí's books. He read me some passages. I looked at him in awe. I couldn't believe my luck in being able to share this time with Fidel, in the silence of that sleeping building. At some point, he suggested that I might be able to help him by giving him certain information he wanted. Specifically, details about the GPP's reaction to the arms he had recently shipped to the Terceristas. I remembered Modesto's rage when he found out the weapons had not been divided equally among the three tendencies.

"If you tell me what you know, I can explain," Fidel proposed. "I can explain everything, but only if you know what I am talking about, because otherwise, what would the point be of giving you an explanation?"

Modesto had made me promise that, no matter what, I wouldn't tell anyone about his reaction. It seemed an odd request at the time, and I had forgotten about it until now. Could Modesto have ever imagined that Fidel Castro himself would want that information? Was it something that Fidel shouldn't know about? I wondered. But that was not my decision. And in this business, silence was golden. I thought Fidel would have to explain everything to Modesto, not to me. I wasn't going to say anything. It wasn't up to me to get involved in this game between leaders.

Moving ashtrays and sundry objects about his desk, Fidel demonstrated his thesis, that a classic war of fixed positions would force Somoza to deploy considerable resources to the south of Nicaragua, giving the Sandinista guerrilla army the opportunity to advance on other fronts. For that reason, he said, the Southern Front needed enough arms for a conventional war: antiaircraft and antitank weapons, cannons. He was sure that this was the correct strategy. It was fascinating to watch how passionately involved he was with this idea, as if he felt he was once again leading a revolution. Except that I was proudly aware and thankful that we Sandinistas had our own ideas. Much as we respected the Cubans, this was our war, and if we were going to win, we would do it thanks to our daring and our strategy. Maybe the Ortegas were willing to go along with him, but there was more to Sandinismo than just the Ortegas. It disturbed me to see that Fidel was so inclined to meddle, so intent on playing a leading role in our revolution. I listened to him in silence. I didn't share his view and I said as much. I felt it made more sense to send the weapons to reinforce guerrilla columns operating around the northern cities. War on the Southern Front didn't look auspicious. We were not a conventional army and had no experience defending fixed positions. That kind of war would cost too many lives. I gave him my arguments but I didn't press them. Nothing that I'd say would change his mind anyway. It was a lost cause. At midnight, Piñeiro returned. He too urged me to tell them what I knew.

"I don't have the information you're looking for," I repeated.

Finally they gave up. Fidel went back to just being Fidel. At the door, he said goodbye to me, affectionately.

"Say hello to Camilo," he said. I was surprised he had remembered my son's name. I smiled.

When I returned to the hotel, I was plagued with doubt as to whether I had done the right thing. I called a cab. Amazed at my own powers of recollection, I guided him from memory through the streets of Havana until we reached the house where Modesto was staying. He was surprised to see me so late. It was almost two in the morning.

"You did the right thing," he assured me. "I'll talk to them later. Don't worry."

Before leaving Cuba, I wrote Fidel a letter. A letter from one *compañero* to another. I had great respect for him, I said, but he had to understand the impossible position he had put me in. I was a member of the rank and file. I couldn't disobey my orders. I thought it had been most inappropriate of him to use his authority and prestige to induce me to do so. According to me it was "revolutionary criticism." I realize now how naive I was.

I saw Fidel again, after the Sandinista Revolution triumphed. He greeted me, polite but distant. Clearly my letter—assuming he read it—had not ingratiated me to him.

The real meaning of that night continues to elude me, but I treasure the memory as one of those entrancing, slightly perverse situations that life occasionally deals us. Instead of becoming clearer, the episode has become more confusing over time. Did Fidel really need me to give him that information? Why had he been so insistent with me? Did he just need a pretext to justify his desire to see me, talk to me, examine me like a butterfly under a microscope, study my reaction to power? Had he wanted to seduce me? I don't know. I suppose I never will.

CHAPTER THIRTY-THREE

Of other trips, events, and adventures

SAN JOSÉ, 1979

MY TRIP TO HAVANA was the first of many. I was rarely home. I went to Puerto Rico to participate in solidarity rallies for Nicaragua and with the secret mission of finding a pilot for Operation Eureka. I continued my courier missions to Panama and Honduras. I got to know Modesto better. He was a temperamental man, given to sharp mood swings, often becoming suddenly hostile and silent, loving me one minute and hating me the next. He baffled me, but each rejection made me cling more tightly to him. Often I would return from those trips thinking it was all over between us. A few days later, he would turn up in San José and seduce me again with renewed passion, or he would phone me as if nothing had happened, as if his love was unchanged.

During those months, I often took him to the Panamanian border, which he crossed clandestinely. We'd leave San José before dawn and cross the inhospitable, fog-shrouded pass known as Death's Peak. It was twelve hours round-trip, and either Paco or Malena usually came along. She was a childhood friend whom I had rediscovered in San José, and who became a Sandinista with the same admirable passion that imbued everything she did, from playing the piano to studying sociology, or taking care of her three children, who were my daughters' playmates. I couldn't help but confide in her about what was happening to me. We had long conversations about fidelity, which, after a few stumbles of her own, she had grown to value. Once trust was lost it was impossible to salvage a relationship, she told me. She was right. I think that relationships only rarely survive once the inner sanctum has been violated. What forges a couple is the shared responsibility to defend that space. Malena tried to bring me back to my senses. She refused to be my accomplice as far as the affair was concerned, but she would keep me company on those long road trips because her loyalty to me was stronger than her censure. When Modesto was in the car, she kept him entertained with interminable questions. After leaving the highway and following dusty dirt roads, through back-country dotted by peasant huts and rickety farmhouses, we would drop him off near the Panamanian border. We'd wait until another car came from Panama to pick him up, then Malena and I would make the long drive back to San José.

But even when I was home, playing with Camilo, cuddling with my daughters, my mind was elsewhere. My long absences are the only memory my daughters have of those days. Years later, on one of her college applications, Melissa wrote an essay in which she spoke of her love for me, but which began: "Once again, her toothbrush is gone." If there were times when I didn't say goodbye before leaving on my trips, possibly I have made myself forget. It seems so terrible to me now, but then, having a family was a luxury we often felt we didn't deserve, and often didn't honor. Reading Melissa's essay broke my heart. I could just see her, staring at the bathroom sink, an innocent and disconsolate little girl. I began to cry, and soon the two of us were crying together. I was inconsolable, and she was the one who calmed me, patting me softly on the back, pressing me tightly against her chest, saying, "It's okay, Mommy, it's over now. You couldn't expect everything to work out perfectly."

My relationship with Sergio was also being eroded by the fact that my heart was elsewhere. I increasingly distanced myself from him as a way to attenuate my feelings of guilt. It pained me that he had no inkling of what was going on. I wondered how it was possible for him not to suspect anything. I thought that in his place, I would have detected the scent of another replacing him on my body. I even speculated that he chose to ignore the affair because he knew it was to end soon: Modesto would return to Nicaragua and I would come back to him.

Toward the end of 1978, the military struggle within Nicaragua was buoyed by a massive wave of popular protests. Women, journalists, workers, and students, all rallied against the dictatorship, demanding respect for human rights. The dictatorship raged on, implacable in its campaign of repression, now aimed at the young people. To be young was to be suspect. On an isolated road which bordered the Esso refinery and from which one could see a magnificent view of Lake Managua, the dead bodies of the young were being found almost daily. Without any warning, the National Guard would raid working-class neighborhoods, carting off anyone suspected of supporting the Sandinistas. Many prisoners disappeared without a trace. Editorial and op-ed pieces both inside and outside Nicaragua blasted the Somoza regime, which found itself increasingly more isolated. The dictator fought back with a vengeance.

On March 7, 1979, the three Sandinista tendencies finally signed a unity agreement. The Joint National Directorate, which would guide the final phase of the war against the tyrant, was made up of nine members: Modesto, Tomás Borge, and Bayardo Arce of the GPP, Daniel Ortega, Humberto Ortega, and Victor Tirado of the Terceristas, and Jaime Wheelock, Luis Carrión, and Carlos Núñez of the Proletarian tendency.

Inside Nicaragua, it meant the consolidation of guerrilla squadrons, weapons, and field commanders. I found it hard to believe: we had been so few at first and now we were a real army able to fight in every corner of the country. Somoza could no longer control the proliferation of clandestine soldiers who hid their weapons during the day while they went about their business as construction workers or salesclerks, and at night ambushed the National Guard, or rallied people in the barrios.

After we all came together, the Sandinista network abroad was reorganized and I became part of the FSLN's Political-Diplomatic Committee, an ambassador so to speak, for what was already a solid and widely recognized national liberation movement.

The preparations for Operation Eureka were moving ahead at full speed. By now we had secured the pilot, the weapons, new radio communications equipment, and the support of the control tower staff at the Juan Santamaría Airport in San José.

Meanwhile, we also had to devote lots of time and effort to the Southern Front—Fidel's pet project. The front had most of its encampments on Costa Rican soil, and we had to attend to the needs of the troops and provide weapons, training, and assistance to the hundreds of volunteers— from Latin America, Europe, and even the United States—who came to join the struggle. Somoza had deployed a battalion of elite soldiers to contain the Sandinista advance in the south. The situation got to a point where both sides were mired defending their fixed positions unable to advance. Every day there were dead and wounded. We had to set up clandestine clinics. It was a logistical nightmare.

Radio Sandino, the Sandinista pirate station that broadcast from Costa Rica, aired the ingenious songs that Carlos Mejía Godoy, Nicaragua's most popular singer, had composed with Modesto's help. The lyrics were nothing other than step-by-step instructions on how to use, assemble, and disassemble the rifles people were capturing from the National Guard in street battles. The entire population of Nicaragua was racing to prepare for the uprising that would soon topple the dictatorship.

For the final insurrection, we needed funds for arms, ammunitions, medical supplies, communications equipment. We had received several offers for aid from Europe, so Modesto decided that Malena and I should travel there. First we would go to Spain to attend the Spanish Socialist Workers Party's (PSOE) congress as guests of Felipe González, who later became Spain's head of state. From there we would go to France, Holland, Sweden, and Austria.

Leaving for Europe meant leaving Modesto for good. When I returned, if everything went according to plan, he would be in Nicaragua heading his guerrilla column again. The idea of parting weighed heavily on us. We hadn't separated yet, but several times we caught ourselves looking nostalgically at the other. "I will always remember this moment. Your scent. I will think of you when I see the Iyas River. It's such a beautiful river," he would say. I would drop him off at the poet Joaquín Gutiérrez's house, where he was staying, and I would just weep at the wheel of my car.

Finally, my departure was upon us. "Keep your eye on the newspapers. If Eureka is successful, you'll see it in the news," Modesto said. Once again I would have to endure the tension of waiting for news in a foreign language. Malena consoled me during the flight. No doubt it was painful for me to leave him, she said, but it was the right thing to do. For the entire flight she talked about all sorts of ideas and projects with remarkable energy, an energy she still has to this day. We arrived in Madrid at ten in the morning. Because I was a fugitive, I had been unable to renew my Nicaraguan passport, and so I carried a "laissez-passer" issued to me by the Costa Rican authorities. It was a legitimate document and I confidently presented it to the immigration officer at Barajas Airport.

"I can't let you through," he said, squarely. "You don't have a visa."

"But Nicaraguans don't need a visa to enter Spain," I replied. "The people at Iberia told me so."

"With a regular passport you don't, but with this document you do. Please, step aside."

There was no convincing any of the immigration officials at the airport. Malena got into a taxi and headed for the PSOE headquarters to arrange for a permit that would allow me to enter the country. But Felipe González wasn't in power yet. And the Suárez government still hadn't stamped out the last vestiges of Franco. Our hosts at the PSOE did everything they could, but their efforts could not make a dent in the rigid immigration bureaucracy. I was detained in Barajas from ten in the morning on Saturday until two in the morning on Sunday, with a Civil Guard watching over me the entire time.

At two a.m. on Sunday, they made me board an Iberia flight for San José. I arrived home that Sunday evening, exhausted and furious. I couldn't believe I had gone back and forth over the Atlantic in the space of forty-eight hours.

"Give me your passport," Paco said to me. "I'll renew it for you."

That Tuesday, with my old Nicaraguan passport renewed—guerrilla-style—I flew back to Madrid. This time they let me through.

Malena and I collapsed in laughter when we finally reunited at the hotel.

"What irony," I said. "After I tried so hard to do all of this legally."

At the PSOE congress, the master of ceremonies saluted the presence of the FSLN delegation, which at that point just consisted of me. I greeted the packed auditorium with a raised fist, and the public responded with a roaring standing ovation.

That day I attended a lunch with Felipe González. The other guests included Rubén Berrios of the Puerto Rico Independence Party, and Darcy Ribeiro and Leonel Brizola from Brazil. The composed, mature Brizola, who would later become governor of Rio de Janeiro, spent most of the lunch trying to play footsie with me under the table. Being a young woman among politicians was to live in a world full of surprises.

Malena and I met again in Paris. We stayed at the home of Francis Pisani, the *Le Monde* correspondent whom I had befriended after granting him several interviews in San José.

A press conference was arranged for me in Paris. It was my first time facing a battery of journalists from the most important French and international news organizations. When I saw how crowded the room was where the press conference was to take place, my hands turned to ice. But as soon as I opened my mouth, the words spilled out with aplomb, as I told myself it wasn't me the journalists were looking at, but my country, my *compañeros*. I managed to give a lucid presentation, in English, on the insurrectional military strategy.

The following night, Malena and I met with Régis Debray, who was famous for a time he spent with Che in Bolivia, and for his book *Revolution in the Revolution*. Régis was thin and blond, with that elegant arrogance so typical of certain enlightened intellectuals, especially French ones. He was thinking about traveling to Nicaragua although he was convinced that the Sandinistas didn't stand a chance. We argued all night to no avail.

Flash-forward to Managua on July 20, 1979: I was in the back of a truck, entering Somoza's old bunker, now the headquarters of the Sandinista National Directorate, when I saw Debray dressed in olive drab, sitting atop a wall inside the military complex.

"Régis, Régis!" I shouted, waving at him. "You see, we were right! We won!"

He waved back absently. Either he didn't recognize me or he pretended not to. "Who is that blond guy?" asked the *compañero* sitting next to me.

"Régis Debray," I said. "A French intellectual who once tried to convince me we'd never win."

Those days brought many moments to savor.

Malena and I traveled to more countries than I could count that May. The lopsided war, young, tattered soldiers fighting against government forces armed to the teeth, aroused tremendous sympathy and opened doors wherever we went.

Malena and I were dizzy from the endless meetings, from repeating the same speech over and over again, but we were possessed by our mission, inspired by the warm, welcoming response we received. We didn't even think about being tired. We managed to find enough energy still to go to parks, eat apple strudel in Vienna, wander through the canals in Amsterdam, to enjoy brief moments as tourists.

Our mission fulfilled, it was time to go home. That was when we found out Eureka had failed. A thick cloud cover had prevented the plane from landing at the appointed airstrip. Without reinforcements, without new equipment, the guerrilla columns had to retreat back into the mountains, but not before suffering a number of casualties.

CHAPTER THIRTY-FOUR

On how forty-five years of dictatorship came to an end

SAN JOSÉ–MANAGUA, 1979

BY THE BEGINNING of June, the advance of the Revolution was unstoppable. In almost every city, all across Nicaragua, people were fighting in the streets. In his bomb-proof office, known as "El Bunker," Somoza clung to the last vestiges of his power.

One day on the radio I heard Modesto speaking from a city in northern Nicaragua. The area was crawling with National Guard soldiers, and air strikes were coming down hard and fast. I was worried, but I was also happy for him. Finally he was back in Nicaragua, fighting with his troops. I wished I was there. The rear guard was important, but I was anxious for the moment when I could join in the one, most basic contribution to the struggle: combat in Nicaragua.

My house was a nerve center of Sandinista activity. All day long, a constant stream of people flowed in and out of the apartment we had moved into after I gave up my job at Garnier and our income dropped. It was a small apartment, not far from the university. Maryam and Melissa continued going to school as usual. Camilo, a chubby, beautiful baby with red hair, was beginning to take his first steps. Things between Sergio and me were strained. Much as I tried to disguise it, my love for him had waned. With so much work and so many trips, we barely had time to resolve the tensions that continued to build between us. He clung to me, but I was worn out by the intensity of my emotions and the obligations of each new day, and was insensitive, even cruel to him. Alone and confused, I ruminated over the alternatives. Sometimes I wished Sergio wasn't so good, so accommodating, so persistent. It would have been easier to let him go.

Despite his dogmatic nature, that purist inflexibility of his that irritated me so, Sergio was an extraordinarily noble man. In many ways, a much better partner than Modesto, whose personality gave off enough danger signals for me to realize how very precarious and ephemeral any happiness he could offer me would be.

Ah, how blind we humans can be when we fall in love!

I loved Sergio. I couldn't help but love him, but my love for Modesto was raw, electrifying passion, blind madness. I didn't know if I could ever choose between the two. I loved them both. Together, they were my perfect man. Unfortunately, I didn't live in some tribe where a woman could have several husbands.

San José had become the safe haven for people looking to escape the war in Nicaragua, or for those who knew the end was in sight and were trying to ally themselves with the winners. Bankers, economists, and private businessmen offered their services to work on the blueprints for rebuilding the country once Somoza fell. We didn't say no to anyone. We were overjoyed to be able to benefit from so many sharp minds and collective experiences. Malena, her husband, Eduardo, and I organized several task forces to elaborate policy for the new government. Other people worked out lists of prospective cabinet members and candidates for other important positions. A lot of juggling went on. In the definitive cabinet, only one woman was included: Lea Guido, minister of social welfare. Some of us expressed our disappointment and protested the absence of women on the list, but our objections went unheard.

The war in Nicaragua reached its peak in June and July of 1979. Various cities were liberated. León was first. Then came Diriamba, Masaya, Matagalpa, Jinotepe, Estelí. Every day small planes made clandestine flights from San José to deliver supplies to the different battle fronts in Nicaragua. Whenever I had a spare moment I would go to Palo Alto, a radio base which kept constant communication with every other important command center at the front lines. It was mesmerizing to hear about the progress of the insurrection, to hear what was happening in real time. Every night at nine o'clock, the commanders of the different fronts would hold a radio conference. Humberto Ortega was at the microphone in Palo Alto. I would get goosebumps as I listened to the reports, the combat updates, the heroic stories of so many fearless young men and women defying the National Guard despite their technical disadvantages. People participated in droves and they were so anxious to fight that often there was no way to organize so much courage and disposition. On June 28 after a brutal National Guard offensive in Managua's poor eastern barrios, the *comandantes* ordered the guerrilla forces to retreat to Masaya. As the combatants slowly began to make their way out of Managua after sunset, thousands of people decided to flee with them. The guerrillas had to herd at least three thousand people of all ages along a thirty-kilometer stretch, walking through ditches and country roads in total silence to avoid being intercepted. The majority of this human tidal wave managed to make it to the liberated city of Masaya alive by dawn. This strategic retreat right under the noses of the National Guard turned what could have been a military setback into a resounding victory. Thousands of lives were saved, people who surely would have perished in the air attacks Somoza unleashed upon their barrios as soon as the sun rose.

June 4 marked the day of the last general strike in Managua. National Guard patrols combed the silent city, waiting for the final battle. Twenty-five cities and towns throughout the country were up in arms, their streets blocked with barricades fashioned from sandbags, cement blocks, doors ripped from their hinges, and overturned trucks. Guerrillas roamed about everywhere.

Then Bill Stewart, an ABC journalist, trying to get to one of the devastated barrios, was assassinated. It happened in such an unexpected and brutal manner that his unsuspecting cameraman had been filming Stewart's approach to the army checkpoint. He filmed the soldier when he ordered Stewart to lie face down on the ground with his hands behind his head, then kicked him, and then killed him with a shot point-blank to the head. Bill Stewart was probably more surprised than anyone at such an unexpected death. His body twitched for a second, and then lay still on the asphalt. The shaken cameraman had the presence of mind to get out of there and ship the film out of the country. That night, television stations all over the world broadcast the footage. I will never forget the spine-chilling image of the soldier, and the absolute ease with which he pointed and fired. This was the hard evidence of what the Nicaraguan people were living with, day in and day out. Susan Meiselas, an extraordinarily brave photographer, had recorded similar horrors for a number of years. Her pictures had appeared on the front pages of all the American newspapers, but the photo of Bill Stewart caused the furor that so many hundreds of anonymous murders could not. His death was the catalyst which finally caused the United States to withdraw its support of Somoza.

Not long after that, the National Guard shot and killed a driver and medic in a Red Cross ambulance. The international community reacted.

On June 17, 1979, Mexico, Costa Rica, Ecuador, and Panama broke diplomatic relations with Somoza. In Costa Rica, the Sandinistas announced the formation of a provisional government, made up of Violeta Chamorro, Pedro Joaquín's widow; Moisés Hassan, mathematics professor and member of the United People's Movement; Alfonso Robelo, a businessman in the private sector; Daniel Ortega of the FSLN; and Sergio Ramírez of the Group of Twelve.

Lawrence Pezullo, the U.S. ambassador, desperately tried to negotiate keeping certain National Guard generals in their positions, in an army without Somoza. At a special meeting of the Organization of American States, the United States proposed that an inter-American peacekeeping force be sent to Nicaragua. Latin American countries rejected his proposal in a resounding majority vote.

From that last month I recall the sensation of unreality that gnawed at me each time I met with politicians and journalists who asked me questions which I could only respond to with improvised answers. Things like, what would the revolutionary government do with private property, with the National Guard? Would we maintain relations with Cuba, with Moscow? Sometimes it seemed as though they couldn't be talking about my tiny country, abandoned by everyone and beholden to a bloody dictator for half a century, but about a major power, able to make policy decisions that would alter Latin America's future. Nevertheless we were viewed with more sympathy than skepticism.

Even journalists gave us advice. I was proud to see how the Nicaraguan struggle had rallied such incredible solidarity. Our supporters were all emotionally involved with the outcome that, at this point, few doubted would be a Sandinista victory.

In the rear guard, there was no time for rest. Everyone did a little bit of everything, whether it was distributing pamphlets, taking turns on the radio, or delivering weapons to soldiers scattered everywhere.

My brother Eduardo's extended family arrived in Costa Rica in early July, fleeing the war. They stayed at our house, and the jovial, topsy-turvy atmosphere they brought with them was a welcome blessing for my children.

On July 15 and 16, a rumor began to circulate that the United States was planning to intervene in Nicaragua. We feared that—as it had been the case so often in the past—a new U.S. military intervention would be the kiss of death for our efforts to achieve a truly independent Nicaraguan government, free of any and all foreign interests. This rumor grew out of Washington's desperate attempt to help the National Guard maintain at least a modicum of power.

The very thought of an intervention plunged me into a state of despair. I didn't want to be in Costa Rica if that happened. All of us outside the country would be isolated, condemned to watch the debacle unfold. I would rather die inside my country than be a spectator witnessing the war in Nicaragua from afar.

I convinced Alfredo to let me request authorization by radio for travel to Nicaragua the next day with Roy de Montis, Malena's brother, who was piloting a plane to deliver munitions and weapons to the front.

"But we need you here," Alfredo said.

"Please, Chichí," I begged, using my affectionate nickname for him. "Don't get in my way on this. Let me talk to José León." That was Bayardo Arce's nom de guerre.

I finally convinced him, and I stayed glued to the radio until I managed to get through. Bayardo responded evasively. He had to check with Modesto, he said. He would have an answer for me later on.

I began to get ready for my departure the following day. I would disobey my orders if I had to. Once inside Nicaragua, nobody could make me leave. I was tremendously excited, nervous and totally determined. I couldn't stand being away any longer. I'd spent enough years in exile. My *compañeros'* machismo was the problem, I thought to myself. If I were a man, they wouldn't stop me. I took out my military uniform and my red and black bandanna, and prepared my backpack. I told Maryam and Melissa where I was going, and they looked at me reflecting the wide-eyed excitement I had managed to convey to them. I ran my hands over Camilo's face, to fix it in my mind and heart.

At four in the morning on July 17, Sergio and I left the house and headed for Pavas, a private airport near San José International Airport. We didn't have a proper scale to weigh the boxes of equipment and ammunitions we would take with us on the plane, and so I brought along my bathroom scale—pink, of all things. It would be ludicrous to use a pink bathroom scale to weigh boxes filled with ammunition, but it was all we had. Roy would at least be able to get an approximate idea of the cargo's weight.

The journey to the airport through this city, cloaked in the early morning mist, was a farewell to the streets and images of a nation which, though it wasn't my own, had become a worthy substitute. I felt a special affection for San José. So much of my own history had unfolded there. I saw the corner building of the Garnier advertising agency, then further ahead, the geometric silhouette of the Hospital México, where Camilo had been born.

Standing on the runway next to the plane, Paco and Roy waited for us.

"So you're going?" Paco asked me, watching me get out of the car dressed in my olive drab and military boots.

"Yes," I said.

"But . . . did José León say it was all right?" He looked at me in consternation. "I need you here. I don't think you should go. You can't ignore your responsibilities, not now."

"Let's weigh these boxes," I proposed. "Alfredo won't be long. Let's see what they said to him."

I prayed that Modesto would let me go. José León probably knew what was going on between us, and that was why he was letting Modesto decide. Male solidarity. Under any other circumstances, José León would have said yes.

Alfredo drove up. He got out of his car. He looked at me and shook his head to say no and what can I do about it?

"You can't go," he said to me. "José León gave me strict instructions that you were not to go. Orders from the National Directorate."

Still, I weighed my options for a moment. Once there, they wouldn't send me back, I thought. But my cursed discipline won out. That bit about the "orders from the National Directorate," the nine-man Sandinista top leadership, had the desired effect on me. When all was said and done I couldn't disobey orders from the Directorate. We closed up the plane and Roy started the engine. The tiny aircraft took off for Nicaragua, and I watched it disappear into the sky like someone seeing a last hope vanish.

On our way home from the airport, mentally disconnected from Costa Rica and my obligations there, I asked Sergio to take me to Milena and Carlos's house. Carlos was my cousin, and Milena was his wife. Both of them were members of our working group. I felt depressed and defeated.

Sergio tried to convince me that I had done the right thing. It wasn't a question of doing what one wanted, he said, but of doing what one was told to do.

"Somoza left! Somoza left!" cried Milena when she opened the door, pointing to the radio. I went in and saw the *compañeros* from our group: Paco, Alfredo, Chepito, Ciro, and Álvaro all huddled in the room, sitting on chairs, on the floor, standing, hanging on to every word of the radio broadcast. Nobody spoke. Nobody moved. Everyone's eyes glittered with anticipation.

"The National Directorate already ordered the offensive on Managua," Paco murmured as I sat down next to him.

So odd, that silence. All I wanted to do was scream, jump for joy. The radio announcer, conscious of the history being made, intoned solemnly as he reported the tyrant's escape earlier that morning. The entire Somoza family had fled along with its ministers, collaborators, and accomplices, who wrestled each other trying to board any available airplane, as if they were on a sinking ship elbowing their way to the few life rafts. Somoza's out, I said to myself over and over again. Maybe we were silent because we had trouble believing it, because we needed to hear every last detail to be sure, and we needed to hear it together so that later we wouldn't think it had been a dream, a crazy illusion. We would know we had all heard it together, on the radio. There was no doubt about it anymore. The Somoza family had even opened the tomb of the first tyrant to take his remains with them to Miami, maybe fearing that the sacrilegious public would wreak vengeance once again on that ghost of the past.

The radio broadcast stopped for a brief moment. Overcome with joy, we fell into one another's arms. "Somoza left!" we repeated to each other, as we kissed, danced, and hugged. I don't know who began crying first, or how the tears spread from one person to the other, but suddenly the tiny apartment was filled with wails and sobs. Alfredo and I looked in each other's eyes, remembering the dinners in Mazatlán with Marcos. I saw Ricardo in the inky twilight at the Poet's house, Pin and his thick eyeglasses, Arnoldo's smile as he left my house, Camilo talking to me about Woodstock and Joe Cocker, José Benito and his white shirt as he waved goodbye to me, Gaspar in his black Basque beret, Blas . . . Multitudes of our beloved dead came to life among us with their empty eyes, their deaf ears, the dust of their bones that could never celebrate with us. From a remote reservoir hidden deep inside of me, a wave of buried tears spilled forth. So many lives, too many lives, had been given up to hear that news flash, that short little sentence: "Somoza left." My God. After forty-five years, the dynasty had ended.

Who knows what kind of flooding we would have provoked with our collective sobbing if the radio hadn't sputtered out the beep-beep-beep of another news flash. Dr. Francisco Urcuyo Maliaño, appointed by Somoza and the U.S. embassy to negotiate the transfer of power to the provisional government, had just announced that he would occupy the presidency until new elections could be held in 1981. What? I exclaimed, swallowing my tears. Urcuyo Maliaño was a doctor, a sad, lifeless figurehead of the Somoza regime.

"This is some gringo maneuver," someone said. "Urcuyo will now request a U.S. intervention to 'pacify' the country."

"It won't be that easy," I said. "No government will recognize him."

We began to speculate about what could happen next. The triumphant mood of a moment ago had suddenly vanished. The meeting broke up. I went with Paco and Alfredo to Palo Alto, the communications base. We listened to column commanders report that the National Guard was fleeing. The military offensive to take Managua had begun that morning. Columns from the various fronts were descending toward the city, but instead of fighting, the National Guard had put up no resistance. Somoza's feared army was surrendering in droves while thousands of soldiers beat their retreat to Honduras.

I returned home. The enormity of what was happening was beginning to sink in. I found my brother, his wife, Kathy, and her sister, Diana, the children, and their nanny, María Elsa, celebrating the news in the living room. All of us hugged and kissed, still incredulous. I went to the refrigerator and pulled out a bottle of champagne that someone had given me years before, which I had been saving just for this moment. I called my parents in Managua, and they were euphoric. In the background I could hear firecrackers going off.

"Everyone's celebrating," my father said. "Setting off fireworks. A procession of guerrillas has been passing in front of our house, hugging everyone and shouting, 'Patria Libre o Morir,' Freedom or Death. You guys won, sweetheart. Congratulations."

"What about Urcuyo Maliaño?"

"They say he's already fled. That man was crazy to declare himself president! He didn't even wear the presidential sash an entire day. No. It's all over and done with. You guys won. When are you coming home?"

The 18th, the 19th of July 1979. Two crazy days. Two days that felt as though a magical, age-old spell had been cast over us, taking us back to Genesis, to the very site of the creation of the world. Journalists besieged me. Over and over again Paco reminded us that even the dispersion of troops had to be carried out in an orderly manner. Sergio, my husband, also exhorted everyone to stay calm. But me? My soul was begging to break free from my body and run all the way to Nicaragua. Nobody could stop me now.

But then Sergio said: "There are no newspapers. Somoza sacked and bombed *La Prensa.* There's no one to print the victory issue. We have to do it here." He was right. The two of us wrote the newspaper. Four tabloid pages. We baptized it *Patria Libre*—Free Country. Sergio did the layout and brought it to the printer. That newspaper was my exit visa. Someone had to take it to Nicaragua and distribute it.

I put feelers out to various collaborators so we could raise money to rent a plane. We would leave the following day, as soon as the newspaper was printed. Costa Rican television stations provided continuous live coverage from Nicaragua. Guerrilla columns entering Managua appeared on the screen. Thousands of men and women in tatters, with red and black bandannas, piled onto buses, dump trucks, pickup trucks. The Sandinista National Directorate talked to the media at an airport that was the meeting place for the northern columns. We saw TV images of plane after plane landing, unloading journalists, exiles, thrill-seekers. The Directorate announced the new cabinet.

At home, I jumped around doing pirouettes, hugging my daughters and Camilo, kissing their astonished, smiling little faces.

THE RETURN TO NICARAGUA

Tiene el mundo otra cara. Se acerca lo remoto
En una muchedumbre de bocas y de brazos.
Se ve la muerte como un mueble roto,
como una blanca silla hecha pedazos.

—Miguel Hernández

Another face to the world. What is distant draws near/In a multitude of voices and arms./We see death as a broken down thing,/a shattered white chair.

CHAPTER THIRTY-FIVE

Of how I entered Managua delivering newspapers

MANAGUA, JULY 1979

THE NEXT DAY, July 20, I arrived in Managua in an old DC-3 airplane with Milena and the nine *compañeros* Paco placed under my command. We all applauded when the plane touched down. If I close my eyes, I can still see it all so perfectly: the reverberation of the noon sun off the tarmac, the heat that blasted us as the plane door opened, the sound of the newspapers flapping in the wind. Forty thousand copies were piled up in the cabin in front of the one and only row of seats. On the strangely deserted runway, a young man in olive drab came running toward us pushing a staircase we used to deplane. Everyone was at the celebration ceremony in the plaza, he said, but the National Directorate had sent a truck to bring us and the newspapers into the city. I saw the familiar silhouette of the airport's modern terminal, built just before the earthquake. The terraces, normally packed with people waiting for the arrival of relatives, were empty. I walked to the immigration office. My senses were jubilant with the welcome heat, the smell, the clouds. In the large, low-ceilinged hall bathed in neon light, one lone girl, dressed in fatigues, sat behind a desk. I felt around in my bag, looking for my old passport. The girl smiled.

"You don't need a passport, *compañera*. This is your country." It had never felt so mine.

As I left the immigration area and walked toward the runway I saw Justine, my long-lost friend from the time of the earthquake, opening her arms. She beamed at me, her big black eyes misting over. I hadn't expected her, and it seemed like an illusion. She wanted to surprise me at the airport, she said. My parents told her I was coming, and there she was to welcome me to my free country, to take me home. I felt odd, as if the lives we had led separately had suddenly come between us, and I was at a loss to explain, without hurting her feelings, that I couldn't go with her. Even though I was deeply moved by her welcoming gesture, I couldn't leave the boys that were waiting for me with the newspapers. I had to tell her this plain and simple, and I watched her react exactly as I had feared she would. Sadness flew into her eyes. It hurt to see her so disappointed, to see her walk away alone. I had already been feeling melancholic because I had hoped to find the airport bubbling over with all the activity I had seen the day before on the television—not the stillness that surrounded me now, the long, white building enveloped in an eerie desolation. Now, over that image, Justine's sad expression would be always superimposed. I managed to shake off my uneasiness. There would be time later on to explain things to Justine, to my parents, I said to myself. They would wait for me, they always did. But history wouldn't. That day would never happen again, and I had to live it.

My squadron and I piled into the back of the truck, among the newspapers. The driver had only received instructions to pick us up. He didn't know where we were supposed to go, nor to whom we should report. The military commanders and the National Directorate had established their headquarters in El Bunker, he said, Somoza's old offices.

"Let's go to the plaza," I suggested. "We can go to El Bunker afterward."

We drove up the north highway toward the city. The penetrating smell of burning tires filled the air. Their flaming circles could be seen everywhere. Piles of paving stones and open ditches marked the places where barricades had been. We had scarcely left the airport behind when the desolate air simply evaporated, like magic. The truck rolled slowly through the crowded shantytowns of Managua's industrial zone—a strip of small factories interspersed with bustling grocery stores, bus stops, gas stations, pharmacies. Beyond this, toward the lake, lay the vast collection of even more marginal dwellings. We were moving deeper and deeper through a sea of people walking on either side of the road wearing bright and colorful clothes, their Sunday best. On seeing us, they waved happily and yelled out Sandinista cheers, *vivas* to a free Nicaragua. The euphoria etched on their faces spread in concentric circles, became one giant, exultant smile, and the celebratory mood was so contagious, the energy of the crowd so jubilant and electrifying, that I knew, as they reached out to shake our hands, this was the moment to begin our mission.

"Let's start handing out the newspapers," I called out to my *compañeros.*

And so we began yelling out "Freedom" as loud as we could, waving copies of the newspaper. People responded "or death," completing the Sandinista war cry they were all so familiar with. They knew it because it was scrawled and painted on walls everywhere, and because they had chanted it so many times before, in battles against the army, and in street protests. That cry was now a symbol of victory, of the courage that had brought about that hot day when freedom finally showed its face in the streets of my city for the first time in half a century. Scores of hands reached up toward us to grab the newspapers. I will never forget the eagerness, the hope, the joyous optimism of those faces. All the grief, tears, everything I had lived through had been worthwhile if only to live through this moment. What more could I ask than to bear witness to so much happiness? What had been the goal of all our efforts, if not these smiles? Whatever existential doubts one had disappeared right here. This was our life's purpose: to see others smile, to take human joy to its full potential. I felt I was floating over a canopy of grinning faces and out-stretched hands. How intimate were all those hands—wide hands, delicate hands—sliding across mine as they reached for the newspapers, how intimate the scent of that woman dressed in yellow and of the man who propped the little boy on his shoulders so he could touch us, and the old lady with the apron tied around her waist, her thick braid hanging down her back, asking, "Pass one to me, sweetheart!"

Suddenly the truck sped up and the faces got lost in the distance, but it wasn't long before more appeared, and once again their joy had the taste of sweet, red watermelon, its juice dripping down my chin. No solitary pleasure could remotely compare with the satisfaction of feeling responsible for at least a minute particle of the gaiety that surrounded me. This time, the dead came alive inside of me. I felt as if they were taking turns to look at the scene through my eyes. Tears rolled down my cheeks, turning to mud as they mixed with the dust on my face. Now my dead friends would finally be consoled. To die is not as terrible as to not know why one lives, and they had known it all along. That slow truck ride into Managua reminded me of childbirth, of the joy after pain. I was witnessing the birth of my country.

Silence set in once again. We had reached the plaza, flanked by the imposing Cathedral and National Palace, and the park at the far end with its gazebo in the middle. But there was no one left. That was when we realized that the crowds we'd seen on the road had been walking home after the celebration. All that was left in the great, deserted plaza were wrappers, trash, the detritus left by thousands of people which scraped the ground noisily like dry leaves swirling in the wind.

CHAPTER THIRTY-SIX

On the experience of discovering that one must start from zero

MANAGUA, JULY–AUGUST 1979

WE HAD TAKEN OVER. The experience evoked images of the Allied troops arriving at towns abandoned by the Nazis at the end of the Second World War. That was the kind of joy the people greeted us with, and that was the power void in which we found ourselves: a clean-slate situation. The state had been completely dissolved. There were no courts, no police, no army, no government ministries. Just abandoned offices, deserted military bunkers. It was an odd sensation to have been subversive guerrillas and fugitives only a day earlier, and now, suddenly—as young as we were, no less—to find ourselves in a city deserted by the ancient regime, conscious that from then on, everything was up to us.

Managua was in a state of euphoric chaos, and some people did succumb to anarchy. The disenfranchised pillaged the uninhabited, locked-up houses of the rich and the military. Guerrillas with their red and black bandannas took the vehicles that the Somoza supporters had left behind in their frantic flight, and drove with glee through the city streets at full speed. Men and women from self-appointed popular militia units decided to assume the role of traffic police or general vigilantes, arbitrarily performing some arrests, and proclaiming themselves *comandantes*. If one had been in the news or had a name people associated with any kind of authority, *compañeros* and civilians would bestow the title upon you. Everywhere I went those days people would call me "Comandante Belli," which I found quite amusing. The only restricted zone was Somoza's bunker, now headquarters of the Sandinista National Directorate. Other military or government installations were accessible to anyone. Nobody stopped us when the truck we were traveling in drove up to La Loma de Tiscapa. The offices of the National Guard staff and Somoza's State Security had been located on a hill that formed the highest point of the city. The hill was really a volcanic crater with a lagoon at its center. Until the 1972 earthquake, it had also been the site of the president's house. La Loma had been a sinister symbol of the dictatorship, an impenetrable fortress. That day, nevertheless, we crossed the empty checkpoint as if we owned the place. Those forbidden grounds that we were seeing for the first time now looked more like a summer camp for young, disheveled soldiers. Hundreds of young guerrilla men and women lay out on the lawn, laughing, singing, hugging, as if they had been students on a field trip.

At a small square in front of the National Guard's recreation center, we got down from the truck. A warm breeze blew gently over the terrace, where we contemplated a panoramic view of the city, with the lake and volcanoes in the distance. I stood there. An etching from a children's book I used to love when I was growing up suddenly popped into my head. It was an image of a little girl lying on the grass, looking out on a beautiful landscape. The caption read: "The world was mine, I felt as if everything belonged to me." At that instant, I physically understood the meaning of the words "take power." I was suddenly filled with an indescribable sensation that was at once revelation, pride, and humble gratitude to life for having granted me that day. When you dream of things like changing the world, there is no power more beautiful than the feeling that you can make it happen, and that day, right there, everything was possible, there was no dream that couldn't be fulfilled. And the joy wasn't even over yet. I was walking over to another group of buildings higher up on the hill, toward the back of the casino, when someone yelled out my name. That was when I saw Freddy walking toward me. Freddy, a *compañero* I thought was dead. He hugged me, lifting me up into the air, spinning me around just like in the movies. I stared at him, incredulous, touching his beard, moved by this magical resurrection, to both laughter and tears. With Freddy I walked into the army's mind-boggling warehouse, feeling like Ali Baba in the den of thieves. I prowled through dark, high-ceilinged rooms filled with endless piles of uniforms, cases of alcohol, canned goods, and more munitions and arms than I had ever seen in my life. Scores of guerrilla soldiers were now changing their old uniforms for new ones in a gleeful melee while they laughed, grabbed pants and shirts from the stacks, and threw their old clothes up in the air. I also helped myself to various uniforms and in the armory I took a Madsen submachine gun from a pile of weapons. Harold, another *compañero* I knew and who seemed vaguely to be in charge, gave me a box of bullets. Content with my booty, I returned to the truck. On the way I ran into more *compañeros* I knew. More hugs, more revelry, more happiness.

That night, my squad and I slept in the rickety dormitory used by the maintenance crews of the telephone company. As night fell, danger returned. National Guardsmen who stayed hidden during the day came out under the cover of darkness to drive by checkpoints while firing at the militiamen stationed there. The young militiamen, on the other hand, would fire for no particular reason, trigger-happy and nervous.

"It keeps me from getting bored," one of them said to me later on.

The next day we finished distributing the newspaper. I went to my parents' house, and they gave me a heroine's welcome. It just didn't seem real that I was there. My house was the same. Nothing appeared to have changed, yet everything was so different. My parents wanted me to stay. They asked if I had brought clothing with me, and when Sergio and the children would come. They told me I could sleep in my old room. I called Sergio. I talked to the girls. Then I took a bath, got dressed, and explained I had to work. Outfitted in one of my new uniforms, my submachine gun next to me, I drove my father's car to Somoza's bunker. I wanted to find Modesto, get to work. There was so much to do.

At the bunker—the luxury bombproof shelter Somoza had built for himself—you could feel the eye-of-the-storm quiet of a command center. The air-conditioned rooms with wall-to-wall carpeting, leather chairs, and massive, heavy wood desks were heaving with activity. Members of the Sandinista Directorate had moved into the offices and were now issuing orders and organizing task forces to maintain order and get the country up and running again. Feeling a bit lost but excited nevertheless, I walked from one end of the tyrant's bunker to the other. In Somoza's bedroom, the young guerrillas were lying on the enormous bed, some of them rolling around like small children. Others were in the bathroom, taking turns calling their friends on the telephone mounted on the wall next to the toilet.

As Modesto told me later on that day, the way we had taken such absolute control was nothing less than astounding. For the several weeks leading up to the victory, the general feeling was that we would have to share power in some way, either with a reduced version of Somoza's army (that was the United States's idea) or in some other sort of power-sharing arrangement. Nobody expected the National Guard to disband so massively after the dictator fled. Sitting in one of the high-backed chairs in the conference room that he had moved into, Modesto looked content, but exhausted. The rectangular room was not very large, and there was almost no space at all around the conference table. A tall window looked out over an interior garden. There was wall-to-wall carpeting, like the other rooms, and the walls were still covered with maps where the dictator had assessed the extent of his defeat during his last days in power.

My reunion with Modesto turned out not to be the memorable event I had envisioned. No longer was he a guerrilla soldier with nothing to lose. Now he was one of our country's leaders. He looked through me. I left him to continue whatever he was doing, and wandered through the bunker, exploring every corner. Because it was a bunker, it was compact and functional, and the little natural light it received came in from a narrow, walled garden that doubled as a kind of protective trench. In a small side office, presumably for Somoza's support staff, I found an Argentinian woman, from the Montonero guerrillas, who had joined our forces on the Southern Front, enthusiastically ripping up photographs of Somoza and pulling diplomas and decorations off the walls, making a great pile on the floor with the idea of eventually setting it on fire. At the far end of the long rectangle of the bunker, a group of *compañeras* toiled away in the little kitchen, serving rice, beans, and cranberry sauce—one of the cans they had found in the pantry and which they deemed the most precious, valuable nectar—to the men conferring excitedly in the dining room next door. There were soldiers everywhere, commanders from all the different fronts. I saw several I knew personally. One of them, Ezequiel, was cuddling an ocelot in his lap—his mascot in the *runga*, or fray, as the insurrection was also known. In the hallways, in the rooms, and in the library, *compañeros* stood around, waiting for instructions. To kill time, they regaled each other with anecdotes of their exploits, telling their stories in a grand display of theatrics, onomatopoeia, and laughter. In the reception area, two stunning young women handled the radio communications with the municipalities and regions that were calling in for orientation, supplies for the citizens, doctors for the wounded.

By the time Modesto and I finally had a moment alone in the conference room, it was late. He told me that the next day I was to receive orders from Bayardo Arce, since he was the person organizing the media. I nodded.

"About you and me," he declared. "We can't go on like before. You have to define your situation, decide. The thing is, I'm not sure if I'm ready to live with anyone. I've told you before, I'm a loner. It would be a question of you living in one house and me in another."

It hurt to hear Modesto proposing that we live apart: I was supposed to leave Sergio so that the two of us could live in separate houses?

"Like the general's mistress," I answered, furious. The men in the National Guard were famous for maintaining houses for their lovers.

We argued and we grew angry with each other, but we ended up on the carpet, making love tangled in chair legs underneath Somoza's conference table.

CHAPTER THIRTY-SEVEN

On how I took charge of the country's TV stations
and aired the first Sandinista newscast

MANAGUA, 1979

THE NEXT DAY, Bayardo Arce sent me to take charge of the state television station, Channel 6. There were only two channels back then in Nicaragua.

"Go with your squad and take charge," he said. "I want you to have a newscast up and running by eight tonight." The television studios were located on the avenue that ran alongside the same volcanic crater where La Loma and the Military Hospital were. The building was an old, ugly mansion to which offices had been added with no particular concern for aesthetics. We went inside the station with our weapons at the ready, since we had been told there might be a fair number of National Guardsmen hiding in the basement, which supposedly had a tunnel that connected with La Loma. But there was no tunnel, nor any soldiers. When we inspected the area, we only found many old TV sets, plus a good number of new ones still sealed in their boxes. Other sections of the building—the studios, the archives, the offices—had been brutally vandalized, as if before leaving Somoza's loyalists had let loose a pack of wild horses to trample the place. When I went back out on the street, I noticed a group of people gathered on the lawn; they were service and mid-level employees of the station waiting to know whether they still had jobs. Since they were the only ones who could guide us through that disaster inside, I held an impromptu meeting with them and delivered a patriotic speech about the need to work together.

"For the moment, we can't offer you any salary other than food," I said as I finished. "As soon as the situation normalizes we'll clear all these things up. But right now we have to air the evening news."

They clapped. I remember that many of them came over to tell me they had never been Somoza supporters, that they had worked there because they needed the money. I remembered some of their faces from my days in advertising.

That night, standing amid the chaos, banging away at a beat-up typewriter, I wrote the script for that evening's news, baptizing it the Sandinista News. (In those days we were using the "Sandinista" label with no qualms, since the FSLN hadn't yet become a political party and "Sandinismo" still stood for a patriotic, all-encompassing movement. That would change later.) The text of my presentation said something like "the Revolution advances; the Revolution gathers strength," and I don't remember what else. What I hurriedly wrote down in ten minutes at the most remained the introduction to the nightly news for several years. As the brand-new director of what I named the Sandinista Television System, I went on the air briefly that night (in an olive drab uniform and red and black bandanna around my neck) to introduce the news and apologize for whatever glitches there might be in the program.

The next day, I disbanded my squad and sent the boys to report for other tasks. I began organizing the TV station and choosing the programming. I decided first to broadcast documentaries and educational programs, which we dug up from the archives. Then in the afternoon my friend Bosco arrived, with Iván García, also a creative executive in advertising. In the days that followed, more men and women, journalists, technicians, cameramen, showed up to volunteer. We came up with ambitious plans for a new era of television in the country.

After complaining for so much of my adult life about how television's tremendous possibilities were just being wasted—not only in Nicaragua, but in Costa Rica as well—I suddenly found myself in charge of designing the kind of state-run television that the new, free, revolutionary Nicaragua should offer. I had complete freedom to implement whatever crazy scheme happened to occur to me. Of course, intellectual romantic that I was, I thought of the obvious: education and culture for the people. None of those canned sitcoms from the United States. *Bonanza* and *I Dream of Jeannie* (even though I actually liked that one) were out. Jacques Cousteau, Chaplin movies, and science and nature documentaries were in, as were programs we could produce ourselves: interviews with guerrilla leaders, debates about the future of the country, a news hour focusing on the people of Nicaragua. The problem was that 60 percent of the dictatorship-era programming came from those American TV series, and the storage rooms were filled with all the shows I wanted to get rid of. The documentaries and educational programs were few and far between. Often we would have to rerun them just to fill up airtime. Sometimes, unintentional but hilarious conflicts would come up. On July 26, the anniversary of the Moncada takeover in Cuba, for example, a week after our victory, we broadcast Fidel Castro's speech and his salute to the Sandinista Revolution. After it was over, the station returned to its regular programming: the movie of the day—Charlie Chaplin's *The Great Dictator*.

I was in my parents' house when I received a phone call, either from Tomás Borge, the recently appointed minister of the interior (national security), or from Bayardo—I can't remember, but it was someone from the National Directorate.

"Gioconda, were you the person who decided to broadcast that dictator satire right after Fidel's speech?"

"Satire about a dictator? What satire about a dictator?" I asked, surprised, running to the television, where Charlie Chaplin, dressed in military garb, was playing with a globe, knocking it around in a buffoon's ballet, symbolically destroying it.

"My God! We never even thought it could look intentional. I'll have it stopped right away."

"You have to be more careful next time, all right?" said the voice on the other end of the line, conspiratorial, amused. "Don't forget, our Cuban friends aren't quite as irreverent as we are. Better to take it off the air, put on one of those science documentaries about the life of tigers."

I laughed. After all, it had been quite a humorous coincidence. I called the station and told them to pull the movie, replace it with some harmless documentary about tigers or elephants. After a week filled with scientific and educational documentaries, no one—not the public, not the *compañeros*, not even I—could bear the tedium any longer. Timidly, telling ourselves that a little further on we would start looking for better material, we began to pull out the sitcoms.

On behalf of the Revolution, I also took possession of the other Nicaraguan TV channel—the private one, Channel 2. The owners had fled the

country because of the war, and left the place in the custody of Dr. Luis
Pasos Arguello, a prestigious lawyer who had some relation to them.

"We need to use the facilities, Doctor," I said to him.

Dr. Pasos, who was also a friend of my own family—his daughter and I
had been classmates—said yes, of course, by all means. Trust and good
faith reigned and the doctor courteously granted us all the access we
needed to the facilities, while his son-in-law Octavio, the owner, made his
return.

Coming to power with such popular support, after a victorious military campaign, gave us a sense of absolute entitlement which presented a
myriad of temptations. There was an agreement, for example, stating
that only the properties belonging to Somoza and his closest allies could
be confiscated. Nevertheless, several months later, Channel 2 was confiscated. It was argued that its owners were Somoza supporters, mainly
because they had some family connection to him, but that was merely a
pretext for a totally unjustifiable action. Because I had been the one
handed the keys with such trust, I regretted the takeover on a personal
level, even if I was in no position to reverse the decision. That kind of
conduct quickly eroded the private sector's trust in the Revolution, and
impeded progress on the road to a new social contract. Other agreements
were "modified" as well, and concessions made to political parties, indi-
viduals, and the private sector were not honored. To maintain the hegemony necessary to push through the radical changes that would benefit
the majority, the Sandinistas excluded those who had hoped to share
power in a national coalition. With the dictatorship out of the way, blame
fell squarely on the shoulders of the bourgeoisie. Sandinistas who came
from upper-class backgrounds felt too intimidated to point out this
policy of exclusion, at the expense of agreements that had been made during the struggle. We were afraid to be eyed with suspicion. The bourgeoisie, I knew this firsthand, was far from innocent and its members
were only biding time while all these young Sandinista leaders revealed
their incompetence. I also knew that if we made enemies of them, they
would never give up. But this did not seem to bother many of my *compañeros*. They felt powerful, capable of handling any situation. Once again,
the notion of the ends justifying the means had won out.

My time as the head of the TV station was not a happy one. Those days
were so full of possibility, but when I look back on them, I regret not hav-

ing had more wisdom, I regret the obsession that possessed me and robbed me of the elation and novelty of that period. I did not breathe in the crisp, fresh air of rebirth that was pervasive in those first weeks. Every poet, I suppose, should fall madly in love at least once in her life, so that she may come to know the shadow side of the feminine human experience, plumb the depth of her own vulnerability and emerge the wiser. But such maddening, all-encompassing love monopolized all my senses and robbed me of energy. I, who had always been a responsible person, one who met her obligations, now found myself inventing the most pathetic excuses to leave my office at the TV station. I assigned myself the task of interviewing all the prominent guerrilla leaders because this allowed me to spend long hours at the bunker near Modesto. His exhortation of "you have to define your situation, decide" hung over my head like the sword of Damocles. I was desperately fending off the arrival of the day I would have to tell Sergio the truth, watch his face, hear the sound of his heart breaking. I felt selfish, cruel. In my heart, though, I knew that his pain wasn't the only thing that stopped me from confessing everything—it was also my own fear that Modesto would reject me in the end. Why take the chance of throwing my entire life overboard if the only thing waiting for me was desolation and heartache?

My redheaded Camilo, his round, chubby baby face, was a living presence that grew larger and larger, pressing on my chest, constricting my breath. I was the arsonist, the one who was about to torch the refuge where my children and I had found shelter.

I was having lunch one day at my parents' house when Sergio called. I don't how he found out. It was barely a week after the victory.

"I think you and I have to talk," he said. "Wouldn't you say so?"

"Yes," I answered.

"There's someone else, isn't there?"

"Yes," I answered.

I could see myself in the mirror we women use when we believe that earthly paradise ended because we bit the apple. I was a serpent-haired, hellish Medusa. Later, I would realize that living by your heart has its price, and that I didn't have it in me to live any other way. I have never been able to bring myself to believe that a woman can save a man's honor by sacrificing her own integrity and lying to herself. For better or for worse, my passions did not lie with Sergio. He had run that risk willingly from the start of our relationship. When he accepted that, if I had not fallen in love with him, he would make me love him by offering his company and consolation. He had loved me on his own terms and that was his responsibility, but I couldn't see that at the time.

Sergio arrived from San José the next day. Patiently, almost sweetly, the recriminations began.

"I trusted you. I trusted Modesto," he said.

"Sometimes I thought you knew," I whispered. "It was so obvious."

"So what do we do now? When a relationship fails, both people are at fault. I don't deny that I have some responsibility in this. But we should give it another try. We can forget this and rebuild our relationship. What we have is solid. I think it's worth trying to salvage it."

"I don't know if I can do it," I said, wanting to cry. "But we can give it a try."

For several months I tried. Then I started to waver, maddened by the dilemma, knowing I had to choose between two men, each of whom possessed qualities I loved and clung to.

But the situation was untenable. I came to a decision: Sergio and I separated for good. Before I put an end to my doubts, I went to Costa Rica to fetch Maryam and Melissa. Before returning to Nicaragua, I locked myself with my three children in the bathroom of our San José apartment (which at the time was serving as a temporary residence for Sandinistas) to talk with them alone. I felt I had an obligation to explain what was going on, so that they wouldn't suffer and imagine worse things than what they had already begun to sense. Just like the apartment, the bathroom was small and simple. Camilo crawled on a shag rug, dragging it behind him, and the girls sat on the floor, looking up at me. Sitting on the edge of the shower stall, I told them that Sergio and I were separating, that I had fallen in love with someone else. Maryam was upset. Melissa said, "That's good. Sergio scolds me too much," which made Maryam and me smile. The two of us ended up amused at the puckered lips on her little sister's face, her childish logic. I reassured them that we would manage. I told them I wasn't the perfect mother, that I was just a woman like any other, that I had fallen in love, but I also loved them with all my heart. We would overcome the difficulties together. Camilo was crawling around, climbing on my legs.

He stayed with Sergio in San José temporarily. Sergio was planning to move to Nicaragua and he wanted our little boy to live with him. He clung to Camilo and I didn't have the heart, after I had denied him my love, to summarily dismantle what had been his life, brandishing the sword of my maternal rights. He had done his share. I was the evil one, Circe, Medusa. Bitterly, I convinced myself that Sergio would give my little Camilo stability. He was a wonderful father. In any case, women don't have a monopoly on maternity. Truly living up to the dream of equality between men and women meant accepting that men could mother too. It was easy to say, and sounded like some airtight feminist rationale, but my body ached as if I were in the hospital all over again, with the doctor ripping my insides apart and telling me my son was dead.

I felt like I was drowning in amniotic fluid. Never before had I experienced anything as painful as that psychic conjunction: on one hand, terror at the loss, and on the other, paralysis of the will. I didn't even dare demand possession of my son. For me, at that moment, Sergio was the incarnation of the masculine archetype, the High Priest, Solomon with his sword, ready to cut the child in half. And I yielded. I gave him up. My little redhead. The child that had taken more of my life than any of the others. I didn't yell that I had been the one who had remained immobile in bed, so that he could live; that it had been I who had enticed him with the beauty of life, whispering to him, encouraging him day and night to hold fast to my womb; that I was the one who had offered my body, the one who had invoked the spirit of my *compañeros*. I didn't hold up any of those rights even though I knew that the wrenching intensity of my desire was at the root of our son's miraculous survival. I wanted to open my mouth and beg Sergio not to inflict that punishment on me, but words wouldn't come forth. Centuries of guilt, of hearing stories about adulterous women stoned to death, my Catholic education, prevented me from seeing any responsibility other than my own. The fear that I would not be a good mother for Camilo paralyzed me, my unconscious submitted to the prejudices against my own gender.

I remember so clearly the looks on my daughters' faces as we drove across the border and entered Nicaragua, as they looked out on the great expanse of green, the banks of Lake Nicaragua, and Concepción and Maderas, twin volcanoes, with their peaks shrouded in clouds. "Nicaragua is so pretty," said Melissa. Despite my mood, once again I felt the breath of freedom and joy that kept my heart in high spirits during those days.

"I want you to know that dreams can come true," I said to them, becoming emotional. "Don't ever forget that; and don't ever let anyone convince you that something you dream of isn't possible. It is. I dreamt of this. Of bringing you here without fear. Of giving you a free country, and here we are . . . and you helped make that happen too. You were my brave little *compañeras.*"

Not long after, Sergio left the apartment in San José and moved to Managua, where he rented a little house. I would visit Camilo there, and sometimes he would spend days in my house. When it was time to separate, Camilo and I would both cry, and I would be left with a sad void in my arms. Slowly Sergio and I achieved some sort of balance. For Camilo's sake, we made an effort to act like a couple, like friends, completely sharing our parental role. Camilo moved effortlessly from Sergio's house to mine, guided by his own emotional instincts and needs rather than a strict schedule of weekend visits. As he grew older, he would spend longer and longer periods of time with me. He was seven years old when it was his father's turn to be the parent in an unstable situation. From that point on until he went off to college, Camilo lived with me.

Melissa, Maryam, and I spent a short period of time with my parents before moving to our own house not far from Modesto's. He had gotten his way. We didn't live together.

"Think about Jean-Paul Sartre and Simone de Beauvoir," he said. "They didn't live together. Look at it that way."

I never could. I raged about it until the very last day.

CHAPTER THIRTY-EIGHT

On the implications of power and on how love made me lose my mind

MANAGUA, 1979

IN MANAGUA the initial chaos subsided relatively quickly, at least on the surface. The capital hadn't suffered nearly as much damage as some other cities, and apart from the boys in olive drab all over the place, Managua's day-to-day life began showing signs of a return to normality. The only exceptions were the nighttime skirmishes, which took longer to let up.

The Ejército Popular Sandinista, the Sandinista People's Army, was made up of the people who had fought in the guerrilla columns. As a demonstration of their recruits' improvement, the military leaders organized their first small, simple military parade sometime around then, in a vacant lot not far from Somoza's old bunker. Modesto and I went to watch it together, and I remember how impressed we were by the discipline of the men and women marching in formation beneath the hot sun, wearing their new uniforms, their rifles resting against their shoulders. We watched the parade go by from a set of improvised bleachers, and I remember hearing various members of the Sandinista leadership comment about how difficult it was for young men and women to live together in the same military barracks. For the first time ever, I heard someone suggest that perhaps women should be barred from active service. I considered that ludicrous and said so. How could they even think such a thing when women had already proven themselves to be as able fighters as men during the insurrection? Nevertheless, some months later, the top army officials, led by Humberto Ortega, decided that from that point on women would only occupy administrative posts. They justified the decision by saying it was a question of money, that keeping men and women soldiers separate was a giant headache that incurred far too many additional expenses. But the Sandinista police, as it was called then, which was being organized with advisers supplied by General Torrijos, chose not to make that distinction and women enlisted in its ranks in great numbers. The same thing happened in the Ministry of the Interior. I liked seeing those women in their olive green uniforms and impeccably shined military boots. Many of them wore lipstick and even painted their nails bright red. These were all signs of a new era for the women in my country.

For Nicaraguans, fear of authority was a conditioned reflex. We were all too accustomed to menacing-looking soldiers wearing combat helmets and patrolling the streets with their weapons drawn. The Sandinista police never wore helmets and their corps was so young and friendly that people would refer to them as *compitas*, buddies. That was nothing short of a miracle. I was nearly moved to tears when, one day, I was stopped by a young policeman who, after he read my name on the driver's license, gave me a mini-lecture on "the revolutionary responsibility of drivers to the people of Nicaragua," and then said: "All right, *compañera*, you can go. Maybe this will make it into one of your poems."

The city changed in other ways as well, including the residential neighborhoods that had once been the sole domain of the haute bourgeoisie. Many homes that had been abandoned by Somoza supporters and military officers on the run—government ministers, corporate executives whose companies were linked to the dictatorship, and wealthy families that had left Managua months earlier when the insurrection had begun to spread throughout the country—were now occupied by guerrillas. I don't know how it happened or who made the decision, but I can only guess that initially it was just a matter of finding a house for the combatants who didn't have any place to live. The obvious solution was to occupy empty homes, based on the assumption that those properties now belonged to the state. The improvised nature of this operation, however, lent itself to abuses as time went by. Those houses were deemed spoils of war taken from a corrupt enemy; at least this was the moral justification for making use of them. One simply took possession of the house and the belongings of the people who had fled. The house I moved into with my daughters had belonged to a colonel in the Nicaraguan navy. It was simple but comfortable, with four rooms, a garden and a guest house in the back, filled with books on navigation. Some of its furniture still remained, and it took me several months to conquer the feeling that time inside the house was stalled, and of having intruded upon someone else's life—there were family photos and children's notebooks everywhere, and you could feel the presence of those people who, when they left, probably never imagined they wouldn't be coming back.

Modesto called me up to the bunker one day, saying he urgently needed someone he could trust to work with him. He wanted me to be that person.

"You'd be making a mistake," Bayardo said when I told him about it. "You're an intelligent woman. The work at the television station is exactly the kind of work you're good at. If you accept what he proposes you'll be following him around, playing a sort of secretarial role . . . the woman behind the man. You'll be setting yourself up for trouble," he warned me with a devilish smile, flashing his sharp canines at me. He was saying it to me as a friend, just between the two of us. He was right. I thanked him for the advice, though I didn't take it. I couldn't. All my inner resolve had degenerated into a kind of gelatinous goo that moved only to accommodate Modesto. I justified the decision by telling myself he needed me. He needed a person to help him organize his time, keep records of his activities—an assistant. And I, a woman who scorned the idea of being any man's secretary, who had consistently refused to study to be a bilingual secretary (the career of the moment when I graduated from high school), suddenly found this prospect unbelievably attractive. To be at Modesto's side as he shaped the future of the country, resurrecting it from the ashes, seemed far more fascinating than any other project I could have undertaken independently of him.

"It was power," says my friend Malena whenever we look back on those days. "Power was what attracted you."

I never would have accepted this reasoning back then, but twenty years later I can't deny that my desire for an intimate brush with power contributed to the sum of my confusions. It would be too easy, of course, to claim that it was my only motivation. My actions were totally primitive, similar to the behavior of females in a pack of apes in the jungle. I wanted to be selected by the strongest male. The thing that fired my mind (and my hormones), betraying all reason, wasn't power itself but rather my *submission* to the power of the dominant male. My rational mind clearly told me that following Modesto would hurt me in the long run. I knew my power rested in affirming myself through my own means, not in staying at Modesto's side. Leaving my job as the head of the television station would hurt my image, erode the respect I had earned from the work I had done up until then.

And so, when against my own better judgment I told Bayardo that I was sorry but I would take the job with Modesto, I felt my stomach twist in a knot. The way he looked at me, with a mix of contempt and compassion, made me feel profoundly ashamed of myself. I turned to leave as quickly as I could and went straight into the conference room where Modesto was meeting with a group of people. As I listened to him—"take notes," he said to me—I felt a piercing disappointment with myself for having given in. In the days that followed, I accompanied him on a trip to evaluate the general conditions in various Nicaraguan cities. Thirty-five thousand people had died in the insurrection, one hundred thousand had been wounded or mutilated, and a million people had been displaced from their homes or towns. The food situation was critical, and Nicaragua had to rely on humanitarian aid from the Red Cross and other international relief agencies. We went to Jinotepe, Granada, Rivas. Dressed in olive drab with my submachine gun slung over my shoulder (which Bayardo always said I carried like a handbag), I went around with the *comandante*'s entourage. The head of the Sandinista Television System was now a bodyguard with a typewriter. Whenever I would start to regret having made such a foolish decision, Modesto would suddenly appear at my side, or someone would mention that I was the *comandante*'s partner, and for one dark, pathetic moment I would feel validated, important. To make matters worse, Modesto's affections for me swung like a pendulum gone mad. At moments he was sweet and affectionate, but, in general, he was distant and acted with pointed indifference, as if to make people think there was nothing but a purely professional relationship between us. Reduced to a crumpled rag of my former self, I followed him around like a house pet, ready to do anything that would earn me a bit of his affection.

It was at Modesto's side, stopping in small towns and bombed-out cities, that I witnessed, firsthand, the extensive damage caused by the war. The hamlets and villages of Nicaragua are sleepy communities where time's passing is barely perceptible. Tile-roofed houses, with high ceilings and adobe construction, are packed tightly together around thickly planted parks, with large trees and the ever present old church. Only the center of town qualifies for paving, otherwise it's all dirt roads where pigs and chickens roam, bordered by houses built out of rough-hewn planks with outdoor kitchens, zinc roofs, and children running around barefoot and in rags. In cities that had been bombed, rubble was everywhere. Crops had been lost and the infrastructure obliterated. Spray-painted revolutionary slogans covered every available wall surface. At spontaneous rallies held in parks, Modesto would talk to people about the reconstruction of the country and the tremendous work it would require. The crowd would applaud wildly when he declared that the young would now have access to free education, and that everybody would receive adequate health care. I was always incredibly moved by the hope and joy I saw in those faces, the firm voices with which the most humble people described their problems, needs, expectations. I would carefully note down the request along with the name of the person in my notebook.

During that trip, I also observed the effect power had over people's behavior. Modesto's bodyguards, who only a month earlier had fearlessly confronted Somoza's tanks, were docile and obedient in their leader's presence. I understood that, besides the respect they felt for Modesto, they were now trying to behave like military men, but it bothered me to watch how they scurried after him whenever he would get up to leave a meeting, without so much as a word in their direction. I resented the assumption that we were to follow him—as if we were obligated to read his mind—the flurry that would ensue, and the yelling: "Move, move, it's time to go, the *comandante*'s already on his way out." We would spring into action, our rifles clicking away as we hoisted them onto our shoulders at full speed, bumping into each other as we hurried to reach Modesto in time before his driver pulled up, as if the doors of the three cars in which our retinue traveled were to open and close in unison, so they could all start their engines at precisely the same moment. Several times I barely made it to my place just before the convoy took off. Often I found myself reacting angrily and rebelling against those rituals of Modesto's entourage. What's wrong with you? I asked the men. What was the point of rushing around like that? What would happen to Modesto if he actually had to wait a few minutes? For God's sake, it wasn't as though we were rushing a casualty to the hospital!

But that military protocol had its grandiose, seductive side. We would arrive at the military headquarters of war-torn cities still reeling from the recent fighting, and Modesto—*comandante*, member of the Sandinista National Directorate, maximum authority in Nicaragua both during and after the Revolution—would move calmly amid the soldiers hurriedly standing at attention. In Jinotepe, the town where Modesto was born, people gathered to cheer him from the street beneath the windows of the building where he held his meeting with the local authorities. In

Rivas, a city on the Costa Rican border, we visited an estate on a sugar mill that had belonged to Somoza's family. We strolled through one carpeted salon after another, contemplating the luxurious, utterly tasteless décor and the inevitable mess wrought by the victorious guerrillas who had marched through the house. In one of the rooms, we found hundreds of photographs scattered all over the floor. We sat down to look at them. Family photos. The dictator's children and nephews blowing out candles on their birthday cakes, laughing before the camera dressed up in ridiculous outfits for a carnival celebration. Photos of pleasure trips and *quinceañeras*, fifteenth-birthday parties. I saw photographs of Valeria, my childhood classmate who married Bernabé, one of Somoza's nephews, in a sumptuous country club reception to which I was invited. It was hard to believe we were actually in this house, looking at the photographs of the deposed dynasty. My *compañeros* laughed and laughed, opening boxes and closets, pulling out dresses, diving into the pool clothes and all, as I stared, mesmerized by the photographs of the young Somoza women: Salvadora, Karla, Carolina, all of whom had gone to the same school as me. Salvadora had even been in my class, a hefty, spoiled girl who wore thick satin ribbons in her hair. I still remember the day when, without any provocation at all, in an act of pure childish cruelty, she walked up to me as I was eating a piece of cake I had bought at recess, and in one movement grabbed the treat from me and threw it down to the ground, laughing as I struggled not to cry.

In the area where the Southern Front had been active—their offensives had been famously repelled by Somoza's best troops, disproving Fidel's hypothesis—we visited San Martín, Cornelio Hueck's hacienda. Hueck, a plotting, corrupt politician, had been loyal to the dictator. When we arrived, we found a Sandinista garrison camped out in his colonial house, perched atop a series of rocks near the beach and with spectacular views of the Pacific Ocean.

"That's where Cornelio hid," said a guerrilla, pointing to a dimple in the terrain. "We weren't going to fire at him, but he took out a weapon and we had to execute him." Modesto looked at him. Then he looked at me and shrugged. There was nothing he could do now. The Revolution prohibited summary executions but some couldn't be stopped.

Regardless of everything else, being with Modesto was to witness close-up the creation of a new power structure. I felt I was living an extraordinary time filled with historic resonance. In my notebook I recorded events, agreements, anecdotes, possessed by my role as scribe and chronicler. I resigned myself to his sour temperament, his sudden mood swings. They would pass, I thought, and when they did, I would still be there. The unbridled, tortured love I felt for him led me to invent the most convoluted justifications to soothe the rebelliousness inside of me. My submissive admiration for the hero all but blinded me to the man. I was no longer Dulcinea, but Sancho Panza gazing up at my Don Quixote.

We returned to Managua. Modesto had moved to the house of the colonel who had been the head of the Transit Police. It was a huge house, with Mediterranean-style architecture and abundant gardens. The inside was a tribute to bad taste. Six living rooms all decorated in different styles: one with red, Louis XIV–style furniture, another completely modern, another Spanish-style, another decked out in wicker from top to bottom, and yet another that was all chrome and glass. In the bathroom, the toilet was mounted up on a little round altar, and the study was dominated by a massive billiard table. Generally I slept at home with my daughters, but I would often have lunch or spend part of the night there. Several of Modesto's old guerrilla friends, from his days in the mountains, also stayed there for a while. Whenever they would see me suffering, they would try and console me, telling me not to take his tantrums so seriously. That was just his way, they said.

"When we barely had food, he didn't eat so that we could," they argued in his defense. They were ferociously loyal to him and I knew why. The man had his demons but he also had his angels; he was a truly noble person.

It took me years to finally acquire the maturity to understand how that period must have been for someone like Modesto. For a long, long time, there had been a great deal of mistrust among the nine leaders of the Sandinista National Directorate. And then, only a few short months after the unity agreements had been signed, we won the war. All the misgivings and conflicts were still fresh in their minds when the political circumstances suddenly forced them to face the task of creating a new country as a unified group. In the power games within the group, some members were too trusting, too quick to soften their opposition to certain decisions, while the more politically shrewd took advantage of them. The Ortega brothers, champions of the insurrectional strategy that set the country on fire, felt superior to the rest. They assiduously placed their people in positions of power by cannily manipulating the tacit recognition of their peers, and situated themselves at the top of the heap: one brother became the head of the government and coordinator of the junta, and the other, commander in chief of the new army.

Modesto's foul mood had its reasons. Yet my obsessive love and insecurity had me so wrapped up in myself that I thought I was to blame for everything that upset him. I would observe his tense silences and dissolve in all sorts of crazy hypotheses, wondering what I had done to anger him.

CHAPTER THIRTY-NINE

On my return to Cuba and on another encounter
with Fidel after the Revolution

HAVANA, 1979

GIVEN THE CONSIDERABLE international relations experience I had accumulated during my years in exile, Modesto asked me to join him on a trip to Cuba, for the 6th Summit Conference of the Non-Aligned Movement. After returning from Havana we would then take off for a tour of several socialist countries.

The summit was held in Havana from September 3 to 9, 1979. Maryam and Melissa stayed with Justine, because my relationship with my parents had grown increasingly tense after my separation from Sergio.

Heads of state from all over the world attended the conference, but the Sandinistas were the novelty, the youngsters everyone doted on. That year, Nicaragua applied for membership to the Non-Aligned Countries, which, ever since its creation in Belgrade in 1961, was a forum for Third World nations that proposed a different, more just, international order, and a position of independence from the superpowers.

International leaders treated us with great warmth, like heroes, as we congregated in the hallways of Havana's beautiful Conventions Palace. Whenever the Sandinistas or Nicaragua were mentioned during the plenary sessions, the entire room would explode in thunderous applause and we would get up, radiant, and raise our fists high. Most of us were in olive drab, but each person wore their soldier's uniform as he or she saw fit. Since it was so hot, I wore my military pants with a halter top. From the waist up I looked like a summer vacationer and from the waist down—pants, boots, and all—I was a soldier. Now I think it must have looked terrible, but at the time I felt beautiful and seductive. I was in that getup when I ran into General Torrijos. He acknowledged me with a curt nod of the head and then quickly walked away.

In the house where the Nicaraguan delegation was staying, there was a constant flow of people. The Cuban Communist Party officials didn't know what to do with us, they were so beside themselves with glee that they now had revolutionary company in Latin America. Fidel came by several times for breakfast, lunch. He barely glanced at me.

"Ah! The poet," he said, courteous and distant as he offered me his hand the first time I saw him since our meeting in January.

He acted like our grandfather. We were the triumphant guerrillas that he had so often dreamt of for Latin America, and we were young and inexperienced besides. We sat around him in rocking chairs, listening to him philosophize about the differences between fighting for freedom and finally taking control. It was obvious that he felt a kind of calling to be our mentor, to guide us down the arduous path of governing a nation. I sat there, watching him pontificate. I noticed how carefully he expressed his opinions: on one hand he didn't want to seem like he was telling us what to do, yet he left no doubt as to how he thought we should do things. It was almost endearing, because you could see how much he would have liked to take charge—he was making such an effort to maintain a statesmanlike distance in a situation that he would have loved to handle personally. But he must have also realized that we felt wise in our own way, that we felt we had both opportunities and the wherewithal to avoid falling into the isolation that the Cuban Revolution had suffered.

The atmosphere in the house was jubilant, electric. At nighttime we would convene to compare notes from the day's activities, laughing at how little we knew about those protocol-laden summits where we were supposed to take a position on so many international conflicts. Our delegates would return from closed-door sessions to madly flip through geography books to figure out where a particular country was on the map, and to read up on the history of some guerrilla movement or other on a remote island somewhere. We would debate about the position the Sandinistas should take on different issues, how to avoid sticking one's foot in one's mouth, and how to act as if we knew everything about the complexities of world politics.

———

As we walked through Havana in our flashy guerrilla getups, people everywhere would stop to congratulate us. Those were happy times. We were on top of the world. At lunchtime in the official reception house, I would sit down to eat with Modesto, the Ortega brothers sitting at the table next to ours. Daniel would sit there, peering at me out of the corner of his eye, casting me odd, provocative looks which I did my best to avoid. I could hardly believe he would do that right in front of Modesto and Rosario, his girlfriend, but he seemed utterly unbothered. I hardly knew him then, and he was a man of few words, but from that moment on I would always think of him as a conniving, dark character filled with shadows and cobwebs. Years later, when his stepdaughter accused him of sexual abuse, I remembered how uneasy I felt with him ever since that day. Rosario, who had always been such a strong woman, was now timid and frightened, a bag of nerves. She had lost a considerable amount of weight since I first met her, and bit her fingernails incessantly, following Daniel around like a faceless, sad little shadow. Maybe that was what I looked like with Modesto, I thought to myself, ashamed. She and I, each in our own way, were the victims of a treacherous spell that had us chasing after them like beggars trying to catch the love crumbs those men dropped for us here and there, crumbs which we accepted as if they were manna from heaven. I remember how we observed one another cagily— we were both conscious, I think, of our utterly unjustifiable behavior, of the perverse, hateful pleasure of submission. We had regressed to being cavewomen, totally beholden to our male partners. Months later Rosario and I would trade stories and we were astonished at the similarities of our situations.

The 6th Summit of the Non-Aligned Movement was brought to an end by Hurricane Fifi. The raging fury of the tropics descended upon us. The little lake bordering the hospitality houses overflowed and our house was suddenly filled with ducks swimming through the living room. We were forced to evacuate in minibuses, the water almost reaching the level of the windows. Our final days in Havana were spent in the Hotel Habana Libre. There, Modesto's mood improved. He would talk passionately of the faith he had in our ability to achieve a new, benevolent kind of revolution, a synthesis of the positive elements of the other revolutions, yet without falling into the same traps. When society's objective was collective happiness, when it began to function as a community of ideas and hopes, the people would adopt a new set of values. We spent all our time in the hotel room, reading and talking, and listening to Omar Cabezas's amusing stories.

At the time, Omar embodied the happy, irreverent spirit that gave our Revolution an innocent, mischievous kind of vitality. He was the chief of Personal Security, the secret service that protected the Sandinista leaders, but such a serious position inspired no solemnity on his part. I will never forget how hard we laughed when he recounted his adventures from when the Costa Rican president, Rodrigo Carazo Odio, paid a visit to Managua shortly after our victory.

"Just picture it, Gioconda: the Costa Rican secret service arrive at the airport with the president, all of them flashing their walkie-talkies. We didn't have any of that, you know? Nothing. So I go behind one of the airline counters and borrow a walkie-talkie from one of the girls I know there. No way, I said to myself—we're not going to be left out of this. So there I am, talking the whole time into this walkie-talkie as if I'm giving orders to my men, but it was all a big sham. Nobody heard a thing I said, of course. I mean, I wasn't talking to anyone, but I just acted serious, even though inside I was cracking up at this big farce I had staged!"

That's what those days were like, full of improvisation and a desire to fit into the roles history had cast for us.

CHAPTER FORTY

On how the shadows of the past came to cloud the present

Managua, 1979, 1981

I GREW UP with the idea that American ambassadors were powerful figures whose function was to protect the tyrant against any popular attempts to get rid of him. I remember one in particular, Turner B. Shelton, with his unforgettable toad eyes, always hovering behind Somoza like a sinister, ugly, Machiavelli.

Our victory was only a few days old when everyone in the bunker began speculating about what to expect from the United States. The consensus was that they would come after us.

"Why be so pessimistic?" I argued.

"Because that's what they've always done. They're the empire. The minute we don't do what they want, they'll pounce on us. You'll see. Don't be naive. The best thing we can do is get ourselves ready."

In one of his first press conferences as minister of the interior (state security), Tomás Borge spoke, ironically, of how the new government would warmly welcome U.S. aid to arm the Sandinista People's Army.

"All revolutions inevitably generate a counterrevolution," he said. "Somoza's National Guardsmen who left the country will return. That's the way it is. And that is why we must be prepared. We would be very pleased to receive President Carter's assistance."

In that same press conference, he announced that there would be no capital punishment in Nicaragua. He said that the Sandinistas were "relentless in combat" but "generous in triumph." He announced his willingness to pardon his tireless torturers, the people who kept him chained to a wall for seven months and in solitary confinement for over a

year. There would be no summary executions in Nicaragua as there had
been in Cuba. The tiny figure of Tomás Borge shook with the emotion of
his fiery words. He gave a long, eloquent speech about forgiveness as an
integral quality of the revolutionary character. Many of us in the audience were moved to tears. His discussion of weapons and the United
States got lost in the magnanimity of what followed. Nobody there actually thought that the United States would ever be willing to aid the Sandinista army.

One afternoon, while chaos still reigned in the old bunker, there was a
great commotion. A rumor had spread that a delegation of U.S. senators
and congressmen were about to arrive to meet with the National Directorate. Everyone was ordered out of the room, we all were told to disappear. Once the meeting was over and I was back at the office I saw
Modesto, Humberto Ortega, Daniel Ortega, and Bayardo Arce in the
waiting area just after the U.S. delegation left. They looked like mischievous, gleeful little boys. All they could talk about was the incredible
twist of fate that put them in the position of being recognized as powerful
leaders, when only recently they had been nothing more than guerrilla
fighters. But hadn't anyone noticed their tone? someone asked. American
mistrust had been evident from that very first meeting, they had wasted
no time in demanding to know the Revolution's intentions, as if it was
suddenly their job to supervise a country that they had left in the hands
of a tyrant for so many years. They just assumed they would continue to
exert the same influence over Nicaragua that they had had during the
Somoza years, one of them added, but they were wrong. Very wrong.

The childlike, triumphant, mischievous delight I saw in their faces
that day will remain etched in my memory forever. I don't know if it was a
premonition, but in the course of those years and in light of all the troubles that eventually came our way, I have often thought back to those
faces and I have always felt the same, unsettling intuition that these men
had been seduced by the spell of their own self-image, the vision that
they saw in the eyes of the masses on the day the Revolution was won.
They felt eminently astute and capable, a cross between political bright
boys and heroic, strapping knights-errant. That was the attitude with
which they confronted dangerous challenges that deserved closer, more
cautious judgment and a maturity that the dazzling spell of power placed
beyond their grasp.

The bold spontaneity they exhibited in the beginning eventually became their downfall when the moment arrived to confront the United States—paradoxically, another nation that clung to its own grandiose vision of itself. There was a clash of images from the start, each government rejecting the way the other saw it. The Sandinistas were unwilling to accept the way the United States referred to us, and the United States was equally unwilling to accept the way we referred to them. How could they possibly swallow the verse of the Sandinista anthem, which we sang at the top of our lungs, and that said: "we fight against the Yankee, enemy of humanity"—a quote from Che Guevara about the Vietnam War. It was pointless to argue that our perspective originated in a decades-long history of U.S. interventions in Nicaragua, of the very struggle that Sandino himself had waged against the U.S. Marines. The rhetoric we used didn't help. "We aren't communists," we argued, fighting the label the United States had pinned on us. And it was the truth: for all the Marxism and Leninism we had studied, for all the love or respect we may have felt for Cuba, Fidel, and even the Soviet Union, we had different dreams for Nicaragua, we wanted a new kind of socialism— Nicaraguan, libertarian.

For as long as I could remember, among ourselves, the Sandinistas, there was always a lively, open debate—and rather sharp criticism— regarding the Soviet and Cuban models. No doubt the Sandinista rhetoric was the product of the radical times we lived in, of our self-aggrandizing identity as heroic champions of truth and justice and of our desire to change the world on behalf of the exploited and the oppressed, but we were not dogmatic leftists. We wanted a new kind of revolution that would be original and open, the product of a tropical, irreverent left-wing movement.

With time, the Revolution's stance grew more and more rigid. Powerful economic groups and the extremist Left began to challenge the revolutionary reforms—the former because their own interests were being threatened, and the latter because their extremist demands were not being met. But their criticism was not met with an open mind. It was hard to forget previous Latin American experiences, like Chile in 1973, where leniency had ended in a bloody coup. Rather than working toward an all-inclusive social pact, we decreed a new order because we felt it was the only way to remain true to the impoverished masses. Lacking a democratic tradition of our own, we took advantage of the authority we wielded. We might have considered ourselves very benevolent, but the truth was we had inherited a long legacy of authoritarianism.

I would like to think that with time, the Revolution could have muddled through its own confusion to eventually arrive at a fair, equitable balance. Sadly, we will never know what would have happened to our nation if Nicaraguans had taken full responsibility of the country's future, without foreign intervention. Ronald Reagan began his presidency in 1981. His electoral platform stated: "We deplore the Sandinista takeover of Nicaragua, as well as Marxist attempts to destabilize El Salvador, Honduras, and Guatemala."

All too quickly, the bad omens had become a reality.

CHAPTER FORTY-ONE

*Of my travels to the socialist countries and of
my meeting with Vietnamese General Vo Nguyen Giap*

OCTOBER–NOVEMBER 1979

AFTER SPENDING a few weeks in Nicaragua following the summit in
Havana, we left on a tour of the socialist countries. As time went by the
official delegations grew larger and larger, with bodyguards, secretaries,
and photographers, but in the beginning everything was much simpler.
Five of us went: Modesto and Luis Carrión of the National Directorate
and Juan Jované, Julio López, and I as advisers, observers, translators—
whatever was needed of us.

In Moscow, we were met by Constantin Kurin, the official in charge of
Nicaraguan relations for the Central Committee of the Soviet Communist Party. He was a very tall, thin man, with the kind and melancholic
face of a Tolstoy character. It was the first time that someone from the
Soviet Communist Party met with the Sandinistas; their links with
Nicaragua for many years had been through the Nicaraguan Socialist
Party. We were still an unknown quantity. We spent a week at a special
residence for distinguished guests, a beautiful, lavish mansion several
stories high with elegant furniture, heavy velvet curtains, and a sumptuous dining room with crystal chandeliers and a long wooden table polished to a high luster. Modesto told me that we couldn't stay in the same
room because we weren't legally married and the Party officials were
quite strict and old-fashioned about that sort of thing. The men were
given rooms on the upper floors, while I was assigned a small room on the
ground floor, as the "secretary." I had no choice but to bite my lip and
contain the anger I felt toward myself, the Russians, and Modesto.

I remember our time in Moscow as a succession of lunches and dinners. In between the sumptuous meals they served us, Party officials would parade through the house, quizzing us endlessly on various topics.

"The Soviets are like elephants," Modesto said. "They're slow to move but when they do, they put all their weight into it."

We toured the Kremlin, and walked in Red Square by John Reed's and also Stalin's tombs. In Lenin's mausoleum, I was awed by the imposing Red Guards, custodians of a pervasive silence, while people tiptoed around the glass case where Lenin seemed to be sleeping so peacefully.

We were in the Rome of the Left, with all its saints and pontiffs. Communism was a kind of religion too. It smelled like one, complete with magical beliefs of a heaven on earth. On every avenue and street corner, history showed its marks. With a little bit of imagination, you could easily travel back in time—to Napoleon's siege of Moscow in 1812, or to the days of the Nazi attacks during World War II, or to the scenes of the Russian Revolution described by Trotsky.

Toward the end of the trip, when we returned to Moscow for the flight home, we attended the anniversary celebrations of the Bolshevik Revolution, on November 7. At the military parade in Red Square, we saw the legendary missile launchers known as Katyushas, Stalin's Organs, which had played a decisive role in Hitler's defeat. The city was bedecked in huge red flags, and the people marched en masse, their children on their shoulders, everyone singing patriotic, nostalgic Russian folk songs. Later on that day, I went to the solemn session of the Central Committee of the Communist Party in the Congressional Palace, and saw Brezhnev in the distance, reading his speech. When he was done, the people in the auditorium stood up and sang the "Internationale," the socialist hymn. The party following the session was majestic. The tables were decorated with huge ice sculptures festooned with fruit, flowers, caviar. The guests were all dressed in formal clothes, the military officers' uniforms heaving with an almost obscene quantity of decorations and pins, the Orthodox priests in their regal vestments. There, I met the cosmonaut Valentina Tereshkova, a small, smiling, attractive woman.

I saw the other side of the coin as well, when Constantin invited us to his home to visit his family and bid us farewell. He and his wife shared their tiny apartment with his daughter, who had recently been married. That was where I learned that in Moscow, the residential quarters were restricted to only a few square meters per family. The daily life of the Kurins was humble, confined. Constantin's wife was a doctor, but at home she was the classic wife, taking care of all the usual domestic tasks. The submissive quality of Russian women shocked me, given that they lived in a system which for so many years had proclaimed the emancipation of women.

Besides the Soviet Union, I visited East Germany and Bulgaria; all of these countries were then part of a socialist world that no longer exists, but that, at the time, seemed sure of itself and immutable. My impressions of those places were colored by the earnest hope I harbored of finding in the socialist system the humanistic utopia I had imagined—an egalitarian, just society, moved by values such as solidarity and mutual respect. In none of those places I visited did I feel I was behind the so-called Iron Curtain of the Cold War. Maybe people wore less fashionable clothing, but their daily lives didn't seem particularly adverse: I saw young people relaxing in the parks, mothers taking their babies out for a stroll, flocks of schoolchildren scampering out of school in the afternoons. The one thing that did lend a flat, shabby quality to the atmosphere in those cities was the total lack of markets, shops, billboards. The absence of commercial activity in the city streets made those places seem like anonymous, numbing suburban neighborhoods. It isn't hard to get an idea of the feeling in those countries—all you need to do is picture the place you live in without the little corner store, without the shop windows, without street vendors, without flower shops or little cafés. I wanted to think that the absence of the market and consumerism allowed people the freedom to dedicate their time to more transcendental pursuits. I wanted to convince myself that the greatest goal was to establish a fair society where everyone worked for the progress of the community as a whole, but I found myself doubting that it was possible to be happy in an environment that seemed so controlled, in which the simple act of buying a pair of shoes was an onerous, bureaucratic enterprise. I couldn't agree with all the restrictions on people's freedom of movement, and I was uncomfortable with the omnipresent specter of the Party, that patriarchal authority that seemed to follow everyone to the grave.

It would be different in Nicaragua, I told myself. We would find the formula to achieve the balance between the individual and the community, we would build a system that would allow for different varieties of property ownership, and a choice of political parties. That would be our contribution to these utopian projects that had not been able to shake off their grim, coercive atmosphere.

The real adventure of that trip began for me when we left Europe for northern Africa. The minute our plane touched down in Algeria, I felt as though I had been delivered to the Thousand and One Nights. On either side of the red carpet that was laid out for us, Harun al-Raschid's soldiers stood at attention with their scimitars held high, forming a resplendent arc over our heads. Dressed in flowing trousers and satin shirts beneath their aquamarine-colored capes, with their white turbans, feathers, and pointed shoes like those Aladdin wore, the Royal Guard accompanied us to the VIP room, another scene of luxuriant splendor. This magnificent show was their way of welcoming the dignitaries invited to the celebration of the twenty-fifth anniversary of the Algerian Revolution.

Until then, the only images I had of Algiers were the concise descriptions in Frantz Fanon's *The Wretched of the Earth*. I was totally unprepared for the vision that reverberated before my eyes in the noontime sun that day. The luminous bay, rising up from the deep blue Mediterranean Sea, was a perfect crescent that cradled the whitewashed buildings, stuccoed houses, palm trees, and coconut groves dotting the landscape.

I was interviewed by a number of female journalists who wanted to know if in Nicaragua the men would cast aside the women who had participated in the Revolution, as they had in Algeria. Their lot was better than that of women in other Arab countries, but they still had to fight tooth and nail to avoid constantly being pushed to the sidelines. I told them that their experience, and that of many other women as well, would serve as a warning sign to us, to help us keep from being sent back to the kitchens, to the margins. They could hardly mask their skepticism. We'll see, their expressions seemed to say.

On the day of the Revolution's anniversary, after a dazzling, colorful military parade along the seashore, we attended the official reception that the Algerian government had organized in a multistoried, modern hotel at the far end of the bay. The diplomats from the Cuban mission introduced us to the various dignitaries. At a certain point, the Cuban ambassador called us over and we followed him into a room, a suite with a balcony. There, chatting away in the living room, were Raúl Castro and the Vietnamese general Vo Nguyen Giap. I couldn't believe my eyes. Giap himself, the general that led the battle of Dien Bien Phu and, fourteen years later, the Tet Offensive. The legendary hero of the Vietnam War, who had managed to defeat the powerful United States. His book, *People's Army, People's War*, was classic reading for guerrillas the world over. Giap was a slight, delicate man, with one of those typically Asian smiles, sweet and impenetrable at the same time. Dressed in a khaki military uniform with red stripes, he looked like the benign grandfather of a children's fairy tale. Since he was resting, he wore slippers. When he stood up, I noticed that his socks slid forward, and his bare heels peeked out. "Eating one's socks" we called that phenomenon when I was in school. That one detail completely humanized him for me. He asked us lots of questions about the situation in Nicaragua. I was especially aware of how he looked at me the same way he looked at everyone else. Not once did he ever treat me as if I were inferior to the others because I was a woman—something I experienced many times during that trip. When we told him about our various problems, he shrugged resignedly and cheekily admitted to us, through an interpreter, that those were the problems of victory.

"If you hadn't won, you wouldn't have them," he said, smiling.

I still have a photograph from that meeting. I am on the balcony of the hotel standing between General Giap, General Raúl Castro, and Modesto.

We returned to the reception hall with General Giap, Raúl Castro, and Gabriel García Márquez. I hadn't been with García Márquez since the celebrations in Havana, and seeing him walk into the suite was a wonderful surprise. Raúl Castro exuded a more military image than his brother Fidel, yet, oddly, was more accessible and down-to-earth. I warmed up to him, his utter lack of pretensions, his paternal quality, and his sense of humor. I felt comfortable with him, as if I was with an old friend. From that brief interlude when we returned to the reception with Giap and Raúl, I remember the odd appearance of a U.S. military officer, I think he was a colonel, who was part of the U.S. delegation. He approached Giap with unctuousness and admiration.

"I'd like to shake your hand, General," he said. "I fought in Vietnam."

Giap nodded his head by way of a greeting. Courteous but cold, he did not extend his hand. Nevertheless, the colonel insisted on talking to him. He tried several times. He had learned to speak Vietnamese, he told Giap. The scene made all of us incredibly uncomfortable. I understood the admiration he felt, a soldier in the presence of the triumphant general, but I couldn't believe how he could be so obtuse and insistent.

The evening ended with the night sky lit up by the grandest and most spectacular fireworks display I have ever seen. We left the party when the cascade of lights began to open wide, like incandescent umbrellas above our heads. When we arrived at the hotel Modesto and I went out onto the balcony to continue watching the great, colorful arcs illuminate the skies above the blue Mediterranean Sea, which reflected them like a mirror, igniting the Bay of Algiers in a dazzling finale of ephemeral light. Modesto sat at the far end of the balcony, not saying a word. He had been acting like that ever since the night before, when I returned to the hotel following an interview with three Polisario guerrilla fighters that Julio López and I had conducted for the FSLN newspaper in Managua. I had come back to the hotel happy, and told him about the three-tea ceremony that the Saharans had prepared for us. They said that the first tea was as strong as life, the second as bitter as death, and the last, as sweet as love. They explained how these three varieties of tea enabled them to withstand the hardships of guerrilla war in the desert, quelling hunger, thirst, and fatigue. The teas had an effect on me that was something like being drunk, but it was a lucid drunkenness. I felt as though my head had separated from my body, and was floating above my neck, oddly light, happy and alert.

Modesto was not amused by any of this. He grunted. He invented some irrelevant complaint about a pair of pants which needed hemming, a task I performed as best as my domestic shortcomings would allow, and then he fell silent. So there we were, on opposite ends of the balcony, contemplating the multicolored splendor of the illuminated skies. I watched the fireworks through a veil of tears that glittered in my eyes. Such hostility was so absurd on such a beautiful, special night. The tangle of rosebushes along the balcony wall, the scent of brine and black powder commingled, and the two of us there, separated like enemies because of some stupid triviality.

From Algeria we flew to Libya, the end of civilization as we knew it. The comedy of errors began in the airport, where we were welcomed by the minister of agriculture, who thought we were Nicaraguan agricultural technicians. Baffling us with his descriptions, in broken English, of the agricultural techniques expanding the agricultural frontier into the desert, he finally left us in the hands of an escort who only knew how to say "wait for me five minutes." Tripoli was a dusty place where camels and automobiles traveled the city streets together. Our escort delivered us to the hotel in a car with a loudspeaker on the roof which the driver used to yell curses at the pedestrians and camels that got in the way.

Once at the hotel, we realized that they had definitely confused us with another group. And because our interpreter couldn't interpret anything, I wrote our names on a piece of paper, and explained what we were there for. We wanted to see Khadafi, or one of the other leaders of the Revolution.

"Take this to your boss," I told the man, who tirelessly repeated his bit about the five minutes. "Take it to your boss. *Boss*," I ordered him, shaking the piece of paper.

Finally he left, and while we waited for him to return, we watched television: odalisques dancing and singing to the sharp, keening sounds of traditional Arab music, a relative of flamenco. There was nothing else to watch. The Revolution in Libya was a cultural one as well—nothing foreign there.

At ten in the evening, one of the commanders of the Revolution finally appeared. Praise Allah! we said to ourselves. Finally we had made ourselves understood.

We never did manage to meet Khadafi, though. The next day the minister of foreign relations took us under his wing. He was a small, thin man with white hair who moved like lightning and smoked nonstop. Trikki was his last name, and he spoke English. The exhausting task of translating the meetings fell to me. A cooperative agreement between Libya and the Nicaraguan Revolution was eventually reached, but the complicated, convoluted negotiations almost broke down when we refused to agree to a paragraph that denied Israel's right to exist and declared the territory to be Palestinian. There was no way we could sign something like that, we said. The paragraph would have to be rewritten. In the end, they conceded. Meanwhile, Trikki had left, only to reappear later with his entire family, who wanted to take photographs with the Sandinistas. As a woman, of course, I didn't count. At mealtimes, I was placed at a separate table. According to the Koran, women don't have souls, Modesto explained to me, laughing at my fury that they, my *compañeros*, would allow such a thing.

"This is another culture, come on, don't be like that," he said, trying to calm me down.

But we too were another culture—why not tell that to the Libyans? All I could do was resign myself to the situation and try not to lose my sense of humor about it. The whole situation was so ridiculous. To tell the truth, I don't think we stopped laughing the entire time we were there. After all the protocol in the other countries we visited, Libya was like a disorganized tribe of recently arrived nomads. Tripoli was filled with buildings under construction. Oil was the source of a tremendous amount of money which they still hadn't decided exactly how to use.

Our visit to the market was an unforgettable experience for me. It was an incredible bazaar filled with sumptuous clothing, Bedouin capes with magnificent borders, fabrics of every color imaginable, and all kinds of trinkets. "I love you, I love you" were the only words I could elicit from the one vendor whom I eventually managed to communicate with.

At the end of the trip we had succeeded in securing the cooperation of several new allies, exercising our sovereign right to maintain relations with any country in the world and to prepare to defend ourselves for the possibility of future aggression from the deposed National Guard, or even the United States. We didn't realize, however, that in our efforts to prevent these prophecies from materializing, we were actually setting the stage for them.

CHAPTER FORTY-TWO

On how a cycle in my life came to a close

MANAGUA, 1979–1981

MY LAST MEMORY of the year 1979 is New Year's Eve. Everyone was out in the streets, celebrating together in a great collective party. I had never seen Managua so alive. Everywhere you looked, men and women dressed in olive green and black and red bandannas danced to the rhythms of the music blasting from the radios on every street corner and sidewalk. At midnight, pandemonium broke out. Everyone in the city was armed to the teeth and every last gun went off. On the sidewalk in my neighborhood, Los Robles, we pointed our machine guns skyward, irresponsibly, not thinking that the projectiles would eventually fall back to earth. We fired away enthusiastically against the past, emptying every last clip. The tracer bullets ripped through the sky in brilliant trails of orange light. Firecrackers and bottle rockets exploded, but most of all, weapons of all kinds fired. The rattle of automatic weapons thundered for at least fifteen minutes, reverberating through the city in a collective madness that was unforgettable, gleeful, and never to be repeated.

The next day, the newly created Sandinista People's Army issued an ordinance that prohibited soldiers and anybody carrying a weapon from firing up in the air without just cause, declaring it an offense punishable by imprisonment.

In early 1980 Modesto was named minister of planning. His mission was to formulate a plan to reactivate the country's economy, which had been devastated by the Somoza regime and the recent war. We felt that our success hinged on the Nicaraguans' understanding and willingness to assume the jobs that corresponded to each sector. In this respect, my experience in advertising and mass media was extremely useful. I enthusiastically went to work, learning as much as I could about the complexities of macroeconomics to put together an educational campaign.

The new government slowly found its way. By this time, those of us who were civilians had shed our olive green uniforms. When the Ministry of the Interior issued an order commanding us to hand over our weapons, I returned my submachine gun though I held on to the Makarov pistol inscribed with my name in the Cyrillic alphabet, a gift I had received in Bulgaria.

"To think we had to go through so many trials just to end up as civil servants," one of my *compañeros* said with an amused grin.

In February the National Crusade for Literacy began; it was the most amazing and moving patriotic enterprise I was fortunate to witness. Thousands of teenagers, between twelve and eighteen years old, left the comfort of their homes, their beds, and the security of their families, and scattered out all over the country to teach Nicaraguans, 70 percent of whom were illiterate, how to read.

Neither Maryam nor Melissa was old enough to join the contingent of literacy volunteers, but together we went to the plazas to see the multitude of young people, armed with pencils and primers, say goodbye to mothers and fathers and girlfriends and grandmothers amid a flurry of kisses and songs. With their backpacks on their shoulders they boarded trucks and buses, heading out to villages and towns all across Nicaragua. Going deep into all four corners of the country, they would live for three months with their humble hosts, the *campesinos* and workers who would be their students. The government and the military's entire fleet of vehicles mobilized this teenage army, a monumental effort that absorbed the energy of thousands of people. It was about fulfilling one of the Revolution's fundamental promises, and a way of showing the younger generations that solidarity and generosity, not weapons, were the things that would change our country and its persistent, age-old backwardness. People would learn to read! The older people would understand the meaning of the written word, *campesinos* would be able to read the labels on their fertilizers and reap greater harvests, the workers would improve their technical abilities. Besides deciphering the mysteries of their finances and improving small businesses, women would finally exercise control on the cycles of their bodies, reading birth control instructions, and they would be able to use the soy food supplements to improve their children's nutrition. That was the beginning of the real revolution—teaching Nicaraguans to read. That was why the young people trained themselves, like warriors of literacy, with uniforms and military-style battalions and squadrons, setting out to fight ignorance.

During this tremendously energizing undertaking, I joined Modesto on a trip to visit the literacy brigades stationed in the remote regions where he had spent years as a clandestine guerrilla. It was on that trip that I finally realized how my love for him was like a disease that was slowly consuming me. If I didn't exorcise him from my body, my identity would burn away into nothing. We left in a caravan that included some of the *compañeros* who had been with him during those long days in the jungle. We entered via the mountains in the north, following a trail of rough country roads, hidden in the thick underbrush, branches arching over our heads. It felt as if we were going back into a virginal world. Birds with orange and blue feathers watched us, sullen but curious, from the tops of immense trees with leafy green manes. Finally I saw the Iyas River (Modesto always called me Iyas), clear and wide as it flowed between banks filled with wild ferns that opened up like giant fans. Lianas with orchids hung down from the trees that swayed on the river's edge.

We spent our first night in a settlement of Cuban engineers who were working on a stretch of road that would connect the Pacific to the Atlantic zone. In the simple wooden structures that served as their shelter, they cleared a space for us. I remember when night began to fall, how the air was lit up with thousands of fluttering fireflies. I sat down next to Modesto on a low wall facing the huts. It was hot, humid, sticky heat. I took off my boots, my socks. Modesto studied my feet for a long time. My long, thin, white, bourgeois feet. I could just imagine what was going through his mind. He had already admitted to me one day that he was afraid his men—his troops—would never understand that he had fallen in love with me. He was mortified by the idea that they would consider him weak for loving someone like me. "But it's to your credit that someone like you, from the bourgeoisie, joined the Revolution. Instead of continuing to enjoy all your privileges, you came over to our side," he admitted. Nevertheless, in that newfound world where the disenfranchised recovered their rights, class privileges had been turned topsy-turvy. People like me were subtly made to feel the burden of their class origin. It was a shame one was supposed to grow accustomed to, a primeval sin, pardoned but never fully erased from the record.

Modesto didn't want to pay a price for his choice. He was steeped in doubt and his attitude hurt me deeply. I hadn't chosen my birth or skin color—I could only be responsible for the way I led my life. After casting me that look, as eloquent as an insult, Modesto distanced himself from me. And I realized that I could no longer endure those days filled with his hurtful and cutting remarks. Every so often I would reach my limit but then he would pull out his bag of magic tricks, the colorful scarves, and on a starry night or in a moment of euphoria he would think he could erase it all with his sweet nothings, his caresses, and his vision of a bright future. He made me vacillate because I loved him, but I felt the pain of a thousand sharp splinters inside me. The glass was broken and nothing could mend it. The resolve I felt on that trip would fail me on many occasions. Months passed before I would finally dare to leave his house determined not to go back. I decided to do what I had to do: I destroyed all the bridges that could lead me back to him.

"You're going to have to leave the country," a friend said to me. "How will you manage to forget him and rebuild your life seeing him everywhere?"

I admitted I was wounded, broken down, I felt as if my legs could barely hold me up. But I wasn't about to leave my country. I wasn't dead. If I had survived earthquakes, wars, the deaths of so many friends, I knew I could withstand the loss of a man. I didn't consider the emptiness I would feel, or the way nostalgia cleanses one's memories of sorrow, leaving a dazzling gem where darkness had been.

La mente se resiste a olvidar las cosas hermosas,
Se aferra a ellas y olvida todo lo doloroso, mágicamente anonadada por la belleza.
No recuerdo discursos contra mis débiles brazos
Guardando la exacta dimensión de tu cintura;
*Recuerdo la suave, exacta, lúcida transparencia de tus manos.**

* Mind shall not forget beauty,/It will cling to it and forget sorrows dazzled by beauty's radiance./I don't remember words of reproach belittling the weakness of my arms/I remember the exact curvature of your waist/the soft, transparent light of your hands.

I wrote. I wrote poems of love and songs of desperation. I became so depressed that some days I couldn't get out of bed. Yet I venture to say that this crisis marked the closing of a circle in my life, it made me hit bottom, and I emerged with an understanding of myself I probably wouldn't have obtained otherwise.

I remember the terrible days of sitting next to the telephone, resisting the temptation to dial his number, listening to the torrential downpours of the tropical rainy season crash down outside my window. I remember my bedroom, the open window and the hundreds of flying ants buzzing around the lamps. I was consumed with loneliness and anguish.

I didn't know how to be alone. I had exposed myself to bullets, death; I had smuggled weapons, given speeches, received awards, had children— so many things, but a life without men, without love, was alien to me, I felt I had no existence unless a man's voice said my name and a man's love rendered my life worthwhile. It was not a question of denying men a role in my life, but I was determined to stop being emotionally dependent on them. I no longer wanted a man to have life-or-death power over me. I forced myself to examine my vulnerabilities: I had filled a raw emotional void, tried to make up for affection I had lacked, by asserting myself and my femininity mostly through my sexuality and my powers of seduction, ignoring and underestimating my other gifts. I thought nothing of my tenacity, or my optimism. I didn't see what I was capable of when a dream took hold of me, I hadn't even taken full possession of the facility I had with words. I didn't give it much importance, as if it were something that came easily, like a child riding her bike, saying, "Look, no hands."

I also understood that I loved my children, but only as reflections, only in two dimensions, as if they were just simple, sweet creatures, and I could not see that below the surface they too had fears, complexities. It was easier for me to think that I could still protect them, take them back into my womb, convey my love to them just with a touch. I had not seen them thrust by life so far from me, so apart, beings with their own names, suffering their own wounds, falling from that tree in the garden, alone with the questions only they could answer. But how could it have been otherwise? It wasn't fair, really, to blame myself like that, to be so hard on myself. I was practically an adolescent when they were born. "You've been like a sister to them," said the therapist. "What they need is a mother." I needed a mother too, one who didn't threaten to withhold her love if I deviated from her plans or her way of doing things. I didn't need the real mother who, after all, only did what she could; I needed the mythic "mother" within me to free me from my compulsion to always push the limits. I didn't want to keep reinventing myself over and over, drawing in red lipstick over my reflection in the mirror. It wasn't necessary anymore. I would never again be the demure, well-behaved little girl I was forever trying to escape.

The time had come for me to inhabit myself and learn to accept and enjoy who I was. "Until now, you've loved like a child. When you are able to give love not because you need it, but because you've taken control of your own freedom—that's when you'll know what adult love is." This is what Gisella told me. Gisella—who, besides being a psychologist, was a shaman, a seer, a wise woman, who helped me with incredible generosity when I was battling this crisis. To her I owe the death-defying leaps that at last catapulted me into a new period of my life, the most fruitful, the time when I learned to enjoy the crowded solitude of my thoughts and the aroma of my own experience, a time when I found I could be good company for myself and love my children not as their playmate or friend but as their mother. Eventually I would be with a man again, not because I needed him, but because I loved him.

It took me three years to weave a new tapestry, unraveling, starting anew. Three lonely years of falling down and picking myself up.

It was also three years before Modesto and I spoke again. When we did, there was no anger left between us. There was just this nostalgia for what we had been: a man and a woman in search of utopia, who imagined that all that was needed to save the world was good intentions and a magic formula. Together we took an inventory of all that happened between us, a sad but unavoidable process, that finally allowed us to shed our old skins and become friends. I think no love gets completely wiped out from the soul. Of the love I felt for Modesto, I kept the knowledge that neither he nor I had had the wisdom to navigate through an untimely passion which touched obscure recesses and unnamed needs in our psyche. The affection we felt for each other, the moment in history we lived together, allowed us to create a new bond. We became friends; partners in memories, dangers, and dreams.

CHAPTER FORTY–THREE

Of how dreams were transformed into nightmares

MANAGUA, 1981–1982

TEN DAYS AFTER assuming the presidency on January 20, 1981, Ronald Reagan canceled the final $15 million payment of a loan President Carter had granted to Nicaragua. On February 10, he also withdrew another loan for the purchase of sixty thousand tons of wheat. And on April 1, upon discovering that Nicaragua was sending arms to the Salvadoran guerrillas, the Reagan administration cut off all our lines of credit, and the following year blocked loans from institutions like the Inter-American Development Bank.

This chain of events marked the beginning of a downward spiral in the relations between the two countries. I think the Sandinista Directorate felt a moral obligation to support the struggle in El Salvador. Solidarity among guerrilla movements took precedence over caution, or maybe the Nicaraguan leaders thought the United States would find fault with them one way or the other. In any event, after the Salvadoran issue came to light it opened the way for the Reagan administration to get aggressively involved in undermining the Nicaraguan Revolution. The threats from the United States and the diplomatic arrogance of its secretary of state, Alexander Haig, clashed sharply with the obstinate, nationalistic pride of the revolutionary government, paving the way for a lopsided confrontation. With financial backing from the U.S. Congress, members of Somoza's National Guard began to regroup in Honduras. The Revolution responded by confiscating more property, toughening its stance, creating more and more enemies within its own borders. It's hard to say how things began to escalate in this tragedy of errors. The majority of us were left to watch as little lead soldiers were assembled on the chessboard of our future. After barely a year of peace, we were at war again. And not just against our old enemies: now we were being threatened by a U.S. invasion as well.

By 1982, I had left my job with Modesto at the Ministry of Planning and was working in the Media Department at the Sandinista party headquarters. My boss was a very intense, good-looking, high-ranking cadre, Federico López. He had been a member of the Socialist Party until shortly before the Revolution, when he and other Socialist Party members joined the ranks of the FSLN. Although Federico was at heart a true hard-liner, he enjoyed political maneuvering and was a capable negotiator. He ran the department while also holding a position in the Council of State— what would later become the National Assembly, Nicaragua's legislative body. When I began working for him I was to be the liaison between the Sandinista party and the radio and television station managers. My job was to keep them informed about party activities and to make sure they understood the party line and went along with it. Once a week, Federico and I met with them to analyze the events of the week and give them our spin on the news. The FSLN had a direct involvement in the TV station—the Sandinista Television System, as I had baptized it—and in Radio Sandino, but other independent radio stations run by Sandinista members or sympathizers willingly participated in our efforts to develop a new style of "popular communication." The idea was to find ways to facilitate a more active involvement of the population with the media to generate news that mattered to them, instead of just feeding them whatever was in the government's or the media's agenda.

It soon became clear to me, however, that, aside from our weekly meetings and my periodic contacts with the media bosses, there was not much I needed to do to extend the party's influence. If anything I had to remind them of the virtues of creativity and independence. Federico then assigned me to come up with a media strategy to rally the population to protest against military exercises the United States was doing in Honduras simulating rapid delivery of U.S. weapons to Honduran forces operating close to the Nicaraguan border. What was really going on at that point was the supplying of weapons to the newly organized anti-Sandinista forces, the so-called Contras, by the United States. The Sandinista leadership wanted the Nicaraguan people to beware, and to reject this covert U.S. operation by going out into the streets. Having worked in advertising, it wasn't difficult for me to come up with spots for radio and TV, catchy chants and slogans. Federico added some patriotic harangues to my copy, and there was no way to convince him we shouldn't make people feel war was imminent. Those U.S. military exercises with the Honduran army marked the beginning of a frantic period of activity within the party's ranks, prompted by the rapid growth of military Contra activity throughout the country. There was not a minute of rest.

Suddenly gears had shifted and the whole country was getting ready for the war that threatened to destroy the revolution we had barely managed to begin. Federico embarked me on a series of projects to prepare the different radio stations and the TV for a time of war. The office was a nuthouse with people coming in and out all day.

Around that time a state of emergency was decreed, and in one of those strange party-state confusions so common in those days, I ended up having to go to the TV and radio stations to check the news before it was aired to make sure there was nothing that would endanger "national security." I would finish checking the last radio broadcast around eleven p.m., and arrive home exhausted. With Federico in command, there were no Saturdays or Sundays to speak of, nor any distinction between office and home time. He'd often call me at two or three in the morning, his voice always a blend of calculated irony and sweetness. "Gioconda, are you awake?" he'd ask. I came to dread those phone calls summoning me to the office for extemporaneous meetings, either on the weekends or late at night.

My only solace at the time was Ruth, a Dominican *compañera* who worked in the office and who could weather Federico's crazy schedule better than I because she was also a nocturnal bird. Besides she had no children or boyfriend to make any demands on her time. "You are a nun of the Revolution," I used to say to her. But Ruth had a great sense of humor, an unbridled love for the revolutionary ideals, and she liked Calvados and opera. It was she, in fact, who taught me to appreciate opera, an art I had never been particularly fond of. Listening to a series of opera tapes someone had given me, she patiently explained the concept of the human voice as an instrument, told me to distinguish tenor from baritone, soprano from mezzo-soprano; told me the stories of the different librettos. She did a lot for my musical education. Until then I had often listened to opera with Modesto, who loved it, and assumed I knew it as much as he did, a belief I never corrected.

The Contra war became a full-fledged confrontation by the end of 1982. The preparations for a time of war advanced to the point where Federico decided that, in the event of an invasion, my house would become the child care center for the sons and daughters of the Media Department. One day I arrived at my house to find it flooded with army mattresses I was supposed to stack and keep for the appropriate time. "Tomorrow we'll start digging a bomb shelter in your backyard," he announced to me that afternoon. Fortunately he backtracked the next day. I suspected he did some of these things just to test me.

I was tired and dismayed. Instead of the things we had hoped to be doing, here we were getting ready for battle again. Somehow, however, all the frantic time of war preparations didn't make much sense to me. I could understand getting ready to face the counterrevolution, but preparing for a U.S. invasion was another thing. It disturbed me that each time the Reagan administration admonished Nicaragua, Daniel Ortega would respond with one of his defiant speeches, accusing the United States of imperialism and interventionism. It was counterproductive, and many times during the Contra War I would ask myself why certain influential Sandinistas who knew full well how the United States operated didn't offer better counsel. The revolutionary government's reactions to the United States only provoked the Reagan administration to adopt a tougher, more aggressive position.

"We have to dissuade them. The Americans move according to the number of casualties they think they'd suffer. If they figure that invading Nicaragua would cost them too many American lives, they won't do it," Federico would argue. "We have to convince them we are ready to resist a long time."

Sleep-deprived and depressed, I dragged myself through militia training sessions, night watches, volunteer work in storm drains, and Sundays picking cotton under the hot sun during the harvest. There were moments when I was happy. I especially enjoyed the camaraderie of volunteer work, being in the back of a truck returning from the fields, singing the tunes I had sung in exile when the idea of triumph seemed distant or far-fetched. But I'd come home to face my daughters' recriminations.

"Mommy, you said that when we won the Revolution we would have more time to be together."

"But there's so much to do," I would say. "Things will get back to normal soon. Just be patient."

But I said it without conviction. I didn't have the faintest idea of when the situation would normalize, or when we would have more time together.

It was around then, I think, that I began to entertain myself with an idiotic fantasy. At night, lying on my bed alone, hoping that the phone wouldn't ring, I'd imagine being able to choose another life the next time I was born. I'd have deserved a totally different experience and so maybe I'd choose a pampered life. I'd choose, for example, to be the cherished lover or wife of a gentle, good-looking man, an Englishman perhaps, an artistic soul who would own a cottage, with a thatched roof, set in the countryside near Oxford or Cambridge, in a green, humid, hazy landscape with carefully groomed hedges, berry bushes, and the aroma of a pine forest nearby—I had spent a summer in Ixworth learning English when I was in school in Spain, and had fallen in love with the soft contours of East Anglia's verdant fields and the Norfolk broads. I'd imagine my lover and me riding on beautiful horses in the afternoon, returning at sunset to our cottage to have tea by the crackling fireplace.

This fantasy became a kind of meditation for me. It was like "the place" I would retire to when I wanted to set my mind at ease and give myself some relief and comfort from the daily struggles. I had no idea then that my mind had the power to conjure realities that would look like my fantasies. I never would have believed it was possible to bring to life such a fairy tale, white horse and all, nor did I know the perils of wishing a different kind of existence, so similar in many ways to the one I had chosen to abandon. I guess I was so convinced nothing like that would ever come my way again that I saw no harm, or felt any guilt, in indulging my imagination.

CHAPTER FORTY-FOUR

On the idea I had to improve the Revolution's image abroad and give myself a new job

MANAGUA, 1982–1983

AT THE END of 1982 or thereabouts, Federico left the FSLN's Media Department, and we got a new boss, my old friend Roberto, the one who had been my contact in Managua in 1973. I thought it would be easier to work with him, but after a few months I began to get impatient. Although Roberto did not keep up the frantic pace of his predecessor, I continued to feel that my job had no content and that I was wasting my time. Because of my decision in the early days of the Revolution to quit the TV station to become Modesto's assistant, I was aware that I had slipped in the party's hierarchy and I knew I had to make merits if I wanted to be eligible again for any important responsibility. But by then I felt I had already gone through Purgatory. Ruth and I had many conversations about what the Media Department should have been doing, and from these long chats an idea began to take shape in our heads: the FSLN had to dedicate some cadres to face off the propaganda war the Reagan administration was waging against the Sandinista Revolution. The Media Department had to have an office that would make it its business to respond to the Reagan administration's portrayal of the Sandinista Revolution as a communist threat in the region. The FSLN had to make sure that the mainstream media from the United States and Europe would have sufficient access and information to tell our side of the story. We were appalled by the malicious and tendentious reports divulged by the State Department, satanizing the Revolution as an evil regime, and overlooking every effort we had made to improve the living conditions of

Nicaraguans. The United States, which supported a bloody dictatorship for forty-five years, now was demanding that the new Nicaraguan government, in less than two years, establish a fully working democracy. Although Nicaragua was being attacked by armed counterrevolutionaries who were crossing through the Honduran border by the thousands, we weren't supposed to put any restrictions on the press, even if it was a matter of national security. We were being scrutinized, while the Salvadoran government, guilty of horrible crimes, was receiving millions of dollars in aid.

It's easy to look back now and say, "oh, if only we had done this, or that." But beyond the mistakes caused by our inexperience, I will never cease to be appalled at the utterly venomous, unwarranted manner in which the United States acted toward a tiny country that simply tried to do things its own way, even if this meant making its own mistakes. The Reagan administration's foreign policy was simply unforgivable, and we wanted the world to see what the Sandinista Revolution was really about. Ruth convinced me that my time of feeling guilty and keeping a low profile was up. I had all the qualifications to run such an office, and we just had to write a proposal and convince the National Directorate to let me set it up. She didn't need to use much coaxing to convince me. I couldn't have been more aware of the need, and her encouragement emboldened me to make the case.

It so happened that the National Directorate was backing a diplomatic offensive carried out by the government's foreign minister, Miguel D'Escoto. The minister had hired a public relations firm in Washington, run by two former Maryknoll priests (D'Escoto was a Maryknoller himself). The National Directorate not only gave me the go-ahead to organize the office, but sent me to Washington to coordinate the work with the public relations firm on behalf of the FSLN.

The memories of that trip are full of laughter. I traveled in the company of two men: José Pasos and Saul Arana. The first was an FSLN functionary at the International Relations Department and the second worked at the U.S. Section in Nicaragua's Foreign Ministry. Their conversation was full of irreverent references to each and every member of the Sandinista leadership and the governing junta. They had made up fantastic and hilarious nicknames for all of them, and, during the long flight, they kept bantering back and forth, until my stomach ached from laugh-

ing so much. I guess one of the things that have kept us going in
Nicaragua in spite of so many hardships is the playfulness and sense of
humor inherent in our national character. It's not in our nature to be unc-
tuous or ceremonious, or to cry over spilled milk. On that trip it helped
to have some fun with my traveling companions. It relieved the stress of
our mission.

Aside from meeting with the PR firm at the Nicaraguan embassy in
Washington, I accompanied José and Saul as the newly appointed head
of the Sandinista Foreign Information Office to several meetings on Capitol Hill. We felt like boxers trying to avoid the punches. We were questioned about governmental and partisan politics and subjected to intense
scrutiny. Even congressmen who strongly disagreed with the policies of
the Reagan administration raked us over the coals in a mild-mannered,
affable way. They were wary they could be accused of siding with a "communist" regime, and wanted to make sure that that was not the case. The
Reagan administration's emphasis had shifted. The issue was no longer
to stop arms shipments to El Salvador, but to impose "democracy":
to make sure we held elections, liberalized the economy, enforced judi-
cial processes, suspended the special tribunals created to judge former
Somoza National Guardsmen or henchmen, stopped the military build-
up. The problem was not that we were asked to be democratic, but that
we were being asked to do so while the United States spent millions of
dollars—$79 million between 1982 and 1983—in training, arming, and
advising a military force made up not only of the remnants of Somoza's
National Guard, but of every group of discontented citizens willing to
oppose the revolutionary government. After many years of a one-man
authoritarian rule in our country, we were supposed to build a perfectly
functioning democracy—at gunpoint. But we had no institutions, no
experience. And we wanted to do it on our own terms, we needed to be
given the chance to prove our commitment to improving the lot of the
Nicaraguan people. But it was not to be. We had been branded as a threat
to American values, we had become the prime target for Reagan's sacred
crusade against "communism." As would become clear later on during
the Iran-Contra scandal, not even the U.S. Congress would be able to stop
Reagan's obsession.

Because we weren't expecting much understanding from any of the
functionaries we met, since we had read history and knew the cost of
challenging America's hegemony in Central America, we were neither
surprised nor excessively troubled at their reaction.

At the Nicaraguan embassy on Massachussets Avenue, everyone had stories and funny anecdotes to tell about adjusting to life in Washington. The ambassador was a friend from my years in Costa Rica, Antonio Jarquín. I was staying at his house and had gone shopping with his wife the same night I arrived because, with my meager salary of approximately fifty dollars a month, I had no presentable clothes to wear. My boss had given me five hundred dollars to get outfitted for my new job and we went to one of those stores that sell slightly faulty things for much less money. I used my allowance judiciously, and managed to look fairly well groomed.

I had never been in Washington before. I was very impressed by the beauty of its tree-lined avenues, the green lawns at the banks of the Potomac, the glimpses I caught of long, elegant avenues as we drove from place to place.

That Sunday, Angela Saballos, the embassy's press attaché, a beautiful, petite woman who had recently been accused by some Washington tabloid newspaper of being a sort of Sandinista Mata Hari, organized a barbecue at her home in Chevy Chase. She wanted Saul, José, and me to meet a group of journalists and talk to them in a relaxed, informal setting. It was hot in Angela's backyard, the Washington summer was beginning. I made the rounds and recognized some familiar faces, a correspondent from Agence France Press I had met in Paris in 1979, others I had seen in press conferences in Managua.

In a different tone, the American journalists echoed the functionaries we had been meeting with, and after a while, tired from standing up so long and being questioned, I went to sit on a truncated log on a terrace next to the house, in the shade. Angela came by with a good-looking man I had not seen before.

"Gioconda, this is Charlie Castaldi. He is the correspondent for National Public Radio."

Charlie Castaldi looked Italian. Medium-built, a pastel-color shirt with rolled-up sleeves, khaki pants, loafers, no socks. He had very nice, manly features, a head of curly dark hair, and a very good-humored, ironic, flirtatious gaze. I felt a bit self-conscious in my new dress, but met his eyes with an equal measure of playfulness.

"You have an Italian name," he remarked.

"So do you," I responded.

It was a relief to talk about my ancestors' voyage to the Americas. He was very attentive and curious and soon I was telling him details about my family, my upbringing, a bit about how I had gotten involved in the Revolution, things about the history of Nicaragua. There was something different about Charlie Castaldi but I couldn't put my finger on it. I just felt he wasn't the typical kind of journalist. His interests were broader and he seemed more relaxed, not as fixated on getting background information or a story out of me. I knew little then about the quality and importance of National Public Radio in the United States. In principle, a radio station seemed less important to me than the print or television media.

Perhaps judging him less threatening, I also relaxed and got him to tell me about his family. He talked happily and evocatively of his childhood in Paris, where he was born, then about his parents moving to Milan when he was eight, and to the United States, when he was twelve. He had lived in Washington since then, and for a few years he had been covering the news in Capitol Hill and most recently the conflicts in Central America. His father, he said, had been a partisan in World War II. He had defected from the Italian army to join the anti-Fascist resistance in Yugoslavia.

Charlie knew a little Spanish but I preferred when he switched to English. His voice was deep and pleasant and I smiled looking at the way he moved his hands. Very Italian, in a measured kind of way. I think it began to get dark or somebody came and interrupted our long tête-à-tête.

"I will soon come to Nicaragua," he said before he left, handing me his card.

I handed him mine.

"Call me if you do," I said.

I remember catching myself looking longingly at him as he went out the door, wondering if I would ever run into him again.

When I returned to Nicaragua, Ruth was waiting for me at the VIP lounge at the airport. I had always been wary of getting special privileges, but she dismissed my reservations. I was now the head of a party's section and these kinds of status symbols were important to assess one's own importance. "I think the same way you do," she said, "but the others don't. Besides, we need this kind of access to do our job." She was very pragmatic and I saw her point. By then I had learned that being self-effacing and meek was not the best way to serve the Revolution. I had seen how we women had been losing ground, giving up leadership positions out of fear of being considered ambitious, or power-seeking. It was a trap. If I wanted to change things, I had to have the power to do it. Men know this instinctively. We learn it.

I relished the sense of possibility I felt in my new job. Ruth and I worked feverishly setting up our office. We began the process of creating an agile and efficient communication flow with the foreign press, the diplomatic corps, our embassies around the world. We wrote and printed fact sheets, put together mailing lists, and tried to coordinate our efforts with the Ministry of Foreign Affairs, which handled press accreditations, interview requests, and the like. I began to deal with American and European journalists, to select the access each one should have in accordance with the importance of which newspaper or TV network or station they worked for, to recommend who should be granted interviews with whom, to supply the party functionaries with ideas on subjects they should bring up with journalists. But I had little say in what I considered to be the most crucial aspect of my job: advising the leadership on the overall tone they should employ to convey an appropriate picture of what Sandinismo was about. It was very hard in those days to keep a cool head. Although aid to the Contras had become a contentious issue in the U.S. Congress and the Reagan administration had been reined in somewhat by the Boland Amendment, which specified that the United States couldn't take it upon itself to seek to overthrow the Sandinista government, aid to the Contras kept flowing masked under the "humanitarian" label. In Nicaragua, military clashes were a daily occurrence. The Contras had become a full-fledged mercenary army.

Moreover, that year, 1983, William Casey, the head of the CIA, impatient with disparaging reports about the rebels' abilities to strike in urban centers, got the CIA directly involved in masterminding two large operations. One was the bombing of military installations in Managua's Augusto C. Sandino Airport—the plane, downed by Sandinista antiaircraft fire, crashed into the airport building, causing considerable damage. The other was the attack on Nicaragua's oil reserves. On October 2, 1983, shots from a motorboat destroyed fuel tanks in a port on the Atlantic coast. On October 11, in a similar kind of attack, five fuel tanks were blown up in our ports on the Pacific coast. The tanks, which contained more than three million gallons of gas, went up in flames and the fires spread uncontrollably through the small and poor port city of Corinto. More than twenty-five thousand people had to be evacuated. The men who carried out these attacks were employees of the CIA, "unilaterally controlled Latino assets," not even Nicaraguan Contras. After that, the CIA also decided to mine Nicaraguan ports to strangle our economy. The understandable outrage at these acts of aggression on the part of the United States found its way into an increasingly defiant rhetoric on the part of the Sandinista leadership, to which President Reagan would respond, comparing the Contras with the United States's founding fathers and calling them "freedom fighters." It was hard for me at that point to convince anybody we were just making things worse by responding in the same testosterone-driven manner. The main players on our side were proud, hardheaded men who somehow got the idea that they were invincible. It was a shouting match that I had no power to stop.

It was a terrible period. I had to juggle spending time at the office and driving here and there looking for food for my children. Everything was scarce: groceries, medicine, toilet paper, gasoline. In the supermarkets, now frequented by more than just wealthy housewives, the shelves were empty. For weeks on end at home we ate nothing but locally produced spaghetti; the instant the noodles touched the water they would be transformed into a round, sticky pile of mush. It was like eating plastic. The milk, reconstituted and watery, tasted like cardboard. Since the best coffee in the country was sold for export, we had to consume a substitute made from toasted corn, which tasted like ashes. Rice, beans, sugar, and grains were all rationed. Once a week you bought your rations with a card. The hardest thing for me was going without toilet paper, using newspapers or napkins instead. I would drive anywhere, any distance, just for a roll of toilet paper. They were prohibitively expensive, even though they were primitive and lumpy rolls made of recycled paper. Instead of meat, which we almost never ate, we had canned Russian sardines. Eating chicken was a big deal. Even bread was scarce and I remember months in which eggs where impossible to find. Whatever free time I had, I spent in the long lines we had to make to get anything. So much energy was wasted just in ensuring daily survival.

Those of us who understood this war strategy—christened by the CIA as "low-intensity war"—could at least use our rage to strengthen our determination. We could decide not to attribute so much importance to material things, convince ourselves that living only with basic necessities isn't as hard as it may seem to those used to abundance. We could appeal to our deepest, most patriotic reserves of strength so as not to lose our faith and get depressed. Among the general public, however, the shortages and the restrictions were the signs of impending doom. The Sandinistas had brought the country head-to-head with the United States and everyone was paying the price. The Revolution's main base of support began to erode, slowly but irrevocably.

Ruth and I kept trying to show the positive side of the Revolution. Small achievements were enough to renew our energies. A beautiful anonymous Vietnamese poem became my personal credo:

> *We fill the craters left by the bombs*
> *And once again we sing*
> *And once again we sow*
> *Because life never surrenders*

ANOTHER LIFE

After a furious conflagration . . . we have sunk to ashes, leaving no relics, no unburnt bones, no wisps of hair to be kept in lockets such as your intimacies leave behind them. Now I turn gray; now I turn gaunt; but I look at my face at midday sitting in front of the looking-glass in broad daylight, and note precisely my nose, my chin, my lips that open too wide and show too much gum. But I am not afraid.

—Virginia Woolf, *The Waves*

CHAPTER FORTY-FIVE

On how it was that a casual encounter
turned into many dinner invitations

MANAGUA, 1983

A FEW MONTHS after we met in Washington, when Charlie called me at the office, I was able to match his face with his name without difficulty. He seemed pleased about this and asked if we could have dinner together. I was used to foreign journalists' fondness for restaurants. They liked to kill two birds with one stone. We could have a nice meal and I could give them background information in an informal setting without the constraints of whatever was said "on the record." It was tricky sometimes, though. When one is a "source," anything one says can find its way into a story and on several occasions I regretted trusting someone who then turned around and printed personal anecdotes I had told in confidence. On the other hand, there were some fine men and women in the press corps and with them I often felt we could relate as human beings. For me it was important to make a more personal kind of connection in order to convey to them that it was lives, not stories, which were at stake in Nicaragua.

Charlie took me to an aspiring French restaurant in Managua. I was glad to see that the tropical setting had not made him unrecognizable, as was the case with other journalists I had met while traveling, who then appeared in Nicaragua in Hawaiian shirts and dusty sandals. He had another one of his pastel shirts on and looked the same as when I had last seen him. He seemed amused by the pretentious decor of the restaurant and touched by the ceremonious courtesy of our waiter. Much as we tried to maintain a proper, professional distance, we kept running into the realization that our eyes were doing their own kind of talk. They wanted to say they were really glad we had met again. How was it that we had waited this long to see each other. They were having so much fun exchanging glances. Somehow the conversation veered to continue what we had begun telling each other in Angela's backyard. It seems that if animals smell each other, we humans probe into memories as a courting ritual. Warning flags should go up when one finds oneself sharing childhood tales and discoveries with a stranger. More so when time is forgotten into a reality that suddenly becomes unreal.

We had traveled far away from the faux French ambiance. I was in the bay of Santa Margarita in Liguria seeing Charlie's grandparents' summer house, the walls covered with bougainvillea blossoms. I was going with him to meet his friend Alessandro and racing through the twisted trunks of olive groves up the hill until we could look down on the transparent waters of the blue Mediterranean. I was then taking him by the hand to a very different place: the coffee hacienda were I used to spend part of my summer holidays. I was a little girl in an uncle's coffee plantation. I was forbidden from going anywhere near the dormitories where the coffee pickers lived, a prohibition that only made me want to see them more. One afternoon, I surreptitiously slid out from my nanny's watchful eye to have a look. It was like discovering one of the circles of hell. The rustic wooden barracks, dark and foul-smelling, had only a couple of crude openings just under the roofline and housed God only knows how many families. Each family occupied a kind of shelf set into the wall. There were many, stacked closely together. Crammed into that small space, the coffee pickers slept with their wives and children, lying on top of dirty rags. I told him I would never forget that stench of humidity and filth, of being closed in, airless. The spectacle had left an indelible impression upon my memory and shattered any childish illusions I may have harbored that the world I lived in was a happy one.

I could see that my recollection had abruptly brought us back to the present. Charlie stared at me and then looked down, moving his head. He said he had wondered, just looking around in Nicaragua, how we could tolerate to witness such dismal poverty every day. Driving on the highway at sundown, he often stopped to give a lift to people hitchhiking in throngs at the sides of the road. He talked to them. They were students, women, men, and the hardships they described broke his heart.

Charlie proceeded to say that he didn't understand why the Sandinistas had chosen to provoke the United States by helping the Salvadoran guerrillas when Nicaragua itself had so many of its own problems. I denied the part about supporting the Salvadoran guerrillas—although it was an open secret—and tried to explain to him a bit about the history that had driven us (and so many other Third World countries) into an endemic poverty that was impossible to remedy with short-term plans. A long discussion ensued.

"Your country has supported this continent's most ruthless tyrants," I said to him, "and has viciously attacked all the governments that offer solutions for real social change, accusing them of being communists."

He didn't take my critique of the United States humbly, as was the case with most Americans. He wanted me to accept that we Sandinistas also had our share of responsibility. We had done certain things that were anathema to the concept of democracy that Americans had. Like censoring the press, for example. "What about when your country invaded Grenada. Press censorship was imposed on the American media as well," I argued. "But our media was able to come out and critizice this executive order," he said. "And what about Ray Bonner. He was fired from the *New York Times* for his coverage of El Salvador . . . And you must remember the complicity of the Chilean press in Allende's demise. There's not such a thing as an objective, impartial media," I declared.

That was the subject of our first discussion, as I remember. Between arguments and counterarguments, Charlie suddenly said: "What the heck. If I had been born in this country I would have ended up in the guerrilla movement too. It's very easy for us Americans to judge from the outside, but we are used to a system of law. If we had to deal with a tyrant I am sure we would have done the same thing you did, and feel entitled to defend tooth and nail our newfound freedom."

Clearly, whatever disagreements we had about form, we surely agreed when it came to content.

At some point we realized we were alone in the restaurant. Everybody else had left. Tired of waiting, the staff had begun to clean the place and were noisily stacking the chairs on top of the tables.

On his frequent trips to Nicaragua, Charlie would ask me out to dinner just before he would leave to go back to the United States. Every time, we were invariably forced to leave the restaurants when we thought we were just getting going with our discussion.

CHAPTER FORTY-SIX

Of how it happened that I found love and a new job in election times

MANAGUA, 1983

I DIDN'T THINK much about Charlie when he was gone. Life on the edge is not conducive to daydreaming and I wasn't about to start having fantasies about an American journalist. I remember seeing him briefly at the Revolution's fourth-anniversary party. I had on a dress my sister Lucía had bought for me in Panama. It was kind of satiny and girlish, not exactly my style, and he looked at me up and down and told me I looked like I probably did when I was a *"burguesa."* I smiled nonchalantly and made some ironic remark about the notion that revolutionary women could only be true to themselves when dressed in fatigues. He told me he was leaving the next day and would be gone for a few months.

"Be good," I smiled mischievously. "Don't do anything I wouldn't do . . . that should give you a wide margin." I kissed him on the cheek and left him to join the party.

I don't know what it was about those days. Maybe it was because most of us Sandinistas were young and unafraid; maybe it was that we had actually dared the United States, or that the majority of us were seriously committed and believed fiercely in our right to be sole owners of our destiny, but we lived in a constant high. We did everything with passion and felt a strong sense of entitlement, of pride in what we had accomplished. I think that, in spite of their misgivings, most of the journalists, who were young like us, couldn't help but be drawn to the romantic notions we symbolized. They were also seduced by the irreverence and constant bantering we carried on, by the way we made fun of our own hardships. American journalists especially were often amazed at how, in spite of their country's aggressive policies against us, we were mostly open and caring with them. There was no hostility either in official circles or among the people in the streets. They often remarked to me that they felt safer in Nicaragua than they did in El Salvador, Honduras, or Guatemala, countries that had governments which were U.S. allies.

Among the journalists themselves and with those of us who worked closely with them, strong ties were forged during the years of the Sandinista Revolution. To this day, many of my dearest friends—American, English, Spanish—are journalists I met then. For all of us, those years left an indelible mark. Emotions were so raw, death was such a close neighbor, life was so stripped of artifice that we came to understand and cherish the value of a good laugh, a good cry, or a meaningful conversation. In the end, the Nicaraguan experience taught us all that life is about being with others, about building strong friendships, about people.

Given that people's well-being was the primary objective of the Revolution, it was clear that the most serious consequence of the Contra War and the conflict with the United States was that it had completely derailed the Revolution from its goal. At the beginning of 1984 I had begun to question the wisdom of the Sandinista leadership. It could feel good to be tough, but it was proving to be far too costly. Something had to give. Many of us who held high or intermediate positions of responsibility within Sandinismo devoted quite a bit of energy to point out that people's resilience was failing and that we had to offer some hope, look for a sensible solution. We wanted to play a constructive, critical role. Unfortunately, to be critical was becoming increasingly difficult. The more cornered the leadership felt, the more they tended to expect that we close ranks. To criticize was to play into the hands of the counterrevolution, they warned us. Worse yet: we could create a rift within the party, sabotage Sandinista unity.

Within the nine-man National Directorate, not all were equal. Each of its members had his own particular vision, and although they were all supposed to have the same share of power, Humberto and Daniel Ortega kept their hegemony, astutely waving the flag of unity as a pretext to silence any opposition. The other members had no choice but to submit to them, since it was generally assumed that divisions within the Directorate would have dire consequences in the midst of the Contra War and the conflict with the United States. Paradoxically, the United States gave the Ortegas the perfect excuse to silence the debate raging within the Sandinista movement. The rank and file would urge one or another member of the National Directorate to oppose this or that policy, but whenever the situation reached a crisis point, the nine members would resolve things among themselves, generally giving in to the Ortega brothers. Those of us who had trusted any one of the nine *comandantes* to state our position would suddenly find ourselves alone, fighting hopeless battles that only made us feel bitter, sad, and betrayed by the very *compañeros* we had hoped would act on our behalf in their closed-door meetings.

The diverging positions within the nine-man Sandinista Directorate were a blessing during the first years because they opened the Revolution up to a variety of perspectives. But as the Ortegas took over, monopolizing power, the Revolution slowly lost its steam, its spark, its positive energy, to be replaced by an unprincipled, manipulative, and populist mentality. The Revolution rocked between moderation and radicalism. Nobody—neither allies nor adversaries—knew what to expect. The Contra ranks were growing with the incorporation of more and more disgruntled *campesinos*, young people who refused to serve in the army, and soldiers who defected. The upper classes, the businessmen who felt they had been marginalized, complained to the U.S. ambassador, or abandoned the country entirely to join the directorates of the counterrevolutionary groups.

In the cities, we were feeling more and more like spectators to a process that continued to live off its heroic, idealistic image even though, in practice, it was being gutted and turned into an amorphous, arbitrary mess. Obligatory military conscription had been put into effect. Brave, young, tenacious Nicaraguans were dying every day on the battlefields, urged to defend a dream that unbeknownst to them was being torn to shreds. For a long time I refused to acknowledge the irreparable damage the Revolution had suffered. I was too close to the situation. My love wasn't blind, but it was tolerant and unconditional; I was like a mother seeing her daughter stumble, thinking that, in the end, she was going to learn her lessons and overcome it all. A process that was the product of so much love and sacrifice would amend its mistakes and resume its course. "Hold on," I would tell myself, "we just need to end the war, which corrodes everything." We had to get the United States to backtrack and leave us alone, then we would be able to turn revolutionary dreams into realities.

In those days we were encouraged by the solidarity of a variety of people who came to Nicaragua and made us feel we were not alone. Young "sandalistas"—the press called them—as well as intellectuals and artists like William Styron, Allen Ginsberg, Alfre Woodard, Anne Waldman, Adrienne Rich, Lawrence Ferlinghetti, Susan Sarandon, Richard Gere, Jackson Browne, Joan Peters. European and Latin Americans came as well. That was how I met Harold Pinter, Salman Rushdie, Eduardo Galeano, Juan Gelman, and so many others. They were like a flock of birds hoping to spread their wings and protect the good they saw in the Revolution. They would return to their countries, denouncing Reagan's politics, writing articles and books, and organizing groups of people to come to Nicaragua to build schools and houses or to join the teams of volunteers working in the coffee and cotton fields. The advocacy of people like them was instrumental in making the Reagan administration think twice about invading us. Over and over again opinion polls showed that the majority of the people in the United States opposed the idea of direct military action in Nicaragua. International opinion was also mounting against U.S. involvement.

Even though there were many urgent needs regarding people's basic welfare, the Sandinista leadership felt it had to give a clear signal that the Revolution really meant to be democratic. On December 4, 1983, Daniel Ortega announced that presidential elections were going to be held in 1984, a year before they were supposed to take place. In a country that no sooner had finished a war when another one began, it meant dedicating enormous human and financial resources to satisfy outside pressures. It was a huge concession to the United States, but we hoped it could improve the overall situation.

I was called to Comandante Bayardo Arce's office. He asked me if I would be willing to work with him in the National Directorate's Electoral Commission. I would be in charge of ensuring that its guidelines were properly executed within the party structure. I would monitor the work that had to be done internally for the coming election. In addition, I would be the Sandinista spokesperson and would represent the party at the National Assembly and the National Council of Political Parties. I accepted right away. I had a very good team at my section in the Media Department. I was confident that they could continue the work. Besides, with all the attention of the foreign media focused on the electoral process, we certainly had to keep in touch.

I was just settling into my new office at the Sandinista National Directorate headquarters when I got a phone call from Charlie. My secretary came in all smiles to let me know he was on the line. I hadn't heard from him in several months.

"I can't believe my ears!" I said. "I thought you had vanished."

"I would never do that without saying goodbye," he replied in the same playful tone.

He inquired about my new job. I could tell he was happy for me and impressed. He asked if we could have dinner as usual.

We met that night at a restaurant tucked on one side of the crater of an extinct volcano. Getting dressed I had felt nervous. When I saw him sitting at the table, before he saw me, my heart leaped. I could tell, when I met his eyes and we exchanged greetings, that a subtle shift had taken place. We didn't banter. We looked quietly at each other. I remember that Angela—who had introduced us—came by our table to say hello. She gave us a mischievous glance. "You are both flirts," she said. "I can tell." And she left.

"We are not flirting, are we?" Charlie asked me.

"Of course not." I smiled.

Toward the end of the evening, when I inquired whether he was leaving soon, he said he wasn't leaving, that NPR had stationed him in Managua. He had been appointed their correspondent for Central America. At the bottom of the crater, we could see the moon reflected in the still waters of the Tiscapa lagoon.

"What good news," I said, feeling a combination of joy and anxiety.

"Yes. I'll be around. We can have dinner more often." I could feel his hand lying very close to mine across the table. I felt like holding hands with him, but I caught myself.

A few days after our dinner by the lagoon Charlie came to my office to interview me. The office was large and handsomely furnished. Bayardo, my boss, told me it had been meant for one of them (meaning one of the nine leaders). "I don't know if you'll become one of us someday, but at least you have the office," he joked.

Charlie and I sat in the small sitting area. He pulled out his cassette recorder, microphones, earphones, and all his journalist paraphernalia.

I answered his questions thinking of his audience: Americans listening to the radio as they drove to work, or took showers, or ate breakfast. The opposition was threatening to pull out of the elections, coming up with impossible demands. They knew that they had the Reagan administration's support. Anything that chipped away at the Sandinistas' credibility was warmly received in Washington. I found it difficult to reduce such a complex reality down to the few short quotes that the journalists always wanted, for out of context they could easily come off sounding like simplistic anti-American rhetoric. Yet I knew how little he would use if I came up with a long-winded explanation. It was the same with all foreign correspondents, and I had no illusions about Charlie. I could tell he was not the type who would let me or anybody influence his work. I suspected that he was bound to be more careful with me because he liked me. I insisted: The quality of democracy in Nicaragua should not be measured using U.S. standards. After a dictatorship, democracy was a slow learning process for us. One that had been slowed down even further by the Reagan administration and the war it financed.

From my conversations with Charlie all through that period, I confirmed my first impressions: beyond nationalities, on a purely human level, we basically felt the same way about the important things in life.

We began seeing each other more often. He introduced me to John Lantigua and María Morrison, a fellow journalist and a photographer with whom he shared a house in Managua. He invited me to meals he personally cooked there with great flair, his manly hands with square fingers expertly handling shrimp, chopping onions. We laughed at his failed attempts to cook Nicaraguan pasta at a dinner where he wanted to show off before his guests, among others, Angela, Bianca Jagger, and me. He ended up with an inedible purplish mass and we had to lick the sauce and seafood off the spaghetti. We went to movies where the film would rip in the middle of the projection, or there would be bats flying blindly up in the ceiling. One night I couldn't come out of my house to meet him because it had begun to rain and my street had flooded. He came with rubber boots and carried me out in his arms to the car. He invited me to an oldies disco once and we danced very formally in that funny American way, rocking from side to side, keeping a distance, while I, used to the more sensuous Latino way, tried in vain to come closer and sway to the rhythm of the music. It was all very sweet, discreet, measured. We loved talking to each other. That was all. We would say good night at my doorstep.

"A pleasure, as always," he would say.

During the day, I often would see him at official functions, press conferences. He was there when I took my oath at the opening sessions of the National Council of Political Parties. I liked to watch him work his microphones, the black square tape recorder, the earphones. His hands fascinated me. So strong, so different from mine. After my stormy relationship with Modesto, I had gone out with other people, but I had felt a dullness inside, a lack of echo. I had thought I would never fall in love again. Maybe because I never thought of Charlie as someone I could have a relationship with, given who we were, I lowered my defenses. I was able to open myself to him. I saw no reason for the politics of our countries to stop us from being friends, or from sharing the pleasures of a rainy May evening discussing literature or regaling each other with childhood stories. But I had fallen in love. I didn't admit it to myself then. I took it as a nice flirtation, a platonic romance that didn't threaten me. Charlie was transient, fleeting, a ship in the fog that blasted its mellow, deep horn, a beautiful man with the face of a Roman statue and expressive hands, who knew how to make me laugh. He was a welcome respite from the macho men who were constantly hovering around me, attracted by the scent of my solitude.

One day, after countless dates and dinners and conversations, he came to my house to watch a movie on video. *WarGames*, of all things. We sat on the sofa in my minuscule study. My girls came to say hello. They had already met him. Camilo was at his father's. Hours went by. We got lost in conversation. By the time we turned the video on it was very late. We had to sit close on the sofa because of the angle of the TV. We touched. We never saw the end of the movie, nor did we sleep that night.

The next morning I had to meet an Italian journalist at the Intercontinental Hotel for breakfast. I was sleep-deprived but happy and buoyant when I arrived for my appointment. I must have been in the middle of buttering my toast when I saw a large group of American journalists walking into the cafeteria, Charlie among them. Without flinching, he came up to me and shook my hand.

"It is so nice to see you this morning," he said, full of mischief.

"Who's he?" the Italian journalist asked, surprised because Charlie had addressed him in perfect Italian.

"Well, he is American, but he knows many languages," I replied with a smile.

CHAPTER FORTY-SEVEN

On the complications brought about by love in times of war

MANAGUA, 1984

CLOSING MY EYES, not giving it much thought, I surrendered to loving Charlie. By that time, I had become an expert at ignoring the future and focusing on the present. My whole life seemed like one long lesson in the ephemeral, fragile nature of human existence. In those days, my *compañeros* and I would invent the most absurd scenarios involving what might happen if Ronald Reagan decided to send the 82nd Airborne Division over Nicaragua. We would find ourselves bantering about the "Johnnys," the soldiers that would rain from the heavens to kill us and whom we would meet armed with garden tools. If they knew, we would laugh, that it would only take a few airplanes dropping Milky Ways to disband us. We hadn't seen chocolate in months. The bantering got so bad that one day the staff in the office was summoned to the auditorium and lectured by Carlos Núñez, one of the nine, and president of the National Assembly. "I am just going to read to you the weaponry and personnel of the 82nd Airborne. See if you feel like laughing after this." We had to admit it was pretty scary.

With the same nonchalant feeling prevalent then, I slid into Charlie's arms. Who cared about the future, who cared if someday he would return to his country to the north, when I could run my fingers through his hair right now, cuddle up next to him and pretend that we were like any other couple in any other part of the world? Charlie had a room at the back of the house he shared with John and María. The house came fully furnished and equipped when they rented it, and Charlie slept in a twin bed that, along with the linens, had belonged to the owner's child. It became a source of permanent amusement to make love on top of Raggedy Ann, Goofy, and Mickey Mouse bedsheets. Whenever we turned on the ancient air conditioner, the entire room would rattle and shake, rumbling like an airplane taking off. All of Charlie's journalist paraphernalia—notebooks, tapes, pens, what-have-you—was piled high on a large metallic desk in one corner of the room. There was a large *Romeo and Juliet* poster resting on the tank of the toilet. Charlie had baptized his room as "the hellhole." One night, he got nostalgic and told me he was used to quite a different life. A brownstone house where he lived with his father, near Dupont Circle in Washington, or his family's farm in Virginia, which he loved and missed terribly. Every weekend he talked to his father and asked about the trees, as if they were family pets.

María and John's house in Managua was quite a hub for foreign correspondents and for other American visitors to Nicaragua. Often I would be invited to have dinner with them. It was good for me to listen to the conversations at the table, the different perspectives. I especially remember meeting Pete Hamill, the New York columnist who was then editor of the English-language newspaper in Mexico. I immediately liked him. He has a very clear gaze, as if he owns every experience he's lived. His friendly, intelligent face made me think of Hemingway. I also met Jacobo Timmerman, the Argentinean journalist, and I was reacquainted with Bianca Jagger, whom I had seen several times on her sporadic visits to Nicaragua. Aside from the celebrities, I met other people there, like the truly remarkable Karen Brudney, a young doctor who came to Nicaragua to volunteer and launch an antituberculosis program, or Stephen Kinzer, who was the *New York Times* correspondent for Central America, but who also became quite a connoisseur of Nicaraguan literature and Nicaraguan baseball, and was able to not lose sight of the many facets of a culture that was still vibrant in the midst of war.

Through my job and later on my relationship with Charlie, I ended up spending quite a bit of time with journalists in Managua. We used to watch movies together—videos, because the movie theaters didn't have foreign exchange currency so could only show cheap or old films. And we also played games and talked and came to know each other's trials and tribulations pretty well. As I said, some of my most dear friends to this day are those journalists: María Morrison, John Carlin, Mathew Campbell, Joe Gannon, to name a few. I was not the only Sandinista who fell in love with a journalist. There were a few cases. In Charlie's own house a woman who also lived there, the CNN correspondent, was in love with a journalist from the Sandinista newspaper, *Barricada*. Every so often I would feel a wave of anxiety about the potential conflict of interest of being involved with an American journalist, but since it wasn't only happening to me, I clung to the belief that I was entitled to freedom and autonomy over my personal life. Our sex life was our business, not the party's, as Bayardo, my boss, would say. The nature of my work was highly sensitive, and I knew that discretion was paramount. After my years of experience, I was confident I could guard classified information. Besides, Charlie and I were aware of the distance we had to keep.

I don't remember how many months had gone by after Charlie and I began seeing each other—two or three, I think, because we were edging toward July 19, the fifth anniversary of the Revolution—when Tomás Borge called me.

"Come to my office, child. I need to talk to you," he said over the phone, in his baritone voice.

Through the years that had passed since 1979, Tomás and I had remained close friends. I barely saw some of the *compañeros* I knew from before, but Tomás had kept me under his wing. He had cared for me when I broke up with Modesto, providing me with the plane ticket to go to Mexico and seek therapy with Gisella. Tomás loved literature and writers. He wrote good poetry and very inspiring speeches. The last remaining founder of the Sandinista National Liberation Front is a charismatic man who can easily be arrogant and authoritarian one moment and tender and sentimental the next.

I arrived at his home office in one of Managua's middle-class developments. He had connected a number of these small mass-produced houses and created an enclave for himself. He had moved there when people started to criticize the lifestyle of Sandinista leaders. As always, he greeted me effusively, and then led me to a small office. He sat down behind his desk, and I sat down in front of him.

"Is it true, my girl, that you are going out with an American journalist?"

"Yes," I said. His question caught me off guard. I hadn't expected that. The worried look on his face disturbed me. My God, please don't tell me that Charlie works for the CIA, I thought.

"Are you in love with him?" He looked at me as he leaned back in his chair, smoking.

"I like him," I said, cautiously. "I don't think we've been together long enough for me to say whether I love him or not. Why, what's the problem, Tomás? *Is* there a problem?"

"The problem is that your job is a very delicate one. You handle all the information dealing with the elections. Journalists are after that information. It would be better if you stopped seeing him. He has friends . . . people who could pass things on to U.S. intelligence . . . I trust you," he said. "You know that, but I can't ask the same of other people. This could get you in trouble."

I looked at him, not knowing what to say. I asked him to please tell me, if he had any evidence, whether Charlie was working for the U.S. government. He repeated that they weren't sure. I remained silent for a long while. I felt flushed. My face felt hot. Was I ashamed of myself? I just felt that if I had been wrong about Charlie, I wouldn't forgive myself. And I was nervous and uncomfortable. I couldn't believe this was happening to me. Was he suggesting I was in on it? I understood their concerns, but the mere hint of suspicion was painful. My first reaction was to dispel his doubts. Even if he was a secret agent, I had not revealed anything, I said.

"But all right, Tomás," I added. "Don't worry. I won't see him anymore."

He hugged me. Once again, he said he trusted me. I didn't feel resentful toward Tomás. It was just that goddamned situation we were in. The war had sown so much suspicion. Other people had lost arms, legs, loved ones. I'd lose Charlie.

I left Tomás's with the bitter taste of mourning in my mouth. Love would have to be one more casualty of war. Why the hell did it have to be a journalist, and a gringo at that, the man who I thought held underneath his magnificent dark curls the equilibrium I had sought for so long. I, who had been fighting for freedom for so many years, was forced now to sacrifice my own to avoid being tainted by suspicion, so that none could accuse that, on rainy nights, curled up against my journalist-lover, my pillow talk would include state secrets. I was enraged and anguished. It was natural that state security would be zealous about maintaining secrecy. But they could also harm me. It could have consequences for my job, my standing, and the confidence granted to me within the Revolution's ranks. I couldn't conceive of being ostracized from the Revolution. Sandinismo was a fundamental element of my identity, as mine as my last name. My ties with it were emotional as well as political. It was my family. My head was spinning. I resented what I considered unwarranted suspicions but I was also overwhelmed by the fear that my friends, my *compañeros*, would reject me.

I returned to the office. I sat down at my desk, unable to stop the tossing and turning of thoughts in my head. I scrutinized my conversations with Charlie, his psychological profile. It didn't fit, although now I would be more vigilant. Regardless, was I ready to be a soldier and obey my orders? Would I be a woman in love or a revolutionary? Would I let my emotions rule or choose to be a "new person," that utopian, Che Guevarista paradigm, ready to renounce everything for the love of country? Maybe Tomás was right, I thought. Maybe I knew from the start that this was a dumb idea and just refused to see it. Charlie, personally, was not the enemy, but his country was attacking Nicaragua. Just in March, a scandal had exploded in the U.S. Senate when a staffer from the Intelligence Committee had supplied Senator Goldwater with conclusive evidence that President Reagan himself had approved the mining of Nicaragua's harbors, which had been carried out directly by the CIA. Later on Nicaragua would take the United States to the World International Tribunal at The Hague for this and win the case. But the United States neither acknowledged the verdict, nor paid the indemnification. It was such a disgrace to have the most powerful nation on earth so intent on destroying what had been my poor little country's best opportunity to start anew. And it was the poor who were paying the highest price: their sons' lives, to start with; the hope of a raise in the minimum wage; even the right to strike had been curtailed because the country could not bear those costs in the midst of such a crisis. Every ambitious project had been set aside because of the war. *Campesinos* had gotten land but no money to work the land.

And sure enough, on my desk, in my files, in my drawers, I had the FSLN strategy for the 1984 elections. I knew what had transpired at the meetings with other political parties to negotiate the terms of a campaign that Washington and the CIA were shamelessly trying to sabotage. None of that information was at risk with me. I was sure of that. But how could I convince the operatives at State Security, whose judgments were based on appearance and prejudice? I called Charlie. I had to see him, I said. It was urgent.

I picked him up in front of his house. We drove around and around in my car. I didn't tell him about Tomás's vague insinuations that he could be an agent. As far as I was concerned, journalists were habitual sources of information for diplomats, and the only real connection I could see

Charlie having with intelligence sources was through the diplomats he, and other journalists, befriended. But I did say that given the nature of my job, the type of work I did, the secrecy I had to preserve, I had been asked by my people to stop seeing him. Our liaison could have negative repercussions for me, I said, and probably for him too. Sooner or later his superiors would bring it up and call him on it. They would give the matter their own spin, but one way or the other, we were not meant to be. I couldn't put in question my loyalty to the Revolution, even if it meant something as painful as not seeing him again.

I could tell he was shaken by the news. He looked downtrodden, his back against the passenger seat, his head resting on the headrest as if a great weight had been dropped on him. He was so sorry to have caused me trouble, he kept saying, he should have known better than to compromise my standing, my job. Of course he understood if I couldn't see him anymore, he said, exhaling all the air out of his lungs.

We felt caught in a drama much larger than ourselves, victims of some ancient, tragic script. We looked at each other with eyes burning, tearful. I parked on the street a few blocks from his house. We talked for a long time inside the car. We kissed. Over and over we said goodbye, although neither he nor I moved. It was as if I had gone back in time to a clandestine rendezvous during the dictatorship. I kept looking around to make sure we were not being watched, thinking how ironic it was to feel like this when Sandinismo, not the dictator, was in power.

A good hour or two went by before he got out of the car and walked toward his house.

I felt like getting out and running after him. Instead I watched him as he walked away, slowly dragging his feet, and I cursed Ronald Reagan with all my heart.

CHAPTER FORTY-EIGHT

On how female solidarity brought Charlie back into my life

MANAGUA, 1984

EVERY YEAR, as another July 19 grew near, I would be swept into the celebratory spirit that preceded the big rally to commemorate another anniversary of the Revolution in Managua's largest plaza. Radios blaring music from the time of the struggle, banners on the streets, neighborhood campfires, would rekindle my best memories and revitalize my notion of belonging to a valiant, proud people.

Nicaragua. *Nicaragüita*. A free country. And I had lived to see it.

The fifth anniversary found me—and I guess the entire country—in a different spirit. Too many people had died. Too many young people were being forcibly recruited into the army and sent off into battle. The poor were paying the highest price, as is often the case. *Campesinos* resented the economic measures which banned them from selling their crops in the open market. They were supposed to sell to the state so that the grain would be affordable for everyone in the general population. But they didn't see it that way. They yearned for the old, traditional way of doing things: the middleman exploited them, yes, but he also supplied them with their basic necessities: batteries for their radios, rubber boots, machetes. When the usual suppliers disappeared, they felt deprived. Despondent, many of them joined the Contras. To the so-called patriotic businessmen and large-scale producers, on the other hand, the government granted all sorts of extraordinary concessions.

At the National Council of Political Parties that I attended as the Sandinista representative, I used to converse with the leaders of the radical left-wing Movimiento de Acción Popular (MAP)—the Marxist-Leninist Action Party. They considered that we Sandinistas had made too many concessions to the bourgeoisie and had betrayed the Revolution.

"You are making us pay the price of a Marxist-Leninist revolution for one that doesn't even qualify as a social democracy," they would say to me. They had a point. Sandinismo's fiery rhetoric did not mirror what was taking place in real life, yet it gave Reagan the excuse to satanize the Revolution.

Sandinista leaders always remarked that the Nicaraguan masses were now the protagonists and principal actors of the country's history. But it was clear that the masses were asked to make many sacrifices in the name of a future that never seemed to materialize. In the quest for the "rivers of milk and honey" that the Revolution had promised Nicaraguans, obstacles were becoming more and more insurmountable.

The rallies celebrating the Revolution's anniversaries drew multitudes. The Plaza de la Revolución, right next to the ruins of the National Cathedral, which had been wrecked by the earthquake, would fill beyond its capacity. People also crowded in the small park along its side—the same park where I used to go on Sundays as a little girl to listen to live music played by the municipal orchestra. The rally was festive. Old protest songs, the same ones that were emblematic of the struggle against Somoza, blasted from the loudspeakers or were performed live. Memories were reawakened of when the Revolution was just beginning and we were all brimming with pride and euphoria. For a few hours we forgot about war, food shortages, hardships as we looked out at the boisterous young people with red and black bandannas on their foreheads, laughing, dancing, climbing on top of each other to form ephemeral human towers at the center of the plaza. In the crowd's milling, I found friends, *compañeros*. Our spirits rose in defiance of the many difficulties we faced, and one felt reenergized with the strength and warmth of so many thousands of people vowing that the Revolution would not be turned back. Like a dying flame, the belief that a new day was upon us was rekindled. Mythical David would once again defeat Goliath. Just like Sandino had done, fighting in the mountains of northern Nicaragua in 1933 with a ragged, tiny army, we would also beat the Contras, and overcome even a U.S. intervention.

I spotted Charlie at the grandstand raised above the public, in the space designated for the press reporting the celebration. He was only a few meters away, but such a chasm it seemed. We inhabited such different worlds. And yet I was consumed by longing. The notion that we were citizens of nations in conflict had such minor importance when nostalgia brought back to me the look in his eyes—so genuine and intense—when he said: "I think I'm falling in love with you."

After the rally, sunburnt and tired, I went to my cousin Pía's house. I needed her special warmth and comfort. We had shared so many deaths, so many separations, and a great deal of happiness too. She lived with her mother, who had a large rose garden in her house. From the terrace there was a beautiful view of Lake Managua in the distance and behind it the Chontales mountain range, its bluish peaks only a faint outline on the horizon. Pía and Alfredo, who had two girls and one boy, had been separated for several years. The little girls, running through the house in their bare feet, were tiny and fragile—they always made me think of Tinkerbell, Peter Pan's fairy. Pía was affectionate and welcoming as always, talking nonstop as she bustled around, slender, practical, and motherly, preparing something for me to eat and drink. Sitting on a stool in the kitchen, I decided to tell her about my conversation with Tomás. She was outraged. How could I just accept such an insult to my intelligence?—she blasted, slathering mayonnaise on bread. Hadn't I noticed that my male *compañeros* were never questioned about the female company they kept? Was I not aware that even those who had jobs far more sensitive than my own slept with foreign women, women journalists, whoever they felt like sleeping with? Perhaps I didn't know that the chief of one of the State Security divisions was married to a gringa? The same went for other men she mentioned, all of them holding important government positions. She was on a roll and kept at it. Are you trying to tell me that after so many years risking your skin for the Revolution, you're just simply going to sit back and calmly accept their lack of trust? That you will accept without flinching the insulting notion that because you are a woman you can't keep your head when you drop your underwear? A bunch of self-righteous male chauvinists, that's what they are! That's all there is to it!

If Charlie was really an agent, they had to prove it to you. Why would you be expected to drop somebody you feel for just on a presumption of guilt? Remember Sergio? Didn't they try to tell you that about him too? She kept firing away. They want to be able to do whatever they want, but God help us if we try to do the same!

I sat there, staring at her. I had forgotten what had happened with Sergio. It never amounted to much because—paradoxically enough—Modesto had vigorously intervened on my behalf much before he and I had anything personal. As time had proved, to cast a shadow on Sergio had been a tremendous injustice. How could I, who was the feminist militant, have not thought of all these things until Pía brought them up? It was embarrassing. Pía was right. I had reacted in a most traditional way, accepting, without a whimper, prejudices about women that dated from the time when Adam bit the apple. I jumped up and hugged her. I love women, I thought. We had to stick together so that men's ideas about our "duties," what we could or couldn't do, wouldn't cloud our thinking. It was good to remember that political power, even when it was considered revolutionary, had been for the most part a man's job, tailored to his needs.

"You're so right, Pía. I will tell Tomás that if I can't be trusted, they can just fire me. I will tell him that I will personally give Charlie his due if it turns out he works for the CIA."

I telephoned Charlie. The sun was setting when he arrived at Pía's house. The three of us had dinner on the terrace, looking out at the lights of Managua on the horizon. He and I decided to keep a very low profile, avoid public places. For his sake also.

Tomás didn't fire me. I remained in my job through the November 1984 election. During the electoral process, I occasionally felt wisps of mistrust coming at me from State Security. Nothing substantial. I might have been a bit paranoid. I didn't like it, but I was determined not to recast my life to dispel someone else's unfounded prejudices.

Soon enough, it was Charlie's turn to face the limitations of freedom even in the country that prides itself on being its beacon in the world. At a meeting in Washington with the executive and foreign editors of National Public Radio he was confronted by Otto Reich. Reich masqueraded as a State Department official, but in reality he worked for Oliver North in a secret White House outfit created to divulge black propaganda about the Sandinistas and to go after journalists whose coverage was deemed unfavorable to the Reagan administration's policies in Central America. Before Charlie's editors, Reich accused him of using his news reports to spread "Sandinista propaganda." He tried unsuccessfully to rake Charlie over the coals by misrepresenting his work, but neither NPR's editors nor Charlie allowed him much slack. Reich's allegations were dismissed, but he didn't relent. Shortly after that he started a rumor that Charlie had received money to work as an agent for the Sandinistas and that that was the real motive behind our relationship. We were flabbergasted at this fabrication and the total lack of decency of these people.

"Your fellow Americans have no problem lying," I said. "Yet, we are supposed to be the villains."

In November, Daniel Ortega won 60 percent of the vote, but the United States didn't recognize his victory. The Reagan administration had backed one of the opposition candidates, who, at the last minute, pulled out of the contest. That had been the plan since the start: to find a way to question the legitimacy and fairness of the elections. In a propaganda strike, meant to dismiss any discussion over the Nicaraguan electoral process in the media, two days after results were announced, President Reagan interrupted the Super Bowl broadcast and went on national television to accuse the Sandinista Revolution of breaking the tactical equilibrium in the region by accepting a shipment of Soviet MiG jets—an accusation based on the CIA spotting some crates that actually contained combat helicopters.

I was having breakfast with my kids the next morning when a loud explosion startled us out of our chairs. Windowpanes and the china on the table rattled loudly. It was the sonic boom of an SR-71 Blackbird spy plane over Nicaraguan airspace, a warning from the United States. The scene was replayed each morning for several days. It made everybody extremely nervous, reviving the fear of a U.S. invasion. Charlie would wonder what we were to do if that happened. Would he leave? Would I go with him? Would he get the children out? Would he have to take sides? Daunting questions with no easy answers. I just knew I wasn't going to leave Nicaragua in a situation like that.

CHAPTER FORTY-NINE

*Of the trepidations I endured at other airports and the surprises
granted to me by the power of my imagination*

UNITED STATES, 1984

THE FIRST TIME Charlie and I were together in the United States after
the beginning of our romance was when I was invited by the Nation Institute to visit New York and take part in a conference they named "Dialogue of the Americas." I flew to New York via Miami. As I waited my
turn in front of the immigration cubicles, I felt restless. I was aware that
growing up under the Somoza dictatorship I had developed, by a quasi-
Pavlovian reflex, an instinctive, irrational fear toward men or women in
uniforms. It was pointless to remind myself that I wasn't under any particular danger in Miami. Traveling to the United States had become
troublesome for me since a previous trip, during the electoral campaign,
when I toured several universities lecturing on the Nicaraguan electoral
process and the Sandinista program. The United States consulate had
unduly delayed granting me a visa and finally had issued one for thirty
days and one single entry. The visa document itself had a mysterious
series of numbers on the bottom. Upon my arrival in Miami then, the
immigration official had eyed me with suspicion and inquired if I was a
communist. "You have a waiver in your passport," he indicated. I had no
idea what that meant, but since then I would often be escorted to a room
marked "Secondary Immigration Inspection," where men and women
mostly from the Third World fidgeted in their seats. After a long wait, I
would be asked more questions, usually in a hostile way, and they would
finally stamp my passport and allow me to proceed to the baggage claim.

For the most part I considered that these delays and humiliations had little to do with me personally and were just another expression of the Central American conflict. Only sometime later an immigration lawyer told Charlie and me that the numbers at the bottom of my visa identified me as an "excludable alien," a foreigner not allowed into the United States except if the State Department waived the exclusion, which was based on Section 28 of the McCarran-Walters Act. The act had been passed during the McCarthy era, to deny entry into the United States to anyone deemed a communist. Since the Reagan administration labeled Sandinistas as communists, each time I applied for a visa, the State Department had to waive the "ideological exclusion" clause. They usually granted the waiver to people invited to the United States by a university, grassroots, or political organization, which requested it invoking the Freedom of Information Act.

The long waits at the airports, the questioning, the impediments made me very uncomfortable and brought back the feeling of helplessness and anxiety I used to feel during the dictatorship, and that I had thought I would never experience again.

When I finally got to New York, I spent three exciting days with well-known writers and intellectuals who had arrived from countries ranging from Canada to Argentina. On panels and roundtables we discussed the cultural differences in each region of the American continent and what we could do to propitiate a productive inter-American dialogue. I especially remember a lively debate with Susan Sontag and E. L. Doctorow. It comes to mind not only because I felt culturally close to them, but also because someone stole Doctorow's car and he returned to the salon, quite distraught, to call the police.

On the last day of the conference Charlie flew to New York from Managua. It was fun to see him in his milieu. I could barely match the rhythm of his pace on the streets. He seemed distracted, overstimulated, like he couldn't get enough of the sounds, the smells, the abundance of New York—the place, he said, where he was most at home. He had to feel very deprived in Nicaragua, I thought. It was such a contrast to be surrounded by so many lights, so many things, so many choices. It made me dizzy. There was no harmony in a world where one could jump in a five-hour journey from abject misery to excess. We took the train from Penn Station the next day to go to his home in Washington. After that we would spend a few days in Virginia, at "the farm." Charlie settled in the

Metroliner with a bunch of newspapers, magazines. He brought me coffee, cookies in a paper tray. I remember feeling a surge of tenderness as I watched him fall asleep. It all seemed to me like an out-of-body experience.

Charlie's father, Lou, whom I would meet at the farm, lived in a beautiful brownstone, a three-story house decorated with exquisite Italian antiques, porcelain vases perched on illuminated stands, kilim rugs. There was a piano on the second floor. A tasteful collection of Chinese cloisonné, enamel plates with intricate, delicate designs, hung on the dining room wall. His grandfather had collected them, Charlie explained. The parquet floors shone, and a thin housekeeper, from the Seychelles Islands, with the voice of a little girl and a French accent, served us a very formal dinner on an elegant white porcelain service. I was reminded of the quiet, polished rooms in my grandparents' house. The decor, the Venetian engravings on the walls gave me the feeling I was in Milan, not Washington. It was definitely a European sensibility. Charlie's bedroom on the third floor was filled with books and the general disarray of papers and random objects accumulated since adolescence, an upscale version of his room in Managua. No doubt he found his cramped little room there amusing. Charlie's father, who was retired, had been the head of IBM in Europe, and his maternal grandfather, a powerful Italian magnate. His mother had died of cancer when Charlie was twenty-four. He had only one brother, Peter, who had come to visit in Managua and arrived the night that a powerful explosion blew up a munitions storehouse close to some military installations, just a few blocks from where Charlie lived.

At dusk, we drove to the farm, where Charlie's father waited for us. We took Route 66, heading toward Virginia. After passing through a town called Warrenton, we began to enter an entirely rural world, a shadowy, sylvan realm with the smoky profile of the Blue Ridge Mountains on the horizon. Eventually we left the main highway and turned onto a narrow country road, dotted with pleasant Southern-style country houses. Summer had just begun. A quiet green landscape enveloped us, deeper and denser than the scandalous brilliance of the tropics. Every now and then we would pass by pristine, picturesque little churches—Baptist, Methodist, and other denominations—nestled among the rolling hills. We drove by red barns, tidy white fences, ponds. I could sense my mind intent on trying to grasp the familiarity of an image that, although I was seeing it for the first time, seemed to exist already in my memory, as if this was a place I was revisiting. Where have I seen this? I asked myself.

Where? I had traveled or was going to travel that road many times in my life. I was certain of it. Still trying to come to terms with such a singular sensation, all of a sudden a flash of understanding came over me. This landscape was almost exactly the same one that served as the backdrop to my fantasy of living another life somewhere in the English countryside.

I am one of those people who firmly believe in the untapped powers of the mind, but to drive down country lanes in Virginia with Charlie, and discover how much he and his whole world resembled my fantasy, was like entering an episode of *The Twilight Zone.*

"Do you have horses at your farm?" I asked.

"Yes," he said.

"Would you believe that I imagined myself in a place like this? I hadn't even met you when I had a vivid vision of living in a place like this, with a man who looked like you."

He smiled. I smiled too. Back then, we had not even remotely considered that we could have a future together. I described it to him like a surreal, fantastic dream that would never really happen, that had no place in the life of a Sandinista woman like me.

At the cozy house at the farm I had long conversations with Lou. He was seventy-two going on forty. A strong, charming, inquisitive man and a tireless conversationalist. He wanted to know everything about Nicaragua. I spent time with him while Charlie, turned into a farmer, bush-hogged on the tractor and pruned.

CHAPTER FIFTY

Where I return to New York City on a sad mission with Charlie

NICARAGUA–NEW YORK, 1985–1986

A YEAR WENT BY. Reagan imposed an economic embargo on Nicaragua. Charlie moved into my house and became best friends with my son, Camilo, who had also moved back in with me. For New Year's we went to the beach. I thought he would be thrilled to spend New Year's by the ocean. "The ocean, you know? On the beach. When have you, inhabitant of winter, citizen of the snow, ever been able to lie on the sand on December 31 and gaze up at the stars?"

The party in the house of some friends, on the shores of the Pacific, was casual: rum and Cokes in paper cups, guests in jeans and T-shirts dancing cumbias and merengues, music blasting from the stereo. When midnight came we bid farewell to 1985 with kisses and shouts and patriotic cheers. "Long live freedom in Nicaragua!" I went to look for Charlie, who had gone to the beach and was sitting on the dunes, contemplating the ocean with a nostalgic look on his face. He missed the snow, he said, the log fire in the fireplace that his father and brother would light in the farm. I was taken aback by his sadness. I was so happy that he had decided to stay in Nicaragua to spend Christmas and New Year's with me. My daughters were spending the vacation with their father, who now lived in Guatemala. Camilo was with us, sleeping inside, in one of the upstairs rooms. I convinced Charlie to join the party. That night I didn't feel like sharing his melancholy.

In the chill of the wee hours of the morning, we made a bed in the sand. We didn't have sleeping bags, only sheets and blankets. Finally he emerged from his distant gaze, his yearning to be somewhere else.

Together we smoothed out the sand, making a square depression for the sheet, a bed at the foot of a sea that bellowed like a happy ruminant with great white curls, flinging its tangled mane against jutting rocks. There, on the fresh, dry sand we snuggled beneath our blanket. Pressed up against each other, we listened as silence descended over the house. On the Pacific coast of Nicaragua, the beach colonies are small hamlets, with rustic vacation homes and fishermen's shacks. The absence of city lights keeps the night sky dark, crisp and resplendent. Above our heads a myriad of stars shimmered. The Milky Way unfolded, like a woman's veil flowing carelessly in the wind. The constellations—the Southern Cross, Libra, Orion's Belt, the Pleiades—were so clear and sharp that a child might have easily connected the dots. Too beautiful to sleep. Beneath the blankets, our bodies created their own nocturnal, amphibious world, living creatures rocked by ebb and flow, moaning like the wave-swept sea. The sky was a deep indigo by the time we fell asleep.

It was the beginning of February when I realized I was pregnant. A major scare I hadn't anticipated. I had been extremely cautious ever since Camilo's birth, but there were months in which the war, the shortages, and the lack of medicine left me without birth control pills, forcing me to rely on the age-old rhythm method. This time the calculations failed. What would we do, what *could* we do? We were living together in Managua, but our future was far from certain. Neither of us was willing to give up our lives in our respective countries. We couldn't imagine how either of us could make that concession, or how we could reach any sort of compromise.

I went to the doctor, and the prognosis was not good: the pregnancy was likely to have complications. Charlie suggested we go to New York, to hear some better-informed medical opinions. There, no matter what our decision, we would have more resources at our disposal. We waited for my visa, which was expedited because of health issues. New York in February was a labyrinth of chilling gusts and drafts. I had imagined the doctors' offices would be more or less like those in Nicaragua, only nicer. Ample, sunny places filled with plants and friendly secretaries. I was unprepared for those tall, mysterious buildings with endless corridors, heavy doors, and gloomy, antiseptic waiting rooms, where secretaries far too busy to smile made us fill out forms and questioned us about medical coverage, of which I had none. It struck me as rude, especially in a country as wealthy as the United States, that financial concerns had to be taken care of before anything else. In Nicaragua, money is dealt with at the end, just before leaving the doctor's office. At the doctor's office on Park Avenue, however, my having no insurance didn't seem to be a problem. Young and friendly, the doctor very plainly stated after examining me that she wouldn't be able to help me, no matter what my decision. Because of my scarred cervix, I would require special attention. Whether I decided to have the baby or not, I needed to see a doctor who specialized in high-risk cases. Mine was sure to be a delicate, difficult case, and without medical insurance, it would also be costly. Even if I was lucky enough not to miscarry, the baby would probably be premature. This meant at least six hundred dollars a day for the use of an incubator which could very well be needed a long time. I knew the routine all too well. Camilo had been in an incubator for two months, except that it hadn't cost me a penny.

For almost two weeks, anxiety consumed every last bit of warmth I had brought with me from the tropics. The bitter cold of New York and its gray days were the perfect metaphor for how I felt. The high-risk specialists presented us with a spine-chilling scenario: the entire pregnancy in bed, in the immediate vicinity of a hospital specializing in premature births. The doctor explained that in the United States, premature babies often survive despite the damage caused by low birth weight. Quality of life was the issue at hand, meaning potential cerebral paralysis or severe mental retardation. In the Third World, the survival rate was lower, but the babies that made it frequently managed to live normal lives, something my own son's experience had proven. There was also a considerable risk to my own health. In the best of possible worlds, it would be a repeat performance of what I had already been through.

I don't know how many coffee shops Charlie and I went to during that trip. I still remember Madison Avenue and its Greek coffee shops, each indistinguishable from the other. We drank cup after cup wondering what we should do. Where would our child grow up? How would I manage if I had to stay in bed? Where would I stay? And what would I do with my other children? Who would take care of them if I had to wait in the United States to give birth? And if the baby was born with problems? We wanted to be responsible, to summon up some kind of Solomonic wisdom, but what we really wanted was that someone would withdraw the chalice of that terrible decision, to be spared the need to play God, thanks to modern medicine. I was already forming a bond with the little creature cradled in my belly—an ambiguous bond which was sometimes love and sometimes rejection, depending on the day, the hour, whether the sun was shining or not. In the end, I came to the grim realization that the only person who could make that decision was me. Charlie struggled in a sea of doubt and anxiety, but he had the consolation—as all men do—that the problem did not reside in his body. My body would pay the consequences. I was terrified by the idea of going through all that pain again, frightened by the interminable list of risks the doctors so descriptively enumerated. I didn't understand why they had to be so cruel; later I realized they explained things so carefully to protect themselves from lawsuits. The prospects were far too dangerous, and I had other children—three others—for whom I had to safeguard my place in the world of the living. I made my decision.

I still remember the emptiness I felt on the flight home to Nicaragua, like a gutted house with only its facade left standing. For many years I cried over what could have been. I suffered for every woman who has ever found herself torn by life-or-death decisions, decisions that are our right, but that forever leave a bomb crater in our hearts, a disaster zone where the ghost of a child wanders, laughing the laughter that never was, forever gazing at us wistfully for the life we denied it.

The plane landed in Managua and taxied down the runway. Deep in my sorrow, my forehead pressed to the window, I was the first to see the flickering lights, the thousands of oil lamps lining both sides of the runway. Those humble, primitive oil lamps had been the only beacons to guide our descent. The plane had touched down on an altar filled with votive candles! After New York with all its lights and highways, this seemed totally surreal. Charlie and I could hardly believe what we were seeing— it actually cheered me up, it was so touching. Such a wonderfully simple solution.

"The airport was inundated by the latest storms. The lights on the landing strip blinked once and went out. We don't have the money to replace them," said the immigration officer.

"What happens if it rains?" Charlie asked.

"We close the airport. What else can we do? Your country's embargo is doing this to us," explained the young official with a smile that was both ironic and resigned.

And in New York, such an abundance of lights! The contrast was enough to make you cry. When I went out into the streets, I finally understood why Charlie always said Managua was so dark. Ah! But the heat of the tropical night soothed my bones, and to me the darkness felt intimate, restful. Surrendered to its blackness, the night was what it was supposed to be. Nothing was as comforting as returning.

CHAPTER FIFTY-ONE

Of the memories I revisited with Charlie
and of my daughters' many exploits

MANAGUA, 1985

I REVISITED the road to Mazatlán—my grandfather's coffee hacienda, where I used to meet with Marcos—at the beginning of 1985. My life and my country were so different now, but that road that threaded through ravines and coffee plants had not changed. The tilled earth, the smell of roasted coffee, the wind whistling through elongated yucca leaves. Perhaps there were fewer trees. Since almost all Nicaraguans cook with firewood, the depletion of the forest is merciless. It was mid-morning, Charlie and I were driving in my Lada on the way to visit my daughters. It was January, and school was out. Maryam and Melissa had both decided to join the brigade of boys and girls from their school who spent their days out in the coffee fields. The war had had a drastic effect on the supply of manual laborers, and the government issued a call to students, seeking their help. If that coffee wasn't picked at just the right time, the country's main export would be lost. It was the second year that Maryam, now sixteen, had joined the Sandinista Youth Coffee Pickers Brigade. The first year, 1984, I had to repress my anxiety: she would be in the north, near the war zone, in a mountain hacienda which was connected to the outside world by only the rockiest of country roads. I went to visit her at Christmastime and was amazed at how happy she seemed during those months, so filled with hard work, but also with the incredible camaraderie of her fellow coffee pickers. Now her brigade as well as Melissa's had been assigned to a hacienda just outside Managua. Because she would be with her sister, and not far from the city, I relented and allowed Melissa, at age twelve, to participate.

From the moment I turned onto the road, the past floated through the brisk air: childhood Sundays with my family, lunches with my grandparents during their long visits to the hacienda, nighttime trips with Marcos. Such different times, now coming together. Who would have ever guessed that my daughters would close the circle, that in the new, revolutionary version of my memories, they too would hold fast to the smells and sounds of the wind in this landscape? There they were waiting for me, their cheeks pink from the sun and cool wind. The coffee hacienda was a lot like my grandfather's place. Wooden structures, with weathered outdoor decks, large cement plazas used to dry coffee, and whitewashed walls. Scores of teenagers everywhere: one group sitting around a boy playing guitar, and another group of girls lying in the sun.

"Did you bring food?" asked Melissa, peering inside the car. I took out what I brought and suddenly we were surrounded by a sizable group—all provisions brought by parents were spread around for everyone to share. During the entire week the volunteer pickers lived with the *campesinos* and ate what they ate: rice, beans, a tortilla, and coffee. The same thing, breakfast, lunch, and dinner. By Sunday, visiting day, any other food was a banquet to them.

Maryam and Melissa led us to the barracks where they slept. Just like me, Charlie was intrigued by the surroundings. It was inspiring to see so many young people, tired but enthusiastic and happy. The workday began at four in the morning, Melissa explained. The younger kids planted young coffee plants in black plastic bags, so they could mature in the nursery. The older ones, like Maryam, carried big baskets around their waists to collect the coffee beans in the ravines, moving up and down the steep hills, eating in the fields and returning just before midday. This way they avoided working in the intense afternoon heat.

Entering the dormitories sent me reeling back to the scene at my uncle's hacienda years before. The barracks where my daughters slept were exactly the same, except that they had a little more space between shelves, and each person had his or her own space and a little mattress to sleep on. Melissa had to use a rough wooden ladder to reach her mattress because her shelf was the fifth up from the floor.

"This is a very good experience," she said, trying to alleviate the horrified look that she saw come across my face. Her expression was sweet, solemn, and serious. "The *campesinos'* lives are hard, and I will never drink another cup of coffee without thinking of them. We only spend three months here, but for them this is life."

I gathered all my strength so as not to weep. Pride and tenderness mixed in with the old wound left by the injustice I had witnessed as a child. Another circle had closed. I too had fought for this, fought so my daughters could, as Che said, "deeply feel any injustice committed against any human being anywhere in the world."

"You should see, Mommy, what it's like to wash up with the freezing water from the tanks, or to use the latrines," Maryam said, laughing off the hardships. "And falls we take on the hillsides when it rains and the ground turns to mud."

Later on, we found a spot near the barracks to sit down and have an improvised picnic with Maryam's and Melissa's friends. With the abundant humor of youth, they joked and shared anecdotes about the various calamities they survived daily.

I watched Charlie as he observed everything, visibly moved by the scene, while I, enraptured, contemplated my daughters, my two formidable little women.

"The world would be a different place if all young people did things like this," Charlie said to me just after we said our goodbyes. "Although it's sad that there's such a need for it at all."

CHAPTER FIFTY-TWO

Where I take the risk of making a marriage proposal

MANAGUA, 1986

CHARLIE OFTEN TALKED to me about what his life would be like when he returned to the United States. Living in the realm of the present, at first I didn't find his bouts of nostalgia particularly threatening, but the more we fitted into each other, the more our lives and our bodies became intertwined, the less able I was to take his remarks lightly. On the contrary, his words began to pierce me, like needles on my skin. I began to ask myself if there was any point in devoting so much love to a man who, at any moment, could get up and say goodbye. How much longer would it be before he decided to burst the bubble we had built around ourselves, a bubble that defied the vagaries of time, that grew walls and floors, that solidified every day into something more permanent, more protective? Would I, once again, be forced to accept the absence of a future, or would I have to seek this chimera, this male partner for the rest of my life? After so many lost loves, errant searches, and mortal leaps in quest of greener, illusive landscapes, I had finally accepted the precipices that exist in each human topography. The real challenge was not in finding one's match, but in settling the territory, the tender labor of two imperfect beings who accept one another and agree to work the land, lay bridges, and not escape at the earth's first shuddering. I had come to this knowledge just when the path before me was full of uncertainties.

With Charlie, more than with any other, I was able to dismiss the feminine vice of excessive second-guessing: "If I do this, he's going to think that; if I say that, he'll think this"—such a weary, futile exercise. With Charlie I dared to be exactly who I was. To say exactly what I felt. To assume the risks of my emotions. I don't know when, but at some point I made a vow never to act according to how I thought he might react. I would call him when I wanted to, reveal whatever it was that was passing through my head at any given moment. At first, it gave me vertigo to reveal my raw emotions. From the time we are little girls, women are taught to please. We are trained to be chameleons for our men, adapting to them. But if we don't stop ourselves, we risk losing our identities. I had come to this realization after a slow and painful process and I didn't want to regress.

"What is it that you want?" one of my wisest friends asked me one day. I began a long, complicated explanation.

"Do you want him to marry you? Is that what you want?" she interrupted.

Well put. I sat there, mute, looking at her.

"Well, yes," I said. "The truth is, that's what I want. I want him to marry me."

"Tell him. That's all you have to do. Why wait for him to ask? Why can't you be the first to say it?"

I was fortunate to have fearless friends! But I give myself credit too: seldom have I dismissed good advice or refused to listen to and trust other women.

"Do you want to marry me?" I asked Charlie.

I still laugh whenever I think of the expression on his face. We were sitting in the love seat in the tiny studio next to my bedroom. I have kept that seat as a memento of the discussions to which it has been witness. Charlie and I had been practically living together for more than a year, but whenever we had long talks we couldn't seem to agree about what to do with our relationship. Neither of us was willing to give up life in our respective countries. He maintained that he thought he could never adjust to life in Nicaragua. He took for granted that I would never adapt to life in the United States.

"What?" he asked. "Are you serious?"

"Yes!" I smiled. "This is a marriage proposal!"

"I have to think about it," he said.

I chuckled. He was the first man I had ever proposed to, I protested, and he said he had to think about it! We went out to dinner. I told him that I just couldn't go on living as if the future didn't matter. I didn't want any more uncertainties, short-lived relationships. I had accepted conditions of romantic uncertainty too many times in my life and I couldn't do it anymore. I would rather put an end to it, make a clean break and start over—anything but live in fear of the day when he would tell me he had to leave. We either had to get married or go our separate ways. That was the choice I gave him.

I begged fate to press him to accept my terms, because in this man who held my hand and gazed at me across the top of his wineglass, I sensed I had found the safe harbor for the wanderings of my heart.

Charlie didn't take what I said lightly. Unfurling every rationale he could think of, he began to dissect my proposal, to see the pros and cons of a marriage between us. I could see he was not a person to commit easily precisely because he took his commitments very seriously. About marriage he was quite the Italian—before divorce was legal. I knew the idea challenged every imaginary scenario he had ever envisioned for himself. I was a divorcée, a woman with baggage, with three children. He had never been married, although he had lived a few years with a woman. I was aware I had to give him time to think, to overcome his fears.

CHAPTER FIFTY-THREE

On how Charlie and I constructed a bridge
that spanned our separate geographies

MANAGUA, 1986

CHARLIE HAD LEFT his job at NPR and was now working as a freelancer for other news organizations. He traveled frequently to Washington. On one of his trips I told him on the phone that time was running out. If he didn't think he could commit, I didn't want him to return to me. He might as well stay. Begin his life anew. We could both start over. That began a round of daily, long phone calls. He would call to propose different formulas which, he thought, would prevent us from breaking up. I didn't give in. I knew it would hurt me to part with him, but I also knew I would survive. I had survived every time. Like the brain, the heart has an amazing capacity for recovery. I was absolutely determined not to waste myself on another relationship without a future. I think he could tell mine were not empty words, that I meant what I said. And he couldn't accept parting with me. He loved me as much as I loved him. "We'll get engaged," he offered. I accepted. Two or three days later he was back in Managua with a computer in lieu of a ring.

Who knows how our story would have ended, if that year I had not found myself possessed by the urgent need to write. It might have seized me at the office on a day like any other, when I suddenly realized I was becoming a bureaucrat, or it might have been the awareness that I was overflowing with some unnamed emotions that needed to be spelled out. Maybe it was both things at the same time. Whatever the cause, the truth is that my literary vocation unexpectedly surged within me. I didn't quite know what it was, but something was asking to be written. I could see its contours, an island in the mist, whose precise shape would only become clear after I built a bridge and took possession of it.

Following the 1984 elections, I had become the director of a state-owned communications company. But my heart wasn't in it. After a while, I just wanted to escape, and use my time to think and reach my island. Sometimes it seemed to me that a long theatrical poem with a chorus would emerge. But finally the mist lifted. I sat down at my typewriter one afternoon and began to describe what I used to see—back when I was a newlywed—while I walked to work every morning from my apartment to Publisa, the advertising agency where I met the Poet. My hands took on a life of their own. It wasn't me who was walking anymore, but another woman. Five pages later, the island began to take shape. A story that had simmered for fifteen years finally found its voice. That was the beginning of my first novel, *The Inhabited Woman*. From that moment anything not connected with writing ceased to matter.

I spoke to Bayardo Arce and asked him if I could take a leave of absence from my job. I offered to continue collaborating in the design of advertising campaigns for social projects or political races. I could be available at specific times, but I needed to dedicate myself mostly to writing my novel. I could count on the royalties from a book of poems recently published in Germany to supply some income. Bayardo approved and encouraged me. He thought it was a brave thing to do. I will always be grateful to him for understanding me, for not telling me that writing was a petit bourgeois indulgence when one lived in a country that was slowly being torn apart by a counterrevolutionary war. After a few weeks, arrangements were made and my responsibilities were assigned to someone else.

Shifting the focus of my life from politics to literature felt like taking a death-defying leap without a safety net. I understood what Rilke meant when he said he had to write in order to keep on living. Had I not started writing, I would have been asphyxiated by the words trapped in my throat. But the decision troubled me and I felt guilty. When people asked me where I worked, I felt embarrassed, as if writing a novel were a point-less occupation. But it was a tolerable discomfort because the unfettered joy I felt pecking at my keyboard every day more than compensated for my misgivings.

Suddenly I had the freedom to think, to reflect. I thought that aspiring to be happy was as valid a goal as making a revolution; without the wisdom to forge my own happiness, how could I presume to save the world?

"Let's make a deal," I said to Charlie. "When Reagan is no longer president, I'll go with you to the United States. Then, after a few years, we'll come back to Nicaragua. We'll take turns. That way neither one of us has to forfeit their country."

"But will you be able to live in the United States?"

I said yes. I wasn't sure, but I thought it would do me good to dedicate myself to literature, to writing, reading, going to libraries, doing research.

In Managua, on April 10, 1987, Charlie and I became husband and wife. The judge, echoing the patriotic rhetoric of the time, married us in the name of the heroes and martyrs of the Revolution.

Getting married in the midst of conflict between our two countries got us into a few imbroglios, the first, in fact, during our honeymoon. On our way to Venice, we stopped in Granada, Spain, where I had been invited to attend a week of literary celebrations. One night, in a packed theater, I participated in a reading with the poets Rafael Alberti, Ernesto Cardenal, Mario Benedetti, Claribel Alegría, and Julio Valle-Castillo. As we stepped off the stage, I found Charlie waiting for me with a mischievous smile on his face. He told me a man had approached him, thinking that because he was my husband, he had to be Nicaraguan.

"I didn't want to disappoint him by telling him I was a gringo," said Charlie, who by now spoke perfect Spanish.

The man, an engineer, wanted to go to Nicaragua to help the Revolution. Charlie, assuming his role, told him yes, absolutely, that an engineer would be of great use to Nicaragua.

"No, what I want to do is help, really help," the man insisted.

Charlie stayed in character, and carried on about the importance of building schools, roads. Finally, the man grew impatient and leveled with him. In a conspiratorial whisper, he leaned toward Charlie and said, "Look, man, what I want to do is go to Nicaragua and kill some gringos."

"I came that close to telling him he could start right then and there with me," Charlie said. "Can you imagine how shocked he would have been? Don't worry, though. I told him that the Revolution wasn't out to kill gringos, just persuade them to leave Nicaragua alone."

We had a good laugh with that episode; it was to be the first of many.

It was midnight, on a deserted canal in Venice, when we exchanged wedding rings, the silence broken only by the gondolier's rhythmic oar stroke and his deep, melancholy call at every corner. Venice, like the fog hovering over its canals, felt unchanging and timeless. But that languid romanticism seemed alien to me; Nicaragua's frenzy felt more tolerable and real. In that gondola, I realized that I would no longer be satisfied by passive and sensory pleasures, that for me nothing would compare to the vibrant passion of pursuing collective dreams.

CHAPTER FIFTY-FOUR

*On how I witnessed the fall of the Berlin Wall in
a Miami hotel, and on the death of my mother*

MANAGUA–MIAMI, 1989

CRUCIAL POLITICAL and military developments took place in Nicaragua between 1986 and 1989. On October 5, 1986, a Contra supply plane was shot down over Nicaragua and the pilot, Eugene Hasenfus, was captured. The documents in that plane and a hostage who was released November 2 in Lebanon were to be the beginning of the Iran-Contra scandal. The Reagan administration's illegal sale of arms to Iran to obtain funds for the Contras was exposed. Aid to the Contras stopped and the Sandinista army gained ground, pushing large contingents of the rebel forces back to their camps in Honduras. With the Nicaraguan economy in shambles and the threat of diplomatic isolation over their heads, after the failure of a number of peace initiatives, the Sandinista leadership began talks with the Contras in Sapoá, near the Costa Rican border. Peace was desperately needed. We were all exhausted after so many years of war. Reagan was to leave office in 1989, and we hoped there would be more favorable conditions for the Contras to disarm. The Sapoá talks, which Charlie covered for NPR, achieved an end to the war. It was also the beginning of a democratization process, since democracy had greatly suffered as the Sandinista leadership hardened its stance in response to anything deemed a threat to the survival of the Revolution. In February 1989, Daniel Ortega agreed to hold free and fair elections under international supervision by February 25, 1990.

Again I was called by the Sandinista party to work in the electoral campaign. I wrote the first draft of a proposal stating that we had to pre-

347

pare for the "worst possible scenario." Nobody agreed with me. Daniel
Ortega had his own proposal, which I objected to. I had already been
involved in several head-to-head clashes with him over the role of his wife
in the Cultural Workers Association. Alleging that I was a contrarian, he
had me dismissed from the Electoral Commission.

Marginalized from political life, I plunged into work on my second
novel, *Sofía de los presagios*, but I was quite depressed. Charlie suggested we
spend the last few months of the year with his father in Virginia. He came
with me to the U.S. consulate in Managua to apply for a visa, hoping that
it would be easier to obtain now that we were married. I, however, had no
such illusions. Our lawyer had warned us that our marriage would not
alter my "non grata" migratory status. The embassy, protected by a double fence crowned with rolls of concertina wire, was a true fortress. The
consulate official at the window was very friendly until she saw the code
printed on my previous visa. Then her expression changed completely.

"But she's my wife," Charlie said.

"In this, she stands alone," the woman said.

We had to wait for authorization. "Unbelievable," I said to Charlie.
"Your country that prides itself on its freedom is in essence limiting
yours. They accuse us Sandinistas of being communist, but you can come
in and out of this country with total freedom. Meanwhile, you cannot
bring your wife to your country."

Deeply disturbed, Charlie traveled to Washington alone. He wrote
letters to the State Department and spoke to several lawyers. Finally,
weeks later, I was granted the famous waiver, and a one-month, one-entry
visa.

We arrived in Miami on November 9, 1989. As soon as we settled in the
hotel, Charlie turned on the television. To watch CNN was a treat for
him. It made him feel that he was back in civilization. There was no cable
television in Nicaragua. There were still only two TV channels at the
time. A crowd at Berlin's Brandenburg Gate appeared on the screen. The
Wall was being torn down. Mesmerized, I watched images of euphoric
young Germans, men and women from East Berlin and West Berlin, looking at each other, stunned, celebrating, hugging those strangers who had
lived in such close proximity for so long, inhabiting such distant worlds. It
was a truly momentous occasion. We were watching history take a gigantic leap, the beginning of a new era. Charlie and I sat, not saying a word.

I remembered the chill and apprehension I felt on my first trip to Berlin as I faced the barbed wire and crossed Checkpoint Charlie with my mother. I remembered the official visit Modesto and I made to East Berlin: the documentary they showed us at Brandenburg Gate, the sad feat of building the entire Wall in one night. I had felt a pressing anxiety on my chest just to imagine the terrible desperation suffered by the people who that night had been forcibly separated by that brutal rift. Children, wives, lovers. "A tragedy that was inevitable." So had said the Party official who accompanied us.

A sense of relief came over me. It was great to see that shameful Wall come down. It had been such a symbol of pain for people on either side of it. I got teary-eyed. My mind started to spin the implications it would have for the Nicaraguan elections coming up. Maybe perestroika, the fall of the Eastern bloc, would open room for my country to slip out of the East-West rivalry. Maybe President Reagan and President George Bush would realize that the Sandinistas were not planning to invade the United States, that we weren't going to try to slip in through Texas, as Mr. Reagan so seriously warned. Maybe all of them would understand how ludicrous it was to consider Nicaragua a threat to their national security.

That night we went for a walk and had dinner in Coconut Grove, the fashionable area in Miami at the time. I had been in the city years before, but now it was almost unrecognizable. In the streets, lit up with neon signs of bars and shops, store windows displayed all sorts of garish, brightly colored clothes. Carefree young people strolled down the streets speaking a mix of English and Spanish. Shiny motorcycles, driven by well-dressed, smiling couples, weaved in and out of traffic. It was a mix of Caribbean and shopping mall influences, *la Cubamérica*. Miami was also the Mecca of the Nicaraguan upper classes who opposed the Revolution, a city populated by those who had been evicted from their countries, a giant waiting room where people bided their time until revolutions came to an end. Charlie often wondered what kind of culture would eventually emerge from the mix. The immigration phenomenon in the United States fascinated him. I, instead, felt alienated in such a noisy, brightly lit environment. In Berlin people were tearing down the Wall with their bare hands, yet here the nightlife seemed to go on as if nothing had happened. People weren't piling up in bars to see it on TV. They continued drinking their beer as if it was business as usual.

———

My mother became ill in December. I waited until after Christmas to return to Nicaragua, since my visa didn't allow me to go see her and then return to the United States. After what Charlie had gone through so that I could spend Christmas with him, I didn't want to leave. I was generally the one who cared for my mother and father, given that my brothers and sisters all lived abroad. But since some of them were in Nicaragua at that point, I didn't think she needed me as much this time around.

I returned to Nicaragua on December 27, 1989. Two days later, my mother died. The exact cause of death was never very clear. According to the doctor she had developed a lethal sort of anemia due to bouts of anorexia nervosa she had had through the years. I think that a mix of things—diagnostic inaccuracies, her feeble condition, her lack of will to live—resulted in her death. There were also other factors: the Revolution that brought me so much happiness meant many losses for her. Her family dispersed. My two brothers had left Nicaragua, disillusioned by the Sandinistas, my sister Lavinia was doing her master's at Cornell University, Lucía lived in Spain. My mother became increasingly apathetic and sickly, and fell into a deep depression. She spent most of her time locked up in her room. Even though she translated into Spanish and adapted Shakespeare's *The Comedy of Errors*, and even directed several plays, she barely ate at all, growing thinner and thinner all the time. She refused to admit to her depression and always attributed her physical condition to other factors, which was why it took us so long to discover the real source of her problems.

Before leaving in November, I convinced her to face her depression and to stop pretending she was stronger than she felt. I made her promise that she would go to the doctor so he could prescribe her some antidepressants. When the doctor examined her, he detected the anemia, which required not one but several blood transfusions. The last time I saw her alive, when she was in the intensive care unit at the hospital, it was as though our roles had been reversed. Like a little girl wanting to please her mother, she told me about how hard she was trying to eat more. I held her hand as she dozed, and she came to after a few minutes, trembling. My mother didn't love life any longer but death terrified her, even though she'd never admit it. She wanted to be strong to the end. "I'm freezing to death," she complained. I wrapped the blankets around her and rubbed her feet to warm her up. Once she fell asleep, I left the room. Lucía and Eduardo, my sister and brother, stayed with her while I went to the airport to pick up my bags, which had arrived late. When I returned to the hospital, my father was crying. My mother had died. I found out that when her heart monitor began beeping its alarm signal, the doctors ordered Lucía and Eduardo out of the room. I will always mourn the fact that none of us was allowed to be present, that she had to be alone at that moment. I would have liked to take her hand, be at her side as she took that mysterious journey—just as she had always been at my side during the difficult junctures in my life, loyal and steadfast above all else.

During the last years of her life, our relationship was like a silent tug-of-war. Once we were confidantes, but slowly we became adversaries in a never-ending conflict, forever sizing each other up from a distance. In my determination never to be a conformist, even when it meant walking on fire, I broke many of the codes she believed in. She never understood the risks I took. Perhaps she sensed me fighting to cut the umbilical cord once and for all, something that meant she would ultimately lose her power over me. She never understood that she would get me back after losing me. She never understood that I had found strength in the very same vulnerability she had denied herself for so long.

I would fight my last battle with my mother in 1994 after the Los Angeles earthquake, which caught me in Santa Monica. A flood of buried fears, unresolved conflicts, and accumulated deaths came crashing into my consciousness. I was possessed by uncontrollable panic attacks that sent my heart galloping at breakneck speed, making me fear for my life. The terror, that constant sensation that a disaster or sickness might suddenly kill me, finally led me back to therapy. That was when I discovered that I was still searching for common ground with my mother, looking for ways to bring her closer to me and to purge all the guilt I felt. I was doing it by putting myself through all the anguish I imagined she had gone through. After a very long process, I finally managed the separation I needed to finally reconcile my self with hers. Without guilt I accepted my happiness, my survival in the face of so much death, my dedication to literature. I reclaimed my romantic idealism, with all the consequences it implied.

One day, sometime in 1995, I went with my friend Sofía to visit her grave. The two of us sat on the gravestone and began talking about the passions that gave our lives meaning—passions we vowed never to renounce. We talked for a long time. The afternoon turned into dusk while we threw the apple of knowledge back and forth, the good and the bad we had experienced. I envisioned our words falling noiselessly on the earth, descending in the afternoon heat like weightless messengers that my mother would receive in her dark resting place. Sofía and I smoked and laughed. We shared the sorrows as well as the jubilant exhilarations that are inescapable elements of the female vocation. It was like visiting a sleeping friend who could hear us from a little crevice deep within her slumber. That was my homage to my mother. My ceremonial peace pipe.

CHAPTER FIFTY-FIVE

On how the most intense years of my life drew to an end

MANAGUA, 1990

ON FEBRUARY 25, 1990, the Sandinista Revolution—the heroic deed of the Nicaraguan people to dethrone a legacy of tyrants, the cause that filled the most intense, difficult, and happy years of my life—came to an end. I remember how it rained the day before. A dust storm blew over everything just before the downpour, coating the volcanoes and lakes with a thin film of light brown soot.

"I don't like this rain," I said to Charlie.

Political campaigning ended three days before the actual election date to comply with electoral law. After the last heated months of the race, silence fell on Managua and I went around in my car feeling shivers travel up and down my spine, as if my skin knew something unexpected was about to happen. I wasn't as sure as my *compañeros* that the public would vote overwhelmingly in favor of the FSLN. I had voiced my concerns when I said we had to prepare for the worst possible scenario, that we had to acknowledge people's feelings after years of scarcity and loss. But Daniel Ortega and the others had insisted on a bright, cheerful, Coca-Cola–style campaign. The slogan they used was Daniel's very own creation, "Todo será mejor"—everything will be better.

In December, after I returned from the United States, I watched the advertising on television in disbelief, wondering how they could have put together such an incredibly tactless, obnoxious campaign, complete with rock and roll music. While people mourned so many young kids who had died in the war, while they endured hunger and terrible hardships, the

FSLN's propaganda conveyed such a festive atmosphere: kids dancing around in plazas as if the Revolution was still one big party.

I prayed that my predictions wouldn't come true. I tried to scrutinize the faces I saw in the traffic to find—I don't know how—reason to hope, but all I wanted to do was run away, hide, anything but live through the days that were hurtling toward me, fast and unstoppable. Even the most sensible, most reasonable, most critical of my *compañeros* scowled at me when I would even suggest the possibility of defeat. "Don't be crazy. Of course we're going to win." Everyone was so loyal, up until the last moment, despite everything. I guess it was hard for us to accept that one, two, or three men could derail a process that had cost so many lives. With a visceral faith they were betting that nothing—not the war, not Reagan—could defeat us, that the Nicaraguan people would support us to the end. Once the war was over, we would right all the wrongs, patch the misunderstandings, temper the authoritarian tendencies. We would demand democracy from within, consistency, no more sudden changes in direction. We hoped that the elections would create an opportunity to move forward, without any more pretexts. We hoped people would not be asked to put up with any more disproportionate sacrifices. I hoped my daughters wouldn't have to attend any more of their friends' funerals. I wanted my *compañeros* to be right. My friend Sofía, who was so stubborn and defiant, she just couldn't be wrong. I had to be the one who was mistaken.

But on Election Sunday, people lined up in silence to enter the polling stations; there was none of the typical gleeful Nicaraguan bantering. Silence was the order of the day. And when I returned home, the three foreign journalists staying with us were already back, crestfallen, from doing their exit polls, which were worrisome. From what they could tell, Violeta Chamorro, who was leading UNO, a coalition of political parties, had won. Even they looked distressed. I think they felt somewhat responsible for the way their country had mercilessly pounded a revolution that, though they didn't consider perfect, they had grown to like.

"People must feel like they are voting with a gun to their heads," one journalist said to me. "They know that if they vote for the Sandinistas, the war will continue. That's what people say, they don't want any more war."

I think it was around ten in the evening when my sister Lavinia called.

"Gioconda, the Sandinistas lost. They just called Humberto to Doña

Violeta's house. President Carter is on his way there now to tell her the FSLN accepts the defeat, that she won."

My hands went cold. President Carter was the highest ranking person among the many international observers supervising the fairness of the electoral process.

"Let's go," I said to Charlie. "Let's go to Sofía's."

Sofía Montenegro, my partner in women's meetings and crying spells, feminist, courageous, brilliantly eloquent, greeted us at her front door in slippers. We sat down in the living room.

"We lost," I said. And I told her about Lavinia's phone call.

It's not true, she kept saying. Why would I believe those rumors? They are just ploys to demoralize us. It isn't true.

There was no way to convince her. I returned home with Charlie. The city, the air, the traffic—everything seemed so hostile to me.

We didn't sleep at all that night, staying up to wait for news from the Supreme Electoral Council. The Sandinista station was broadcasting live from the FSLN's campaign headquarters, where a giant victory party was scheduled to take place. The orchestra had been playing music for several hours, but the cheerful mood that had reigned in the early evening was all gone. The crowd had also grown quiet, there were no more slogans chanted by the multitude. Melissa's boyfriend came over and told us that, instead, people were hugging each other and crying. My girls were at home. The two of them had grown up with the Revolution, they had witnessed its history, they had come to love it as much as I did. Maryam was a member of the Sandinista Youth. Melissa's first boyfriend, David, was a polite, sweet boy who had just completed his military service. Camilo was spending a few days in Costa Rica with my brother Eduardo. As I found out later, my eleven-year-old boy cried inconsolably while his uncle's family celebrated the Sandinista defeat.

At six in the morning, Daniel Ortega gave the speech of his life as he accepted electoral defeat. For the first time he sounded like a true statesman. He spoke with sincerity and pain, but he was calm, and asked people to keep the peace and not to riot, and he called upon the Sandinistas to accept the decision of the Nicaraguan people. Our new victory would be to achieve the first peaceful transfer of power between contending parties in Nicaragua's history.

In the living room, where we could see a magnificent view of the sunrise parting the clouds and waking up the birds, we all felt as if our backbones had been snapped and could no longer hold us upright. We were hunched over, stunned, anyone could see the sadness in our bleary eyes and our sallow faces. When I looked out at the city beyond, I was disturbed to feel a hostile emanation rising from my own land. The people had rejected us. I never thought I would live to see this day. My desolation filled with the presence of all my dead friends, but this time the feeling was devastating. I felt they were dying again, dying in vain, their deaths futile, their lives wasted. So many lives had been lost. And now there were more. With the counterrevolution, the death toll was up to fifty thousand. And it had to end like this!

People didn't celebrate in the streets the victory of UNO and Violeta Chamorro. On the contrary—in the days following Election Sunday, the city was enveloped in an air of mourning. The streets looked the same as when everybody left for the holidays at the height of the summer months. Some said people were afraid of a violent reaction from the Sandinistas; personally, I think people granted Violeta her electoral victory conscious that they were exchanging their sense of power for peace. They must have sensed that once again they would be relegated to being the "poor people," and not the "popular masses" the Sandinistas had championed. Violeta's victory was celebrated by the upper classes, the Miami exiles, the people who would now regain their old privileges, and they held their parties behind closed doors, not in the streets or the plazas.

I thought my mother would have been so happy. It saddened me to think she had died only a month before her friend Violeta's victory. One of her theater friends, Gladys Ramírez, was named director of the Cultural Institute. Oh, my mother! I sighed. She would have been beside herself with joy. Instead, I was bereaved. It was a stunning blow to all Sandinistas. At least I had been lucky to have harbored some doubts about the certainty of victory. These helped mitigate my surprise. But my friends—Sofía, for example—were in total shock. We were desolate, gripped by uncertainty over a future we had imagined would remain revolutionary through the ages. Nevertheless, not one Sandinista disputed or tried to sabotage Violeta Chamorro's victory with riots or demonstrations. Never before had we witnessed such civility in Nicaragua, a country where the strong had never voluntarily surrendered power, never surrendered to the will of the weak unless it was at gunpoint. No Nicaraguan had ever lived through a change of guard brought about by an electoral process, and that in itself was a Sandinista victory. After having been decried as a communist, authoritarian, and absolutist regime, that the FSLN would relinquish power despite the support of the army, the civilian organizations, and 42 percent of the votes had momentous importance for the democratic future of our country.

But I didn't want to witness the dissolution of the Revolution I had so passionately upheld. When Charlie proposed that we move to the United States, so that I could fulfill my part of the bargain—after all, he had spent six years living in Nicaragua—I accepted. My primordial instinct was to flee, close my eyes, not see what would happen to my country.

Violeta turned out to be a maternal figure whose simple words cradled and consoled the broken, divided country. Displaying a perceptive, nuanced wisdom few thought she possessed, she was able to appease the warring factions and force them to coexist. Risking the support of her allies, she chose to make Nicaragua a homeland for all, with no exceptions. That was how old enemies were brought together, sat at the same table, and wept over their shared sorrow. It was odd, but incredibly encouraging, to see such a battle-scarred, defiant country capable of such civility.

CHAPTER FIFTY-SIX

Of how I lived my first year in the United States

MANAGUA–WASHINGTON, 1990

THE IDEA OF LEAVING my home, my friends, everything that rooted me and gave me reason for being, made me feel like the cowardly captain of the *Medusa* who abandoned his ship as it sank. But I had made a promise and I felt I had to honor it. I had to wait three months for my visa, but it finally came through. Grudgingly, unwillingly, I packed our bags and interviewed potential tenants to live in the house Charlie and I had set up together, with the view of my volcanoes and my lakes. I gave away furniture and clothing, feeling as though I was being stripped naked. Weeping, I said goodbye to my father, my sister, my beloved friends, the dogs, the cat, the palm tree, with her fronds flapping like wings. The plane lifted off. It was June 9, 1990. The foliage, the mountains faded away, soon replaced by the turquoise-blue waters of the Caribbean, then the Everglades, the flat Miami landscape, and then the obelisk in Washington, the Potomac River. Had my life come full circle? I wondered. I could almost see its ironic smile as it granted me another existence disquietly similar to the one I fantasized about during the hard times of the Revolution. The taxi dropped us off at Hillyer Place, at the brownstone on the quiet, tree-lined street. My children were filled with the excitement of young people embarking on a great new adventure. "Be careful with the furniture, don't make too much noise, behave yourselves." We settled into the rooms with their shiny wooden floors and Italian furniture, my children in the bronze-frame beds in the guest room, Charlie and I in his teenage bedroom. My father-in-law, Lou, now a dear friend, welcomed us warmly, with his crackling humor. He happily accepted this invasion of his privacy, of the solitude that he had mastered and learned to enjoy as so few people can. Together, with his friends and Charlie's, we would spend many weekends at the farm, Charlie and my children riding horses, while I took long walks through the woods.

Two months later we rented a house. I wasn't prepared for the overwhelming sense of loss I felt when I found myself living in that leafy, protected neighborhood in Bethesda, Maryland, with giant trees that blanketed us with their golden leaves in the fall, a silent neighborhood with ghostlike neighbors whose furtive shadows I saw only occasionally, when they left for work in the morning or came back in the evening. I felt anonymous and lonely, even when surrounded by people, and those were new experiences for me—like wearing clothes that were too large and, no matter how hard I tried, I just couldn't make fit.

In Washington, whenever Charlie and I went out to dinner or coffee, I was always imagining that someone in the surrounding crowds worked for the State Department, or some other arm of the U.S. government. That serious-looking man reading the newspaper at the table next to us, for example, maybe he had been the person responsible for writing the recommendations for the thousand and one ways the United States waged its covert war against the Nicaraguan Revolution, my revolution. As my mind wandered off on those tangents, I would suddenly be startled by the arrival of the waiter, and the determined, purposeful air with which he recited the daily specials. I came from a country where there wasn't enough of anything, and here ordering a beer or a simple ham and cheese sandwich required a level of decision making that I found utterly baffling: first I had to pick from an endless list of brands I didn't recognize, then there were all the different types of ham and cheese, and did I want my sandwich with white, whole wheat, or pumpernickel bread, and did I want it with mayonnaise or some other kind of mustard. I would sit there staring at the waiter like an idiot, wanting to burst into tears as I thought of the monumental lengths one had to go to in Nicaragua just to get a car-ton of eggs.

Although fluent enough in English, I couldn't bring myself to have very deep or intellectual conversations without my vocabulary failing me at some point. The experience was even physically exhausting, and I always ended up feeling like I was retarded. Frustrated and furious, I chose silence. Sometimes if I liked someone, I would find myself inadvertently switching to Spanish, as if friendship and affection could miraculously break the language barrier. When winter came I grew terribly depressed. All my leaves fell to the ground, just as they fell from the trees. When I would open my eyes in the morning and look out at the sad, naked tree trunks, I would ask myself in desperation what kind of trap I had fallen into. I missed my tropical foliage, my volcanoes, my lakes. More than anything, though, I missed my friends, forever busy with their crazy dreams of changing the world. The people I knew in Washington seemed guarded and reserved, and in their eyes I read a message that warned me not to cross the boundaries protecting their privacy and their existential doubts, the great abstractions that nobody talked about, as if all of life's roads were well marked and every one of them knew the path they were on. Conversations were mostly about events happening around them, not inside of them. Wit substituted for intimacy. Irony took the place of dreams. Every so often I would find someone I could be close to. That happened with Billy, one of Charlie's oldest friends.

There are sweeter, happier memories too. During that time I nurtured my children more than ever before. The loneliness we felt forced us to rely on each other, and for all the tears we shed together we also laughed a lot, complicit in our bewilderment. I planted African violets on the windowsill in my studio, caring for them as they blossomed with their little pink and purple flowers. In the afternoons I would walk beneath the trees in front of the houses, peering into the occasional open windows, seeing families in the warmth of their daily routines. But it still felt strange to be surrounded by so many people, and barely hear them or see them at all. On the day of the first big snowstorm I finally saw how many children there were in the neighborhood, as I watched them run from their houses with sleds to go sliding down the hills. My son, Camilo, followed suit, and that was the day he made friends with a little boy in the neighborhood, Andy, a serious child who insisted on drinking only skim milk with his afternoon snack.

I began to understand that one of the more salient aspects of American middle-class culture was privacy, the nuclear family as a tiny, protected haven from the outside world. In big, anonymous cities, many people don't have the reference point of a common history, of a long road of family friendships passed down from generation to generation. Lots of them were as foreign as I was in that city. After the long working day, people in our kind of neighborhood didn't have the time to chat with each other or forge bonds of friendship. This social dispersion, this lack of community and collective living, was another, second exile for me. I realized that in the United States, too often you enter into society as if entering a hostile, highly competitive territory. You leave your home dressed in armor, with your heart shielded, well protected.

This exile—the lack of intimacy with others, the lack of belonging, the absence of a common purpose—was the most difficult one for me.

One morning that winter we all woke up at the crack of dawn to get in line outside the immigration building in Virginia and wait our turn for the interview the United States required in order to grant us residency. The immigration authorities would only see a certain number of people each day, and to get in you had to arrive early. As we stood out on the street with the children in the frigid cold at five in the morning, waiting for the offices to open at seven, Charlie received a harsh lesson in the less-friendly realities of his great nation. The interview brought few surprises. Melissa and Camilo were granted their residency papers soon afterward. Mine, however, took three years and I was lucky that the Cold War was ending and that the U.S. Congress revoked the ideological restrictions imposed by the McCarran-Walters Act. During those three years, every time I wanted to leave the country I had to apply for a document granting me "advanced parole," a term generally applied to prisoners, a kind of preliminary pardon in which my reentry was contingent upon the approval of immigration authorities at the airport. This meant long waits on the return; I would be ushered into the Secondary Immigration Inspection waiting area again. Inevitably, we would miss our connecting flights, cursing U.S. bureaucracy. Of course, all this only made me feel even more unwelcome in the country that, thanks to my marriage, was ostensibly my second home. And out came all the bottled-up resentment I felt toward the United States for the damage it caused Nicaragua.

After finishing high school, Melissa decided to go back to Latin America to study medicine in Mexico, where Maryam was studying architecture. Going with Melissa to register her at La Salle Medical School in Mexico City was horribly depressing for me. She was my companion, my solace, my conspirator. When she left, I felt more alone than ever.

I think I would have died of sadness if we had stayed in Washington. It was too violent an experience for me to live with the symbols of an authority I could never come to perceive as benevolent or friendly. I would travel back to Nicaragua and return to lonely Bethesda teary and mournful.

After a brief foray into the world of theater, Charlie decided to pursue his dream of making movies, and we moved to Los Angeles. A city with palm trees, street uprisings, and earthquakes, it felt much closer to the world I was accustomed to. So we packed up our belongings and hired a moving company. Instead of flying we decided to drive cross-country, stopping in Santa Fe, the Grand Canyon. I remember how astounded I was by the vastness of it all. The diversity of the landscape, the tiny towns with their authentic, idiosyncratic little touches. "Antiques Made Daily," announced a sign in southern Virginia. "Hitchhikers Might Be Runaway Inmates," warned another sign somewhere near Oklahoma. In the Grand Canyon, tears filled my eyes as I watched the sun set over so many geological eras in a spectacular explosion of pink and purple hues. We laughed a lot on that trip. Camilo was endlessly, tirelessly fascinated by all the parks, the rock formations, the hamburgers. And when we arrived in Los Angeles, a city of low buildings and gardens, the warm sun, green foliage, and palm trees shook free all the eastern cold I had stored up in my body. I felt like a little dog being taken out for a walk, looking out the window, wagging my tail. My heart grew tight, however, as we arrived at the house Charlie had rented a few weeks earlier. The architectural style was exactly like the homes of all my teenage friends in Managua: one story, 1960s-style, with straight lines, a yard in the back, a pool. I felt I was back in the past after such a long, circuitous trip through so many other dimensions. I thought of T. S. Eliot:

> *We shall not cease from exploration*
> *And the end of all our exploring*
> *Will be to arrive where we started*
> *And know the place for the first time.*

Funny, I thought, that my life would take such twists and turns. But I remained the same.

CHAPTER FIFTY-SEVEN

Of how an earthquake made me realize so many differences

SANTA MONICA, 1994

ONE EARTHQUAKE is more than enough for one lifetime. For that reason the first thing I felt was rage when, in the early dawn of January 17, 1994, I was rudely awakened by the angry rumble of the earth shaking beneath our home in Santa Monica. We had bought the house and moved in just a month before. For over a week I had barely slept, trembling with this premonition. A slight tremor the previous Sunday was all it took to convince me that an earthquake was on its way. My son, Camilo, and Charlie had laughed at my disaster preparations, at the suitcase filled with chocolates and canned food which I placed in the trunk of the car along with water and blankets. They laughed too at the flashlight I carried in my pocketbook, at the sweatshirts I slept in for a week. I would have been just as glad to have been wrong, but when my intuition became a reality at least I was relieved of the horrible tension I had felt all week long, waiting for the inevitable to happen. This gift of intuition is a double-edged sword: until the things you predict actually happen, nobody has any sympathy for you; you have to live alone with the fear.

The Los Angeles earthquake did not destroy our house, nor was it anywhere near as apocalyptic as the one that hit Managua. But the earth shook with the same force. Books, objects, plates, the television—everything came crashing down to the floor. Our path downstairs was shrouded in a thick cloak of darkness, lit up only by the flashlight that I—practical woman that I am—had been carrying in my purse. We walked over broken mirrors and glass, but once we reached the street, instead of finding a city destroyed, all we found was a cluster of frightened neighbors, the smell of gas from the burst pipes, and a vaguely tense calm. When dawn broke, I took Camilo and Roberto, his Nicaraguan friend who was spending his vacation with us, to look for my friend María Morrison—who had also ended up living in L.A.—and her daughter, Ana, to make sure they were all right. As we turned onto San Vicente Avenue, I was shocked by what I saw: people walking and jogging, doing their morning exercise as if nothing had happened at all. Even the mail arrived that morning and we actually went out for lunch, eating prepackaged sandwiches from Café Dana, a coffee shop around the corner, that had opened for business.

I was dumbfounded. There was such a wide gulf between the state of terror I was in and the prevailing atmosphere that I wondered if I wasn't going mad. It was as if everyone just wanted to forget about the previous night and return to normal life. I watched people go back into their houses to take showers and go about their business and I couldn't believe they weren't terrified that another quake wouldn't come ripping through the earth. This was nothing like Nicaragua! Since 1972, whenever there are tremors there everyone panics and waits for the worst. In Santa Monica, it seemed Charlie was the only person who felt as afraid as I did.

Instead of a mass exodus like the one in Managua, this time we only left our neighborhood for a night. We spent it in the house of a friend, a film producer who lived in an area where the damage had been minimal— nothing, not even loose objects, had fallen off his tables. Jeff Bridges, the actor, had gone there with his family as well, and at dinnertime we all joined hands in a simple act of thanksgiving. Two days later, every one of our neighbors was back home, sleeping in their beds as usual. Charlie and I, meanwhile, camped out in our living room, ready to bolt if necessary. We barely slept a wink. For me, the isolation was utterly nerve-racking. Our neighbors had been very kind—we all helped one another turn off the gas and double-check the chimneys that had caved in. With the help of his girlfriend Lorri, Bob, the architect who had built our house (and now one of our best friends), helped us clean up all the broken plates and glasses that had tumbled down from the cupboard and wipe up all the spilled milk and broken eggs in the refrigerator. That was when I realized that they—like everyone else in our residential neighborhood—shared a legacy of civic trust and public safety that I completely lacked. I came from a place where life was so much more fragile. There, when tragedy strikes, the one (and only) thing you can count on is solidarity, the company of others. It was probably the case also in poor neighborhoods in

L.A. But here, my neighbors were confident that their houses were well built, that the firemen would always answer their call, that the police were there to protect them. I, however, was frightened by the possibility of anarchy and chaos. All my senses were in a constant state of high alert, ready to defend my life and that of my family, all alone, if necessary. My reaction, primitive as it was, was the result of years of war and uncertainty.

That year which began with such a commotion brought into our lives the joy of a child. Some months before, Charlie and I awakened and realized we had both had a similar dream that night. I dreamt I was swimming with a beautiful little girl next to me. He dreamt he was playing with her in the garden of his grandparents' home in Santa Margarita.

By then, even if we still talked occasionally about trying to have a child, we weren't pursuing it aggressively. We worried about the consequences for my health.

In March I went to Nicaragua, and by one of those mysteries of life, the child I had dreamed of came into my arms. Adriana was four months old. I had not considered adopting a child, but the moment I held her and we made eye contact, a surge of motherly love inundated me. I felt exactly the same sensation as when I had first held Melissa, my second daughter, after her birth. I think Adriana felt it too. Her beautiful black eyes looked straight into my heart. She wouldn't take her eyes off me. I felt with overwhelming certainty that she was my child, and I her mother. It took a few months to get all the paperwork done. I waited in Nicaragua with Adriana, first at my friend Nelba's house, and then in an apartment I rented. It was like a collective birth, all my friends coming by and bringing me baby things their children no longer needed. Charlie had also fallen in love with her just from my description on the telephone. He couldn't stop imagining her big black eyes, he said, as he prepared to come to Nicaragua and meet her. The first morning he spent with Adriana, playing on the bed, I could see in both of them a love that, to this day, often moves me to tears. They are so well suited for each other. Yet, between her and me there's magic, true wonder. We know something inexplicable and deep brought us together. As I often say to her, I might not have had her in my womb, but my heart was pregnant with her. Somewhere within my soul she had her place; a love that was waiting to bloom years even before we actually found each other.

EPILOGUE

Where this female Don Quixote brings her memoirs to an end

SANTA MONICA–MANAGUA, 2002

As I step out of my house in Santa Monica, all I have to do is walk half a block to arrive at Montana Avenue. A street dotted with a succession of boutiques, cafés, antique shops, furniture stores, homeopathic pharmacies, organic food markets, and yoga and fitness centers. During the day Montana bustles with pedestrians. The majority are the loveliest of Californian specimens, tanned, muscular men and women, disciplined soldiers of healthy diets and exercise regimens. They walk down the street in their tight-fitting clothes, entering and exiting their personal training sessions with bottles of Evian water tucked under their arms. Sometimes, in the confusion of pedestrian traffic up and down the avenue, I think of the days when I transported weapons, carried a machine gun on my shoulder, I think of my years of political passions, and I wonder if I am the same person. The places that witnessed that existence have so little in common with the places I find myself in now, and I can't help but wonder if a stroke of fate granted me not one but two lives.

Passing by the exclusive shops where a dining room table costs more than one person in Nicaragua earns in an entire lifetime of hard labor under the hot sun, I am filled with nostalgia for the difficult times I lived through, for the clear purpose that inspired us, for the feeling of possibility and hope that I shared with so many other people. I yearn for that unbridled energy, the incredible, crazy, impossible dreams that took me out of myself in search of a common experience. I know that the obsession to redeem humanity can be just as dangerous as the fanaticism I see in the faces of those who dedicate themselves to perfect bodies, pure, unadulterated food, and the quest for immortality. I try to think that each and every one of us is responsible for finding meaning and purpose in life, and that it's arrogant to think that my solution is better than the rest. On the other hand, I don't think anyone could ever convince me that the kind of pleasure that begins and ends in oneself can even remotely be compared to the exaltation and joy that comes from joining others in the effort to change the world.

I realize that for me the Revolution was more than just a mere flirtation—a trip to the other side—in my journey on this earth. It was a crucial fact that changed me forever. When I decided to join Charlie in the United States, I was often tormented by the fear that I would become soft and compliant, assume the attitude that people term "realistic," hang up my gloves and resign myself to the idea that we lost the battle or, in the best of all worlds, that the fight to achieve new utopias would now fall to other people. But reality taught me otherwise. Life has shown me that not every commitment requires payment in blood, or the heroism of dying in the line of fire. There is a heroism inherent to peace and stability, an accessible, everyday heroism that may not challenge us with the threat of death, but which challenges us to squeeze every last possibility out of life, and to live not one but several lives all at the same time. To accept oneself as a multiple being in time and space is part of modern life, and one of the possibilities enjoyed by those of us who live in an era in which technology can be embraced as a liberating rather than alienating force. Human aspirations are no longer constricted by geographic limitations. In constant contact with my friends and the political life of Nicaragua, I feel that my little country has become portable and near despite its distance, that the horizon is open wide, and that I define the limits of my pursuits.

It took time for me to find the man that could truly be my mate, and a relationship devoid of somersaults, farewells, and sudden flights. Charlie and I have been together many years now. Our skins recognize each other even in the deepest sleep and darkness. When we are apart or I go away to Nicaragua for long periods of time, there is a delicate but strong and resilient thread that connects us in our solitude.

I lead two different lives, in two very different worlds which coexist within myself. My three oldest children are already walking down their own roads. Maryam and Melissa are now two beautiful, sensitive, mature women, but they are also dreamers. Maryam is an architect. She works in Los Angeles, but one day she wants to go back to Nicaragua and apply new techniques to building earthquake-proof adobe structures for a country with so few resources. Melissa is a doctor and wants to revolutionize medicine by incorporating holistic practices into a viable public health policy. Camilo is the most political of the group. He wants to go back to Nicaragua and finish what his parents started. With Adriana I have experienced the mature kind of motherhood I wish I could have given my other children. Adriana has an age-old wisdom in her eyes. Tenderness and happiness flow out from her athletic little body that so loves trapezes and acrobatics. Ever since she was tiny, she has hung on to my words and the stories I invent night after night as she curls up with me before falling asleep. She's sugarcane and cinnamon to sweeten my memories. She is Nicaragua for me: daring and full of life.

I have written two more novels: *Sofía de los presagios* and *Waslala*, as well as a book of poems on middle age. Sometimes this calm, sustained happiness scares me, but within its natural constraints I have grown to see it as the product of a lifelong labor which implied difficult and often daring choices. My life isn't free of conflict or pain. Often, my life in the United States seems like a parenthesis of introspection, an existence within a community of people in whose eyes I see profound loneliness and an aching desire for community, for purpose. I often feel distant, a prisoner of my own prejudice, a reticent inhabitant who fights with herself to not ignore the experiences of a country in which, every day, more than two hundred million people are trying to find meaning in their lives. Here I have come to recognize that any model of society must be based on absolute respect for individual freedom, that this inalienable right is the foundation of the large and small joys of any people.

Every three or four months I go back to Nicaragua. As soon as I arrive I am drawn into the vortex of the things to be done, the telephone that rings constantly, the friends who come over and fill me in on the latest political maneuverings, the latest struggles, the plans, the love affairs, the hatreds, the anxieties, the occasional small signs of a promising future. I insert myself in battles that never end, the same ones that caused me to leave the FSLN and to raise my voice against opportunism and the philosophy that the end justifies the means. I continue to be another of the many citizens of this world who are passionately convinced that our planet will only survive if we eliminate the gross inequalities that divide its people. In a spot that looks out on my beloved Managuan landscape I have a cozy little house. Just looking out at the volcanoes and the lake, my soul returns to my body, and I revel in the familiar sensuality, the atmosphere and the sounds of the tropics that are my passion. The hot and fiery afternoons nourish my roots. Nicaraguan society is a touchstone for who I am as a social creature, and its collective experience remains a source of strength and satisfaction.

I dare say, after the life I have lived, that there is nothing quixotic or romantic in wanting to change the world. It is possible. It is the age-old vocation of all humanity. I can't think of a better life than one dedicated to passion, to dreams, to the stubbornness that defies chaos and disillusionment. Our world, filled with possibilities, is and will be the result of the efforts offered up by us, its inhabitants. Just as life was a consequence of trial and error, the social organization that brings us the full realization of our potential as a species will issue from the ebb and flow of struggles we jointly undertake across the globe.

The future is a construct that is shaped in the present, and that is why to be responsible in the present is the only way of taking serious responsibility for the future. What is important is not the fulfillment of all one's dreams, but the stubborn determination to continue dreaming. We will have grandchildren, and they will have children too. The world will continue, and whether we know it or not, we are deciding its course every day.

My deaths, my dead, were not in vain. This is a relay race to the end of time. In the United States, just as in Nicaragua, I am the same Quixota who learned through life's battles that defeat can be as much of an illusion as victory.

Index